Surabaya, City of Work

This series of publications on Africa, Latin America, Southeast Asia, and Global and Comparative Studies is designed to present significant research, translation, and opinion to area specialists and to a wide community of persons interested in world affairs. The editor seeks manuscripts of quality on any subject and can generally make a decision regarding publication within three months of receipt of the original work. Production methods generally permit a work to appear within one year of acceptance. The editor works closely with authors to produce a high-quality book. The series appears in a paperback format and is distributed worldwide. For more information, contact the executive editor at Ohio University Press, Scott Quadrangle, University Terrace, Athens, Ohio 45701.

The Ohio University Research in International Studies series is published for the Center for International Studies by Ohio University Press. The views expressed in individual monographs are those of the authors and should not be considered to represent the policies or beliefs of the Center for International Studies, Ohio University Press, or Ohio University.

Surabaya, City of Work

A Socioeconomic History, 1900–2000

H. W. Dick

OHIO UNIVERSITY CENTER FOR INTERNATIONAL STUDIES
RESEARCH IN INTERNATIONAL STUDIES
SOUTHEAST ASIA SERIES NO. 106
OHIO UNIVERSITY PRESS
ATHENS

Printed in the United States of America

10 09 08 07 06 05 04 03 02 5 4 3 2 1

The books in the Ohio University Research in International Studies Series
are printed on acid-free paper ♾™

Library of Congress Cataloging-in-Publication Data

Dick, H. W. (Howard W.)
Surabaya, city of work : a socioeconomic history, 1900–2000 / H.W. Dick.
p. cm. — (Research in international studies. Southeast Asia series ; no. 106)
Includes bibliographical references and index.
ISBN 0-89680-221-3 (pbk. : alk. paper)
1. Surabaya (Indonesia)—Economic conditions. 2. Industries—
Indonesia—Surabaya—History. I. Title. II. Series.
HC448.S87 D53 2002
330.9598'2—dc21

2001036347

To the memory of Pak Adi Sukadana

Contents

Illustrations

Figures

Maps

Tables

Preface

The city is the frontier of modern Asian society. Aggressive urban skylines stake the claim. By the mid-1990s investment in urban land and buildings had become so huge and so speculative as to destabilize entire national economies. Industrialization and inmigration had concentrated around the main cities; an expanding middle class clustered in suburbs and new satellite towns.

Nowhere was urbanization more dramatic than in Indonesia under the New Order (1966–98). A few figures tell the story. Urban population increased from 17 percent in 1971 to 32 percent in 1995 (Hugo 1996, 150). Greater Jakarta (Jabotabek) became a region of 20 million people, Greater Surabaya of around 5 million (BPS, Supas 1995a,b,c). Rapid spread of urban areas and transformation of land use within them, along with the steady growth in traffic, was part of the texture of New Order development. Yet while the boom was in full flight the urban phenomenon was little remarked except by demographers and geographers. Elsewhere in the literature these large and dynamic cities are still barely visible.

The modern economic history of Indonesia—and especially of Java—can be read as a tale of two cities, Jakarta (colonial Batavia) and Surabaya. In the nineteenth century, when eastern Java was the frontier of an expanding plantation economy, Surabaya, with its natural harbor, became the larger city. With the application of steam power to sugar milling, as well as to railways, dockyards, and industry, Surabaya grew into one of the great port cities of modern Asia, ranking alongside Calcutta, Rangoon, Singapore, Bangkok, Hong Kong, and Shanghai. After the turn of the century, the trend began to reverse as the land frontier closed in eastern Java and plantation investment shifted toward more sparsely settled western Java. By the 1920s Surabaya had slipped to second place in terms of population but remained the commercial center. Its international standing was evidenced by excellent transport and communications links, the range of foreign business houses, the number of its consulates, thriving journalism in several languages, openness to current trends in architecture and the arts, and radical politics.

Thus it is remarkable that after the 1920s Surabaya faded off the world map. Fifty or sixty years ago anyone with knowledge of world shipping and trade knew the location and importance of Surabaya. Sugar! It was the collapse of the sugar export industry, beginning with the world depression of the 1930s, that eliminated Surabaya's stake in the international economy. Loss of economic momentum had fateful consequences. A weak local market discouraged investment in new manufacturing industries, which established mainly in the province of West Java. In November 1945, at the close of the Japanese occupation, a furious battle between revolutionary soldiers and vengeful British forces left the city devastated, whereas Jakarta prospered under restored Dutch control. After Independence, Jakarta's growth was further boosted by the growth of the public sector, while Surabaya, stagnated. By the 1960s the dilapidated heart of Surabaya's old business district attested to marginalization. Grand façades unpainted and flaking away, behind which little business was now done. The offices of once well-known companies divided up among small firms. Rivers and canals silted up and full of rubbish, their banks lined with squatter shacks. A city in decay. And—though less visibly—a city traumatized by the violence of 1966, when this bastion of the Communist Party had again been bathed in blood.

On my first visit to Surabaya, in April 1972, the city nevertheless seemed a vigorous and charming place where one could still sense the ghosts of the past. There was bustle, but little of Jakarta's worsening congestion. It was no difficulty to explore the city for the first time by bicycle. Yet Surabaya was not, like the old royal capitals of central Java, a city living in the past. The economic recovery of the New Order was slow to spill over from Jakarta, but by the mid-1970s development had begun to impinge. Most evident was the growth in traffic: first motorcycles, then cars and jeeps. Roads were restricted to one way and *becak* (pedicabs) banished to the side streets. Then roads began to be widened, the picturesque old colonial façades of verandahs and wrought iron replaced by bland concrete, while the interiors of offices and houses were altered to suit the modern fashion of air-conditioning, carpets, and plush furniture. The city began to explode in size, with new housing projects and industrial zones spreading over an area more vast than the old colonial town. Within the old urban core there appeared in the 1980s palatial new shopping centers and the first modestly high-rise buildings. Almost from week to week, familiar old buildings were being knocked down for redevelopment. As in Jakarta, anyone returning from even a few months' absence would find things not quite as they had been.

In the 1990s the pace of change accelerated and the skyline was reconfigured with office towers, condominiums, five-star hotels, and shopping malls. Generating all this activity was a structural change in the economy of the city and its hinterland, a shift from the production and processing of cash crops to factories and warehousing, more and more oriented toward foreign markets. This structural change is recognizably the development pattern of the Indonesian economy under the New Order. Surabaya did not just participate in this process but, next to Greater Jakarta, became its second leading edge, Indonesia's other industrial heartland and metropolis. After a long and difficult transition from plantation to industrial economy, Surabaya at last regained its dynamism.

Since the meltdown of the Indonesian economy in 1997–98 and the accompanying political turmoil, Soeharto's New Order is no longer regarded as a triumph of sustained development. The once vaunted economic achievements are now discounted and weighed against institutional weakness and political repression. The task of scholars is to understand the transformation in the longer term. A marvelous overview has already been provided by Anne Booth (1998). *City of Work* is a more eclectic study, with the gaze lowered from the national level to the city. Jakarta and Surabaya have been both bases for modern sector development and the essential gateways to and from the emerging global economy. They have also been the crucible of modern Indonesian society. A twentieth-century socioeconomic history of Surabaya, read with an eye to more than economic indicators, suggests that the New Order boom was not a new phenomenon to be construed in its own terms but the belated continuation of a late-colonial pattern of development. The historical puzzle is not the sudden and sustained vitality of the period after the 1970s but the long hiatus between the 1930s and 1970s.

Nationalist and developmentalist ideologies exaggerate the discontinuity between the colonial period and the New Order. Each attempts to close a period of history—one at 1945, the other at 1965—and to discourage backward journeys, not because there is nothing to discover but because knowledge might erode the simplicity of official truth. Nations and regimes are constructed in the mind. Like private construction firms, the state clears the old ground before it lays foundations for the new edifice. Yet, as the example of mainland China also shows, societies are robust even after prolonged trauma. History demands to be written across generations and to test the self-referencing assumptions of each time. After a decent interval, we can now revisit the colonial period and see something more complex than a discredited colonial experience. An urban lens allows us to do so within some consistent framework, which the construct of nation most assuredly is not. Administrative decentralization from 1 January 2001 reinforces this logic.

Here is a story, but how is it to be told? The city is as difficult a unit for economic analysis as it is logical. Governments collect economic data at a highly aggregated level: even provincial-level data merge the city with its rural hinterland. This is no problem for city-states, such as Singapore and Hong Kong, or for capital cities, such as Jakarta or Manila, which are elevated to provincial status in their own right. For a provincial city, however, it imposes very narrow limits on the scope of rigorous quantitative analysis. It is hardly surprising that economic historians have preferred to focus on countries, leaving urban history to historians and geographers. This is especially true of writings on the Third World, leading to the absurdity that a great deal is written about agricultural and industrial development but very little that acknowledges the importance of cities and towns as the main concentrations of economic activity. The economy, though invoked as if having tangible form, is treated as a peculiarly disembodied thing, having a sectoral structure but no identified spatial structure. The economy of a city has therefore to be discovered before its history can be analyzed.

The extensive literature on Indonesian development gives little insight into how to approach an urban economic history. Indeed, with few exceptions such as Nas 1986, it barely acknowledges the urban dimension. Indonesian economic history, a small but expanding field, focuses on the colonial period and stops, like the sources themselves, in 1940; it also has little to say about cities and hinterlands. There are three good histories of Indonesian cities. Abeyasekere 1987 is a short general history that only touches on economic trends. Vuldy 1987 is a fine-grained ethnographic history of Pekalongan, an old port and textile center on the north coast of Java. Colombijn 1994, a detailed twentieth-century history of Padang (West Sumatra), is an interdisciplinary study that emphasizes politics and society rather than economics. Apart from a series of very good Dutch-language pictorial works and various specialist articles and theses, most other material on Indonesian urban history is a by-product of studies in demography, urban anthropology, or urban sociology and tends to accept the framework of standard general works.

Nor does the comparative literature offer much guidance. Insofar as the city has been studied at all, it has been mainly by historians and sociologists, for whom the city is a logical frame of reference. Economists and economic historians have virtually ignored such mundane affairs. It is deeply ironic that economists, who have had so much influence upon public policy, have paid so little explicit attention to management of the urban environment in which they actually live. In the case of historians, Asian cities have not yet attracted the same level of academic interest as Western cities, though since the 1970s there has been a rapid expansion of the field. Unfortunately, preoccupation with the colonial city and the port city as types, together with a fairly casual approach to economic history, has been not at all productive. Despite the confidence of the 1976 Santa Cruz conference that the colonial port city was "a meaningful ideal-type that deserved further exploration and study" (Basu 1985), collections such as Ross and Telkamp 1985 and Broeze 1989 and 1996 confirm that such research is still a rather uninteresting backwater. The accumulation of case studies has given rise to no methodological breakthrough because the frame of reference is too weak.

An alternative approach closer to mainstream economic history is to use urban economic history not as an end in itself but as a frame of reference for a more spatially explicit analysis of the development process at a national or subnational level. In a Southeast Asian context the best example is still Doeppers 1984 on late-colonial Manila, which uses the concept of the export base both to highlight the relationship between the city and the international economy and to integrate economic and social change. Also notable as good economic as well as social history, in this case of the Philippine provincial town of Iloilo, is McCoy 1982. In scope, rigor, and eclecticism, these are excellent works, even though the questions asked and the approach taken here are rather different.

In the absence of any appropriate model for the task, and subject to the limitation of sources, this book seeks to blend my fascination with Surabaya as a living city with the professional concerns of the economic historian and development economist. The study was conceived out of interest in the rapid industrialization of Surabaya and its hinterland since the mid-1970s, in effect a second front in Indonesia's industrialization. The task would have been more manageable within the time horizon of the New Order, but a starting point in the 1970s would have ignored Surabaya's long experience of light and heavy industry, dating back to the mid-nineteenth century. Contrast of New Order boom with Old Order stagnation would have been cliché rather than history. The relevant precedent for the New Order seemed rather to be the boom of the early decades of the twentieth century. My research confirmed that growth in these two periods had similar characteristics, which focused attention on the reasons for the prolonged hiatus after 1930. By taking such a long-term perspective, it was possible to bridge the chasm between studies of the late colonial and postindependence periods and to show that, despite all the political turmoil, Surabaya's twentieth-century *economic* history displays continuity as well as change. Because industrialization is only one facet of Surabaya's complex economic history, the book tries to round out the picture with analysis of the socioeconomic profile of the city, the growing role of government, and the spatial pattern of development. It draws upon the very useful antiquarian works of Faber (1931, 1936) and complements the superb social history of the 1945 revolution by Frederick (1989).

The outcome is a twentieth-century economic history of Surabaya that is loosely structured and idiosyncratic. It does not attempt a single chronological account but explores key themes by taking several cross-sections of the historical experience, each subject to its own chronology. Chapter 1 introduces the city: where it is, what it looks like, and the rhythms of daily life; chapter 2 highlights some of the main economic and political events that have shaped the city's economic history from the beginning of the twentieth century to the rise and fall of the New Order; chapter 3 uses census data since 1930 and more recent expenditure surveys to reveal long-term socioeconomic trends. These first three chapters provide context and texture. The next three outline processes of change: chapter 4 examines the changing structure and role of government in public health, education, and housing; chapter 5 studies industrialization; chapter 6 documents the spread of the city and conflicts in the evolution of land use. Chapter 7 explores the relationship between Surabaya, its hinterland of eastern Java, and interisland and international trade, showing that the city's twentieth-century cycle of boom-stagnation-boom coincided with its involvement, disengagement, and reintegration with the world economy. Photos are used extensively to illustrate and reinforce the text.

Like the city itself, the book holds in tension different ideas and perspectives and is not to be read as an evenly paced narrative. Some chapters (1, 2, 4) are accessible as sections of narrative. Others (3, 5, 7) are a dialogue between statistical sources and narrative, while chapter 6 is a dialogue between maps and narrative. The reader is invited to view the book as a series of treks across difficult terrain, using the guides and mode of conveyance best suited to each stage. At the beginning of the twenty-first century, the least familiar terrain may in fact be the city. Urban dwellers are familiar with their own circuits yet may be quite ignorant of the rest of their urban world, catching only glimpses from word of mouth and trusting the roving but erratic eye of newspapers and television.

While any history is a point of view, this is especially true of an attempt to portray the evolution of such a complex and multifaceted society as a large city. Citizens of Surabaya may well feel that, as an outsider, I have given them less than their due. Academic colleagues may claim that important issues that have been skimmed over. I have my own frustration that amid other tasks it has taken more than ten years to finalize the manuscript: some detail and interpretation may now have become dated. Yet with hindsight the book—or was it the author?—needed to ripen. At the outset the focus was very much on industrialization as the engine of economic development, which is to say an economist's conventional, production-oriented view of society. Only much later, as the real estate boom accelerated, did conflicts over land use come into the foreground. I now see control of land to be as fundamental to urban society as to rural society. Periodic real estate booms, like tidal waves, are one of the elemental force of destruction, reconstruction, and redistribution in urban society. The century's dramatic closure with the Asian crisis, Soeharto's downfall and the popular elections of June 1999 have given the book its necessary frame.

Acknowledgments

Research began as long ago as 1986 with a three-year secondment from the University of Newcastle to the Research School of Pacific Studies at the Australian National University. Its context was the Industrialisation Project, a large interdisciplinary study of recent industrialization in East Java and West Malaysia that was convened by Jim Fox, Tony Reid, and Harold Brookfield. A joint product was *Balanced Development: East Java in the New Order* (Dick, Fox, and Mackie 1993). Tony, colleagues, and staff in the Department of Pacific and Asian History provided a congenial academic home away from home. In the hard slog of chasing sources and data processing, I was fortunate to have the help successively of three very competent and good-humored research assistants in Marion May, Liz Drysdale, and Loene Doube, while Jane Lindsay freelanced on the more difficult computer work. In my new home at the University of Melbourne, Malaya Papworth, Mudrajad Kuncoro, and Wahyu Sutiyono assisted in the final stages of completing the manuscript. Peter Gardiner generously provided maps and statistical calculations. Sue Blackburn, Charles Coppel, Peter van Diermen, Andrew Gunawan, Hal Hill, Terry Hull, John Ingleson, Ispurwono, Gavin Jones, Kai Kaiser, Peter Koffel, Heath McMichael, Peter Rimmer, and Thee Kian Wie gave timely and valuable support. Of especial value were the advice, assistance, and friendship of Radin Fernando, whose research into the adjacent residency of Surabaya in the late colonial period greatly informed my own work. Rosemary Beckett lived with the work in progress and never lost faith in its eventual completion.

More than superficial coverage of the colonial period would have been impossible without the opportunity to work for several months in 1987 on archival sources in the Netherlands. Staff of the Algemeen Rijksarchief (Tweede Afdeeling) and Jan Scholte were generous with their advice and the Ministry of Foreign Affairs kindly gave permission to consult some restricted sources. The KITLV in Leiden and the Tropen Instituut in Amsterdam were other treasure troves, while the International Centre provided a comfortable base in Leiden, where I enjoyed the stimulus of a widening circle of university colleagues. A highlight of my all-too-brief stay in the Netherlands was two visits to Haaksbergen, where I was privileged to meet the late Ir. Dirk Schaap, former managing director of NV Braat. Leonard Blusse, Peter Boomgaard, Freek Colombijn, Cees Fasseur, Gerrit Knaap, Willem Korthals-Altes, Thomas Lindblad, Peter Nas, and Willem Segers all helped guide me along the way.

Fieldwork in Indonesia was sponsored by the Social Science Faculty (FISIP) of Universitas Airlangga and supported by the Indonesian Institute of Sciences (LIPI). Faculty colleagues provided a stimulating academic environment and good friendship. I benefited greatly from the insights of Dede Oetomo, Hotman Siregar, and Sutandyo Wignjosubroto in the Faculty of Social Sciences and from Edi Slamet, Tjuk Sukiadi, and Suroso Imam Zadjuli in the Faculty of Economics. The Research sections of the East Java Provincial Government and the Municipality of Surabaya gave access to government offices, of which the Regional Planning Offices (Bappeda) and the Statistical Offices (Kantor Statistik) were most helpful. The socioeconomic profile (chapter 3) relied heavily on population census, economic census, and expenditure survey (Susenas) tapes provided to the Australian National University under agreement with the Central Bureau of Statistics. Photographic material was made available by Arsip Nasional in Jakarta. Without being able to mention by name the many officials, businesspeople, and private persons in Surabaya who patiently responded to my inquiries, I would like specifically to acknowledge the assistance of Ir. Moehtadi and Budi Daroe, the good fellowship of several of the city's Rotary Clubs, and the assistance from the libraries of the *Surabaya Post* and *Jawa Pos* newspapers.

Finally, some very personal acknowledgments. Is Moritis explored Surabaya with me in 1973–74 during several months' fieldwork for my Ph.D. on interisland shipping, and the seeds of this book took root in that shared experience. Lea Jellinek has been a constant intellectual companion. By happy accident of timing, I began the research as she was writing her Ph.D. on the Jakarta *kampung* (urban village) of Kebun Kacang, since published as *The Wheel of Fortune* (1991). This interaction not only gave much sharper insight into kampung life but also changed my way of imagining Indonesian cities. The late Dr. Adi Sukadana, as incoming Dean of the Faculty of Social Sciences at Universitas Airlangga, agreed sight unseen to sponsor my research and then with his wife, Maria, and family became my host and mentor. The news of his sudden death was a terrible shock. His energy, wisdom, good humor, and generosity remain fresh in memory and to him by way of tribute the book is gratefully dedicated. The late Fajar Notonegoro, whom I first met in 1973–74 as Dean of the Faculty of Economics, was always willing to make available his wonderful memory, wisdom, and old-world hospitality and brought alive the city many years before my own experience. Ir. Johan Silas of the Faculty of Architecture helped make the task almost manageable: his immense knowledge of the city, his commitment to socially and environmentally responsible development, and his boundless energy in promoting a better Surabaya have been an inspiration to me, as to so many others, and his continued support has been invaluable. Freddy Samalo more than twenty years ago helped me find my way around the business world of Surabaya and has remained a good and cheerful friend and opened many doors. Such friends make even so large a city as Surabaya seem like a village. A very long manuscript would never have become a book without the support of Bill Frederick, the commitment of Gillian Berchowitz, and the cheerful dedication of my editor, Nancy Basmaijan and her team. Banyak terima kasih.

A Note on Spelling

Indonesian spelling is according to usage since 1972, except in the case of organizations and persons adhering to the older Dutch style. Thus Surabaya instead of Soerabaja or Soerabaia; Jakarta for Djakarta; but Soeharto rather than Suharto.

Gresik, the port town northwest of Surabaya, may also be rendered as Grissee or Gersik.

Municipality when capitalized denotes the local government or administration of the city of Surabaya, known in the colonial period as the Gemeente, after Independence as Kota Pradja, under the New Order as Kota Madya (or Kotamadya), and now as Pemerintah Kota (Pemkot); municipality in lowercase denotes the administrative area of the city.

Independence when capitalized denotes Indonesia's Declaration of Independence on 17 August 1945. Its recognition by the Netherlands on 27 December 1949 is referred to as the "transfer of sovereignty." The intervening four years of warfare is known as the Revolution.

Chapter 1

ASPECTS

Surabaya makes few concessions to the casual visitor. A turn-of-the-century tourist guidebook offered not even faint praise:

> [W]e would advise travellers to stay no longer at Soerabaja than necessary, the more so as a single day is amply sufficient to reach several attractive spots in the highlands. (KPM 1903, 82)

Little has changed. For the foreign tourist, Surabaya is still a staging point en route to or from Bali or the spectacular volcanoes of Java's interior. Efforts to promote the city as a tourist attraction have been halfhearted and almost embarrassed. The postcards on sale are mostly of Jakarta or Bali, with a view of Mount Bromo or the bull races on Madura for local interest. For those who just pass through, the city seldom gives rise to fond memories. However, the perspective of the foreign tourist has no intrinsic merit. Although in the late twentieth century a city's tourist appeal confers legitimacy and status, like shrines of famous saints in earlier times, these public images are much contrived. Most people who visit Surabaya do so not as tourists but on business. When business boomed during the 1990s, luxury hotels proliferated. In 1990 the city had one five-star hotel: five years later it had nine (*SP,* 9/5/95).

For a large agglomeration of people to perpetuate itself in a certain place despite great vicissitudes there has to be some economic rationale, which in turn gives that society its unique character. An Asian commercial directory of the mid-1920s far better captures the spirit of Surabaya:

> Sourabaya is to be judged in its own category. It would else be a disappointment to the visitor who arrives there from Batavia; for Batavia is old and dignified, but Sourabaya is a young city "on the make"—Batavia is a home, Sourabaya is a mart and a factory. The song of Sourabaya is the song of labour. No more hard-working place can be found east of Suez. All day the streets are busy, and the roar of traffic is never stilled. Nor does the night bring quietness, for . . . the inhabitants seek to recuperate their tired energies in pursuit of pleasure. With brilliant suns and gharish nights, Sourabaya lives on its reserves of nervous energy. (Macmillan 1926, 543)

No one would any longer describe Jakarta (Batavia) as old and dignified but this remains an apt depiction of Surabaya. Much of the appeal of Surabaya to those who know it well is that it is not self-conscious, that it goes about its business and pleasure in a vigorous, practical way. Surabaya is Surabaya.

Arrivals

BY SEA

The best way to arrive in Surabaya is by sea, allowing time for reflection and a sense of anticipation. The low coastline of Java, which all day has demarcated the horizon on the starboard side, appears to extend as far as the eye can see. There seems no good reason for the course to veer toward the jagged hills of what is in fact the island of Madura. As the ship comes nearer to the coast, the deep blue of the Java Sea gives way to a lighter, milky brown. Only when the ship turns sharply to enter a marked channel does one notice that there may indeed be a passage between the mainland

and Madura, a fact confirmed by the passing of an outbound bulk carrier (fig. 1.1). On the port side just beyond the channel appears a low, sandy island with a latticework lighthouse and a pilot station. As the ship slows to pick up the pilot, immaculate in white drill, one observes large chunks of rusting metal strewn around the shallows, the remains of wartime wrecks cleared from the approaches. Beside a low training wall, the ship gathers speed into a swift-flowing and now chocolate-brown stream. In the nineteenth century, Dutch engineers diverted the course of the mighty Bengawan Solo from the main shipping channel to an artificial outlet to the northwest but the tides still flush out much of the silt from the equally large Brantas River, in whose delta Surabaya lies. Opposite the old river mouth, the tall, white lighthouse of Tanjung Piring marks where the training wall joins onto Madura. Here the ship enters the narrowest part of the channel, with mangrove swamps close by on either side. Tiny fishing boats (*prahu*) bob past or make patient headway under blue nylon sails as the ship begins the long, wide turn that will bring it up to the industrial port of Gresik.

Off the starboard side, nestling at the foot of an outcrop of dry limestone hills, Gresik is a historic trading and handicraft center that in modern times has been eclipsed by nearby Surabaya. Close by the mouth of the Bengawan Solo, the main artery to the heartland of central Java, Gresik may have been founded by Chinese in the fourteenth century as a transshipment center for the spices of the Moluccas (Reid 1992). The Portuguese traveler Tomé Pires attested to its prominence in the sixteenth century but two devastating conquests by the armies of Sultan Agung of Mataram early in the seventeenth century ended its era of greatness. It survived because of its religious importance as the burial place of two of Java's nine early Muslim "saints" (Malik Ibrahim and Sunan Giri), which helped to sustain a merchant community of devout Muslims (*santri*). For the Dutch East India Company (VOC), it was a logical place to establish a trading factory and little attention was paid to Surabaya until late in the eighteenth century. In the narrow streets of the old commercial quarter, the size and rich decoration of the

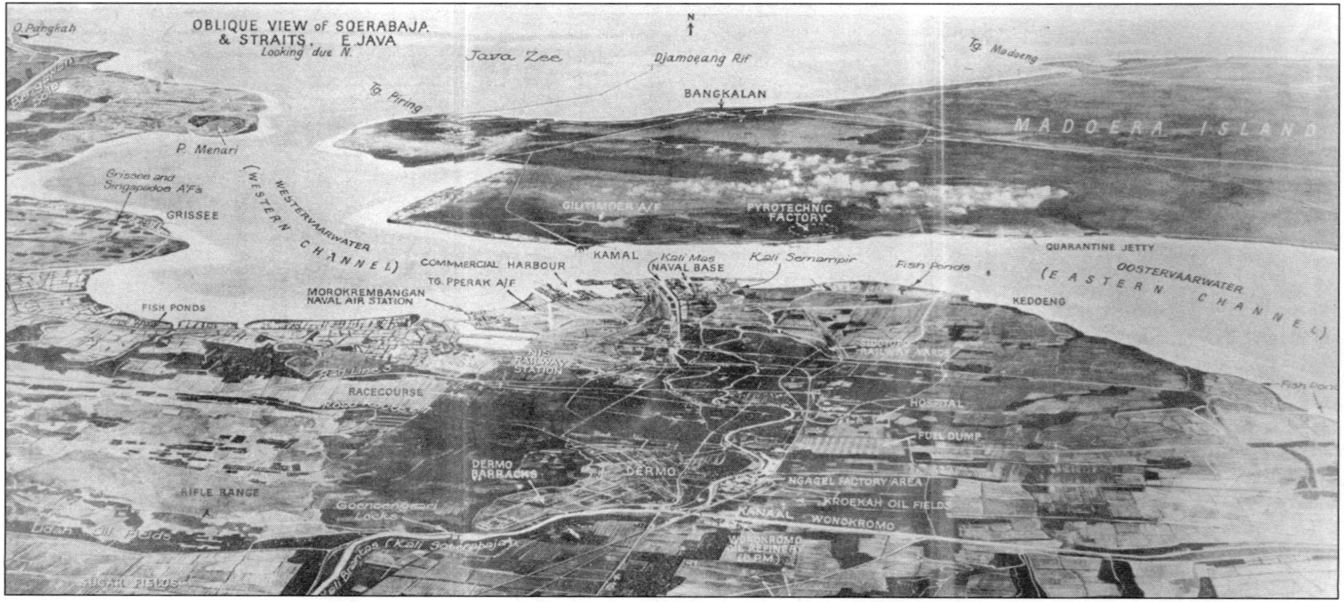

Figure 1.1. Surabaya: composite aerial view, ca. 1944. From AGS 1945.

houses attests to former prosperity. Now even the handicraft industries have withered away. The wooden hand looms that once wove fine sarongs are silent. The little birds that wove their precious edible nests—a delicacy in Chinese cuisine—in the lofts of the big old houses have all but succumbed to industrial pollution. Gresik has stubbornly maintained its separate identity but today is little more than an industrial outer suburb of Surabaya.

As Gresik passes abeam, the heavy industry becomes apparent. The low-lying town is dwarfed by the Petrokimia fertilizer complex, the tall red-and-white-banded smokestacks of the power station, and the belching chimneys of the cement works, whose voracious appetite for limestone is slowly consuming the hillsides. The little prahu harbor, shelter to the handful of prahus that during the dry season still bring copra from the Moluccas, a last echo of the old spice trade, is lost among the modern wharves with their large tankers and bulk carriers. At anchor, a timber carrier discharges logs for one of the plywood mills. Then the coast reverts to mangrove, concealing the carefully tended salt- and fishponds and the little fishing hamlets along the creeks.

As the ship rounds up to enter the broad roadstead of Surabaya, the first sighting is unimpressive. Unless it is an unusually clear day, when the towering blue mass of Mount Arjuno makes a spectacular background, the only striking feature is the tall wheat silos beside the Bogasari flour mill. From there stretches the clutter of wharves and ships typical of any large port. Yet as one sails into the roads, past the lines of anchored ships, there is some quickening of the pulse. The low green hills of Madura give a sense of shelter, reminding that this is indeed a great natural harbor, the only one on the north coast of Java. The size of the port and the amount and range of its shipping, the naval base and dockyard, the bustle of ferries to and from Madura all convey purpose and activity (fig. 1.2). At low tide, just breaking the surface, a keen observer might note a couple of rusting, capsized wrecks, a quiet echo of the turmoil of the Japanese invasion in March 1942.

Before World War I, when Surabaya was still a roadstead port,

Figure 1.2. The busy Madura ferry terminal at the mouth of the Kali Mas, 1992. Photo by author.

Figure 1.3. The roadstead of Surabaya, ca. 1900. KITLV no. 8577.

the ship would have anchored among many others off the mouth of the Kali Mas (Golden River), the arm of the Brantas that flows through the city (fig. 1.3). Its sluggish, muddy waters belie the name, though apt enough for its rich flow of commerce. Here passengers disembarked awkwardly into milling bumboats (*tambangan*) or steam launches for transfer a short distance upstream to the small customs station, from where they could board the steam tram for the three-kilometer journey into town. Those better off or in a hurry could hire a launch and travel up the Kali Mas, past the rows of sugar warehouses and the clutter of tugs, barges, and prahus, to the Red Bridge (Jembatan Merah) at the center of town. In the 1920s the modern deepwater port of Tanjung Perak was constructed at great expense in the mudflats just west of the river mouth, enabling deep-sea ships to moor alongside. Passengers could then travel to town by electric tram. These days, interisland express ships berth at the new passenger terminal beside the quaint old harbor office. As soon as the gangway is lowered, a crowd of porters rush aboard and pounce upon passengers with offers to carry their luggage ashore to waiting taxis.

The first kilometers into town offer few strong impressions.

This is all reclaimed land, spaciously laid out in the 1920s according to modern town-planning principles. One speeds along a wide, tree-lined boulevard divided by a plantation where once the electric trams used to run, the graceful pylons still in use for street lighting. On either side the road is lined by modest colonial-style bungalows, many since disfigured by ugly modern accretions or displaying office signs of shipping or forwarding companies. As yet there is nothing of the crowding one associates with Indonesian cities. At the end of the boulevard, in front of an old coconut oil factory, one reaches the coast road, right to Gresik, left to enter the old central business district or, as known in Dutch times, the lower town (*benedenstad*) of Surabaya. At the beginning of the twentieth century, Heerenstraat (now Jalan Rajawali) was, as the name suggests, lined with the mansions of wealthy merchants and military officers (fig. 1.4). The porticoes of these dilapidated old buildings can still be made out behind more recent clutter. A little further along the buildings become more imposing: offices of once great banks, trading houses, and plantation companies. Where the street has not yet been widened, the original façades remain, little altered in fifty or sixty years, a miscellany of pillars, arches, and follies. Behind them lie narrow streets of two-story houses with high-pitched roofs, wide eaves, and big windows—until early in the twentieth century the houses of European merchants and now mainly godowns (warehouses).

Before there is time to take in this decayed grandeur, one is already at Jembatan Merah (fig. 1.5). The famous little bridge with its red iron railings, which used to link the European quarter on the west bank with the Chinese and Arab quarters on the east, has recently become a memory, replaced by a functional ferro-concrete structure. Beside the bridge on the west bank is a small square dominated by a stiff, white mausoleumlike building completed about 1930 for the Dutch trading house Internatio. In November 1945, during the British occupation, the square was the scene of the assassination of General Mallaby, the spark that ignited the Battle of Surabaya. This is commemorated by a huge revolutionary statue

Figure 1.4. The Dutch quarter, ca. 1900. KIT alb. 340, bl. 3, neg. 149/6.

Figure 1.5. Jembatan Merah from the old Red Bridge, looking across the square to the former Internatio building, 1987. Photo by author.

rising up in the middle of the square as if about to hurl itself upon the hated colonial masters. Since 1995 the square has looked startlingly different. A huge shopping mall, Jembatan Merah Plaza, has opened on the site of the old Customs warehouses, opposite a four-star Ibis hotel; the formerly jostling public transport terminal buses with its buses, *bemo* (jitneys), and *becak* (pedicabs) has been banished to the outskirts and the square with its revolutionary statue has been landscaped and (exquisite irony!) fenced off.

The taxi does not cross the smelly, badly silted Kali Mas to the Chinese quarter but turns left along the west bank past more old colonial office buildings (figs. 1.6, 1.7). At the next main crossroads, the taxi stops at traffic lights. To the left is the clock tower of the former Lindeteves building, to the right the more modern Bank Indonesia on what was once the City Theatre and Gardens (Stadstuin). Beyond the railway viaduct—in November 1945 the defense line against the invading British forces—is a large open space surrounding the tall Heroes' Obelisk (Tugu Pahlawan). Originally the site of the Palace of Justice, during the Japanese occupation it became even more hated as the headquarters of the military police or Kempeitai. At the first opportunity it was gutted by angry Indonesians and subsequently, like the Bastille, razed. Yet if this side of the street symbolizes revolution, the other side symbolizes continuity. The whitewashed governor's office, an attractive example of late-1920s art deco or de Stijl architecture, is still the seat of government in East Java and the starting point for the measurement of all road mileages (fig. 1.8). In the main foyer is a marble plaque inscribed Gouverneurs van Oost Java that in a nice continuity lists all governors of the province from its inauguration in 1928 to the present day. The Japanese interregnum is acknowledged as a discrete gap between the Dutch governors before 1942 and the Indonesian governors after 1945.

Beyond the governor's office, in what in Dutch times used to be a center of public entertainment, were still until quite recently a couple of old cinemas and an expensive restaurant, although the once-famous Grimm's has long since been a naval canteen. Beyond

Figure 1.6. Central business district, Jalan Niaga, 1987. Photo by author.

Figure 1.7. The Chinese quarter, 1987. Photo by author.

Figure 1.8. The governor's office and electric tram, 1952. Courtesy Arsip Nasional.

Pasar Besar (Main Market), a modest traditional market that perpetuates a very old institution, one enters the street of that name. Early in the century it was the elite European shopping street. As the elite moved southward, Chinese merchants set up shop-houses. Recently widened like so many narrow thoroughfares, it has lost all the charm of old verandahs, shutters, and billboards. With another glimpse on the left of the Kali Mas, one enters Gemblongan, guarded by the fortresslike offices of the electricity utility PLN (formerly the Dutch-owned ANIEM), also built in the austere character of de Stijl. Otherwise, widening has destroyed the original character of this street as well. It is now occupied almost entirely by furniture shops.

From Gemblongan one crosses a broad intersection into Tunjungan. Between the wars this was the European shopping district, with department stores, boutiques, restaurants, ice-cream parlors, tailors, bookshops, and dancings, the more elegant predecessor of the modern discotheque. On the left-hand corner is the well-known Siola department store, formerly the British-owned Whiteaway and Laidlaw. Gutted during the fighting of November 1945, it stood as a gray monument to the Revolution until refurbished and reopened in 1964 (fig. 1.9). Since the 1980s adjacent sites have been redeveloped as more modern shopping complexes and the street has lost its former prestige and charm. Road widening and conversion to several lanes of one-way traffic has turned it into a speedway that is terrifying to cross, choked by exhaust fumes and with only a narrow alleyway for pedestrians. There is no longer any pleasure in strolling. Nor are the furniture shops, electronics shops, and automobile showrooms the kind of stores conducive to such a pastime. The situation became so bad that the Municipality examined ways to restore the character of the street, culminating in December 1994 in a trial closure to evening traffic, perhaps the first (momentary) setback that the motor car has suffered in Surabaya. The southern end of Tunjungan has better retained some life. Toko Nam, until recently a sprawling department store, dated back to before the Second World War, as opposite did the smaller Toko Metro (formerly Piet) (fig. 2.4). Just beyond lies the showpiece Tunjungan Plaza, which opened in 1986 as Surabaya's first multistory, air-conditioned shopping palace and ten years later

Figure 1.9. Surabayans marching through Tunjungan on Heroes' Day, 10 November 1950 (note gutted Siola building). Courtesy Arsip Nasional.

completed its third phase of expansion, including the five-star Sheraton Hotel and an ice-skating rink.

Until the 1970s the traveler would most likely have found a hotel in this part of the city. For many years the leading hotel had been the Hotel Majapahit (in Dutch times the Oranje). Its white-washed 1930s façade, which crowds onto the southern end of Tunjungan, is a deceptive screen—behind is an even older-style hotel laid out around a spacious garden courtyard. Each high-ceiling room, once cooled by a lazy ceiling fan, opens onto its own verandah. Even well beyond its heyday, it was still a haven of tranquillity. The sound of birds in the early morning, of the afternoon rain on the bare earth, carried one back to a calmer *tempo doeloe* (olden time), to village Java far from the big city. There used to be many other more modest such hotels in the vicinity: most have been demolished, for the land is too valuable for such low-density accommodation. Fortunately the Majapahit survives after extensive renovation as the exclusive Majapahit Mandarin.

BY AIR

Nowadays the traveler of means arrives in Surabaya by air. Civil aviation began in 1929 with an air service between Batavia, Semarang, and Surabaya. Two years later, Surabaya became a stopover on the international mail route between Amsterdam, Java, and Australia. Yet for many years the development of air links was hampered by lack of a good airfield. Not until 1965 were basic but adequate facilities provided at the present Juanda airport, well south of the city in the neighboring district, or *kabupaten,* of Sidoarjo. Meanwhile, the government's policy of restricting the gateways for international aviation to Jakarta and Bali meant that, until the boom of the 1990s, Surabaya remained just a domestic gateway. Jakarta and Denpasar are the main destinations but direct flights to Singapore and Taiwan are well patronized by business travelers.

The flight from Bali is perhaps the more spectacular. Flying above Madura Strait along the north coast of Java, on a clear morning one can enjoy a wonderful bird's-eye view of the whole of that fertile region that the Dutch called the Oosthoek (East End). Until the mid-nineteenth century it was a sparsely populated frontier. Then the narrow coastal plain was taken up for sugar and tobacco plantations, the mountain slopes and plateaus cleared for tree crops such as coffee, chocolate, and later, rubber (Elson 1984). From fifteen thousand feet one observes that cultivation now spreads right across the narrow island and up the lower mountain slopes. The volcanic massif dominating the eastern tip of Java gives way to a broad expanse of cultivation broken only by the jagged Iyang plateau, place of the gods, an uninhabited wilderness with patches of *alang-alang,* a coarse tall grass. Beyond this plateau, one flies over the north-coast port town of Probolinggo, from where the eye travels across the mountain saddle to the southern rice plain of Lumajang and the Indian Ocean (map 1.1). To the west this broad expanse is blocked by a high-humped ridge stretching almost across the island. At its southern end soars the awesome cone of Semeru, its bare, lava-encrusted summit shining in the morning sun like gray snow. Remote in its majesty, it is aptly named after the sacred mountain of Hindu mythology, the bridge between heaven and earth. At the northern end lies the vast sandy crater of Bromo, the remains of some ancient, cataclysmic explosion. From behind this ridge emerges the recumbent form of Kawi and to the north the massive bulk of Arjuno. Cradled between these two ridges, invisible beneath a blanket of cloud lies the fertile highland plain around the city of Malang, East Java's second largest city. Surabaya lies some eighty kilometers to the north.

By now the aircraft is commencing its descent. Beside the slopes of Bromo and its vast crater of sand lies the coastal town of Pasuruan. Once an important port for the export sugar, it became a sleepy place, overshadowed by nearby Surabaya, but is now reviving as an outer industrial suburb. The fanlike siltation off the old river mouth is very evident and looks to merge eventually with the

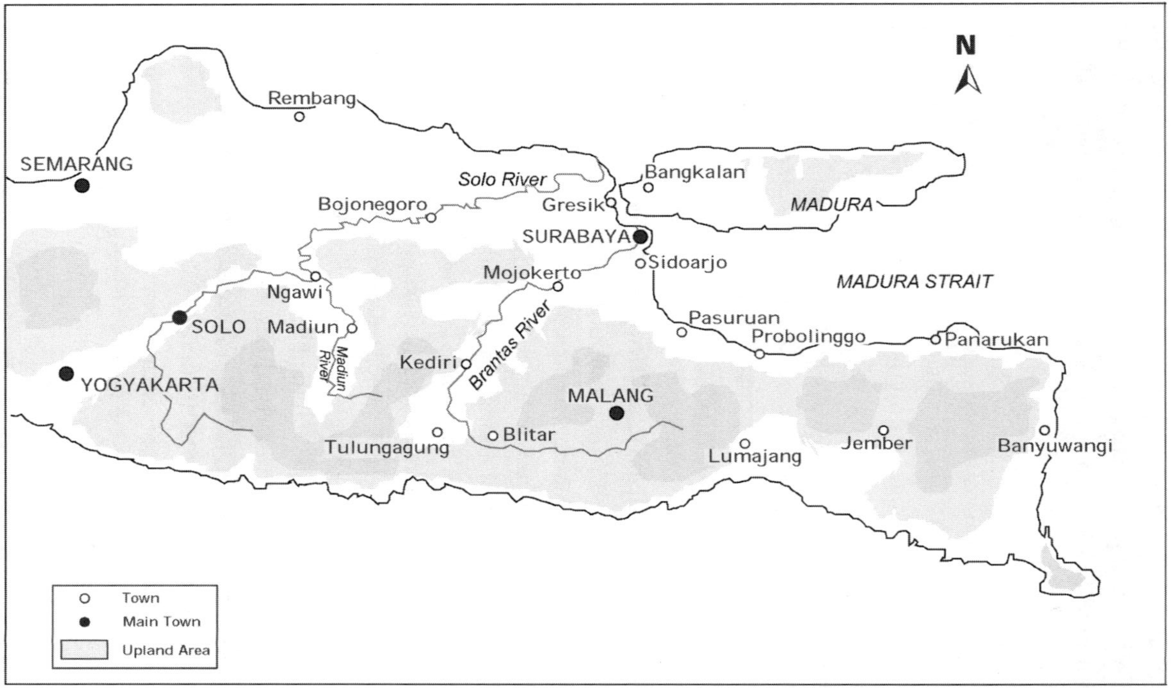

Map 1.1. Eastern Java: Rivers and main towns, ca. 1900. Source: Based on *Officieele Reisgids, 2 November 1939–1 May 1940.*

more extensive siltation spreading from the mouth of the Porong River, the main outlet for the mighty Brantas, the lifeblood of Surabaya. To protect the city against flooding, in the mid-nineteenth century Dutch engineers diverted the main stream due east into Madura Strait, into the corner where the coast bends north toward Surabaya. Here the terrain is obviously that of a delta. Behind the shoreline, fringed with mangroves and lapped by a mud-colored sea, appears a jigsaw of ponds (*tambak*), broken into irregular shapes by the seaward meanderings of small creeks. Mirrorlike when filled, opaque when drying into salt, these tambak are a rich source of fish and prawns, now one of East Java's main exports. Beyond this wide belt of tambak, along an irregular seam, begin the rice fields and the signs of human settlement. But little more is to be seen as the aircraft banks to land and taxis to the terminal against a backdrop of banana trees and tall bamboo.

The drive by taxi from the airport was until quite recently through countryside. Beyond the cluster of airport buildings and housing, the road was lined on either side by rice fields. Only one isolated complex of bungalow housing suggested the proximity of a city. In the 1990s development began to take hold with new projects for hotels, housing, and even a Shoe-Mart, plus many roadside advertisements. The pace quickens when one emerges via a roundabout onto a busy divided highway, the main route to Surabaya from the east, south, and west. This Aloha roundabout, named after a popular roadside restaurant, used to be the southern terminus of the city bus line. For some miles northward one observes the kind of untidy ribbon development so typical of cities in East or West. Factories, government offices, warehouses, shops, kampungs, a university, bungalows, and vacant blocks of land succeed each other in no apparent order. Much of the land behind these buildings is still farmland, once cultivated for long-closed sugar mills, though side roads lead off to housing complexes and other new developments. Eventually one descends by a short overpass into the densely packed settlement of Wonokromo, until the 1960s both the actual and the official southern limit of Surabaya.

Separated from the rest of the city by the northern arm of the Brantas River, it has always been something of an outpost, with a reputation as the haunt of criminal elements. It used also to be the main market for fruit and vegetables brought in from the hinterland. Nowadays Wonokromo is divided even from itself by the highway and its high steel fences. Communication between one side and the other is possible only by overhead walkway, a parable of the modern transport revolution.

Within a minute or two one has sped through Wonokromo, passing over the low bridge across the Brantas lined with squatter shacks, and enters Surabaya proper. On the left is the crowded bus station of Joyoboyo and then the shady enclosure of the zoo. From there one turns into the wide, straight, tree-lined Darmo Boulevard, pushed through in the 1910s as the grand approach to the new garden suburb being laid out in what was then still rice field. Despite modernization, the bungalows and mansions along either side still betray their Dutch origin with high-pitched roofs and large windows—many have been converted into banks, offices, or showrooms. Suddenly the wide center strip disappears, the left-hand lanes diverge, and again the scene changes. Large buildings in garden settings give way to a jumble of single-story shops, the pavement alive with becak, pedestrians, and hawkers. One has crossed over the old edge of the city into the world of crowded kampungs. Only on the right, where the kampungs burned down in the fighting of November 1945, are there any substantial buildings, a long, two-story row of shops, offices and a run-down hotel. As the taxi bears left along what is popularly known as Kaliasin—but like so many other streets bearing the official name of a deceased general—there appears the shining white façade of the luxury Bumi Hyatt Hotel, since 1979 the prestige hotel and a popular venue for society weddings. There follow on both sides a variety of commercial premises: automobile showrooms, new multistory banks of aggressive design, offices, the city bus depot, and a few surviving small stores, shops, and stalls (*warung*). Vacant premises and buildings under construction suggest vigorous redevelopment. On the left one passes the Gelael supermarket, the first in Surabaya, and then the tall Tunjungan Plaza shopping mall. Just beyond, at the aptly named junction of Simpang (Crossroads), our two journeys merge in the heart of modern Surabaya.

Rhythms

In Surabaya, as throughout Indonesia, the day begins very early. Households begin to stir while it is still dark. Typically it is the women, and most notably servants, who are first to rise. Around 4 A.M. the stillness is broken by the universal Muslim call to prayer, the chant of Allahu Akbar distorted through the loudspeakers of nearby mosques. Together with the sounds of roosters crowing, this call marks the orderly beginning of a new day. For those who have not already risen, it is time to bathe and drink in preparation for the dawn prayer (*subuh*), a simple observance in the privacy of the home. Surabaya was one of the towns of the north coast (*pasisir*) from which Islam spread into Java, and the grave of the pioneer missionary Sunan Ngampel at the Ampel mosque is highly revered (fig. 1.10). Despite a sprinkling of Christian churches, Islam remains fundamental to the city's identity, especially among Javanese and Madurese.

As color creeps into the sky and streetlights fade, the streets begin to come to life. By the time the sun peeps over the horizon, around 5 A.M., there is already bustle in the local markets as women arrive on foot or by becak to buy the daily needs of vegetables, fruit, eggs, chicken, and soybean curd (*tahu*) and soybean cake (*tempe*). Most households still shop every day, some because that is all they can afford, some because the food is fresher. Women who cannot afford the time and have no servants to shop for them can buy from peddlers who each morning come around on skillfully overladen bicycles. Bakeries send out fleets of bicycles with clear-glass

Figure 1.10. The Ampel mosque, in the classical style, beside the grave of Sunan Ngampel. Photo by author.

panniers to distribute the sweet white breads that have become popular for quick breakfasts (in colonial times the eating of bread was confined mainly to the European population).

Dawn also brings out a quite different group of people, followers of the modern cult of physical fitness. Among the sedentary but more health-conscious middle class, male and female, jogging has become a popular form of exercise. People of all ages, smartly clad in tracksuits, walk briskly or jog with varying degrees of enthusiasm along streets still empty of traffic. Around five o'clock it is still safe to walk to market or jog in the middle of the road. Sports fields and tennis courts are also fully occupied. Business executives and top officials mingle on the golf course. Those who have to catch the early flight to Jakarta make their way to the airport in time for a 6 A.M. departure.

By six o'clock the exodus to work and school has commenced. Washed clean of the previous day's dust, bemo and becak are scouting for custom. First to leave home are mostly schoolchildren. Because of the pressure on classroom space, school buildings are used twice a day. Morning classes begin about 6:45 (half an hour later for primary school). Since competition for good schools is keen and some students, especially at senior level, have to travel far, from six o'clock onward the streets are full of uniformed schoolchildren waiting for public transport, riding their own bicycles or motorcycles, or being escorted by becak or private car. Along main roads, countless newspaper stalls, cigarette sellers, and hawkers of snacks and drinks ply a busy trade.

First to begin work are those in factories. Before six o'clock the roads of the industrial estate at Rungkut are occupied by a stream of workers, many of them women, from surrounding kampungs and boarding houses. Some factories, such as the Soempurna *kretek* (clove cigarette) factory, employ thousands. Government offices open officially at 7 A.M. but until 7:30 or 8:00 it is often only the cleaners who are in attendance. Only an optimist would try to do business much before about 8:30. Most private offices do not open until about eight o'clock, though to miss the rush hour traffic many managers do not arrive until 8:30 or even 9:00. Appointments are usually made from about nine o'clock onward. Banks, however, now open at eight, so that staff have to report for work up to an hour earlier. In the port of Surabaya, where many thousands are employed, the daytime shift also begins at eight, though customs officers have long been notorious for their tardiness in allowing access to the godowns.

Because they stay open until quite late at night, the last businesses to open are shops and department stores. It is about 8:30 before the boards begin to be removed from the windows and shutters and grills are opened. Most stores do not open for trade until 9 A.M. Anyone who wants to shop before then can go to the multistory market complex of Pasar Turi, a warren of small booths where most kinds of consumer goods are on sale from about seven o'clock. As these are also wholesale markets, it is quite feasible for out-of-town buyers to arrive early in the morning, make their purchases, and return home in time for their normal opening of business. Local fruit and vegetable markets, however, are already quietening down by nine and by midday the last traders will be closing up.

In the middle of the day there is something of a pause in activity. In factories the lunch hour often begins at eleven o'clock, which allows strict Muslims to absent themselves briefly for the midday prayer (*luhur*) about half an hour later. In larger factories and on the waterfront, meals are usually provided by the company, typically a helping of rice and side dishes wrapped in banana leaves or some modern equivalent. In government offices, those who have eaten only a light and early breakfast take lunch or at least a snack from the canteen, perhaps eating at their desk.

From about noon, public transport again becomes crowded, initially with schoolchildren, as morning school finishes and afternoon school begins. Primary school ends at noon, except for students in the first two grades, who return home two hours earlier, and middle and senior school students, between 12:30 and 1 P.M. By the time this rush has subsided, civil servants are already beginning to drift home. Although the official workday does not end until two o'clock, most offices are manned by only a skeleton staff after 1:30. Senior officials, however, may be engaged in their offices, in meetings, or at seminars until the late afternoon. By 2 P.M. government banks are also closing for business, though private banks remain open an hour later. Except in the new air-conditioned shopping plazas, many stores also close, then reopen in the evening. There is no longer, as in colonial times, a general siesta to follow what used to be the main meal of the day. Many factories do not change shift until 3 P.M., without allowing for overtime, and many private offices now remain open until four or even five o'clock. Many bank officers also do not leave work until after four. The return from work in the afternoon is therefore very staggered and hardly resembles the Western phenomenon of the rush hour. Yet even in the absence of a general siesta, mid-afternoon is still a sluggish time of only desultory activity, reflecting the oppressive heat of the dry season and often the chaos of a torrential downpour in the monsoon.

In late afternoon the city comes back to life. The sun has lost its strength and disappears behind a bank of cloud and smog. Asphalt, concrete, and brick still radiate heat but there is at last some breeze from the sea. Those early to return home have rested, bathed, and taken some refreshment, such as a glass of tea and a sweet snack. It is time to relax. In the kampungs, children play on the pathways while their parents sit around smoking and chatting. Especially for young people, it is the opportunity to get together in couples or small groups to go visiting, shopping, or in search of entertainment. In more leisurely colonial times this was the hour when people dressed in their best to promenade, a Mediterranean custom the Dutch had adopted in Batavia as early as the seventeenth century. Nowadays the traffic is such that the street is no longer the place to be and evening recreation is more focused. Cinemas begin screening their evening programs from 4:30 onward. By five o'clock all shops, department stores, supermarkets, and ice-cream parlors are ready for their busiest time of day. The outlets for the national lottery do a thriving trade. Photocopy services are crowded with students. Also busy are the private surgeries of doctors and dentists, who typically work in public hospitals during the day but hold private practice from five to seven in the evening, generating a steady stream of people to nearby pharmacies (*apotik*). Sports fields and tennis courts are again fully occupied, while in the kampungs young people play badminton, volleyball, or football in any vacant patches of level ground. As dusk approaches, those homeless who squat along the riverbanks, beside the railway tracks, or in the parks and plantations begin to bring out their possessions and to reassemble their makeshift dwellings, safe until daylight from the risk of being cleared away by a police raid (fig. 1.11).

By six in the evening it is already dark and the city takes on a very different aspect. The night markets such as Pandegiling are now in full swing, their wares colorfully arranged on trestle tables, protected from the weather by canvas awnings and lit by the soft light of kerosene pressure lamps. In front of the cinemas, food and drink stalls cluster together awaiting the end of the early-evening session. Along the main streets and in front of other strategic locations such as hospitals, food stalls are brightly lit with pressure lamps, which show up in sharp relief the menus painted on their cloth signs advertising *sate,* noodles, rice, or *martabak* (omelette). Cigarette stalls, newspaper and magazine vendors, gasoline and oil kiosks, and tire repairers are also strung out along the side of the road like so many gay decorations. Because the more dimly lit buildings recede into the darkness, these informal-sector activities now stand out with reassuring prominence, keeping at bay the uncertainties of the night. More garishly prominent are the neon lights of the main shopping areas. The old central business district, however, is now quiet. The back lanes have been closed off to become the living areas for the families of Madurese becak drivers, hawkers, guards, and workmen who camp in a semipermanent existence away from their home villages. In the more settled Javanese kampungs, one can walk along the pathways and observe that almost every second house now has a television set, which has become the main focus of household entertainment.

Figure 1.11. Homeless people setting up overnight camp, Gubeng railway yards, 1987. Photo by author.

After eight o'clock the activity begins to decline as shoppers return home, and an hour later the last shops put up their shutters. This is the time when many middle-class households sit down for the evening meal. In the main shopping complexes it is only restaurants, cinemas, and amusement parlors that remain open. On weekdays cinemas offer a late show beginning around 9:45 or 10, but attendance is much lower than in the evening. While the show is in session, the situation outside has become very quiet. The food stalls and handful of waiting becak are now each other's only customers. The busiest parts of the city are the red-light districts, especially the big complexes, thronged mainly with young people. For those who seek brief solace but do not crave the exuberance of these rather notorious haunts, there is also the company of the streetwalkers, who are not hard to identify along their usual sections of some main roads. And, of course, there are also nightclubs and, from 10 P.M. onward, a few discotheques. The Youth Park (Taman Remaja) offers a variety of entertainments to suit the tastes of teenagers, or at least those with money. The night life of Surabaya does not lack variety, even if it is short on sophistication. Officially, all forms of entertainment, including centers of prostitution, are meant to close at midnight—except for discotheques, which for some reason are allowed to stay open until 2 A.M. In reality, as long as they have money the sleepless can always find somewhere to dally and be entertained into the very early hours.

The other place that remains a hive of activity throughout the night is Pasar Keputran, the wholesale fruit and vegetable market beside the river in the southern part of the city. From around dusk, trucks have been arriving with loads of cabbages and cauliflowers, coconuts and jackfruit, and discharging them in great piles beside the road. There the produce is sorted and haggled over before being carried by shoulder pole through the throng of becak and stalls into the ground floor of the market hall. Inside under lights, in a maze of booths and alleyways, all kinds of produce is laid out in profusion. As is typical of Java, the buyers and sellers are mostly women, often in traditional batik costume, while the men, stripped to the waist, provide the muscle that keeps in motion the jostling circulation of goods and people. In the hours after midnight, as the city sleeps, Pasar Keputran is like a hectic, Brueghelian dream. Few factories work a midnight shift, though at Tanjung Perak one or two ships may still be working cargo under lights. And, of course, the new automated presses of the morning newspaper *Jawa Pos* are rushing out the morning edition to be ready for distribution about 3 A.M.

Otherwise the city is quiet, with few visible signs of activity. Except for the occasional taxi, motorized traffic has all but disappeared. The teams of yellow-uniformed street sweepers work undisturbed. The night becak now have the streets to themselves, even the so-called protocol roads, where they are forbidden in normal hours. There are few passengers, but to travel home by becak in these cool, quiet, early hours is serene. The streets are for once deserted of people. Most street stalls are now locked up, though beside the road, often at the end of a kampung lane, one sees the occasional cigarette or food stall, lit up by a pressure lamp. Their occupants are the eyes and ears of the night, a friendly greeting for any familiar face, a quiet challenge to a stranger. Each kampung musters a voluntary skeleton watch for any suspicious comings or goings—their imagined opportunities for nocturnal philandering is a never-ending source of jokes. The rich in large houses beyond the protection of the kampung often number among the servants a night watchman, groups of whom chat and play cards on the pavement. Offices, factories, and godowns also have their night watchmen—typically Madurese, who are much feared for their fierceness and clannishness. Surabaya has long had a bad reputation for often violent theft and burglary. The army-sponsored "mysterious killings" of the early 1980s brought some respite by eliminating many of the gang leaders, but collapse of the authoritarian New Order has been followed by a resurgence in petty criminality.

Such then is the typical working day, a rhythm well suited to the demanding climate and that, in essentials, seems to have changed very little in a long time. Yet there have been changes. Around the turn of the twentieth century, when electric ceiling fans were the modern thing, the working day started very early, around seven, and ended with a large midday meal, followed by siesta. The hot mid-afternoon was strictly a time of rest. Europeans rose again around four for tea and a light snack before dressing to go out. Women would then discard their informal household sarong and long blouse (*kebaya*) for more "elaborate toilettes" and from five to eight in the evening go driving and make their social calls (McMillan 1914, 93). Looking back in 1950 to these times, one old Dutchman recalled the habit known as Poeter Kajoon (taking a turn around Kayun), whereby to escape the oppressive heat of their quarters a group of young men would hire a carriage at Simpang and enjoy the cooler air along the river at Kayun before completing the circuit along Kaliasin back to Simpang (*NC*, 17/3/50). Then presumably they would adjourn to the club for a beer. The various clubs, known in the vernacular as *soos* (pronounced with long -o-; short for *societeit*), were then the center of European social life and occupied imposing premises (Faber 1931, 354–63).

A quarter of a century later much had changed. A reliable electricity supply after 1911 facilitated the installation of ceiling fans, and by the 1930s even air-conditioning. It also brought cheap lighting, not only street and internal lighting but also bright neon signs, especially in the elite shopping street of Tunjungan. Many European and some Chinese families could now afford an automobile, and everyone could enjoy the regularity and comfort of the electric tram. Working hours now extended to five in the evening, which for Europeans became the rush hour for return from the central business district to villas in the new garden suburbs (Bauduin 1941). Indonesian staff would catch the tram, ride their bicycles, or walk. Shopping and entertainment extended further into the night and became more diverse. The soos, with their predictable routine, lost patronage to more modern forms of entertainment, such as the cinema, ice-cream palaces, dancings, or, at home, the radio (Faber 1936, 384–90). Surabayans boasted that unlike the good burghers of Batavia, who went to bed at eight, they enjoyed themselves until well into the night. On the other hand, Simons (1939, 5575) maintains that except on public holidays the average Dutch person would be in bed by ten. Then, as now, younger and unmarried people probably had more stamina, even if their amusements were not always respectable.

After Independence the introduction of a compulsory forty-hour week again shortened hours of work in the afternoon. Department stores, for example, reduced their hours from eight to noon in the morning and from four to seven in the evening (*SP*, 3/8/53). Fewer and fewer civil servants bothered to report punctually for work at seven in the morning. By the 1960s most were forced by inflation to work at second jobs and attendance became highly erratic. Even factories could work only when raw materials were available. In the so-called formal sector people were no longer ruled by time.

Over recent years, there has been a return to more Westernized working hours. The trend first became apparent in Jakarta and gradually spread to Surabaya, initially in the private sector. Punctuality is again emphasized, to some extent even in the public service. Banks have extended their hours of service to 2:30 or 3 P.M. As in the late-colonial period, air-conditioned offices remain open until four or five in the afternoon. Stores in air-conditioned shopping plazas stay open throughout the afternoon. All this is undoubtedly more efficient, but the change in lifestyle is perhaps to be regretted. The city no longer has the time to catch its breath in the hot mid-afternoon. The traffic at the end of the day consists less of people coming out to relax and is more a rush hour of tired people returning at the end of a long day to be entertained at home by national television. Businessmen, however, are joining the trend to go after work to a fitness club, while their wives join aerobics classes. Entertainments are also changing as middle-class youths have more money to spend in cinemas, amusement parlors, and late-night discotheques. For better or worse, lifestyles in Surabaya—at least in middle-class Surabaya—are becoming much more like those of the West, and more like those of the late-colonial period.

The daily pattern varies somewhat over the course of the week. As though people are too exhausted or too impoverished by the weekend's activities, Monday evening is usually quiet. Friday, when Muslims are expected to pray in the mosque, is a short working day (*hari pendek*). Civil servants begin the day at 7 A.M. with an hour of outdoor calisthenics, and then work only until 11 o'clock. This allows plenty of time to join with people congregating in the mosques and prayer halls (*langgar*) for the midday observance. The holy Ampel mosque is especially crowded (fig. 1.12). Private offices and factories do not close but allow an extended lunch break until 1 P.M. For all offices and factories, Saturday is only a half day. On that afternoon everyone has time to rest. From evening onward, shops and places of entertainment are at their busiest for the week. Crowds throng the shopping plazas. Smart restaurants with live singers and floor show may on week nights be at best half full but now are at capacity. Cinemas are well patronized and many hold a midnight screening. Billiard salons, nightclubs, and the red-light districts do a thriving trade. The main difference with Saturday

Figure 1.12. Friday prayers, Ampel Mosque. Photo by author.

nights in the West is that very little alcohol is consumed. Drunkenness is rare. Next morning there are many tired Surabayans but few hangovers.

On Sunday, the week's one full holiday, there is no necessity to rise early. Although Christian church services begin around seven in the morning, without the rush to school and to work the streets remain quiet and even the main highway out of town is free of its usual early morning traffic jam. Not that everyone stays home. Many take the opportunity to visit family or friends outside the city. The bus terminals are busy indeed. Those having cars may make a family outing to the nearby hill resort of Tretes, where as in colonial times the wealthy keep bungalows for weekend use. For most people, however, Sunday is a day to relax at home or to visit friends, to be sociable without spending too much money. Before the day gets too hot, some parents take their children to visit the zoo or the beach, such as it is—the narrow stretch of sand and mudflats at Kenjeran. Cinemas have an early showing at 10 A.M. and another at 1 P.M. The quietest part of the city is the old central business district around Jembatan Merah, where all offices are closed, though the Chinese noodle restaurants are busy. Because many servants are given the day off, food sellers do good business, while the growing number of ice-cream parlors are also well patronized. In the evening, which sees the return of day-trippers by train, bus, and car, the public transport terminals are crowded—pickpockets do a thriving trade—but most people just go home to recover. There is little public entertainment and even restaurants and cinemas are fairly quiet.

Over the course of the month there are subtle differences in the tempo of economic activity. Because public servants and military personnel are paid on the first day of the month, shops, restaurants, cinemas, other places of entertainment and even public transport do a thriving trade in the first week or so, when people have money to spend. As the month wears on, the tempo slackens. Among traders, the hunger for cash becomes extreme:

credit terms become tighter and goods can be bargained down to lower prices. Traffic police seem to become more active. The whole city, like the rest of urban Indonesia, has become accustomed to this monthly cycle.

The year manifests itself primarily though the pattern of the monsoons. Around the middle of the year, at the start of the dry season, when the east wind blows from the dry Australian continent, the climate is at its best: in the middle of the day the sun is not too fierce and at night, without cloud cover, it becomes almost cold. The distant volcanoes become visible and Surabaya seems for a while to be part of Java rather than some off-lying island. As each month goes by, however, the climate becomes more oppressive. By October strong winds are heralding the arrival of the rainy season. Clouds build up on the horizon in the morning and evening. Temperatures climb to 36 degrees (97°F) in the middle of the day and do not drop below 26 degrees (79°F) at night. Everywhere is dusty, the stagnant drains stink, mosquitoes swarm in voracious hordes. Newspapers begin to carry reports of outbreaks of dengue (*demam berdarah,* bloody fever). By November, it is perpetually cloudy but still refuses to rain. Tempers become frayed. In colonial times, this was the month when those Europeans who could afford it took their vacation. Husbands, who had to remain in Surabaya, sent their wives and children to the hill resorts. From the nightly television reports, one learns that the rains have already begun in Jakarta, but Surabaya continues to swelter in temperatures that are among the highest in the country.

The west monsoon arrives fitfully. Toward the end of November the first unpredictable showers bring welcome relief, cleansing air and earth. Not until December, however, does the monsoon really begin. By January it is raining with a vengeance. Every day it teems. Paper is limp and damp; clothes and shoes sprout mildew; rooms smell dank. Until rehabilitation of the elaborate, Dutch-designed system of drains, canals, and pumps, this was the month when large parts of Surabaya disappeared under water. Asphalt roads broke up as one watched and the dirt paths turned into quagmires. In the kampungs, it was impossible to escape the mud. Wells became polluted and intestinal illnesses, including typhus and cholera, became prevalent. These days the city copes rather better. The high priority given to flood control has resulted in accumulated refuse being cleared from drains and canals at the end of each dry season; pumps are overhauled to meet the deluge. Kampung paths have been sealed and drinking water piped in to avoid the need to use wells. In such a low-lying city, however, temporary flash flooding can hardly be avoided. For adults, it is frustrating, for children just good fun.

The monsoons affect not only people's comfort and temper but also the tempo of economic activity. The east monsoon (dry season) no longer brings the prahu trade fleet from eastern Indonesia (Dick 1975), but the agricultural cycle is still felt. In the long dry season, when much of the dry land to the west of Surabaya and on Madura lies idle for lack of water, there is a traditional drift to Surabaya in search of temporary employment. Before the collapse of sugar exports in the 1930s, the dry season coincided with the peak labor demand of the sugar industry, which milled from May to September. Tens of thousands of extra laborers were then engaged by the mills, railways, warehouse, lighterage, and stevedoring companies. Nowadays such seasonal labor must perforce turn to the informal sector, at the most desperate to begging or scavenging in rubbish dumps. Camping outdoors is no hardship at this time of year and many families settle inconspicuously along the riverbanks or railway lines (fig. 1.13). At the start of the wet season there is a movement back to the village to begin plowing and planting. Until the harvest, some three or four months later, there follows a time of dearth known as *paceklik*. Because of the government's buffer stock policies, rice prices no longer soar but cash is scarce and consumer spending subdued. From February onward, as the harvest begins to be brought in, farmers again have money to spend, debts are paid off, food prices fall, and so does the cost of living. After March economic activity is buoyant. Nevertheless, the impact of the monsoons is no longer as marked as it used to be.

Figure 1.13. Riverbank squatters, Keputran, 1987. Photo by author.

Improvement of irrigation and planting of faster-growing and higher-yielding varieties of rice now enable much land in the Lower Brantas valley to be double- or even triple-cropped (Fox 1993). The rhythm of the economy is therefore now more even through the year.

The course of the year is also marked by the cycle of festivities and public holidays. The highlight is the Muslim feast of Lebaran (Idul Fitri), which, like the other events in the Muslim calendar, drops back ten days each year in relation to the Western calendar. For strict Muslims it is preceded by the fasting month of Ramadan, when no food or liquids may be taken in daylight hours. This is also a time, like December in the West, when people spend on new clothing, presents, and special foods. Salary earners, including public servants, usually receive a thirteenth-month bonus. Retail turnover may be two or three times higher than usual. The government keeps a careful watch on supplies of food and clothing to ensure that shortages do not cause sudden price rises. Officially there are only three public holidays but Surabaya virtually closes down for two weeks. Not only do offices, factories, and schools close, but many drivers, hawkers, laborers, and household servants take the opportunity to make a long visit back to their home villages. Faced with the prospect of having to do their own housework, some rich families move into a hotel. All forms of transport are booked out well ahead as the whole country seems to be on the move in one great family reunion. Despite some flow of visitors back to the city, by the day of Idul Fitri, Surabaya seems a dull, empty place. Afterward people straggle back but for the next month or two have neither the means nor the interest in shopping, so that business is rather slack.

No other holidays generate such activity or excitement. The day of pilgrimage (Isra Mi'raj), about two months after Idul Fitri, the Muslim New Year and the birthday of the prophet Muhammad (Maulud Nabi) are fairly quiet affairs, with religious observances but no festivities. From the West have been borrowed the holidays of Christmas and New Year, which now constitute a minor holiday season, when not only Christians take the opportunity to return home for a few days and public transport is again fully booked. This is also a popular time of year for weddings. Chinese New Year was in colonial times celebrated with fireworks and noisy processions through the streets. In view of not so latent anti-Chinese feelings, it is now celebrated more discreetly but most stores and businesses close down, even though it is not a formal public holiday. Before the renewed ethnic violence of 1997–98, Indonesian-Chinese were becoming less nervous about decorating their premises and non-Chinese more relaxed about enjoying the special cakes and snacks that appear in the shops. If ethnic tensions subside, Chinese New Year may again be taken up, like Christmas, as an almost secular festival for the whole city.

The one unambiguously secular holiday is 17 August, Independence Day. Everyone must hang an Indonesian flag in front of their house—local neighborhood officials will scold anyone who is slow to comply. Civil servants and schoolchildren must attend patriotic ceremonies, which are commemorated on a smaller scale on the seventeenth of every month. Despite the content of newspapers and television programs, it seems to have become a rather formal occasion that has little impact on the population at large. More significant for Surabaya, though not in fact a public holiday, is Heroes' Day (Hari Pahlawan), 10 November, which commemorates the fierce three-week resistance against the British invasion in November 1945. In the 1950s, when memories were still fresh, it was the occasion for huge rallies around the new Heroes' Monument, on the ground where Kempeitai headquarters and the colonial Palace of Justice once stood. President Sukarno, himself from Surabaya, often came in person to address huge crowds from the balcony of the governor's office (fig. 2.5). Ceremonies are still held there each year but, except for the diminishing band of gray-haired veterans, it has become more of a formal observance and less of a spontaneous welling up of emotion, faith, and idealism. The events of November 1945 are not forgotten, but they are no longer imminent. The youth of 1945 are now grandparents. Two generations have now known nothing but independence. What they know of the colonial era is from schooling and oral tradition. The fifty-year anniversaries of Independence Day and Heroes' Day in 1995 were elaborately staged events that somehow failed to capture people's imagination, being formal commemorations rather than embodiments of popular feeling.

Chapter 2

EPISODES

THE YEAR 1900 was marked by no dramatic events, nor was it a turning point in any economic cycle. The sugar industry, producer of the city's staple export, had been established since the 1830s, restructured in the 1880s, and, like Surabaya itself, was again prospering. Apart from brief setbacks of recessions and the blockade of World War I, this boom did not run out of steam until the late 1920s, on the eve of the Great Depression. Compared with the tumultuous events after 1930, the early decades of the twentieth century were a time of normalcy and, with hindsight, seemed to both Dutch and Indonesians to have been a golden age (see Oki 1988). Not until the 1980s did Surabaya again enjoy an economic boom. This pattern of sustained expansion to the late 1920s, a long hiatus until the early 1970s, and then renewed economic expansion until the crash of the late 1990s is the template of Surabaya's twentieth-century history. The particular rhythm of that history is set up by a much more erratic sequence of political shifts.

This chapter highlights a few of the historical episodes that have molded the development of Surabaya over the past century. The sequence is broadly chronological and emphasizes the impact on the city of the obvious international and national events, such as the two world wars, the Great Depression, the Indonesian Revolution, and the strife-torn emergence and collapse of the New Order government. Worked into this historical framework are episodes of more local importance, such as the formation of the Municipality in 1906, the controversy that gave rise to the building of a modern deepwater port, the pains of suburban development on private estates and the strife that accompanied the formation of pioneer labor unions at the end of World War I. These events, controversies, and conflicts, whether explicitly economic or not, had long-term economic consequences.

Of all the periods of Surabaya's twentieth century history the New Order is the most difficult to portray episodically. History seemed to have been absorbed into a long and boring monologue on Stability and Development, like one of President Soeharto's twice-yearly reports to the nation. Only in hindsight did it become apparent that history had for thirty years been suspended. The tension, hyperactivity, and violence that surrounded and followed on the fall of Soeharto in May 1998 were of a piece with the bloody and hopeful transition of the mid-1960s, as though the resumption of a long narrative. The final section draws these events together, leaving the content of the New Order to be filled in by subsequent chapters.

Before 1900

Reflecting its strategic location at the gateway to the fertile valley of the Brantas River, Surabaya has long been an important trading center. The city officially dates its founding to 1293, when a Chinese expeditionary force is recorded as having been defeated in the vicinity by local armies. However, there is no firm evidence of any significant urban settlement. In the early fourteenth century, establishment in the Lower Brantas near Mojokerto of the powerful kingdom of Majapahit led to greatly increased trade through Madura Strait. Both Gresik and Surabaya, first mentioned in 1365, emerged as international entrepots, prospering from their stake in the spice trade of the Moluccas. Toward the end of the fifteenth century, as the power of Majapahit waned, the ruler of Surabaya seized the opportunity to become autonomous. For a century or so, Surabaya thrived as a wealthy city-state with a wide trading network and a cosmopolitan merchant community. Though smaller than the leading port cities of Southeast Asia, it was a large city by European standards, with a population estimated in 1625 to be fifty to sixty thousand (Reid 1993). As in other city-states of the pasisir, Chinese influence was strong, not only in the merchant community but also in the ruling elite, a product of intermarriage and the conversion of many Chinese to Islam (Reid 1992). Early in the seventeenth century, this autonomy came under threat from the rising power of Mataram, a kingdom based in the interior of central Java. For some years Surabaya held out against the armies of Sultan Agung (r. 1613–46), who twice laid waste to nearby Gresik, but in 1625, when the besiegers cut off the flow of drinking water, the city had to surrender at last. It was then razed, leaving a population of barely a thousand (de Carpentier, quoted in Faber 1931, 9). Many of the surviving merchants, Javanese and foreign, fled across the Java Sea to Makassar. A Dutch trading post or lodge set up by the Dutch East India Company (VOC) in 1617 had also to be abandoned (Faber 1931, 9). The trade of Mataram, more and more constrained by the monopoly policies of the VOC, was redirected through ports such as Japara and Tuban that were more under the thumb of its paranoid rulers.

For the next two centuries Surabaya remained a sometimes turbulent backwater. A modest Dutch presence in the form of a palisaded fort had been established in 1677, when VOC forces under Admiral Speelman landed and put to flight the army of the rebel prince Trunajaya, who had made Surabaya his bastion (Ricklefs 1993, 37–39). For the successful intervention on behalf of the king of Mataram and in security of the royal debt, the VOC was granted rights over the revenues of the ports of the pasisir (Ricklefs 1993, 47). The garrison was maintained after the debt had been paid off, as also a trading post at nearby Gresik. By the mid-1700s the population had recovered to some ten thousand families (Valentijn 1726, quoted in Faber 1931, 15). In 1743, after Dutch intervention had restored him to the throne of Mataram, Pakubuwana II ceded to the VOC the whole of the pasisir, including the towns of Surabaya, Gresik, and Semarang, of which the Dutch formally took control three years later (Ricklefs 1974, 38–39). By virtue of its proximity to the court of Mataram, Semarang became the center of the VOC administration and commerce on the north coast of Java. Surabaya was very much subordinate and had to share the local trade with the factory and naval station at Gresik, which was better placed to exploit the interior commerce along the Solo River. Over time, however, Surabaya's star waxed while that of Gresik waned, not least because Surabaya came to be seen as the more defensible settlement. Proclamation in 1795 of the Batavian Republic under French protection brought the Netherlands into conflict with Britain, leading to the loss of Ceylon and imposition of a naval blockade. The dangers of British invasion grew with the accession of Napoleon.

The first steps to strengthen the maritime defenses were taken by the energetic and ambitious Dirk van Hogendorp during his time as administrator of eastern Java (1794–98). His successor, F. J. Rothenbuhler (1799–1809), did not share the same sense of urgency. In December 1807, Admiral Edward Pellew's squadron was able to sail unopposed into Madura Strait and promptly overwhelmed and demolished the pitiful maritime defenses, without bothering to establish occupation. Governor-General Herman Willem Daendels (1808–11), who reached Batavia just a month later, was a man of much military experience in the Netherlands and recognized that Surabaya was more defensible than the open roadsteads of Batavia or Semarang.[1] He bent his energies to improving the city's defenses against naval attack, building a strong fort at the mouth of the Solo River to command the western entrance to Madura Strait, another more modest emplacement at the mouth of the Kali Mas, an arsenal just north of the Dutch town, and a military hospital to the south, beside the river. In the event, the British landing of 1811 was made in West Java and the Dutch forces surrendered near Semarang without testing the new defenses of Surabaya. Five years later, along with the rest of Java, the city was handed back just as peacefully to the Dutch. Daendels's initiative was nevertheless decisive in establishing Surabaya as the key to the defense of Java.

Rapid growth of commodity production in the hinterland began in 1830 with the Cultivation System. Perhaps the most succinct definition of this complex system of state-sponsored plantations is that of Cees Fasseur, namely a "form of agro-industrial exploitation of Java whereby the government used its authority and influence to force the peasantry to grow tropical export products in return for unilaterally set, low payments; these products subsequently were sold for the benefit of the treasury" (1975, 11).[2] The well-irrigated hinterland to the south of Surabaya was reckoned ideal for sugar cultivation and during the 1830s a number of sugar mills were established under contract to the government to mill cane grown by the local peasantry and to deliver the product to the monopoly exporter, the Netherlands Trading Company (NHM). During the 1850s, most mills converted to steam power (Umbgrove Commissie 1862–63).

During the 1860s the sugar industry began to be released from government controls (Elson 1994). The NHM's surrender of its export monopoly allowed the entry of commercial capital. Passage in 1870 of the Agrarian Law, with provision for foreigners to lease village land, enabled mill owners to gain control of cane cultivation and to increase both area and yield. In the late 1880s the collapse of sugar prices caused by the rapid growth of beet sugar production in Europe forced the closure of many smaller and less efficient mills but the industry emerged stronger than before. In the 1890s its scope and productivity was enhanced by the provision of steam tramways to supplement the state-owned railway system. Growth of sugar production was accompanied by the growth of tree-crop production, especially coffee, in the highlands. The Agrarian Law of 1870 had allowed foreigners to take up seventy-five-year hereditary leases (*erfpacht*) of uncultivated "wasteland." The subsequent land rush saw much of the accessible land in the sparsely populated Oosthoek taken up for private estates.

By 1900, Surabaya had become the busiest port and largest city in the Netherlands East Indies. The Lower Brantas valley as far as Jombang and Kediri and more distant Madiun had become an extensive sugar-producing hinterland, all of whose output was exported through Surabaya. Although most of the sugar and tobacco of the Oosthoek was exported through adjacent roadstead ports such as Pasuruan, Probolinggo, and Panarukan, the companies managing the estates were based in Surabaya, along with banks, insurance companies, and trading houses. Of a total population of 150,000 at the 1905 census, there was a prosperous European community of around 8,000, a larger Chinese community of some 15,000, and almost 3,000 Arabs. As had long been the custom in Southeast Asia, each ethnic group still occupied its own quarter or kampungs under its own heads, the Chinese being so restricted by law. The historical novels of Pramoedya Ananta Toer (1980a,b) give a vivid impression of the tensions and cross-currents in this fragmented society as its entered a more restless age.

Formation of the Municipality

Queen Wilhelmina in her 1901 speech from the throne declared her government's acceptance of responsibility for the Indonesian population and foreshadowed a range of measures to arrest its apparently declining welfare. This became known as the Ethical Policy. Although the colonial government did not abandon the structures of indirect rule, henceforth the trend was toward increasing intervention and an expanding European-dominated bureaucracy. Infrastructure (especially communications and irrigation), public health, education, and administrative decentralization were some of the main items on the policy agenda, though the level of commitment and urgency varied a good deal.[3] Municipal government was introduced with some speed, first Batavia in 1905 and then Surabaya in 1906.

Formation of the Municipality (Gemeente) of Surabaya under

its own act with an elected Council (Raad) marked the city's passage into adulthood. Not that there was anything novel about the reform itself. Holland was a bastion of city government and Batavia from very early in its history was given the trappings of an independent municipal government. Despite its fine town hall, however, the municipality exercised almost no power, the VOC being too strong and the Dutch citizenry too weak (Abeyasekere 1987, 19). None of the other north-coast towns ceded by Mataram in 1743 were granted municipal government. In Surabaya there resided a Dutch administrator of eastern Java who was responsible to the governor of the northeast coast in Semarang. However, except in matters of trade, defense, and European affairs, the business of government remained very much in the hands of the Javanese administration, which was taken over more or less intact. During the British interregnum under the governor-generalship of Sir Stamford Raffles (1811–16), Surabaya and much of the Lower Brantas became one of the eighteen residencies of Java but the city as such still had no independent status.

In the nineteenth century, all power and authority was vested in the resident. He worked from an office opposite the Red Bridge and lived in the palatial country mansion built at Simpang at the end of the eighteenth century by van Hogendorp and completed by Daendels (fig. 6.1). Most of the day-to-day responsibilities for "native affairs," however, continued to devolve upon the resident's nominal counterpart, the regent, who until 1912 was a hereditary office of the princely Tjokronegoro family. Chinese and Arab communities were also fairly autonomous under natural leaders recognized by the Dutch in a hierarchy of lieutenants, captains, and majors. The Chinese officers were typically from the elite (*cabang atas*) of Java-born (*peranakan*) Chinese, often intermarried with regent families, and were heavily involved in opium farming, sugar mills, and land (Salmon 1991). By the 1900s, however, their influence was waning with abolition of the opium farms, the penetration of European capital, and the preference of Chinese business to operate under Western law (Rush 1990).

The initiative to establish Surabaya as a municipality did not arise from any groundswell of democratic feeling among even the European citizenry, who seem to have been singularly unconcerned with their lack of democratic rights. It was imposed upon Surabaya as a matter of official policy as an early manifestation of the more active orientation of the central government under the Ethical Policy. The basis for the reform of local government was the Decentralization Law of 1903, proclaimed to achieve both a delegation of powers and popular participation in local affairs (Schrieke 1918; Furnivall 1944, 263–64, 269–72; Niessen 1999). However, the central government took no risk of inciting an outburst of democratic enthusiasm. Surabaya's first council was fully appointed: the majority was both official and Dutch (15 European, 5 Indonesian, and 3 "Foreign Orientals")—of course, no women—under chairmanship of the assistant resident (Faber 1936, 96). The mayoralty never became an elected position, and the role of the elected councillors was only advisory. The locus of decision making came to reside in a small executive committee, the College of Aldermen (*Wethouders*), in which the interests of European commerce were always well represented. Its decisions were normally ratified by the full council.

The powers of the Gemeente were restricted in other ways, some formal, some informal. First, the resident continued to work and live in Surabaya, so that the mayor and council remained very much in his shadow. This situation was reinforced on 1 January 1929, when, under the Administrative Reform Law (Bestuurshervormingswet) of 1922, the province of East Java was called into being as an intermediate level between the central government and local government. Secondly, the taxing powers delegated to the municipality were very limited, so that it always remained heavily dependent on central government funding. Thirdly, the limited powers of the Gemeente did not even extend over the full geographic area of the municipality. Despite the emphasis of the Ethical Policy upon raising the welfare of the Indonesian population, under the Constitution of 1854 the kampungs remained autonomous under their own headmen, subject only to a very loose supervision by the "native" civil service. This status rested on a convenient fiction: "The colonial government . . . did not recognize Indonesians as a genuinely urban people, preferring to think of them as essentially rural folk and leaving them . . . to be ruled as such though they resided in an obviously urban setting" (Frederick 1989, 3).

By the twentieth century, the regent had lost all real power and had almost no funds, so that the kampungs were, in effect, a law unto themselves. The efforts of those who wished to improve the deplorable living conditions of the kampung were frustrated until 1931, when the kampungs were more closely integrated with the municipality (see chap. 4). Even then, urban kampungs on private estates remained exempt (see below). Until the collapse of civilian government in 1942, the municipality therefore remained a patchwork of authority rather than a true citywide government. Abolition in 1931 of the now mainly ceremonial functions of the Chinese and Arab officers recognized these groups as part of the mainstream of government but the council remained under control of the European community.

Nevertheless, the Municipality did have an increasing impact. Above all, it focused Surabaya's identity as a city, albeit of first-, second-, and third-class citizens. Second, it facilitated decision making on local matters. Although formally of the central bureaucracy, the mayor ruled through the council rather than by decree. The predominantly Dutch business and professional class thereby gained a real influence over decision-making. Third, although the bulk of funds continued to be provided by the central government, local revenues grew very rapidly, as did the local bureaucracy and its functions (chap. 4). The best symbol of this Parkinsonian process was the new town hall and offices. At first the council had been a homeless waif, for several years moving from one temporary and unsatisfactory building to another. In 1915–16 plans were drawn up for a town hall to be built in the Municipal Gardens (Stadstuin); in 1920, at the peak of the postwar boom, these gardens were upgraded to a palatial quadrangle to be laid out on newly cleared land at Ketabang (Citroen 1934). In the event, the financial stringency of the early 1920s forced curtailment of the scheme to just one of the four intended wings. The Municipality nonetheless acquired an imposing two-story building that is still in use (fig. 6.10), though now supplemented by a modern, five-story office block. It thereby established a commanding physical presence, just across the river from the Resident's mansion.

The Great Port Debate

Because Surabaya's raison d'être has always been its function as a port, the turn-of-the-century controversy over the development of the port was of great moment for the city's future.[4] What is intriguing to the historian is that the matter became so controversial and took so long to resolve. Raking over these old coals reveals much of Surabaya's role at that time in both the regional and international economies. It also gives some insight into the attitudes of its business leaders and officials, still poised uneasily between the familiar habits of isolation and the quickening demands of the modern world.

The issue arose because the opening in 1869 of the Suez Canal and the introduction of direct steamship services with Europe transformed the economics of shipping. In the leisurely days of sail, the time a ship spent in port was of little consequence. Any roadstead that provided a safe anchorage could enjoy the status of a port. As schedules became more structured, steamships ever larger, and speed of port turnaround the key to profitability, the impact on the port hierarchy foreshadowed that of the modern container age. Cargo needed to be concentrated at a few protected deepwater ports well equipped with cargo-handling facilities. Since ports along the north coast of Java were merely roadsteads, the last quarter of the nineteenth century saw much discussion of proposals for building harbors. The first big project was reclamation of an artificial deepwater harbor at Tanjung Priok, a few kilometers east of the old roadstead of Batavia. Work commenced in 1877 and was completed in 1886 (ENI 1918, 2:69).

Because of Surabaya's natural advantages as a sheltered, deep-water roadstead, investment was less urgent. Nonetheless, for the colony's main commercial port, Surabaya's infrastructure was fairly primitive. After negotiating the bar at the entrance to the West Channel, ships came to anchor in the lee of the island of Madura, clustering off the mudbanks at the mouth of the Kali Mas, not much better than a muddy creek (fig. 1.2). Especially after construction of Fort Prins Hendrik at the then mouth of the Kali Mas in 1837, the entrance had advanced very rapidly and was now about three and a half kilometers from the town. Cargo was discharged into lighters (*prauwen*) and unloaded at the main customs house (Groote Boom) beside Jembatan Merah. There import goods were piled up for inspection and payment of dues before being hauled away to the consignee's warehouse. This system, little changed since medieval times, was reminiscent of the weighhouse (*waag*) in the market square of any old Dutch town. The main export cargo of sugar, brought down from the hinterland by river prahu or rail, was transferred into large godowns along the Kali Mas to be later put aboard lighters and taken down to the roads (fig. 2.1). Yet, except for the modern port of Tanjung Priok, cargo handling at Surabaya was not much better or worse than other large ports in the region, including Singapore, Penang, and Hong Kong, which for smaller ships continued to be efficient roadstead and lighterage ports until recent times.

By the twentieth century, however, new technologies and the growth in trade had exposed the limitations of traditional cargo-handling methods, especially for sugar exports. As long as most sugar was shipped from the hinterland by river prahu, lighterage to the roads was still an efficient solution. Godown space along the Kali Mas below Jembatan Merah had increased steadily to meet the demand for preshipment storage. What upset the efficiency of this system was the construction of railways, most notably the State Railways, which competed aggressively for the carriage of sugar.

Figure 2.1. Godowns and lighters along the Kali Mas. From DOC 1930.

By the mid-1900s, only five mills still shipped their harvest by prahu (KKNS 1905, 46). Discharge from rail wagons into lighters now involved unnecessary double handling. Efficient use of the new technology required wharves where deep-sea ships could load directly from rail wagons. Import cargoes faced a different problem. The growth in trade volume and size of ships meant that the physical discharge of all import cargo in front of the customs house now caused incredible congestion, aggravated by the fact that the bar off the mouth of the Kali Mas could be negotiated by loaded prahus only at high tide. Everyone agreed that something had to be done. No one agreed on what should be done.

Plans for the construction of deep-sea steamer wharves like those at Tanjung Priok had been drawn up as early as 1875. The first official initiative, however, was the appointment in December 1897 of a committee under the chairmanship of Ir. W. de Jongh of the State Railways. This committee observed that Surabaya played a minimal role as an entrepot. Even to the east of the Archipelago little cargo was shipped from Surabaya and there was almost no transshipment, this trade being dominated by Singapore merchants using direct steamship lines. Citing the need to boost Surabaya's role as an entrepot, the committee urged the construction of a deepwater basin just east of the Kali Mas with facilities for railway berths. This recommendation was supported in September 1899 by the report of the Rotterdam expert Professor Kraus, but the government decided against proceeding on grounds of cost. As congestion in the Kali Mas and especially at the customs area worsened, however, business organizations like the Chamber of Commerce became more vocal in their demands for improvement.

In April 1903 the governor-general referred the matter to another committee consisting of representatives of the departments of Public Works, Shipping, and Customs. Reflecting the views of its political masters, this committee saw no immediate need for a deepwater harbor. It concluded that the entrepot role of Surabaya was now almost nonexistent because the trade of the eastern archipelago was increasingly directed through the improved port of Makassar. With regard to the shipment of exports from the hinterland, the committee observed that Surabaya's lower handling costs were offset by high rail freights, favoring the numerous anchorages along the coast. There was little reason to expect that the exports of Java would be concentrated upon Surabaya in the foreseeable future. The existing level of sugar exports could be handled very efficiently by lighter, which enabled loading from both sides of the ship. Reflecting the demands of the business community, the committee argued that the pressing need was not for a deepwater harbor but to overcome the congestion on the Kali Mas, which at times was so bad that traffic on the river became completely blocked. Accordingly, the committee recommended widening and dredging the river and excavating a new lighterage harbor on the west side. This plan (later known as Plan C3) was accepted by the government and the first allocation was approved in the 1907 budget.

Just when it appeared that the matter had at last been settled and work could begin, opposition began to be heard. As early as October 1905 the head of the main shipping agency in Surabaya had written to the head of the local division of Public Works, Ir. W. B. van Goor, urging the need to develop Surabaya as a central point of shipment. The branch agent pointed out that since the suspension of government coffee exports, the small rivers and creeks along the north coast of Java had not been maintained; most were now difficult for lighters to negotiate even at high tide, and, apart from Panarukan, none was worthy of being called a harbor. This must have been music to the ears of van Goor, who was committed to the idea of a deepwater harbor. Citing voices being raised against Plan C3, he recommended that it be scaled down to a modest improvement in the Kali Mas pending construction of a proper port. In August 1907, at a meeting in the resident's house at Simpang, he aired his proposals, specifically to dredge the entrance channel to a draught of eight meters (sufficient for the largest ships) and to construct a railway pier with a basin on the south side for the new floating dock. His main argument was that lighters had become an unnecessary link in the transport chain between rail and ship. Against this the Chamber argued that, as long as much sugar was still stored and shipped from godowns along the Kali Mas, lighters remained indispensable and were especially valuable in overcoming congestion at times of peak shipment. The Chamber summarized its objections: "The roadstead of Surabaya is the best natural harbor imaginable. . . . Business therefore regards a wharf for ocean ships as unnecessary and seeks only improvement of the entrance to the roads, so that they can be reached by larger ocean ships, and of the Kali Mas, so that the roads will be accessible to lighters at all times. . . . In the view of the Chamber, further execution of Mr. van Goor's plans, which give Business not what it asks but something that it does not ask, makes no sense" (KKNS 1907, 38). While not opposing construction of a harbor, the Chamber's prime concern continued to be with the state of the Kali Mas and the congestion at the customs house. In April 1908, when the municipal council approved plans of van Goor for renewing the quay walls along the Kali Mas, both the Chamber and the Trade Association actually opposed the measure on the grounds that it was only a palliative. They still wanted a prahu harbor according to Plan C3. These views were no doubt colored by the involvement of key members with the profitable lighterage firms, a vested interest that Abeyasekere (1987, 49) cites as instrumental in the opposition of Batavia's Chamber of Commerce to construction of the new port at Tanjung Priok. At root, however, was probably the association's preoccupation with removing obstacles to their familiar business. Proponents of the deepwater harbor were more oriented to the future, seeing the potential for Surabaya to develop as an entrepot and to draw business away from Singapore.

After the battle of the plans had raged indecisively for over two years, in August 1909 the government attempted to resolve the "deep difference of opinion" by calling in the two Rotterdam engineers, Prof. J. Kraus and G. J. de Jongh, Director of Municipal Works. In March 1910 the pair visited Surabaya and was soon able to convince both the Chamber and the Trade Association to support the harbor project. They made the obvious but hitherto overlooked point that, in the modern world, it was no longer necessary to discharge all import goods in front of the customs house: it was quite satisfactory to bring customs officers to any godown where goods had been discharged. In other words, the problem of congestion in the Kali Mas was in large part an artificial problem caused by an outmoded system of customs control. The engineers' final report was a thorough document that canvassed the arguments of the long controversy and set Surabaya in its international context (Kraus and Jongh 1910). Their proposals were essentially an elaboration of those of van Goor on a somewhat grander scale, with a large harbor basin instead of just a finger pier parallel to the shoreline. As in their proposals for the other main ports in the archipelago, the elements of the Rotterdam model were apparent: alongside berthing for deep-sea ships with rail access and large deepwater godowns with secondary godowns for entrepot cargo.

On receiving the report, the government acted quickly. Of the estimated project cost of 14 million guilders, 2 million were allocated in the colonial budget for 1911. The tender was let and the governor-general himself inaugurated construction on 6 October of that year. According to the original schedule, the work should have been completed within five years. Because of wartime constraints, the northern finger pier was not ready until 1916 and it was actually 1920 before the new facilities were fully operational (fig. 2.2). The unanticipated demand arising from the postwar boom led to extension of the bulk-handling berths and steps were taken to expedite completion of the two inner-harbor piers, for which berth options were fully allocated. Then the boom collapsed. It was too late to cancel the contracts without payment of exorbitant damages. The best that could be achieved was to cancel one pier and press ahead more slowly with work on the other, which was finally ready in 1925. By then Surabaya was unquestionably the best-equipped and most efficient port in the whole of Southeast Asia. No one could have predicted at the time that, because of the vicissitudes of the world economy and changing conditions in Indonesia, the capacity of the port would remain adequate until the 1970s. If anything, the port was overdeveloped, but van Goor's vision was well and truly vindicated. While he received his reward in promotion to head of the Department of Public Works in Batavia, he is one Dutchman who might well be honored by modern Surabaya.

The significance of the decision to build a modern port rather than a small lighterage basin can be appreciated from the striking

Figure 2.2. Loading sugar in the modern harbor of Tanjung Perak. From DOC 1930.

contrast with Semarang (Stevens 1984). In the 1900s business and government there were also preoccupied with the improvement of port facilities. In Semarang the decision was taken to proceed with a lighterage harbor. Work began in 1910 and, after wartime delays, was completed in 1920. Meanwhile plans were also being drawn up for a deepwater harbor. Implementation was delayed first by World War I, then by the financial stringency of the 1920s, the depression of the 1930s, and World War II. Semarang did eventually obtain its deepwater harbor but not until the 1980s. The inadequacies of an unprotected roadstead, in which cargo handling was all but halted during the rough west monsoon, were a great handicap not only to Semarang but to the whole of what became the province of Central Java, whose trade was instead drawn off by rail and road to Tanjung Priok and Surabaya.

Of course, it cannot be deduced that Surabaya would have stagnated in the absence of port improvements. As a sheltered all-weather anchorage it could have remained an efficient lighterage port and, at least until the Depression, would have been assured of a large tonnage of export cargo. Yet had the far-sighted proponents of a deepwater harbor not staged an eleventh-hour comeback and had the construction works been limited to a new lighterage basin, Surabaya might well have lost its status as an international port and, like Semarang, lapsed into stagnation, its trade drawn off by the better-equipped ports of Singapore, Tanjung Priok, and Makassar. In the event, as sugar cargoes dwindled, the excellence of its port maintained Surabaya's status as a gateway and in the 1970s helped the city to revive as Java's second growth center (chap. 7).

The Private Estates

At the beginning of the twentieth century, the town of Surabaya, like Batavia and Semarang, was still ringed with private estates (*particuliere landerijen*). Most of this formerly state land had been alienated under the administrations of Daendels (1808–11) and

Raffles (1811–16), partly as a means of quickly raising revenue and partly to improve the provisioning of the town. Those estates in the delta plain (as opposed to the dry southwestern hills) typically produced rice and sugar, with some tree crops and vegetables. Under the Cultivation System, sugar became the main cash crop and estates along the Kali Mas such as Ketabang, Bagong, Ngagel, Kupang, and Karah-Ketintang had their own mills.

The terms under which estates had been sold and the rights and obligations of landowner and inhabitants were never codified, as in 1836 had those in West Java lying to the west of the Cimanuk River.[5] Over time, however, a degree of de facto uniformity seems to have come about. The larger estates had something of the character of manorial domains. Villagers were entitled to farm the land in perpetuity in return for payment to the landlord (*landheer*) of a land rent (in money or kind) and provision of labor, partly in cultivation of cash crops such as sugar cane and partly in personal services to the landlord, such as housework, gardening in his mansion, or cutting grass for his horses. In practice the landlord or his manager appointed village officials and administered law and order; the native civil service was loathe to interfere unless called upon by the landlord. The main obligation of the landlord to the government was to keep in good repair the public roads and irrigation canals running through or along the boundaries of his land. Over the course of the century, some estates were divided among heirs leaving little more than a compound of garden, house, and servants, while parcels of land were sold off for the mansions of wealthy Europeans. Estates adjacent to the town were often subdivided and more and more took on the features of urban kampungs through the influx of rural dwellers seeking work in the town; household heads discharged their obligations to the landlord by paying land rent and an additional sum in commutation of traditional labor services. Owners of such estates, by now mainly Chinese, thereby took on the character of rentiers.

By the turn of the century the private estates had become an anachronism that satisfied nobody. In the vicinity of Surabaya there were forty-four private estates, varying in size from a single residential block to seven hundred hectares, with a total population of about fifty thousand (*RANI,* 1900). The alienation of powers restricted the authority of a more active bureaucratic state, including the new municipal government. Estate owners, who were now more commonly speculators, eyed the profits to be earned from converting their land into suburbs of European housing and chafed under their obligation to respect traditional land rights. Rents were often increased sharply to drive kampung dwellers off their land. The Arab merchant and land developer Ibrahim Baswedan, who in 1913 purchased the Bagong estate, doubled the rents: those who could not pay forfeited their land rights. Kampung dwellers therefore found themselves in a new and very uncertain situation, without the limited protection of the old paternalism but having no rights in the face of arbitrary landlord power.

Nevertheless, in 1910 kampung dwellers discovered that they did have some rights at law.[6] A courageous kampung dweller, Pak Salekah, refused to abandon his house and land to a Dutch development company, which then applied to the Landraad (Native Court) to evict him. Pak Salekah testified that he had been born in the kampung and, after his marriage, had built his own house adjacent to that of his parents. He had always regularly paid his land rent and additional sums in commutation of various labor services. The amount of Fl 20 offered as compensation was but a fraction of the Fl 70 he had paid for his house and the Fl 100 that he now estimated it to be worth after various extensions and improvements. Much to the astonishment of the developer, the court found that Pak Salekah had an "inviolable autochthonous right of habitation." The ruling had a precedent in the finding of the Raad van Justitie (Supreme Court) at Semarang in May 1903 but had never been applied in Surabaya. Then in 1912 a draughtsman by the name of Prawirodihardjo succeeded in his appeal to the Raad van Justitie against an order of the Landraad requiring him to move off his land. In this case the new landowner was reportedly offering the inhabitants only about one tenth of the value of their houses and land. The Supreme Court found in his favor on grounds that, although he had not lived long in that location, he enjoyed the rights of a traditional inhabitant and had fulfilled his obligations to the landlord. A third surprise was a term of imprisonment imposed upon the Arab landowner Baswedan, who had removed a holy grave without the permission of the local inhabitants.

These judgments started a ferment. Unscrupulous landowners could no longer rely on the support of the courts in evicting kampung dwellers for token compensation. On the contrary, Indonesians could now turn to the courts to defend their rights to land. In 1914, Prawirodihardjo, now described as a solicitor, and one Pak Siti (alias Sadikin), an ex-foreman with the State Railways, encouraged the inhabitants of the Bagong estate to refuse to pay the sharply increased rents to Baswedan, the new landlord. According to Dutch sources, Prawirodihardjo and Sadikin then began to propound the view that land belonged to the Javanese and therefore no rent was payable. During 1915 there emerged a general resistance on the private estates to the payment of rent or the performance of compulsory labor. The landowners were thoroughly alarmed. On 7 December 1915 seventeen of the main landowners in Surabaya—Dutch, Chinese and Arab—came together in an unprecedented meeting and decided to write to the governor-general seeking his intervention and, specifically, the imprisonment of the ringleaders of the revolt. The government's response was cautious. The resident was asked to advise the inhabitants that they were obliged to perform their traditional obligations but, at the same time, raised the prospect that the government would eventually buy out the private estates. The landowners tried to pursue the matter through the courts but met a further setback. In June 1916 the Supreme Court ruled that even nonpayment of rent did not entitle a landowner to evict: he could only demand payment of the back rent against forfeiture of removable assets.

This unrest was encouraged by the swelling Sarekat Islam movement. Early in 1912 leading Islamic merchants in Solo, alarmed at Chinese penetration of the batik industry, had founded Sarekat

Dagang Islam (Muslim traders' league) as a cooperative association dedicated to progress (Shiraishi 1990). On the initiative of Tjokroaminoto, a well-educated Surabayan, in September 1912 it was legally reconstituted in Surabaya as Sarekat Islam, with the triple aims of promoting indigenous commerce, living standards, and Islam (Van Niel 1984, 88–93). As a mouthpiece the vernacular newspaper *Oetoesan Hindia* (Indies Courier) was launched at the end of the year (Adam 1995, 171). Then in January 1913 Tjokroaminoto organized an unprecedented rally of some ten thousand people, which was followed later in the month by the party's first congress (Shiraishi 1990). From these roots Sarekat Islam quickly grew into Indonesia's first mass nationalist party. By 1915 it had co-opted Prawirodihardjo and Sadikin. The party provided legal and financial aid and arranged for kampung representatives to go to Batavia to meet the governor-general (Frederick 1989, 51). Around Batavia as well, discontent on private estates (also owned mainly by Chinese and Arabs) became a focus of Sarekat Islam activity (Abeyasekere 1987, 103–6). The enlightened attempt, in the spirit of the early Ethical Policy, to provide the Indonesian population with rights at law thus facilitated a collision between an adolescent nationalist movement and some of the cruder manifestations of capitalism, thereby also calling into question the legitimacy of colonial rule.

Resistance to the estate owners came to a head in 1916. Inhabitants not only refused to render personal service (*pantjendiensten*) to their landlords but also chopped down fruit trees, erected houses without permission, failed to report for work in the fields, and refused to deliver the landlord's share of the rice harvest. Landowners attempted with mixed success to meet these problems by calling in police, hiring outside wage labor, and in retaliation even refusing to permit marriages and burials, a measure declared invalid by the assistant resident. A more sophisticated tactic was applied by the Dutch-owned tramway company (OJS) on its Dermo (or Darmo) estate. Household heads were advised that a permit to build or rebuild a dwelling would be granted only in return for an agreement specifying that no other rights were claimed than hiring and letting land and dwelling, either party to give one month's notice of termination. By mid-1917 the company had discovered a more elegant solution: an agreement by household heads to renounce all customary rights to their land in return for payment of lump sum compensation of Fl 50–100 per household and relief from any further obligations to the landowner. This commutation transformed the relationship between the landowner and family heads into a simple rental agreement, terminable by either party but with the obligation on the landowner to meet the costs of rehousing in the event of notice from his side. As the OJS observed, the Dermo estate thereby in large part lost the character of a private estate. By August 1917 most inhabitants of Dermo had been persuaded to sign such an agreement. It is doubtful that they had much choice. This convenient solution seems to have met no opposition from government officials, who were anxious to calm down a volatile situation. By 1917 open unrest on the estates seems to have died away. During 1918 most of the five hundred inhabitants of the Dermo estate were paid off and moved off the land with almost no fuss. The next outburst of nationalist frustration would come through the nascent labor movement.

World War I

For the Netherlands Indies, World War I was no cataclysm like the later Japanese occupation. The Indies remained a zone of peace, as indeed did neutral Holland. Yet just as an earthquake on one side of the ocean may fling a tidal wave at the opposite shore, so the Netherlands Indies were affected in ways that could hardly have been predicted in August 1914. The effects may loosely be classified as psychological, economic, and social. Psychological, because eventual isolation from the mother country both kindled ideas of an independent Indies and awakened fear of vulnerability, especially from a nascent Japan; economic and social because the war generated rapid inflation that shattered the stability of Indonesian society.

The initial impact was predictably a jump in prices for imports and a softening in prices for exports.[7] The decline of trade with Europe, however, was soon compensated by the blossoming of trade with the United States, Japan, and Australia. Import volumes were thus maintained, though export demand slackened and by 1916 unsold stocks of perishable tobacco and maize were piling up in warehouses. After Germany's declaration of unrestricted submarine warfare on 31 January 1917, the shipping situation worsened rapidly. With Dutch shipping now also at peril, sailings to and from Holland were sharply restricted and many civil servants and military personnel had to extend their tour of duty. Not a bale was sold of the 1916–17 tobacco harvest and stocks of sugar and coffee also began to accumulate, causing the government to rush to construct semipermanent godowns on the newly reclaimed harbor terrain. In July 1917, soon after entering the war, the United States imposed an embargo on neutral Dutch ships, which severely restricted the burgeoning trade across the Pacific. Three months later, Britain imposed a telegraphic blockade, breaking daily contact with the Netherlands. The heaviest blow fell in March 1918, when the Allied countries seized all Dutch ships trading with or sheltering in their ports, including Singapore. Although the ban was lifted within a few weeks, foreign trade was almost suspended for several months. Such vast quantities of sugar, coffee, and tobacco now filled the warehouses of Surabaya that the 1918 sugar harvest had to be held in storage at the mills. No textiles at all were received from the Netherlands that year. Virtually all imports were now obtained from Japan. It was February 1919, several months after the Armistice, before shipping links were restored and at year's end were still below normal frequency.

Peace brought not a return to normal conditions but a frenzied worldwide boom, followed by a spectacular collapse. The boom was driven by export prices, which had stagnated during wartime but now took off, the index of twenty leading export articles doubling from 107 to 214 (1913 = 100) between 1918 and 1920 (Gonggrijp 1957, 155). Sugar prices (prime quality), which had soared from Fl 5.5 per picul (just over 60 kg.) in July 1918 to Fl 48 by the end of 1919, doubled to a peak of Fl 75 in May 1920, and then plummeted to Fl 15 by December (HVS 1920). During 1919 accumulated commodity stocks were therefore able to be sold off at almost unimaginable prices, leading to a great surge in domestic demand and spilling over into a pent-up demand for imports that trading houses, flush with funds, were more than willing to meet. Because of time lags and the lack of shipping, however, few orders could be met in 1919 and a ten-week dock strike in Rotterdam in the first half of 1920 imposed further delay. All this was conducive to overordering, so that by the second half of 1920 Surabaya's godowns were bursting at the seams with goods for which importers were reluctant or unable to pay (ARA, NHM 1920, 10). Prices for imports, which since 1914 had followed a steadily upward trend, now collapsed, prices of textiles falling to about half their peak level and prices of steel products to about a third (20). As domestic demand began to flag, importers incurred huge losses and many were forced into bankruptcy.

These times were all the more traumatic for the sudden onslaught of the influenza pandemic of 1918. The initial outbreak in July had little impact on East Java but a second outbreak that began in October, at the end of a long dry season, was devastating. Brown (1987) has calculated that the residencies of Surabaya and Gresik were among those where death rates in 1918 exceeded the annual average by up to one standard deviation. Among Europeans, the death rate in Surabaya was higher than in Jakarta and Semarang combined. Among Indonesians, the mortality rate may have been ten times as high: across Java the death toll was estimated as 1.5 million, almost 2 percent of the total Indonesian population. In East Java, where the disease was most virulent, Brown (1987) reckons that the death rate could have been up to twice as great, with a heavy bias toward young children and the aged. These figures nevertheless fail to convey the full horror of a disease of which the cause was unknown, the onset sudden, the symptoms alarming, and, in the absence of any known treatment, the result often death.

Labor Strife

With the Java Bank persisting in an easy monetary policy, wartime cost pressures fed through into domestic inflation. By the end of 1920 the money supply was 4.6 times greater than in mid-1914, much exceeding the threefold increase in import prices and the twofold increase in export prices (Gonggrijp 1957, 154–55). Food prices were especially vulnerable. After two years of heavy importing, in 1917 the Indies faced not only shipping problems but also suspension of imports from British Burma. In the following year, as the Indies came under a virtual blockade, the government took control of rice distribution and brought in measures to boost domestic food production, partly at the expense of the sugar industry, whose product was unsaleable (Creutzberg 1972–75, vol. 2). The rapid increase in secondary food crops (*palawija*) in particular avoided any physical shortage of food, but rice prices increased about 60 percent between 1918 and 1920 (CEI 1978, table 1). Little of the impact of inflation was offset by cost-of-living adjustments, so that urban wage earners in particular suffered a drastic decline in standard of living. After mid-1920, this distress was aggravated by the contraction in economic activity and employment in the modern sector of the economy. As elsewhere around the world, workers responded with industrial action.

During World War I, Java's urban work force had been organized with remarkable speed, especially in the public sector.[8] The first unions had been organized and led by Europeans as associations of skilled workers rather than mass organizations. In 1917 a more radical Sarekat Islam had began to organize trade unions. With this political backing and the encouragement of several dedicated Dutch socialists, Indonesian leaders emerged to form indigenous trade unions in key industries such as the railways, posts and telegraphs, printing, and the pawnshop service. Semarang was the center of political radicalism, trade unionism, and industrial action. Surabaya had the larger industrial work force and was the headquarters of Sarekat Islam yet lagged in unionization. Its urban Indonesian workforce was not organized into trade unions until the latter part of 1920 and then mainly through the efforts of one man, Jahja, the young, Dutch-educated son of a State Railways conductor. Beginning with an advertisement in the vernacular press that he was available to organize trade unions, he was engaged successively to set up organizations of printers, tailors, harbor workers, metalworkers, household servants, and signwriters, all of which were grouped into a central Union Association (Perserikatan Kaoem Boeroeh) with its headquarters in a house in kampung Peneleh. In November and December 1920, just as the downturn in economic activity was being felt, a wave of strikes suddenly engulfed the printing, engineering, and clothing industries. All were defeated and Jahja's union movement broken, but a degree of political awareness had been achieved. Reorganization of the trade union movement was coordinated by the more militant leaders through the Indonesian Communist Party (Partai Komunis di Indonesia, PKI), formally established at Semarang in mid-1920 on the basis of the former Indies Social Democratic Association.

Under PKI leadership, the next big strike of this era, the railway strike of May–August 1923, was centered on Surabaya. The railway workshops at Gubeng were one of the city's main industries and several thousand people lived in the adjacent railway kampungs. The strike began in Semarang on 8 May, following the arrest of the PKI and union leader Semaun, and on 10 May spread to Surabaya, where it was almost total. A day later some four thousand people turned up for a strike meeting at the Sarekat Islam building. Forewarned and prepared, the government and railway management reacted with "coordinated repression." Workers not returning to work by 15 May were sacked and evicted from their government housing. The resident reported 920 workers were not reemployed, of whom some eight hundred remained in Surabaya by July and more than half without work. As late as August, police, soldiers, and marines still patrolled the streets and guarded public buildings.

The next and final wave of industrial strife was the climax of intensive organization by the PKI. According to Dutch analysis, the party's secret policy deliberations held at Yogyakarta in December 1924 determined not only more actively to pursue the organization of the urban work force but to concentrate these efforts on Surabaya. From Yogyakarta, party leaders traveled to Surabaya to organize formation of a single maritime workers' union (Sarikat Pegawei Palaboean dan Laoetan, SPPL) and held a public meeting of some fifteen hundred workers and union representatives. Over the next few months the PKI headquarters became the offices for the unions of postal workers (Sarekat Postel), maritime workers (SPPL), metalworkers (Federatie Sarekat Boeroeh Bengkel Electrisch, SBBE), sugar workers (Sarekat Boeroeh Goela, SPG) and the local branch of railway and tramway workers (Vereeniging van Spoorweg- en Tramwegpersoneel, VSTP). Following the ban of 5 August on public meetings in Semarang and the collapse of plans for a Java-wide general strike, PKI activists moved to Surabaya to intensify their activities.

After a preliminary skirmish in the printing industry, the showdown took place in the metal industry. Here the communist-led union was strong. In October 1925 the SBBE had been formed by amalgamation of two smaller unions to cover almost the entire engineering industry. Its local membership, estimated by the Dutch at some two thousand, was the largest in the city. Moreover, it had just emerged victorious from a brief wildcat strike against one of the biggest engineering firms, the Nederlandsch-Indische Industrie, which had dismissed a communist trade union official. On 23 November 1925 a strike began at the Braat factory over the dismissal of a worker. The SBBE proceeded to serve on all the leading engineering companies a log of claims including a daily instead of hourly wage, an eight-hour day, double wages for overtime (including Sundays and public holidays), a half day's work on

Saturdays for a full day's pay, wages increases of 25 to 50 percent, two weeks' annual leave, and a pension scheme. The Surabaya Association of Engineering Companies rejected all these claims out of hand and refused to negotiate with communist-linked trade unions or officials.

An industry-wide strike was called to begin on 14 December but soon collapsed in the face of government repression. On 26 November the resident had already imposed a ban on public meetings by the PKI and affiliated organizations (including the metal industry union) and over the next few weeks took into detention no less than seventy-three PKI and trade union leaders. Deprived of both leadership and income, workers drifted back to work after Christmas and by January the industry was more or less back to normal. Over the next few months employers dismissed any known PKI or union organizers. In May 1926 the government banned its own employees from being members of the PKI or affiliated organizations. Together these measures were so effective that Surabaya, which in 1925 had been the center of Netherlands Indies communism, was unaffected by the PKI rebellion of November 1926, which was confined to West Java and West Sumatra. The rebellion nonetheless marked the end of any organized trade union activity until after the Japanese occupation.

The 1930s Depression

The 1920s was a decade of narrow and fragile prosperity. It began with a severe worldwide recession, which the colonial government made worse by drastic expenditure cuts. Assisted by a speculative boom in rubber prices, the economy began to recover in 1924 and reached a peak in 1928. Yet outward prosperity had weak foundations (Furnivall 1944, 428). The value of exports peaked in 1925, stagnated until 1929, and then fell almost 10 percent. In Surabaya, so heavily dependent on sugar, these trends were magnified. At the end of 1927 the local trade association had no more confidence than "at best it may be concluded that we are over the worst of a series of malaise years" (HVS 1927). During 1928 domestic demand was high and the value of imports through the port grew by 22 percent, but world sugar prices, which had fallen by about a third in the previous year, continued their downward slide (HVS 1928). Despite record shipments of 1.2 million tonnes of sugar in both 1928 and 1929, their export value was static in 1928 and fell by 14 percent in 1929 (*IV* 1930). By late 1929 the signs of the imminent depression were unambiguous. From then on it was downhill all the way until the trough in 1935. The Dutch government's refusal until 1936 to countenance devaluation meant that the colonial government was obliged to pursue stringent deflation (Korthals Altes 1979).

Because of the crisis of the sugar industry, the world depression affected Surabaya more than any other city in the Indies.[9] Java's sugar exports fell from about 3 million tonnes in 1928 and 1929 to just 1 million tonnes in 1936; shipments through Surabaya fell correspondingly, from 1.2 million tonnes in 1928–29 to less than 0.4 million tonnes in 1936. Between 1931 and 1934, as the Chadbourne international sugar agreement took effect, the area of East Java planted to cane fell by 81 percent. In the four main sugar-growing regencies of the Lower Brantas (Sidoarjo, Mojokerto, Jombang, and Kediri), the proportion of irrigated land planted to cane fell from about 27.5 percent to less than 5 percent (based on Levert 1934, app. Z). It may be presumed that the reduction in the number of man-days of planting labor fell by not much less than the all-Java average of 93 percent (Levert 1934, 279). Many less efficient mills in the hinterland closed down while others operated at reduced output and manning levels. Maintenance was kept to a minimum and as far as possible replacement parts were cannibalized from idle mills. All this led to downward multiplier effects through reduced demand for transport and warehousing, cessation of orders for the heavy engineering industry, and the overall contraction in income and consumption. Until 1931 the full impact of the depression was cushioned by ongoing government expenditure programs, but after 1931 drastic expenditure cuts reinforced it. The city's European façade displayed a semblance of vitality, as did the continuing development of the new Tunjungan shopping precinct in contemporary art deco style. Less visible signs bore witness to the social distress, as in the hundreds of empty houses (Ziesel 1939).

The impact on urban income and employment is obscured by the almost complete absence of statistics (Scheltema 1936, 97). The few available data apply just to urban unemployment, which is the tip of a very large iceberg. The phenomenon applies disproportionately to the European population because, in the absence of any form of social welfare, few non-Europeans could survive without some source of income. Yet even here the statistics are hard to interpret. The numbers registered at the Surabaya labor exchange were already fairly high at the first reported count in January 1930 and, with heavy layoffs by the sugar factories, trading houses, and the metal industry, rose steadily during the year (Vreede 1931b). Thereafter numbers actually fell away as the obvious collapse of the labor market discouraged people from maintaining current registration. After subtracting those of pensionable age and allowing for some hidden unemployment, Vreede (1932a) estimated about nine hundred European unemployed. Because the labor exchange in Surabaya served the whole of East Java, this figure overstated the open unemployment rate in the city of Surabaya (Vreede 1931b, 252). However, even taking it at face value it would imply an open unemployment rate among the European workforce of about 10 percent (see table 2.1).

By comparison with an open-unemployment rate of almost one-quarter in Australia (Forster 1988, 295), another country heavily dependent on the export of primary commodities, even this overestimate does not look too bad. It would probably have been ameliorated by a higher than normal rate of repatriation—Vreede (1931b, 254) referred to the liberal retrenchment policies of the larger Dutch houses, including paid passage back to the Netherlands. There was certainly an attitude that European society should not demean itself by showing obvious signs of poverty. Vreede

TABLE 2.1
Unemployment, Surabaya, 1930–32

	European	Indonesian
January 1930	712	717
June 1931	945	959
June 1932 (registered)	812	1,799
June 1932 (estimated)	900	—
Population (1930)	25,900	271,000
Participation rate (1930) (%)	34	42
Unemployment rate (%)[a]	10	1.5

Sources: Vreede 1931a,b, 1932a,b; tables 3.6, 3.11.

[a]Estimated open unemployment for June 1932 as a percentage of 1930 workforce.

(1932a, 672) reckoned that about half the estimated European unemployed could be categorized as "in need." This was nevertheless a small group—only 450 people—who could be identified and given help through various municipal and voluntary schemes. As the most common occupations of unemployed were identified as bookkeepers, clerks, copyists, and typists (Vreede 1931b, 252), it may be deduced that many of these were in fact Eurasian and would have been on the fringe of European society.

More problematic is the fate of the many thousands of Indonesians who lost their jobs in the early 1930s. Little research was carried out into the social impact of the depression on the Indonesian population, making it hard now to draw any firm conclusions as to how the burden was shared.[10] The official view was that unemployment was a specific and individual problem as far as the European population was concerned but a collective matter for the Indonesian population (Vreede 1931b, 246–49). The former required some policy response; the latter could be left to mechanisms of social redistribution.[11] Epitomizing the European view and anticipating the concept of shared poverty later articulated by Geertz (1963) for village Java, the NHM, for example, referred to the "great absorptive capacity of the kampung," but this seems to have been received wisdom and wishful thinking rather than actual knowledge (ARA, NHM 1931, 29; Boomgaard 2000, 33–35). However, it did receive some support from a fairly detailed—though hardly rigorous—study carried out in the first half of 1931 by a Labour Office official, Raden Mas Moeljono (Vreede 1931a). In several main cities, including Surabaya, he went to half a dozen kampungs and through the kampung heads interviewed anyone known to be without work. He reported that none of these people could be classified as in need. All lived either in their own homes or with other families and could still find other kinds of work at lower wages: at the start of the dry season in May and June work was readily available painting and whitewashing (Vreede 1931a, 523–24). On the southern outskirts of the city the local official (*wedana*) complained about the shortage of labor for the rice harvest. Workers laid off in May 1931 by the closure of the British American Tobacco Company factory at Ngagel were reported to have found work in the nearby sugar harvest (Vreede 1931a, 526). Although difficult to interpret, municipal data on building permits suggest that demand for "semi-permanent" housing held up much better than for brick housing, while in 1934 the Municipality complained of unauthorized building in the kampungs (SGS 1934). These scraps of evidence are hardly satisfactory, but they do suggest that Indonesian urban society was by no means reduced to desperate straits.

Explanation of various inconsistencies in the impact of the depression on the Indonesian population in Surabaya must recognize that the labor market was segmented. For those who retained jobs in the formal sector, where money wages were "sticky," sharp deflation in the domestic price level, especially in food prices, boosted real wages (Scheltema 1936, 95–100). The burden fell upon those who lost their jobs. At the end of 1930 a quick survey among European firms gave evidence of heavy layoffs, including over a thousand dismissals in the metal industry in the latter half year; added to this were 250 dismissals in the printing industry and 1,100 among another nine large European firms (Vreede 1931b, 262). Those who lost their jobs in the metal and printing industries would have been mainly skilled or semiskilled tradesmen (*tukang*) with strong kampung roots, the archetypal Surabayan. The aforementioned Moeljono study argued that such people were supported by kampung networks and could find at least incidental employment in other fields. They would have benefited from a shift in demand to cheaper informal-sector goods and services, including small-scale transport, street vending, and cottage industry, though no data are available on any of these activities.[12]

A separate category was that of day laborers. Because this heavy manual activity was scorned by the Surabayan as beneath his dignity, day laborers and their foremen were typically drawn from the poor outlying districts of Gresik-Lamongan, Madura, and as far afield as Lumajang. Such employment was mainly seasonal and on dismissal most laborers seem to have returned to their village. How great was the cutback in the demand for seasonal labor is not known but Vreede (1931b, 526) reports that two thousand laborers had been laid off at the naval base by mid-1931 and had returned to the nearby rural districts of Gresik. The collapse in the volume of sugar exports would also have slashed the seasonal demand for wharf labor. However, the impact would have fallen upon rural villages rather than urban kampungs.

The most distressed group of unemployed seems to have been indentured labor repatriated mainly from the plantations of North Sumatra. In 1930 and 1931 there was a huge net repatriation to Java of sixty-nine thousand laborers plus their dependents, the largest group of whom returned to Central Java, though East Java also received many thousands (Vreede 1932b, 202–4). Some who were not accepted back into the village made their way back to Surabaya, partly in desperation but perhaps also because they perceived income-earning opportunities to be better there. Unable to turn to any extended family, they formed squatter communities living in deplorable conditions:

> Built from small bamboo poles, here and there strengthened by an iron bar, with walls of cartons and sacking plastered over with

> newspaper, [the kampung house] makes a very pitiful impression. In fact most were not more than one and a half meters wide, scarcely two meters long, and around one meter high. They were inhabited by two adults and mostly one or more children. These tiny houses were situated on a small raised area of about twenty meters by three. The water could therefore drain away but in the immediate vicinity formed small breeding pools for mosquitoes. A complete lack of understanding of hygiene causes the place to be swarming with flies and vermin. . . . It seems that these dwellings have been there for some time already (at least three years) but with the increasing number of vagabonds has grown into a kampong. . . . They work as casual laborers on the rebuilding of the city theatre, at a timber yard at Pasar Turi, on the municipal water supply, as porters at the station or the market, as watchmen over bicycles and cars at the cinema, and so forth. Most, however, quickly lapse into the occupations of ragpicker, grasscutter, or firewood collector and finally to that of beggar. (Vreede 1932b, 203–4)

Assistance for the unemployed relied on local initiative. In April 1930 the Municipality opened a Bureau for Poor Relief (Bureau voor Armenzorg) but insisted that relief be paid out only to those unable to find support from private sources, such as the Christian churches and the Salvation Army (SGS 1930, 355–59). Municipal relief increased from Fl 17,000 in 1930 to around Fl 100,000 in 1936 but the main source of funds was an active voluntary relief committee (SGS 1938, 156; Vreede 1932a, 698–99). Some 150 European women solicited monthly contributions from business firms and private individuals. Similar committees were then set up in the Chinese and Indonesian communities (Siauw 1982). The port authority made available a parcel of land for homeless laborers and the Municipality and the electricity company provided amenities. With support from the central and local relief committees, the Salvation Army fitted out an eighty-bed hospice for the unemployed in the vast home of the Chinese major at Undaan (Vreede 1932a, 701). The local committee also organized training courses, including a four-month course in automobile mechanics (Vreede 1932a,

700). Whether such ad hoc and voluntary measures ameliorated the impact of the Depression is hard to say, but they suggest that colonial society had some capacity to respond to the crisis, albeit along ethnic lines.

Because of the continued restriction on the output of its export staple, Surabaya's recovery from the Depression was also prolonged. This stands out very clearly from import figures. By the trough of 1935 the value of imports through Surabaya had fallen to just 22 percent of their 1929 level (34 percent in the case of Batavia); two years later the value of imports through Batavia had recovered sharply, to 60 percent of the 1929 level, but the corresponding figure for Surabaya was only 39 percent (HVS 1937, 50). In the process, Surabaya lost its primacy as Java's leading port of import. Whereas in 1929 the value of imports through Batavia had been only 80 percent of that of Surabaya, by 1937 it was 20 percent greater. Surabaya's relative decline was attributable primarily to the slow and erratic recovery in sugar exports. The trough in sugar exports was not reached until 1936, when their value was not 10 percent of that in 1927–28. Despite the devaluation of 1936 and except for the one good year of 1939, between 1937 and 1940 the tonnage of sugar exports through Surabaya gradually sank back to the 1936 level, while their value stagnated (*IV* 1940).

These trends in exports and imports pointed to a structural weakness in the economy of Surabaya and its hinterland. The heavy concentration on the sugar industry, which for many decades had underpinned the city's prosperity, now hindered its adjustment to harsher times. Although the release of land by the sugar industry permitted rapid growth of peasant production of rice and other food crops and helped restore rural incomes,[13] linkages with the urban economy were much weaker than in the case of the sugar industry. Because consumer demand remained depressed, Surabaya was also a less attractive location than Batavia for the industrial development fostered by tariff and quota protection (see chap. 5). The observation of Furnivall (1944, 428) that the year 1930 marked the close of a period that began with the opening of the Suez Canal therefore applies with particular force to Surabaya. While most of the turmoil of the next four decades was political in origin, the stagnation of the economy of Surabaya and its hinterland from the 1930s until the 1970s reflects an inability to achieve the kind of structural change needed to cope with the fundamental shift in Java's relations with the world economy (chap. 7).

War

During the 1930s the Dutch in the Netherlands Indies had become more and more apprehensive of the military threat from an expansionist Japan. On the outbreak of the First World War, Japan had come into the war as a British ally that respected Dutch neutrality and willingly supplied the imports no longer available from Europe. In 1913, Japan had supplied only 1.6 percent of the value of Netherlands Indies imports; by 1920 the proportion had risen to 12 percent, a share that was maintained during the 1920s (Dick 1989, 246). During the 1930s, however, Japan came to be seen more and more as a threat to Dutch interests. After devaluation of the yen in December 1931, cheap Japanese imports flooded in, a boon to the Indonesian population but a catastrophe for Dutch and British suppliers. By 1934 a third of all imports were from Japan, giving rise to bitter disputes over trade and shipping. Although the Hart-Ishizawa agreement of April 1937 and the van Mook–Kotani agreement of January 1938 restored a façade of amicable trade relations, by the late 1930s the colonial government was thoroughly alarmed by Japan's military encroachment upon China, its fortification of southern Micronesia (Palau), and the evidence of infiltration of the Netherlands Indies, including links with the suppressed nationalist movement (Post 1991).

German occupation of the Netherlands in May 1940 left the Netherlands Indies isolated and much more vulnerable than in 1914. The Japanese government did not hesitate to press its demands. Japan needed oil and rubber and wanted them on favorable terms (I. Anderson 1975). When Japan occupied Indo-China in July 1941, the United States retaliated by imposing an oil embargo and the Netherlands Indies followed suit. The Indies thereby became a prime military target, whose defense was precariously dependent on the United States and Great Britain, neither of whom had a substantial navy or air force in the region (Gill 1957). The capital ships of the Royal Navy had been withdrawn to other theatres and the American Asiatic Fleet in the Philippines was of little consequence. The main Pacific Fleet, based at Pearl Harbor (Hawaii), had been depleted to meet more pressing needs in the Atlantic. No one believed that the small Dutch colonial forces with token Allied reinforcements could offer any real resistance.[14] Outwardly, however, the situation was still calm. In Surabaya the main sign of war was the drab-painting of the white-washed office buildings and intensified air defense precautions (Frederick 1989, 81).

At seven o'clock on the morning of 8 December 1941, a few hours after the Japanese attack on Pearl Harbor, the governor-general came on local radio to declare a state of war between the Netherlands and Japan.[15] At this eleventh hour the government tried belatedly to enlist the support of Indonesian nationalist parties in defense of the colony. On 17 December the governor of East Java, Charles O. van der Plas, called in person upon the executive of Parindra, the main nationalist party in Surabaya, to seek its co-operation. He was told that this could easily be achieved if the government would establish "popular representation based on Democracy, Economy and Social Justice for Indonesia," responding to the campaign of 1939 for an Indonesian parliament. However, unlike the British in India, the Dutch were still not prepared to go beyond the queen's vague promise of May 1941 to review the constitutional situation after the war. Yet in informal discussions at the last meeting of the Municipal Council on 25 January, Parindra observers were surprised to discover how defeatist was the attitude of the Dutch members. All hopes were pinned on Singapore: if Singapore should fall then the Netherlands Indies would be indefensible. Even among Indonesians, panic was felt and people began to leave the city.

On 3 February the first bombs fell on Surabaya. A Parindra observer gives a vivid Indonesian description: "At 10 o'clock in the morning the sirens sounded, indicating an attack. Soon after, all of us in the office saw high in the sky a number of Japanese bombers accompanied by some fighters, coming from the northwest toward Surabaya. Immediately Dutch antiaircraft fire was heard. Only then did we realize that we really were in the middle of war" (ARA, MK 2.10.29, 409: Parindra). The bombing was directed against the port and naval base at Tanjung Perak, but parts of the city were also hit. The same observer recalled, "the whole of Surabaya trembled on its foundations and it seemed as though the empire [*rijk*] itself tottered." The attack touched off a great panic. Buses and trains were stormed by those seeking evacuation to the interior. From that time there were almost daily raids, although they were directed solely against military targets and did little harm to the city.

Once Singapore had fallen, on 15 February, the end of Dutch rule was nigh. By then the Japanese had already occupied the towns of Banjarmasin (South Kalimantan) and Makassar (South Sulawesi), whose airfields gave aerial command of the Java Sea (Gill 1957, 557). Within days Palembang and Bali were also occupied and Java was tightly encircled. Air raids multiplied to three or four times per day.[16] Residents of the city did not witness the Battle of the Java Sea on 27 February, in which the Japanese fleet destroyed the small Allied navy as a fighting force, but the failure of well-known ships to return to port and the heavy loss of life soon became known and added to the feeling of despair. On Sunday, 1 March, as the Japanese army landed on the coast to the west of Surabaya, there were no fewer than seven air raids. The Dutch now began systematically to destroy all surviving military and oil installations. It must have seemed like the end of the world. Towering black smoke clouds shut out the sun (ARA, MK 2.10.29, 409:

Parindra). Even the shore of Madura was barely visible. The fleet of merchant and naval ships anchored in the roads was scuttled. Through the haze loomed ships heeling over at crazy angles. Everywhere were the sight and smell of acrid smoke. Amid the chaos and without check from a much shrunken police force, looting became frenzied as Indonesians helped themselves to the unguarded spoils (Frederick 1989, 87). So perished the colonial order.

In fact it was not until the night of Friday, 6 March, that the Japanese arrived in strength at Wonokromo on the southern outskirts. Despite reports that the Dutch would make a last-ditch stand, there were few signs of resistance. Air raid sirens wailed continuously but there was only a single burst of antiaircraft fire. As Dutch troops evacuated the city, Parindra sources reported seeing many soldiers throwing their uniforms into the Kali Mas: "Surabaya had nothing of the appearance of a large city. On the roads neither cars nor pony carts [*dokar*] were to be found and few people. Everywhere we heard that paper money was no longer valid, while many Chinese warungs gave no change or only very unwillingly" (ARA, MK 2.10.29, 409: Parindra). Outwardly Surabaya remained calm, waiting, though thousands of Indonesians continued to pour out of the city and the looting of factories, defense posts, and offices continued almost unchecked (Frederick 1989, 87–88).

On Sunday morning, while the sirens still wailed, it was reported by radio from the Dutch army commander that there would be a surrender. As the Japanese air force carried out two last raids to drop pamphlets calling for capitulation, the governor and mayor met with the Japanese commander at the Wonokromo bridge and settled the basis for a peaceful occupation (Frederick 1989, 89). Late that afternoon the occupying troops did not march but rode in, some on requisitioned buses and trucks in makeshift camouflage, others somewhat incongruously on bicycles, officers on motorcycles (fig. 2.3). Japanese flags had suddenly appeared everywhere. The streets were lined with Indonesians, many welcoming their liberators, some anxious for the future.

Figure 2.3. The Japanese army entering Surabaya, March 1942. KITLV no. 2629.

Occupation

After the collapse of the established order, it was perhaps surprising that life so quickly returned to something like normal. The Japanese army set up its headquarters in Tunjungan in the exclusive Oranje (now Majapahit) Hotel, which became the Yamato, while the military government was established in the palatial Handelsvereeniging Amsterdam (HVA) building beside the old Dutch business district at Jembatan Merah. On 13 March the Dutch newspaper *Soerabaiasch Handelsblad* was allowed to reappear with a call to all railway personnel to report for work—next day this call was extended to employees of private firms, plantations, oil companies, banks, hospitals, and schools. Within days shops had reopened at controlled, pre-occupation prices and factories were back in production. By the end of the month trains were again running to Jakarta, although it was mid-May before the damaged railway bridge over the Porong River could be used on the line to

Malang. At the beginning of April, even some cinemas were allowed to reopen.

Yet the appearance of normality was deceptive. Nighttime blackouts confirmed that the city was still on a war footing. More ominously, people began to disappear. All Dutch military personnel had been interned on capture. On 18 March the Japanese had sought from Parindra leaders a report of Indonesian intellectuals who could take over from Dutch officials. By 22 April all but a handful of Dutch civil officials had joined their military colleagues in internment camps. The impact on the Dutch community was starkly revealed by the results of the alien registration that began on 23 April. By 21 May, 6,827 European adults (over seventeen years old) had reported, of whom 4,426 were women (*SH,* 21/5/42). Internment was not applied generally to women to European women and children until mid-1943 (Broeshart et al. 1997, 39–43). Chinese aliens were also required to register, but by 21 May 1942 only 2,505 (1,566 men and 939 women) had done so. The reluctance of Chinese to identify themselves to the Japanese was well grounded, as shown by the arrest in mid-May of those identified as Kuomintang supporters (*SH,* 15/5/42).

Initially the Dutch and Chinese communities bore the brunt of Japanese repression but it was not long before Indonesians discovered that they had exchanged one colonial power for another. From 18 March it was strictly forbidden to show the Dutch flag (*SH,* 18/3/42). Late in May, publication of the *Soerabaiasch Handelsblad* was suspended. For the rest of the occupation the main Surabaya newspaper was the Indonesian language *Soeara Asia*. Use of the Dutch language was banned everywhere, even in the home. Dutch also ceased to be used as a medium of instruction in schools, which on reopening in August 1942 were obliged to adopt either the vernacular or Japanese (Frederick 1989, 106–7). Indonesian children moved into the formerly exclusive Dutch schools. Communications were tightly controlled. All radios had to be registered. For those who did not have radios, loudspeakers were set up at busy points to announce news and government orders. Clocks were put forward one and a half hours to Tokyo time (Soeparto Brata 1983). Perhaps the flavor of the new colonialism was best indicated by the order that cyclists passing in front of Japanese sentries were to dismount, take off their hats, and bow (*SH,* 20/5/42). In September 1942 any pretense of liberation was abandoned with the appointment of a Japanese mayor.

For the first year of so Surabaya was spared direct contact with the war, but its indirect effects became ever more apparent. One of the very first measures of Japanese military rule was to forbid the use of gasoline for all but official use and emergency services (including food distribution, medical calls, and newspaper delivery) (*SH,* 13/3/42). Not only private vehicles but also the familiar jitneys immediately disappeared. The last gasoline-powered public transport vehicles were a few buses, which dropped out of operation after about six months. Henceforth public transport was confined to the steam tram, the electric trams, dokar, and a new vehicle, the pedicab, or becak, which found a niche in these strange times. It therefore became a much quieter city.

Another early measure was food rationing. At the end of March a coupon system was introduced for those in need and soup kitchens opened for two hours from noon in five kampungs. After completion of alien registration and establishment of a tighter system of control in the kampungs, food rationing became general. Rice being scarce, the daily ration was set at only two hundred grams per adult, with the balance of carbohydrate made up of a mixture of maize and soybean known as *mutiara* (lit., pearl) (Soeparto Brata 1983). Sugar, which no longer had an export market, was in plentiful supply. Urban dwellers therefore had just enough to eat, even if they could not enjoy their preferred diet. Better availability of food and the reduced likelihood of recruitment as forced labor (*romusha*) are sufficient to explain the rapid growth in urban population (Sato 1994; Steele 1980, 58–59).

War returned to Surabaya in the middle of 1943 with the first Allied air raid. On 22 July bombs were dropped fairly indiscriminately, some landing in the dense kampungs of Pandean and Pacar

Keling.[17] The city was then left undisturbed until the heavy bombing of 8–9 November. The only other heavy raid was 17 May 1944, but from the end of February 1944 almost no month went by without attacks, the number increasing steadily as the end of the war approached (ROD, IC 072 775; Broeshart et al. 1997, 45). Yet all this had surprisingly little effect on daily life. The Allies had good aerial maps of the city and, apart from the initial attack, concentrated on military targets, primarily the port and naval base at Tanjung Perak, the oil installations around Wonokromo, and, occasionally, the industrial estate at Ngagel. Because of the large workforce at the port and naval base and the dense adjacent kampungs, there must have been civilian casualties, but no estimates are available. Elsewhere people seem to have become accustomed to air raid sirens and the sound of bombs and antiaircraft fire.

Revolution

Nationalists in Surabaya had been planning for independence to follow upon the now inevitable Japanese defeat. The radio broadcast from Batavia on 17 August 1945, in which Sukarno and Mohammad Hatta proclaimed an independent Indonesia, nevertheless came as a surprise. The news spread quickly by word of mouth, but it was three days before it was confirmed by a report in *Soeara Asia* and another two days before the Japanese surrender was announced. On 23 August the blackout and curfew were finally lifted and it seemed that peace had come at last. Nevertheless, acting under Allied orders, the Japanese continued to run the government and maintain law and order until the arrival of Allied troops.

The first moves toward organization of a local Indonesian government were tentative. On 23 August a group under the leadership of Doel Arnowo formed the regional Komite Nasional Indonesia (KNI), which on 3 September officially declared loyalty to the Republik Indonesia and occupied the governor's office under the Indonesian flag. A week later a local committee was formed under Ruslan Wongsokusumo to organize municipal government alongside the Japanese-supported administration under the nominal mayor, Radjamin Nasution, a prewar alderman. Meanwhile, youth belonging to the Japanese-sponsored militia (Pembela Tanah Air, PETA), which had been disarmed on 20 August, reformed themselves into the Badan Keamanan Rakyat (BKR), which, with echoes of the French Revolution, translates as Committee for Public Safety.

The prospect that power would be transferred peacefully from Japanese to Indonesian authority began to recede after 26 August, when Europeans and Eurasians began to trickle back from internment camps and attempted to reoccupy homes and offices without reference to the Indonesian administration, for which they were completely unprepared. When tensions arose, they sought protection from the Japanese (Frederick 1989, 193–97). On 11 September a large rally was held to demonstrate against both the Dutch and the Japanese. Resistance to reestablishment of colonial rule acquired a focus after the parachute landing on 18 September of a handful of British and Dutch officers, who established their headquarters in the Yamato Hotel in Tunjungan. Next day, Dutch and Eurasian youths hoisted the Dutch flag on the hotel's flagpole. This provocation drew a hostile crowd of Indonesians, leading eventually to a few daring ones scaling the hotel and tearing the blue section from the Dutch flag. Symbolically at least, this was seen as the start of the armed independence struggle (Frederick 1989; Meelhuijsen 2000).

At the end of September armed youths began sporadic attacks on Japanese posts.[18] In expectation of the arrival of Allied forces, about ten thousand Japanese troops had already been withdrawn from the city, so that their positions were now less well defended. Early successes emboldened the Indonesians, to the point that a general uprising began on 1 October. Frederick speaks of "two days of negotiations, mob action and often bitter fighting" (1989, 214). The climax was the surrender on 2 October, after a thirty-six-hour siege, of the hated Kempeitai (Military Police) headquarters, the former Palace of Justice, opposite the governor's office. This became the headquarters of the Committee for Public Safety (BKR), shortly to be renamed the Army of Public Safety (Tentara Keamanan Rakyat, TKR). The thousands of remaining Japanese were interned. Huge quantities of arms now came into Indonesian hands, perhaps about half into those of the revolutionary youth (*pemuda*) (Frederick 1989, 217). In the final stage of securing the city on 15 October, the pemuda led the rounding up of all thirty-five hundred Dutch and Eurasians in the city (Frederick 1989, 240). This action unleashed horrific mob violence against defenseless civilians, including women and children. In one notorious incident, between forty and fifty Dutchmen suspected of assisting the return of Dutch administration were killed in gruesome fashion at one pemuda group's headquarters in the Simpang Club, ironically the focal point of prewar Dutch society (241). Some Japanese also became victims of the mob (242).

British troops had landed at Jakarta on 29 September but it was 25 October before the 49th Indian Division under Brigadier Mallaby arrived in Surabaya. Relations began on the wrong foot when the British refused to seek permission to land from the Indonesian government of the city. Although an agreement was hammered out for the British to disarm and embark the Japanese, it soon became apparent that they were occupying the city and freeing Dutch personnel. Any doubt was removed on 27 October, when pamphlets were dropped calling for arms to be surrendered within forty-eight hours or those bearing them would be shot on sight. Passions were inflamed. Fearing that the British were a trojan horse for return of the Dutch, the Indonesian population turned on them and overran them. Within a day the 49th Division had ceased to exist as a fighting force, with 38 known killed, 210 missing (presumed killed), and 84 wounded (Frederick 1989, 276n). Frenzied mobs also attacked and butchered Dutch civilians being transferred to safer jails. In the worst incident, some forty to fifty women and children were dragged from their convoy of buses in Darmo Boulevard and battered to death by mobs from nearby Kampung Keputran (Broeshart et al. 1997, 51). On 29 October, Sukarno,

Hatta, and Amir Sjarifuddin flew to Surabaya and patched together a cease-fire. Next day, while trying to implement the cease-fire, Mallaby was shot dead by an unidentified assassin in the square in front of the Internatio building at Jembatan Merah (see fig. 1.5). Now it was the turn of the British to seek revenge. Plans were quickly drawn up to take Surabaya by force. All was now in place for the final act of the tragedy.

The murder of Brigadier Mallaby so shocked the British that no one seems to have reflected that the desire for revenge was now moving the British to pursue a policy quite opposite to that enunciated in September. Then Mountbatten had emphasized to Lieutenant Governor-General van Mook, through van der Plas, that Great Britain would on no account be drawn into internal troubles in Java and that British soldiers would not be used for putting down any revolt or riots (Wal 1971, 1:182n2; van der Post 1996). The British would remain neutral and do nothing to assist the Dutch reoccupation of Java. Yet within weeks his troops had embarked on a campaign to invade and occupy a city in which Indonesian rule was already established. Evidently the British reckoned that it would be a short sharp campaign "to teach the natives a lesson." They could not have been more mistaken.

The British invasion began on 4 November and by the ninth no less than twenty-four thousand troops had been landed with their equipment at the beachhead of Tanjung Perak. Over the same period, about 6,150 Dutch women and children were evacuated, still leaving some 5,000 (about half in barracks at Darmo) and 3,500 men and boys in the safety of Kalisosok prison in the center of the city (Frederick 1989, 263–64). Thousands of Japanese were also still left in the city. On the ninth the British issued an ultimatum, demanding in effect full and unconditional surrender, failing which a full-scale assault would be mounted at 6 A.M. the following day. Faced with such insulting terms, the Indonesians resolved to fight to the death in defense of their freedom.

The British forces quickly broke through the first defense line, about halfway between the city and the port, but from there faced fanatical opposition on densely settled and unfamiliar terrain.[19] Despite a barrage of naval artillery upon the Indonesian positions, not until the fourteenth did they break through the second line of defense, the railway viaduct just south of the central business district. It took another three days to secure the adjacent governor's office, just north of the viaduct on the main central artery. Indonesian forces were then gradually driven southward through Tunjungan and Bubutan. The local people used to the full their knowledge of the buildings and narrow lanes but could not withstand the relentless pressure from British-Indian troops. Each building captured was searched room by room and anyone found inside shot or bayoneted. It was 22 November, however, before the British captured Sarkies Hotel, on the corner of Tunjungan and Embong Malang, and Indonesian forces were displaced from their stronghold of Tambaksari in the east, which they had defended for the previous week. Thereafter the British advance became much easier. Beyond Tunjungan and Kedungdoro the wide boulevards were much harder to defend than the narrow streets lined with two-story buildings in the old town. On the twenty-third the British introduced tanks, which were virtually immune to attack and advanced quickly in the West. On the twenty-fourth there was some of the most bitter fighting of the whole battle beyond Tunjungan along Kaliasin/Keputran, where buildings were destroyed along both sides. Finally, on the twenty-sixth, with a combined tank attack along the river and Jalan Diponegoro, the British broke through the defenses to the zoo near Wonokromo Bridge. Failing to destroy the bridge and prevent the tanks from crossing, Indonesian forces retreated upriver toward Sepanjang. On the twenty-eighth the last republican bastion fell, the formerly Japanese stronghold of Gunungsari, effectively marking the end of the Battle of Surabaya.

What is most striking about the Battle of Surabaya is its historical absurdity. Apart from Manila, whose picturesque old quarter was all but razed in the American reconquest, Surabaya was the only major Southeast Asian city to suffer badly at the end of the

Pacific War. A city that had without much damage survived the invasion and surrender of Japan was shattered by a British army, which had itself survived some of the most bitter campaigns of World War II and whose self-appointed task was merely to accept the Japanese surrender and repatriate Dutch internees. Its newly won independence was bloodily extinguished by a European power that was not its colonizer and that soon withdrew. In effect, the British filled the role of mercenaries, though receiving no payment from the Dutch and fighting as a matter of honor to avenge their dead. The only party to benefit were the Dutch, who after November 1946 were able to reoccupy Surabaya as a battered, deserted, and cowed city. In two months several hundred each of Dutch internees, British troops, and Chinese civilians had lost their lives and untold thousands of Indonesians, some six thousand by one British estimate (van der Post 1996, 225) or perhaps more than fifteen thousand (Broeshart et al. 1997, 53–56). Main streets were left as rows of burnt-out buildings, their blackened façades pockmarked by bullets and shells; behind them many kampungs, built of more flimsy and inflammable materials, had been razed to the ground. The only parts of the city to escape damage were the Arab quarter around the holy Ampel mosque and the newer European suburbs. The Arab leader, Alamoedi, had managed to negotiate an early evacuation of republican forces (ARA, MK 2.10.29, 409: Memo 30/1/46), while the European suburbs around Darmo were saved by the speed of the final British advance. An abiding image is that of a young Greek man, who at the end of the fighting, ventured out by bicycle from his house near Gubeng as far as Tanjung Perak: he found only an eerie silence in the usually busy streets, empty but for the decomposing bodies that lay everywhere, as they had fallen (George Tsounas, pers. comm.).

The significance of this defeat can hardly be exaggerated. The Indonesian people demonstrated to themselves and to the rest of the world their willingness to fight for independence. It took some of the most experienced troops in the British army, with full naval and air support, more than two weeks to advance just ten kilometers from Tanjung Perak to Wonokromo. Though Surabaya was exhausted, the rest of Java fought on for another four years. Too blind to read the signs, the Dutch became embroiled in a long war of attrition and eventually forfeited not only sovereignty but also the prize of economic hegemony. The chaos of war also undermined the economy and fragile civilian administration of the new state. Meanwhile, an army that had barely existed in 1945 was nourished by the armed struggle to grow into a state within the state and ultimately to take it over.

Interregnum

Cities are resilient. Within two months, activity began to pick up. Markets were the busiest places. People bought whatever was available, then scuttled home, avoiding the main roads. The former European suburbs of Gubeng and Darmo, however, were still very quiet. Looting (*rampok*) and arson was widespread, attributed to Madurese gangs and republican infiltration (ARA, MK 2.10.29, 409: memo, 30/1/46). For Europeans, Surabaya had become a tiny enclave besieged by an alien hinterland. As in the days of the East India Company, the Dutch controlled the sea lanes and could keep open the supply lines, a vital consideration for a city now almost completely dependent on imported food. Nevertheless, both sides of the shipping channel from the Java Sea to the roadstead were Indonesian territory. The north shore of the harbor, Madura, was under Indonesian control, as was the town of Gresik on the western side. As late as January 1947 the navy commander was complaining of republican piracy in Madura Strait of prahus bound for Surabaya (Wal 1978, 33). On land the Allied perimeter extended from about halfway along the road to Gresik southward via Benowo and Menganti to Driyorejo on the Brantas River and then east via Waru to the sea (ARA, MK 2.10.29, 447: 22/7/46). This enclosed an area not much larger than the present municipality. Civil administration was introduced throughout the buffer zone except on the front line.

In August 1946 the buffer zone between the city and the front line was estimated to contain about two hundred ten thousand people (ARA, MK 2.10.29, 447, 22/7/46). South of Wonokromo the population was still very dense but to the east, around Sukolilo and elsewhere, about half the population was estimated to have fled. Van der Plas himself, head of the Dutch civilian administration in East Java, made a detour through Waru and Karang Pilang on his way to the airport in August 1946 and reported "appalling devastation and desolation" (ARA, vdPlas 2.21.226.130, 22/8/46). The west monsoon harvest was only 20 to 50 percent of normal, but villagers were evidently able to obtain other staples such as maize and cassava from their house gardens (ARA, MK 2.10.29, 447, 22/7/46). Officials reported no serious food shortage and some vegetables and fruit were sold to Surabaya.

Relations with the hinterland beyond the Allied line were almost completely broken. By various means, including flooding, the Indonesians forced the evacuation of civilians from the frontier and denied the Dutch access to food supplies. Without a supply of commodities from the interior, Surabaya could no longer support itself, let alone revive as a trade center. What trade there was consisted mainly of food items, such as chickens, eggs, fruit, and fish smuggled in by Madurese prahus landing in the mangroves along the eastern shore or in the small creeks along to the west of Tanjung Perak. As far as infrastructure was concerned, trains had ceased to run, roads were blocked, telephones were cut, and power was no longer transmitted from the modern hydroelectric stations in the interior, forcing the city to rely on its old steam-generating plant. With an echo of Sultan Agung's siege of Surabaya in 1624, the drinking water supply from the permanent springs in the foothills was also cut off. The modest output of the river purification plant at Ngagel had to be supplemented by old wells, which were badly polluted and toward the end of the hot season began to run dry or turn salty (ARA, AS 1.I.45.1, 9/10/46). Apart from perpetuating its own existence, heavily subsidized from without, the city's only rationale was therefore as a military base for reconquest of the hinterland (Wal 1979, 8:27).

During the course of 1946, Surabaya, along with the rest of Java, began to return to formal Dutch rule. While tripartite negotiations tried to establish a political framework for British withdrawal, Dutch troops were arriving from Australia (George 1980, 54). On 15 November the Cheribon Draft Agreement was signed, whereby the Dutch recognized the de facto authority of the Republic. This was followed at the end of the month by disbandment of the Allied Command, leaving the Dutch with a free hand. In the interim Surabaya was governed through a body known as AMACAB (Allied Military Administration, Civil Affairs Branch); day-to-day running of the city, including the vital task of rationing, was handled by an Office of People's Affairs (Kantoor voor Bevolkingszaken, BVZ).[20] This quasi-government was headed by a Dutchman, Dr. F. W. T. Hunger, and staffed mainly by Dutchmen. The return to full Dutch administration was therefore a fairly smooth process. By mid-1946 the commanding officer of AMACAB had ordered restoration as far as possible of the prewar municipal administration. This was achieved through the BVZ office. Thus from 1 August BVZ took over responsibility for population registration, markets, land and housing, and subsequently textile distribution, hygiene, veterinary matters, public works, finances, and economic research.

The city was nevertheless slow to recover from the damage of war. Gradually the rubble was cleared away but there were no funds for permanent reconstruction. Shops reopened but had little to sell. Despite British efforts to maintain public order and a continuing curfew, bands of looters remained active and arson was common. The nervous Dutch saw these as symptoms of republican infiltration and were alarmed at the quantities of ammunition that continued to be uncovered. Careful screenings were carried out of ward (*wijk*) administration and some local officials were arrested. Whether out of nationalism or fear of reprisals, few Indonesians were willing to cooperate in the reestablishment of Dutch authority.

Apart from law and order, the government's main task was to ensure that everyone had enough to eat. Virtually all food had to be imported and, because of a shortage of both foreign exchange and shipping, supply was unpredictable. An early act of the Allied administration had been to register the population. By 1 June 1946, 223,000 people had been issued with an identity card, which entitled them to ration coupons (ARA, MK 2.10.29, 447, 22/7/46). Included in A rations were two hundred grams of rice per day plus allowances of salt, sugar, fish, cigarettes, and coconut oil. When rice stocks were low, the balance was made up of flour. As available, B rations were also issued, which included clothing. Officially new arrivals in the city could be added to the ration list only with permission from the head of the BVZ office. Those who returned spontaneously, however, could not be left to starve. The distribution list therefore had to be expanded from time to time. In December 1947, for example, all those who had arrived in the city without permit before 1 June were declared eligible for rations. The distribution system was backed up by price controls: in November 1948 a new Price Control Law replaced the weaker Price Surveillance Law of 1941 and were supplemented by regulations against hoarding of particular scarce commodities (HVS 1949). Since government not only organized the distribution of consumer goods but also supervised the transport of rice and other essential commodities and attempted to control smuggling, allocated raw materials, and rationed foreign exchange, it can be appreciated that the economy was highly regulated.

The BVZ also attempted to gather up the threads of the prewar municipal administration. Health was an urgent priority because of the resurgence of malaria, which was causing very high death rates among the Indonesian population around the urban fringe. This was tackled by spraying with DDT. Rubbish collection was restored, as were sanitary controls over bakeries, soft drink manufacturers, and dairies. Housing was another urgent problem. A Public Housing Trust (Stichting Bevolkingshuisvesting) was set up to take under control about fourteen hundred houses, while a

Municipal Housing Office (Gemeentelijk Huizenbezit) requisitioned six hundred more. The beneficiaries, however, were mainly Europeans. In the case of the Indonesian kampungs, where the housing shortage was even more desperate, the main concern was to thin out the density and prevent unauthorized rebuilding, measures that in practice were impossible to enforce. From January 1948 onward careful efforts were made to restore the municipal archives to determine who held legal title and who owed rent on municipal lands such as Ngagel.

These attempts to restore a colonial system of government were in the first instance meeting the needs of the returning Dutch population. Their immediate need was for food, clothing, and shelter but there seems also to have been a psychological need for *rust en orde* (law and order). The preoccupation with restoring the familiar structure of government seems to have affected more than the administrators themselves. However, in terms of Dutch strategy to regain control of the hinterland, it was essential to demonstrate good government and an ability to meet the basic needs of the Indonesian population. In the battle for what would later became known as hearts and minds, the Dutch government had to be seen to be equitable. Van der Plas, who was a true disciple of the Ethical Policy, and other top administrators certainly had a lively concern for Indonesian welfare, even if it was often hard to see the fruits of it.

Following the British withdrawal in mid-1946, the Dutch moved to extend their perimeter. Already in August 1946 the commanding officer of AMACAB, Surabaya (Dr. Hunger) had written to the lieutenant governor-general urging the need to extend the territory around Surabaya as far south as the Porong River in order to improve the food supply, gain control of irrigation, and establish a natural line of defense (ARA, AS 1.I.45.1). On 27 January 1947, following several days behind the retreating Republican army, the Dutch occupied the deserted town of Sidoarjo, from where they pressed on to the natural defense line of the Porong River, while occupying the rest of the once rich Sidoarjo district with its several sugar factories. Indonesian forces immediately retaliated by opening the sluices just below Mojokerto at Mlirip and flooding much of the delta between the Brantas and the Porong Rivers (ARA, MK 2.10.14, 3531). This defeated the Dutch objective of securing the rice harvest and led on 19 March to Dutch occupation of the temporary republican provincial capital of Mojokerto in order to close the vital nearby sluices. These were, however, essentially local actions.

On 21 July 1947 the Dutch launched a full offensive, the so-called Police Action, against Republican territory throughout Java and Madura. In East Java the main landing occurred on the beach at Pasir Putih (just west of Panarukan) and led to swift occupation of the whole of the Oosthoek, so swift in fact that most infrastructure and crops were left undamaged. On 4 August, Dutch troops also landed on Madura at Kamal, opposite the port of Tanjung Perak, and quickly occupied the towns of Bangkalan, Sampang, and Pamekasan. A cease-fire came into force before the Dutch had occupied the eastern part of the island but in November the Dutch proceeded to do so anyway. Four months later the passenger ferry service reopened between Surabaya and Kamal and by May was providing four sailings a day. Van der Plas was well satisfied and at the end of November reported that "Madura can now become the bastion for the pacification of East Java" (Drooglever and Schouten 1985, 12:47).

By the end of 1947, East Java could be divided into three zones.[21] The first zone, roughly corresponding with the old residency of Surabaya (minus the district of Jombang) plus Madura, was securely under Dutch control. The second zone, the Oosthoek, was nominally under Dutch control but subject to worsening guerrilla activity, especially in the southern hills. The third zone, embracing South Malang, the Brantas valley beyond Mojokerto, and the whole of the Bengawan Solo valley, remained firmly under Republican control. This division was confirmed in the Renville Agreement of January 1948. By the middle of 1948 the Dutch were congratulating themselves on the rapid rehabilitation of the plantation export economy of the Oosthoek. All sugar mills and most upland estates had been reoccupied by their owners, the harvest was bringing down rice prices and most rice mills were back in operation, vegetables were at last becoming plentiful, and fish ponds were being restocked. By June thrice-daily rail service between Surabaya and Malang had resumed and soon after trains were running through to Jember and Banyuwangi. In September it was reported that the return of women and children to the plantations was restoring some semblance of normality. Bungalows were reoccupied in hill resorts like Tretes. A month later, however, there were ominous signs of renewed infiltration.

Having worked to undermine the Renville Agreement and frustrated by guerrilla activity in the Oosthoek, the Dutch sought to strike a knockout blow. On the night of 18 December 1948 they broke the cease-fire by launching a second Police Action to seize all remaining Republican territory, including the Republican capital of Yogyakarta. By the time the operation was terminated, on 31 December, the Dutch had reoccupied the East Java towns of Jombang, Kediri, Blitar, Kertosono, Madiun, and Tuban. The aim was to destroy the Republic as a military and political force. In this the Dutch were seduced by the universal military optimism that one more battle would win the war. In fact, guerrilla activity quickly worsened, a phenomenon that Dutch officers found hard to comprehend.

To their dismay, the Dutch found that they now occupied a vast area they could not control. The mountainous region along the South coast became a kind of Ho Chi Minh trail along which Indonesian guerrillas could infiltrate the whole of the Oosthoek. Isolated plantations were protected only by their own guards. After several planters had been killed, in January 1949 planters and their families had to be evacuated from the interior to Surabaya. In the hill resorts of Tretes and Prigen, not far from Surabaya, many newly rehabilitated bungalows were burned down. Guerrilla activity was directed not only against plantation installations and infrastructure such as railways but also against the "native" civil service (*pamong praja*), paralyzing Dutch administration. Guerrilla warfare bottled up the Dutch in the towns; they were able to move only in daylight and even then not always in safety. Thus, despite their early optimism, the Dutch were unable to consolidate their position and to provide enough security to allow the restoration of normal economic life much beyond the city of Surabaya and its immediate hinterland. By 1949, Dutch authority was being undermined even in once secure areas like Sidoarjo and Mojokerto. The idea that the Dutch were brought to terms only by international pressure quite underrates the effectiveness of the guerrilla war.

Although Surabaya remained a haven of peace and quiet on the edge of a turbulent hinterland, the implications for the city were profound. Aside from the strategic considerations, the logic of reoccupying the hinterland had been in the first instance to secure food supplies and, subsequently, to regain control of the plantations, whose products were the city's lifeblood and the basis of Dutch prosperity. The plantations were the key to the revival of the export trade, and hence the capacity to import. The flaw in the Dutch military strategy was that many of these plantations were located in the countryside, or even in the mountains, where they were especially vulnerable to guerrilla activity. In the Oosthoek many plantations that were recaptured intact were later damaged, along with their supporting infrastructure. During the second Police Action, Indonesian forces put much more effort into sabotaging sugar mills and other plantations before retreating. Of 32 prewar sugar mills in the Republican part of East Java, only one was recovered intact: 5 had suffered light damage, 17 heavy damage, and 9 were destroyed (although the installations of 11 mills had been removed by the Japanese) (ARA, MK 2.10.29, 408, 19/12/48–31/1/49). In both areas, plantations reoccupied by their owners had soon to be abandoned. For the Dutch this was very bad business. The productive capacity of the plantation sector, which though poorly maintained at the time of the surrender was still undamaged by war, was sacrificed to a bitter war in which scorched earth became a necessary tactic. This decline of the economic base held back Surabaya's recovery after the transfer of sovereignty.

Meanwhile, the Dutch pursued a political strategy of trying to entice Indonesian leaders into various kinds of puppet administrations (Kahin 1952, chap. 12; Yong Mun Cheong 1982). The essence of the strategy was to establish a patchwork of nominally self-governing states having equal rights with the Republic in an eventual federation under Dutch supervision. On the initiative of van der Plas,[22] the commissioner (recomba) of East Java, two states (*negara*) were set up within the old province of East Java: the Negara Madoera and the Negara Djawa Timoer (East Java). On Dutch-controlled Madura and with the support, as prime minister (*wali*), of the former Republican resident, A. M. Tjakraningrat, the process went ahead fairly smoothly. However, when elections resulted in Republican majorities and Tjakraningrat appeared to be playing a double game, the Dutch stalled, so that the transfer of powers did not occur until the eve of sovereignty. In the case of East Java, the first preparatory meeting became a fiasco when the committee denounced the proposal! Van der Plas persisted, especially cultivating Islamic leaders, and by dint of gerrymandering and intimidation was able by September 1948 to reconstitute twelve regency councils, all with majorities in favor of the negara (Kahin 1952, 378–81). After many of the inconveniently elected republican sympathizers had been jailed, van der Plas allowed himself to be "persuaded" to call a conference of council representatives at Bondowoso in mid-November (Drooglever and Schouten 1989, 15:764–68). The Negara Djawa Timoer was proclaimed on 26 November 1948 with the regent of Banyuwangi as wali and the regent of Surabaya as chairman of the provisional parliament. Yet despite the great effort that had gone into establishing the negara, in the face of the deteriorating military situation the Dutch made little progress toward transfer of administrative powers.

In the city of Surabaya the Dutch also attempted to set up a democratic façade. Not without misgivings, in March 1947 the Dutch administration convened the first of what were described cautiously as contact meetings with invited representatives of presumably the more tractable parties, ethnic groups, and associations. These monthly meetings generated a good deal of feedback, especially on the perennial problem of distribution (ARA, MK

2.10.29, 447–49). By the beginning of 1948 the Dutch had more or less restored the administrative and technical organs and the bureaucracy of municipal government. However, these could not function on a proper legal basis under municipal bylaws in the absence of the formal institutions of government. Under emergency orders applying to all of East Java, the powers of the local councils were temporarily vested in the senior provincial and local administrators. This mechanism allowed the first postwar municipal budget to be approved for the second half of the year. Significantly, the prewar dualism between European and "native" government now lapsed: the old powers of the regents to appoint personnel and administer the functions of kampung government were transferred without fuss to the municipality. In October elections were held across the city for a Provisional Municipal Council (Dewan Perwakilan Rakjat Sementara). Anyone over the age of twenty-one with an annual income of more than Fl 300 was entitled to vote by ward (*wijk*) for 17 Indonesian, 5 Dutch, 4 Chinese, and 1 Arab representatives. With the addition of six appointed representatives (2 Indonesian, 2 Dutch, 2 Chinese), this made up a council of 33 persons, with Indonesians now being in the majority. Reflecting the changed political context, and in line with the formation of the Negara Djawa Timoer, the provisional council was installed by van der Plas on 5 November 1948. The façade of Indonesian municipal government was completed in March 1949, when alderman Indra Kasoema took over as mayor from C. J. G. Becht.

Independence

On 2 November 1949 agreement was reached at the Round Table Conference in The Hague to transfer sovereignty from the Netherlands to a United States of Indonesia (Republik Indonesia Serikat, RIS), to take effect on 27 December.[23] This federal system, which relegated the republic to one among sixteen equal states, was a house of cards. In East Java sovereignty was formally transferred from the Netherlands to the Negara Djawa Timoer. Even before the twenty-seventh, however, there had been much agitation for dissolution of the negara, which had never gained credibility. After the transfer, the rallies and petitions intensified. On 19 January 1950, four days after a giant rally addressed by President Sukarno, the wali surrendered his authority to the Republic and was replaced by Samadikoen as representative of the Republic. On 24 February the residency of Surabaya was also formally handed over to the Republic and on the following day the parliament of the negara dissolved itself and merged with the RIS. Samadikoen then became governor of the province of East Java while Doel Arnowo, a local revolutionary hero, became mayor of Surabaya (KP 1953, 117–21). Civil rule was not formally restored, however, until the end of martial law on 7 September (KP 1953, 26), about three weeks after dissolution of the Federation in favor of the unitary Republik Indonesia. In Surabaya the new apparatus of government was completed on 4 December 1950 with appointment of a twenty-five-member provisional municipal people's assembly (Dewan Perwakilan Rakyat Daerah) (Kodamil 1976, 9).

Although the transfer of sovereignty promised to open the door to a new and better world, the results were inevitably disappointing. On the eve of Independence, the city and regency of Surabaya had remained fairly peaceful but in the hinterland guerrilla activity continued throughout November, being especially serious in Sidoarjo (ARA, MK 2.10.29, 397). After the disruption of several years of guerrilla war and the collapse of the former plantation-based economy, East Java could not suddenly revert to rust en orde, even after Independence. Indeed, in some parts armed brigandage became the order of the day, with foreign-owned plantations being especially vulnerable. Though fortunate to have enjoyed four years of peace since the trauma of November 1945, Surabaya was not immune to these unsettled conditions. During 1950 the city experienced an unprecedented crime wave, from petty theft to armed robbery. As in the looting of early March 1942, foreign-owned facilities such as the port, factories, and mansions were particular targets. Police were either unable or unwilling to intervene. Periodic raids gave the appearance of action but did little to restore order. The city had become much more difficult to govern.

Underlying this breakdown of law and order were dramatic swings in the city's population and worsening living conditions. During the Japanese occupation, the population exploded by 50 percent, from 403,000 in 1940 to 618,000 in 1945 (Steele 1980, 47). Then the Battle of Surabaya caused the flight of most Indonesian residents, reducing the population to no more than 130,000 in December 1945 (Steele 1980, 59). From early 1946, many of these people filtered back, accompanied by other refugees in search of a safe haven. By mid-1950 the population was reckoned to have climbed back to 633,000 (*NC,* 8/7/50). Yet the housing stock, already inadequate before the occupation, had been greatly depleted by the fighting. Hundreds of thousands of people now lived in crowded temporary dwellings; more and more immigrants squatted in locations where building was not allowed. These people also needed to work. On the streets, hawkers were more numerous and more brazen, while the number of becak swelled to the tens of thousands—by 1953 some thirteen thousand were registered but estimates of the actual number were as high as forty thousand (*SP,* 3/9/53; fig. 1.9). Crime and prostitution also flourished.

A return to normality was more evident during 1952. One factor was the appointment of a new mayor. For all his revolutionary fervor, Doel Arnowo seems to have made little impact on the great problems besetting the city. At the beginning of 1952 it was announced that he had been posted to Jakarta and in his place was appointed the acting resident of Besuki, Moestadjab Soemowidjojo. Born in Tulungagung, he was a forty-three-year-old career civil servant who had recently served a year as mayor of Madiun (*JP,* 15/1/52). He brought to city administration a professional approach that soon showed results in terms of the big problems such as the housing shortage and poor public health. The physical rehabilitation of the city also proceeded apace, with a boom in construction and rebuilding of damaged offices, shops, and markets (fig. 2.4). One project of immense symbolic importance was the construction of the Heroes' Monument (*Tugu Pahlawan*), a tall obelisk on the site of the former Palace of Justice/Kempeitai building opposite the governor's office. Construction was completed in time for an official opening by President Sukarno on Heroes' Day, 10 November 1952.

One striking difference between post-independence Surabaya and the colonial city was the degree of political mobilization. After years of repression, first by the Dutch and then more viciously by the Japanese, the Revolution had ensured that Surabayans became not only politically aware but also actively involved. The change was most visible in the ability of Sukarno to draw huge crowds whenever he visited the city (fig. 2.5). Besides being the recognized leader of the Revolution and the president of a newly independent Indonesia, he had been born and educated in Surabaya and was regarded as a native son, a true *arek Suroboyo.* His infrequent visits were festive occasions. Meanwhile, as the main political parties competed for mass support, politics began to penetrate into all levels of society, including the Municipal Assembly. The workplace was also affected. Trade unions were now freely permitted without

Figure 2.4. Textile distribution, Tunjungan, 1947. Courtesy Arsip Nasional.

Figure 2.5. Sukarno addressing the people from the balcony of the governor's office (see fig. 1.8), January 1950. Courtesy Arsip Nasional.

the restraint of anti-strike legislation. In 1951 the Labour Code introduced the forty-hour week, with effect mainly on the public sector and modern enterprise (Hawkins 1963, 263–65). Those in powerful unions were able to increase their real wages faster than inflation. Especially in the port and foreign-owed factories, strikes and slowdowns were increasingly common as aggressive union leaders pressed for improved conditions.

In all this the most notable trend during the 1950s was the growing strength of the Communist Party (PKI).[24] With its large industrial proletariat, Surabaya had been targeted in the early 1920s as a base for PKI activity. These efforts met with considerable success until the repression of the party and its affiliated unions in the mid-1920s. Still tainted by its attempt to take over the Republic in the bloody Madiun Affair of September 1948, the PKI was apparently not represented in the Municipal Assembly (Dewan Rakyat) appointed in December 1950. The overwhelming majority of the 25 seats was controlled by the combined forces of Sukarno's own Nationalist Party (PNI), with 9 seats, and the Islamic parties, with 13; apart from the Socialist Party (PSI) no other party held more than one seat (*SP,* 24/5/58). After independence, however, the PKI worked hard at building up its electoral base. In the 1955 election it gained 42 percent of the vote and captured 11 seats out of 25 in the Municipal Assembly, while the PNI was reduced to 4 seats and the Islamic parties to 3 (Hindley 1964, 222; *SP,* 17/4/56). However, the PKI was defeated in its quest for the chairmanship because the other minor parties combined to vote for the PNI candidate. Later the PKI managed to gain control with the support of the Indonesian-Chinese party (Baperki) and local hero Bung Tomo's Indonesia People's Party (Partai Rakjat Indonesia, PRI) (*SP,* 24/5/58).

The PKI consolidated its control of the Municipal Assembly in the February 1958 election. After some years of organizing support among squatters and encouraging their movement into the city, it was able to win 48 percent of the formal votes in a 61 percent turnout and, under the system of proportional representation, to gain 17 seats out of a larger assembly of 35 seats (*SP,* 24/5/58). It missed by only one seat winning a majority in its own right but was able to control the assembly with the continuing support of Baperki. The next largest voting bloc was the Islamic parties, with 10 seats (Nahdatul Ulama [NU] 8, Masjumi 2), while the PNI was held to only 4. The PKI's victory was followed on 1 July 1958 by the election of the city's first Communist mayor, Dr. Satryo Sastrodiredjo (*SP,* 1/7/58). Born in Yogyakarta in 1913, he had, like his older brother Ibnu Sutowo (later head of the state oil company Pertamina), trained at the Surabaya medical school (NIAS) and graduated in 1942. In 1947 he had become a junior minister for health in the cabinet of Amir Sjarifuddin and after Independence joined the Municipal Health Department, eventually becoming assistant director of the public hospital. He claimed to have become a member of the Communist Party only in 1953 but to have been a Marxist since his student days (*SP,* 5/6/58).

Although the PKI continued to control the Municipal Assembly and the mayoralty until the turmoil of September–October 1965, it never controlled the Provincial Assembly. Surabaya's large wage labor force and many squatter communities, the strongholds of the PKI, were not replicated in the hinterland. In the 1955 election the PKI gained 42 percent of the vote in the municipality but only 30 percent in the adjacent kabupaten, which left it with only 14 seats out of 60 in the Provincial Assembly (Hindley 1964, 222). Despite impressive gains at the national level, the proportion was almost unchanged after the 1958 election (20 out of 75). Although after 1958 the PKI was a larger bloc than the PNI (15 seats), it was quite overshadowed by the combined Islamic parties (NU 25, Masjumi 8) (*SP,* 16/4/58). Behind these figures lay rising political tension because the PKI was seen to be organizing Surabaya as a bastion to extend control over the rest of the province, much of which was not only conservative but also staunchly Muslim.

During 1958 society changed dramatically, with the repatriation of the remaining Dutch population. At the time of the transfer of sovereignty there had been an estimated 226,000 Dutch nationals in Indonesia, of which about 50,000 were resident in each of three cities: Jakarta, Surabaya, and Bandung. After the early repatriation of military personnel and civil servants, the total had reduced to around 50,000 by the end of 1957, of which 14,000 were in Jakarta, 13,000 in Surabaya, and 9,000 in Bandung (Meijer 1994, 655). Thus within a few years the Dutch community in Surabaya had already shrunk to a quarter of its colonial size. Most of those who remained worked in the private sector. In 1953 the resident Dutch commissioner had carried out a survey of Dutch firms and agencies throughout East Java that identified 9,500 men, women, and children supported by private employment—2,500 on estates, and a balance of 7,000, most of whom would have lived in Surabaya, engaged in foreign trade (2,082), industry (including electricity and gas, 1,960), shipping and transport (1,154), trade and retailing (817), plantation management (661), and banking (311).[25]

The immediate cause of the repatriation was the defeat in the United Nations on 29 November of a motion calling for Dutch withdrawal from West New Guinea. The root of the tension, however, was the perpetuation of Dutch control over the modern sector of the economy, something that the Indonesians had been forced to concede at the 1949 Round Table negotiations (Meijer 1994). In protest of the United Nations vote and the next day's assassination attempt in Jakarta on President Sukarno, on 1 December the government prohibited the landing of Dutch aircraft, banned publication of Dutch-language newspapers, and called a nationwide twenty-four-hour general strike (Glassburner and Thomas 1965). On 3 December communist-led workers launched a wave of seizures that quickly spread to most Dutch enterprises. Worried that so much economic power was being taken under communist control, on 13 December the army intervened to prevent further takeovers and to place occupied enterprises under military supervision (Feith 1962, 583–84). All Dutch-owned industries, trading houses, and banks in Surabaya thereby came under military control (chap. 4). Dutch citizens who were not willing to take up Indonesian citizenship were ordered to leave the country in a mass evacuation by sea and air. Very few stayed behind. Dutch assets (including household goods) had to be registered. Houses formerly occupied by Dutch nationals were taken over by a special government agency and allocated to the armed forces and departments of the civil service. Almost as suddenly as in 1942, Surabaya thereby ceased to be dominated by a European elite. It still looked like a colonial city, but the colonialists had gone home.

Apart from the rapid disappearance of Dutch people, the consequences of the nationalizations of December 1957 were profound. The wave of seizures led by the communist-dominated trade union movement had provoked military intervention. Despite an order of 14 December requiring joint action with the local military, in practice the military took control and, lacking guns, there was nothing much the PKI and trade unions could do about it. The action deepened the cleavage between the PKI, which enjoyed mass political support and exercised control of city government, and the army, which held the monopoly of military force and now controlled most of the modern sector of the economy. This cleavage ran right up to the national government in Jakarta, where after 1958 President Sukarno sought by Guided Democracy to balance these hostile power blocs and maintain his own authority (Feith 1962, 590–92).

After expulsion of the Dutch, anti-Chinese feeling also become overt, as though the xenophobia that hitherto had been concentrated upon the former colonialists sought a new target.[26] Now the Chinese were the haves, the exploiters of the Indonesian people. Even schoolchildren discovered that Chinese features and Chinese names now set them apart, to be no longer regarded as fellow Indonesians. During 1958 this antagonism gained a hard political edge with the closure of pro-Kuomintang schools following alleged Taiwanese complicity in the regional Permesta rebellion (Coppel 1983, 17). Racial discrimination was given official sanction by Regulation no. 10/1959 of November 1959, which banned foreign nationals (primarily alien Chinese) from operating retail stores in the countryside. Somers (1964, 26) estimated that forty-four thousand alien Chinese were resident in East Java and conducted some five thousand businesses in rural areas. Although in East Java the ban was not enforced as strictly as in West Java and was not generally applied to alien residence, many traders were forced to move to the town or city and several thousand accepted the opportunity to be repatriated to the People's Republic (Mackie 1976, 95–96). However, despite a minor outbreak of anti-Chinese rioting in Surabaya in May 1963 (Mackie 1976, 97, 231n45), the growing strength of the PKI and President Sukarno's closer ties with the People's Republic gradually drew the teeth from this discrimination. It may also have helped that in 1962, when under the 1955 dual-citizenship treaty alien Chinese had to choose their country of citizenship, most elected to become Indonesian citizens (Somers 1964, 32–34).

Over the next few years Western firms and consulates continued to be a target for PKI/trade union mobilization. In the midst of the Confrontation campaign against Malaysia, on 18 January 1964 "workers" seized the Unilever plant in Jakarta, followed three days later by the seizure of the Shell head office. On 24 January this movement spread to Surabaya, with seizure of the Unilever, Frazer and Neave, and British-American Tobacco (BAT) factories by unions affiliated with the PKI-led trade union federation (SOBSI) (*SP,* 24/1/64). The final wave of actions began on 7 December 1964. During a demonstration against American policy in the Belgian Congo, a crowd of youths and students stormed the U.S. Information Service (USIS) library in Jalan Pemuda, burning the American flag, smashing windows, breaking down doors, throwing the books into the street, and burning them in a bonfire (*SP,* 8/12/64). This action, which came only four days after the sacking of the USIS office in Jakarta, was repeated on a larger scale on 23 January 1965 by thousands of students, workers, and women affiliated with communist mass organizations (Hughes 1967, 99; *SP,* 8/1/65). The building was seized and converted into an office for the Communist National Front (*SP,* 21/5/65). In March the American firm of P. T. Filma (formerly Proctor and Gamble) was seized by workers of SOBSI/Kaum Buruh Marhaen. Finally, in May 1965, the transfer of the Prodenta, Singer, and Heineken factories to government supervision marked the end of foreign investment in Surabaya (*SP,* 19/5/65).

Flash Point

As 1965 wore on amid rumors of President Sukarno's worsening health, there was a growing sense of crisis, compounded by economic chaos. The acute shortage of foreign exchange meant that even essential commodities such as rice, textiles, and kerosene were more and more scarce. While black markets boomed, prices soared out of control and inflation surged to several hundred percent per annum (Mackie 1967b). The countryside was becoming polarized as land seizures (*aksi sepihak*) led by the PKI sparked Muslim resistance. In Surabaya, left-wing organizations became very aggressive; people's militia, such as the women's league (Gerwani), trained in public and flaunted their arms. Among middle-class people in the civil service, including public enterprises, schools, and universities, there was widespread fear that the PKI had prepared death lists. Mass demonstrations continued in front of the last imperialist targets such as the United States consulate. On 27 September there occurred the most violent demonstration yet when thousands of left-wing demonstrators forced their way into the governor's residence and held him hostage for a short time, besides affixing posters and causing a good deal of damage (*SP,* 30/9/65; Crouch 1978, 146).

The coup attempt in Jakarta on the night of 30 September had its reverberations in Surabaya but the outcome hung much longer in the balance. Newspapers were cautious in their reporting but word spread quickly by radio and by word of mouth. However, unlike Jakarta, where the military uprising was suppressed within two days, in East Java most of the armed forces remained loyal to President Sukarno, who was still a local hero and whose role in the affair remained unclear. The army command was divided but the navy, whose main base was in Surabaya, was strongly loyal. On 2 October the communist labor federation, SOBSI, launched a campaign of takeovers of state enterprises, most hitherto under army control. This led on the eighth to army intervention and two days later to the occupation of SOBSI headquarters (Crouch 1978, 146). The risk of armed conflict remained high but the PKI attempted no general insurrection and the army was able to maintain an uneasy peace. Violence first broke out in the hinterland when Muslim groups attacked PKI offices and Chinese shops.

In Surabaya the turning point seems to have been 16 October, when a mass meeting was held at the Heroes' Monument by anti-communist organizations, among which Islamic and Catholic organizations were prominent (*SP,* 18/10/65). This meeting, calling for suppression of what was already being called the Gestapu (Gerakan September Tiga-puluh, Thirtieth September Movement), came about a week after a similar large rally in Jakarta. The meeting was addressed by Colonel Sukotjo, commander of the Brawijaya Division in Surabaya, yet afterward about two hundred people were detained after marching on the nearby PKI headquarters. This careful neutrality soon collapsed under the example of army-led repression in Central Java and spontaneous killings in rural East Java (Crouch 1978, 151). On 20 October the army issued decrees concerning the supervision of state enterprises and vital private enterprises and the following day banned all strike action. On 22 October the PKI and affiliated mass organizations (including SOBSI) were banned. By the twenty-seventh the list had grown to thirty-seven organizations and on 4 November the Indonesian-Chinese political party, Baperki, was also proscribed.

Systematic repression of the PKI and left-wing organizations seems to have begun about 27 October and to have been more systematic and ruthless than in Jakarta.[27] Besides publication of a comprehensive list of banned organizations, there were reports of orders from the governor to "screen" the civil guard (Hansip) and of the first raids on kampungs such as Kupang and Pandegiling suspected of harboring communists or their sympathizers. Two days later it was confirmed that the mayor had been arrested, along with seven other *bupati* (regents). Next a governor's decree ordered the purging of government offices and enterprises (*SP*, 29/10/65). This action was supported by the twenty non-communist members of the Municipal Assembly, who called for the dissolution of the PKI and punishment of its members. The purge continued throughout November, leaving almost no organization and no part of the city untouched. A decree of 12 November announced that ninety-six vital enterprises in East Java (mostly in or around Surabaya) had been placed under military control. After military occupation of the Gresik cement plant on 5 November about three hundred people (including the managing director) were dismissed (Semen Gresik 1980, 46); another thousand workers were dismissed from the state railways in the Surabaya area (*SP*, 23/11/65). Even Airlangga University was placed briefly under military control, despite claims by the rector that the university had purged itself (*SP*, 8/11/65). Some were arrested but many workmates, colleagues, and relatives just disappeared. No one dared ask what had happened to them.

The army ruthlessly swept through kampungs known to be PKI strongholds. One notorious PKI area, where the streets were named after communist leaders, lay on the other side of the railway from the Ngagel industrial estate. Soon after the purges began, the army occupied a factory near the railway line and marshaled the population along the viaduct: anyone identified as PKI was taken away. The area was later razed for redevelopment. On 26 November it was reported that three platoons had taken two days to "cleanse" the kampungs of Dinoyo and Kalibutuh, resulting in forty-eight arrests (*SP*, 26/11/65). Another target was the dock area around Tanjung Perak and the naval base, where kampungs of squatters and port workers suspected of being sympathetic to the PKI were also cleared, a process that went on well into 1966. How many were arrested and how many killed is unknown. For weeks there were bodies floating in the Kali Mas. Until the government gave orders for a cleanup, it was a brave man who had the courage to give any a decent burial.

The purge of 1965–66 achieved its goal of breaking the PKI

stranglehold over Surabaya. For the army it was the settlement of unfinished business, a final balancing of accounts for the 1948 Madiun uprising after civilian governments had allowed—even encouraged—the PKI's resurgence. For some ethnic groups, such as the Madurese, it was a matter of defending their religion. Among the middle class and intelligentsia, it was widely believed that a PKI victory would have resulted in their blood being spilled. For the survivors it seems, as elsewhere in Indonesia, to have been cathartic, a release from fear but also a blood sacrifice. It completed a cycle of violence that had begun in 1945 with the Revolution and the Battle of Surabaya—the short story "Surabaya" by Idrus (1968) best captures the manic and disoriented behavior of that earlier time. Schama (1989, 859) identifies violence as not incidental to but the motor of the French Revolution. With hindsight it may be judged that Sukarno's romantic ideal of continuing revolution—like that of his contemporary Chairman Mao—was essentially destructive, a license for escalating violence. Vice President Hatta, speaking in November 1956, had seen this very clearly even before Sukarno had introduced Guided Democracy: "Those who say that our national Revolution is not completed are wrong indeed. . . . What is left unfinished is not the Revolution itself, but the efforts to carry its ideals into effect" (Hatta 1960, quoted in Feith 1962).

The Birth and Death of the New Order

Amidst the turmoil of 1965–66 the New Order's founding triumvirate of General Soeharto, Sultan Hamengku Buwono, and Adam Malik promised a return to normality. Politics had degenerated from the euphoria of independence into madness and fear. People wanted to be left to get on with their lives. They sought relief from the shortages, the inequities of black markets and hyperinflation, and a barely functioning public sector. Student organizations backed by Islamic and Christian groups and encouraged by the army held mass demonstrations calling for political and economic reform. The new government's commitment to political stability and economic rehabilitation and development caught the mood of the times.[28] President Sukarno's powers were whittled away, until in March 1967 his dismissal was ratified by a purged parliament and General Soeharto appointed in his place as acting president. Four months later the state of emergency ended officially throughout Indonesia. The extraordinary Supreme Command for the Liberation of Irian (KOTI) was disbanded; in the provinces the powers of the extraordinary regional commands (Penguasa Pelaksana Dwikora Dareah, Pepelrada) were transferred back to the governors. In East Java the official handover took place on 4 September. Ten days later Colonel Sukotjo, since 4 November 1965 acting mayor of Surabaya, was officially appointed to that position by a reconstituted municipal assembly of twenty-one new members (*SP,* 4/3/67). Another key appointment was that of Mohammed Noer as governor of East Java from 15 December 1967. These two men were to be the driving forces behind the rehabilitation of the city and its province.

In Surabaya the immediate concern was political stability. Combining the functions of both local army commander and acting mayor, Colonel Sukotjo proceeded with mopping up operations against suspected communists. Until well into 1966 the Municipality enforced the clearance of squatter dwellings along the riverbanks, fire lanes, and roadways. This was done with the explicit purpose of facilitating the suppression of the Communist Party. The PKI had encouraged such illegal occupation since the early 1950s, so that illegal kampungs were regarded not only as PKI strongholds but also as places where PKI refugees might hide (*SP,* 9/12/65). Vagrants (*gelendangan*) were also rounded up. Those vagrants and squatters who could not find accommodation in other kampungs or villages were shipped to the Outer Islands as transmigrants (*SP,* 9/12/65). In mid-December 1965, Surabaya was officially declared a "closed city" (*SP,* 15/12/65). This was several years before Governor Sadikin declared Jakarta a closed city and in the longer term was just as unsuccessful in stemming the flow of rural-urban migration. From a planning viewpoint, however, these politically motivated clearances were a first step in urban rehabilitation. To provide a long-term planning framework, in 1966 Colonel Sukotjo brought together a group of city officials with young staff from the Faculty of Architecture at the Institute of Technology (ITS). This Master Plan Team, which began work in October 1966, became the brain trust for redevelopment of the city, with an underlying commitment to improving public welfare (chaps. 4, 6).

A side-effect of the assault on the PKI was a new wave of discrimination against the large Chinese community. In the prevailing climate of paranoia, all Chinese suddenly became guilty by association. In March 1966 students attacked the Chinese news agency, cultural building, and consulate (Crouch 1978, 187). To head off the storm, on 23 April 1966 Indonesians of Chinese descent met in Surabaya to express support for Pancasila, the Constitution, President Sukarno, and the armed forces (*SP,* 23/4/66). Nonetheless, on December 23 East Java's martial law commander, General Sumitro, banned alien Chinese from engaging in wholesaling beyond Surabaya, moving home, or using the Chinese language or characters, and imposed a head tax (Coppel 1983; *SP,* 31/12/66). Chinese schools were shut. The Chinese chamber of commerce (Siang Hwee) in Jalan Kembang Djepun was closed down, to reopen in September 1967 as the Indonesian Chamber of Commerce (KADIN) (*SP,* 15/9/67). On 11 January 1967 regulations were issued in Jakarta concerning the naturalization of Chinese citizens and ten days later these rules were promulgated in Surabaya. At the beginning of 1967 it was estimated that there were still 132,229 Chinese citizens throughout East Java (*SP,* 2/2/67). Even those of Chinese extraction who had already taken Indonesian nationality were expected to adopt Indonesian names. By mid-1968 some hundred and sixty thousand Indonesian Chinese were reported to have changed names in the city of Surabaya alone (*SP,* 9/7/68). Because atheism was regarded as tantamount to Communism and Confucian belief was suspect, there was also pressure to adopt a recognized formal religion: many Chinese declared themselves Christians (Coppel 1983). Yet despite the willingness of most ethnic Chinese to legitimize their status, on 21 October 1968 mobs attacked shops in Pasar Turi, Bubutan and Jagalan. This riot was justified as retaliation against the hanging in Singapore of Indonesian saboteurs captured during the Confrontation against Malaysia (*SP*, 22/10/68).

Besides political stability, the municipal government's main priority was to restore the city's ramshackle infrastructure. Despite the rapid growth in population since the late 1940s, there had been little extension of the colonial infrastructure, most of which had been allowed to run down. This was most apparent in public transport. The electric tram system commissioned in the early 1920s for a city of a few hundred thousand people was by the mid-1960s serving a city of well over one million with the same network and less rolling stock. Lack of power station maintenance meant frequent blackouts and brownouts: businesses provided their own generators while households relied on kerosene lamps and candles. Failure to dredge the river and canals meant that the city flooded badly each monsoon, and then the pumps did not work to remove the water.

In the late 1960s it was unimaginable that rapid and sustained growth would be achieved and even come to be taken for granted. Yet by the 1990s the physical signs of development were everywhere: construction of high-rise offices and banks, five-star hotels, apartment towers, and shopping malls; the spread of industrial estates, middle-class suburbs, and low-cost housing estates; the widening of streets and the growth of traffic (chaps. 5, 6). The problems of social infrastructure were being energetically tackled (chap. 4). In the kampungs the proliferation of radios, cassette players, television sets, and motorcycles suggested a general increase in prosperity (chap. 3). Surabaya looked to have become a very different place, to have reemerged as a prosperous, metropolitan city. It all seemed so tangible. What a shock, therefore, when reality faded into a dream.

The crisis that overwhelmed the New Order in 1998 was a destructive interaction of politics and economics at the national level.

In hindsight, the bell had begun to toll during 1996 with a series of strange incidents. On 9 June a local dispute in Surabaya escalated into assaults by mobs of youths on no fewer than ten Protestant churches, a feat that suggested some premeditation and planning (*Suara Pembaruan,* 18/6/96). Several weeks later thugs in pay of the government stormed the Jakarta headquarters of Megawati Sukarnoputri's Partai Demokrasi Indonesia (PDI), sparking a violent street riot. In October all churches in the East Java town of Situbondo were burned down in a few hours by what appeared to be a well-trained group suspected of military connections (Klinken 1997). From the end of 1996 into the election year of 1997 "spontaneous" rioting spread rapidly through towns in West Java to the Outer Islands, taking on strong anti-Chinese overtones. Thick smoke from forest fires, drought, the threat of food shortages, and the tense election campaign all added to a sense of foreboding. Sensing a mood for change, after the elections student groups and a few brave political leaders called upon Soeharto not to seek reappointment for a seventh term.

The Asian financial crisis began to be felt in Indonesia in July 1997. At first the government was confident of the country's "economic fundamentals" but the rupiah kept falling until in October assistance had to be sought from the International Monetary Fund (IMF). This intervention actually worsened the domestic crisis of confidence. Disputes over the IMF package and its implementation, closure of some banks and growing concern over the soundness of the rest of the banking system, in December rumors that Soeharto was seriously ill, and at the New Year an apparently unrealistic budget led to capital flight that drove the currency down from Rp 2,430 in July to Rp 16,000 in January 1998 (McLeod 1998, 42). Share prices crashed while interest rates soared. Construction projects were halted, factories laid off workers, and companies stopped repaying loans. Nevertheless, amid rising civil unrest, in March 1998 Soeharto was reappointed for a seventh consecutive term and defiantly appointed a cabinet that included his own daughter and personal cronies.

The trigger for popular revolution was an increase of around 50 percent in fuel prices and transport fares at the beginning of May as part of the IMF agreement. Students demonstrated in most main cities. Medan's business district was torn apart by rioting. In Surabaya army and police had been on full alert since mid-February, when food riots broke out across East Java; two months later students and police had clashed when a student demonstration was blocked from leaving the campus of Airlangga University (*New York Times,* 11/2/98; *Kompas,* 9/4/98). On 12 May several students were shot outside Jakarta's Trisakti University and next day riots broke out across Jakarta. The news quickly spread to Surabaya. That night, reviving a tactic of the 1997 elections, a convoy of an estimated five hundred motorcycles took to the streets for several hours while students massed at the city's ten main campuses. On the fourteenth Jakarta was convulsed by savage rioting against Chinese property and businesses associated with the Soeharto family.

Surabaya was fortunate that the sparks of riot did not ignite. The army attempted to confine students to their campuses while guarding roads, malls, offices, and shops. In the afternoon of the fourteenth, thousands of students nevertheless staged a "long march" from Wonokromo in the south of the city to the provincial assembly building. Around 7 P.M. a convoy of about fifty motorcycles gathered at Semampir, in the far north of the city beside the naval base, and with shouts of "Reformasi" drew a crowd and incited it to attack and loot nearby Chinese shops and vehicles. As in Jakarta, it was later reported that at least ten Chinese and also Arab women had been raped (*SP,* 1/7/98). From Semampir the convoy moved on to other parts of the city and had some success inciting crowds to stone, break into, and set fire to Chinese stores and businesses. Police and troops moved to quell each outbreak but it was well after midnight before the convoy and crowds dispersed. At dawn further looting was observed and crowds began to return to the streets. After the ritual Friday morning Muslim prayers, the motorcycle convoy grew into the hundreds and was now targeting not only Chinese businesses but also offices of Bank Central Asia, associated with the Soeharto family and business partner Liem Sioe Liong, as well as Tommy Soeharto's Timor car showrooms. By way of protection, shop owners painted crude signs or hung banners proclaiming Pro Reformasi, Muslim, or Pribumi (indigenous Indonesian). Many ethnic Chinese and expatriates fled with their families to the airport hoping to board flights to Bali or Singapore, some sought refuge in the hill resorts of Tretes and Batu, and others sought security in the city's luxury hotels, which were fully booked. In middle-class suburbs men hurriedly formed themselves into neighborhood watches, armed with whatever implements were at hand. At dusk a noisy pro-Reformasi cavalcade of motorcycles, cars, pickups, and other trucks packed with young people paraded around the streets in a show of defiance and then dispersed. Next day Surabaya was like a ghost town, the main streets all but deserted, business boarded up, here and there broken windows, scattered rubbish, burnt tires, and a few damaged vehicles as reminders of the mayhem.

Compared with Medan, Jakarta, and Solo, in Surabaya there was little damage to persons and property. Newspapers reported that unknown parties had attached themselves to the student protest of 14 May and about two hundred of them had incited the disturbance at Semampir (*SP,* 15/5/98). Police subsequently claimed to have information that about two hundred "guests" had arrived in Surabaya to create trouble and that a man arrested while attempting to set fire to the Tunjungan Plaza shopping center had been paid Rp 40,000 by one such person (*SP,* 17/5/98). No mastermind was identified but by implication the provocateurs had come from Jakarta. The pattern of motorcyclists moving around the city and inciting disturbances at many different locations, as also the targeting of Chinese, Bank Central Asia, Timor cars, and the rape of women at Semampir suggest a pattern similar to that in Jakarta. The important question is why in Surabaya all these outbreaks led to so little actual damage—as though the arsonists were trying to set fire to damp timber. The most salient feature is that police and the armed forces, while unable to keep crowds off the streets, acted promptly and firmly to put down each disturbance. In Jakarta and Solo, by contrast, the military either disappeared from the streets or refused to intervene for a whole day while the city went up in flames. Perhaps in Surabaya there was also less alienation, less pent-up rage among kampung dwellers (chap. 4).

The city remained tense and much quieter than usual in expectation of another big demonstration on 20 May, the anniversary of the Day of National Awakening (Hari Kebangkitan Nasional). Students were asked to remain on campus to avoid any pretext for "other parties" to attach themselves and lead to further violence. On the nineteenth an estimated twenty thousand students from twenty-two universities held a rally at the Stiesia football stadium and next day joined with students in massive pro-Reformasi rallies, six East Java generals called for Soeharto's resignation, the East Java provincial assembly urged the national parliament to support reform, and strikes broke out in factories in Sidoarjo. Some students were injured when the army tried roughly to force students back inside campus fences.

News of Soeharto's resignation just after 9 A.M. on 21 May was soon received in Surabaya and quickly disseminated. Prayers of thanks were offered up in the mosques. Traffic began to return to the streets, shops to reopen. A peace convoy of some five thousand students celebrated their victory. The military presence was scaled back. Over the weekend of 23 and 24 May the big shopping malls reopened and the city began to return to the appearance of normality. Flights were full back from Singapore as ethnic Chinese returned to their homes. However, a month later the Department of Immigration reported that of the 11,600 Chinese and expatriates who had fled overseas from Surabaya's Juanda airport only half had yet returned, not counting others who had left on domestic flights to Jakarta or Bali (*SP,* 19/6/98). In mid-July an outbreak of rioting and looting around the district town of Jember and threats of further anti-Chinese violence in Surabaya led to another wave of departures (*Business Times,* 15/7/98).

In 1998, as in 1965–66, Jakarta was the stage for the national power struggle. The biggest student demonstrations, the worst rioting, the byzantine negotiations, and Soeharto's eventual resignation were all played out there and relayed to the rest of the country. Students, the military, civil leaders, and ordinary people in Surabaya knew they could not control events in Jakarta but at the same time, as in 1965–66, knew they could influence the outcome. The strength of student demonstrations in Surabaya kept pressure on the president and his supporters, just as the reluctance of the armed forces in Surabaya to act brutally against the students or to provoke destructive riots helped to tip the balance in favor of reform. Soeharto's son-in-law General Prabowo had associates in senior military positions but did not command the loyalty of troops in East Java. It was also rumored that the leaders of Surabaya's Chinese business community had paid local army units generous protection money to keep the peace, which the positioning of troops during the tense days would tend to confirm. There was also awareness that Surabaya's kampung dwellers had no sympathy for the regime. Students were kept on their campuses out of fear of igniting popular street protests. Islamic and military leaders who advised Soeharto in the final days had all this as leverage. If the president could no longer control Jakarta, if Yogyakarta was virtually in rebellion, and East Java was tacitly pro-Reformasi, his cause was lost except by resort to mass terror.

Soeharto's New Order thus ended as it had begun—in popular demonstrations and violence, hope and fear. A fundamental difference, however, was the direction of change. In 1965–66 repression had been imposed; in 1998 it was lifted. Protected by their status as children of the elite, students had led the pro-Reformasi movement. Once Soeharto had resigned and the military presence scaled back, the people came into the streets with more basic demands. Workers went on strike, taking to the Provincial Assembly demands for higher wages to compensate for the rapid inflation induced by devaluation and in particular soaring prices for rice and cooking oil. From 4 June some twenty-six thousand workers of the local Maspion-group factories staged orderly protests for several days before a settlement was negotiated by the chairman of the provincial assembly. Many smaller strikes followed. Kampung dwellers in and around the city began to protest against corrupt officials, from headmen to bupati, and to reoccupy land from which they had been evicted without fair compensation. This included the golf course on the Citra Raya luxury housing estate. At the New Year of 1999 the local police station at Lakarsantri was stormed after a detainee was rumored to have been killed (*SP,* 3/1/99). Criminal activity also proliferated, especially bag snatchings, muggings, and break-ins. The fearsome word *rampok* (violent robbery) returned to circulation. Even road signs and traffic lights were stolen. Reformasi was a time of hope but also a time of rising insecurity, especially for ethnic Chinese and the asset-rich but no longer prosperous middle class. Kampung dwellers, however, regained a degree of political and economic autonomy. Ruthlessly suppressed for thirty years, social conflict came back to the surface of urban life, cluttering the streets, challenging the social order. Rumbustious as ever, the *arek Suroboyo* sought to reclaim their city.

In the vigorous June 1999 general elections, the first free elections since 1955, the people of Surabaya decisively rejected the New Order. Megawati's revitalized Indonesian Democratic Party (Struggle) (PDI-P) triumphed with 54 percent of the popular vote, earning 21 of the 35 seats in the Municipal Assembly (*SP,* 9/6/99). The three main Muslim parties gained 31 percent of the vote and 11 seats. The government's Golkar Party managed just 8 percent of the vote, roughly equivalent to the proportion of civil servants and military personnel in the adult population, and was reduced to a token 3 seats. The mayor, Sunarto Sumoprawiro, known familiarly as Cak Nur, nevertheless managed to get himself reappointed after aggressive politicking against a weak PDI-P candidate. Why a city that looked to have benefited so much from the New Order should so firmly reject it is a central issue of the rest of the book.

Chapter 3

PROFILE

A CITY is its people. Without people, it is nothing more than an archaeological site. Through war or natural disaster, cities may lose most of the built environment and yet recover, as long as the people remain. In 1945 the survivors in the devastated cities of Germany and Japan crawled out from their underground shelters and with bare hands began immediately and compulsively to clear and rebuild. Within a decade most of these cities were again thriving. By contrast, in Roman Pompeii an entire population was suffocated by the deluge of lava and ash and no one was left to excavate and rebuild; preserved beneath the volcanic debris, the town's physical remains were frozen in time.

The starting point for urban history must therefore be the population, beginning with the issue of scale. We have become accustomed to measuring world population by the billion and urban populations by the million. Yet this is a perspective of the late twentieth century. Only a few decades ago New York was unique as a city of over ten million people. Cities of such size now include Tokyo, Mexico City, Shanghai, and Jakarta. It requires some mental effort to remember that around 1900 the threshold for a very large city was not ten but one million, with the scale marked in units of one hundred thousand. This dramatic increase in scale has to be born in mind. To keep an ever smaller city in focus as we go back in time, we must extend the telephoto lens and foreshorten the field of vision.

An urban population is a highly structured multitude that we identify by the term *society.* The difficulty lies in its sheer complexity. A city of two to three million people cannot be studied in a glass-fronted box like a child's ant nest. Fortunately, the preoccupation of twentieth-century governments with the collecting of statistics makes it possible to go beyond merely haphazard and impressionistic evidence. Censuses and expenditure surveys provide basic socioeconomic data for a representative cross-section of the population and, in the case of a few key demographic statistics, for the entire population. Each variable is like an X-ray exposure of that elusive phenomenon known as society. Put together, from the viewpoint of both production and consumption, they build up a profile that, to some extent, can also be traced over time.

In Indonesia, usable socioeconomic data first became available with the colonial government census of 1930. The first genuine census, that of 1920, contained only basic age and gender data (CEI 1991b, 25–29). The 1930 census was the first to collate key socioeconomic variables for the whole population, including education and occupation by ethnic group. Though sparse, these data throw the first sharp rays of light on the socioeconomic status of the Indonesian population, which hitherto had been to its Dutch rulers an undifferentiated mass. Unfortunately for historians, the outbreak of World War II halted preparations for a comparable 1940 census. Not until 1961 was the government of an independent Indonesia well enough organized to hold its first census, which like that of 1920 was confined to basic demographic variables. A comprehensive and reliable database came into existence only under the New Order. Censuses have been held at the beginning of each decade, supplemented by the 1985 and 1995 intercensal surveys (Supas) and annual household expenditure surveys (Susenas). These data tapes can be analyzed down to the municipal level, allowing construction of a socioeconomic profile. For a few variables, it is possible to identify long-term trends since 1930.

An important question is the extent to which Surabaya is like other cities. This chapter will attempt to provide a partial answer by collating the same socioeconomic variables for Jakarta. As the capital and largest city, Jakarta might be expected to differ significantly from its provincial counterpart. In fact, it turns out that the socioeconomic profiles of the two cities are remarkably similar. By these criteria, Surabaya looks to be a scaled-down version of Jakarta.

The chapter will begin with analysis of the Surabaya's changing position in the urban hierarchy of Java and then look at the city's changing ethnic composition. This is followed by examination of trends in the occupational structure of employment and in educational attainment. The nexus between production and consumption will be drawn out by reviewing the evidence on the distribution of expenditure and long-term trends in housing and living conditions. Where possible, these variables are traced back as far as the 1930 census. Health is considered in chapter 4. The final section of the chapter considers what sort of society has emerged from colonial society, with some reflections on the emerging middle class.

A Tale of Two Cities

At the beginning of the twentieth century, Surabaya was by population and volume of trade the foremost city of Java. A prosperous urban economy based on foreign trade and associated services had been sustained by decades of rapid development of plantation agriculture in the hinterland. By contrast, the colonial capital of Batavia (Jakarta) was held back economically by its small cultivable hinterland, poor transport links with that hinterland, and, until the opening of Tanjung Priok in 1886, a very ordinary roadstead port. Java's third main coastal city, Semarang (Central Java), suffered from similar disadvantages. In modern terms, however, all three cities were still very small: at the 1905 census Surabaya had 150,000 inhabitants, Jakarta 138,500, and Semarang 96,700 (table 3.1). Surabaya's turn-of-the-century population was only three times the estimated precolonial population of 50–60,000 in 1625 and not much above the 100,000 estimated as the early-seventeenth-century populations of the largest Southeast Asian port cities (Reid 1993). Not that Surabaya in 1905 was any Southeast Asian dwarf: the region's main trading center, Singapore, then had a population of only around 250,000.

Contrary to what might have been expected, Surabaya was unable to capitalize on its head start as Java's largest city. Between the censuses of 1905 and 1920, the city slipped back to second place in Java's urban hierarchy. Its population continued to grow, but at a recorded rate of only 1.6 percent per annum (table 3.2).[1] Meanwhile Jakarta's population more than doubled, at a rate of just over 5 percent per annum, and must have surpassed that of Surabaya by 1914. Jakarta's rapid growth had several causes. The new Ethical Policy and the incorporation of the Outer Islands into the colonial state stimulated the growth and centralization of the bureaucracy. With regard to the private sector, the city's hinterland, West Java, was now coming into its own as a frontier for the planting of estate crops like tea and rubber. Between the censuses of 1920 and 1930 Surabaya was unable to make up much lost ground, despite record volumes of trade (chap. 7). When the sugar industry collapsed in the 1930s, the city lost all momentum. After 1930 Jakarta again grew much faster than Surabaya and began to assume the dominant role that became characteristic after Independence.

Absence of any census between 1930 and 1961 means that charting population trends during this tumultuous period is fairly speculative (table 3.3). If the municipal registration of December 1940 can be relied on in place of the canceled census, Surabaya's population had grown to 403,000, implying modest growth in the 1930s of 1.6 percent per annum (Steele 1980, 47). The Depression had probably caused some net migration back to rural areas in the first half of the 1930s, reversing later in the decade. During the Japanese

TABLE 3.1
Census population of main Javanese cities and Singapore, 1905–2000 (thousands)

Municipality	1905	1920	1930	1961	1971[b]	1980[b]	1990[b]	2000[b]
Singapore[a]	250	418	588	1,687	2,075	2,414	2,690	3,263
Jakarta	139	306	533	2,973	4,085	6,072	8,228	8,385
Surabaya	150	192	342	1,408	1,309	1,737	2,410	2,589
Semarang	97	158	218	503	566	820	1,004	1,266
Bandung	47	95	167	973	1,311	1,745	2,026	2,142
Malang	30	43	87	342	365	491	650	735

Source: Censuses; Hugo et al. 1987 (52, 101–2); Straits Settlements (annual); Singapore (annual); Dept. of Statistics (www.singstat.gov.sq) (18/3/01).

[a]Per censuses 1921, 1931, 1961, 1970, 1980, 1990; 1905 interpolated exponentially from 1901 and 1911 censuses.

[b]Figures for 1971 and 1980 are for Javanese cities as adjusted by NUDS (1985) for functional urban boundaries; 1990 and 2000 figures for urban population of municipalities.

TABLE 3.2
Intercensal population growth of main Javanese cities (exponential rates, %)

City	1905–20	1920–30	1930–61	1961–71	1971–80	1980–90	1990–2000
Jakarta	5.3	5.5	5.5	3.2	4.4	3.1	0.14
Surabaya	1.6	5.8	3.5	2.6	3.1	3.3	0.72
Semarang	3.3	3.3	2.7	1.2	4.1	2.0	2.32
Bandung	4.6	5.6	5.7	3.0	3.2	1.5	0.41
Malang	2.4	7.0	4.4	0.7	2.5	2.8	1.23

Source: Calculated from table 3.1.

occupation Surabaya's population soared to 618,000 by September 1945, implying an 8.6 percent rate of growth over the five-year period and probably over 10 percent for the period 1942–45 (table 3.3; Steele 1980, 57). However, the battles of October–November 1945 caused massive flight of Surabaya's population (chap. 2), while that of Jakarta maintained its upward trend. After the Dutch had reestablished control, Surabaya's population began fairly quickly to recover as refugees poured back from a now turbulent hinterland. By September 1948 population had regained its 1940 level and by the transfer of sovereignty at the end of 1949 had regained the immediate postwar level of 600,000. The breakdown of colonial constraints on rural-urban migration and urban settlement affected both cities, but Jakarta's population growth accelerated, while that of Surabaya declined.

The mathematics of a consistently higher base and a higher sustained rate of growth ensured that over the entire period 1930–61, Jakarta's population growth was almost twice as fast. Surabaya's population reached one million on the eve of the 1961 census: Jakarta's population, which had already exceeded one million in mid-1948, was by then almost three million. Whereas in 1930 Surabaya's population had been almost two-thirds that of Jakarta, by 1961 it was only one-third. Surabaya had thereby been relegated unambiguously to provincial status. Throughout both the stagna-

TABLE 3.3
Estimates of population, Surabaya and Jakarta, 1940–61 (thousands)

City	1940[a] (Dec)	1945[b] (Sept)	1945[c] (Dec)	1948[d] (Sept)	1949[d] (May)	1949[e] (Dec)	1950[f]	1961[g]
Surabaya	403	618	209	400	500	ca. 600	715	1,008
Jakarta	ca. 600	844[h]	–	1,050[h]	–	–	–	2,973

Sources: [a]Municipal registration (Steele 1980, 47); [b]Japanese registration (Steele 1980, 59); [c]Allied registration (Steele 1980, 59); [d]ARA, MK 2.10.29, 447-50: BVZ (monthly); [e]Steele 1980 (60); [f]SP, 30/11/64; [g]table 3.1; [h]Abeyasekere 1987 (141, 157).

tion of the 1960s and the boom of the 1970s, the population of Surabaya continued to lag further behind.

The 1980s was the first decade since the 1920s when Surabaya's population growth appeared to exceed that of Jakarta, albeit by a very small amount. These figures are consistent with the upturn in the economy of Surabaya that seems to have begun in the 1970s and gathered pace in the 1980s. However, the apparent slowdown in Jakarta's population growth is a statistical artifact, because the figures for the capital city region do not capture urban sprawl. By 1985 the adjacent districts of Tangerang, Bogor, and Bekasi had an urbanization rate of 68 percent. If their combined urban population were incorporated into Greater Jakarta (Jabotabek), the city's enumerated population would rise from about 9 million to almost 17 million.[2]

The municipality of Surabaya is also experiencing urban spillover. Factories, industrial estates, housing complexes, the airport and other transportation facilities now extend across the municipal boundary into the adjacent districts of Sidoarjo and Gresik (chaps. 5, 6). By 2000, Sidoarjo had the highest level of urbanization (86 percent) of any kabupaten in East Java, followed by Gresik (50 percent). Adding in these urban populations plus the ferry town of Kamal on Madura would almost double the population of Greater Surabaya from the municipal figure of 2.6 million to over 4.5 million.[3]

Ethnic Composition

Like other port cities of Southeast Asia, Surabaya's population has traditionally been ethnically diverse and even now could hardly be judged to be a single community. On the edge of the mainland of Java and adjacent to the off-lying island of Madura, the city has always been an interface between two distinct indigenous cultures, the Javanese and Madurese, each having its own very different language. The Javanese have tended to settle in the southern part of the city, Madurese in the northern part, and each group has filled different occupational niches. Seafaring indigenous peoples such as the Banjar (from South Kalimantan) and the Bugis (from South Sulawesi) still have their own kampungs around the port. Of the foreign communities, the Chinese flourished in Surabaya under colonial rule, though until 1918 they were still officially confined to the Chinese quarter, with the remnants of the pass system controlling access to the interior (Cator 1936; Furnivall 1944, 240–42). The European—mainly Dutch—population was never as large but enjoyed the prerogatives of power and wealth. Since Independence, the Europeans have been repatriated and the residual Eurasian and "Other Foreign Oriental" communities have been absorbed into the Indonesian population. Antagonisms nevertheless remain between the Indonesian and Chinese communities, while the Indonesian community itself remains divided by language and custom.

Colonial rule rested upon ethnic discrimination. The colonial racial hierarchy had Europeans at the top, followed by Eurasians, Chinese, Other Foreign Orientals (Arabs, Armenians, Jews, and British Indians), and, at the bottom, the Indonesian peoples. In the last colonial census of 1930, the ethnic composition of the city was carefully tabulated (table 3.4). The great majority of the total population was Indonesian, of which most were Javanese (84 percent); Madurese constituted a substantial minority (13 percent), and other indigenous groups made up the last 3 percent. The one-fifth of the city's population that was not Indonesian was made up of Europeans (which after 1899 included Japanese) (7.6 percent), Chinese

TABLE 3.4
Ethnic composition of main Javanese cities, 1930 (%)

	European	Chinese	Other Asians[a]	Indonesians
Batavia	6.9	14.8	1.4	76.9
Surabaya	7.6[b]	11.4	1.6	79.4[c]
Semarang	5.8	12.6	1.0	80.6

Source: Census 1930.
[a]Mainly Arabs and British Indians.
[b]Dutch 87%, Japanese 2.4%, German 2.3%, British 1.2%, Armenian 1.0%, "assimilated natives" 3%, and sundry other nationalities.
[c]Javanese 84%, Madurese 13%, Other 3%.

(11.4 percent), and Other Foreign Orientals (1.6 percent). This ethnic composition was not markedly different from that of Surabaya's two sister cities. Surabaya had proportionately more Europeans and fewer Chinese. However, these differences were too small to affect the class structure.

Indonesians constituted three-quarters to four-fifths of the population in all three cities but held no political power. Even in Surabaya's municipal council, where Indonesians were allowed to vote, the income qualification was set so high that very few were eligible. In Surabaya 43 percent of European males were eligible to vote but only 9 percent of Foreign Orientals (mainly Chinese and Arab) and just 2 percent of Native males (table 3.5). The Dutch community thereby constituted over half the voting roll, though barely 8 percent of the total population. This gerrymander, albeit at the humble level of local government, showed up very clearly the dilemma faced by the Dutch in even modest attempts to legitimize colonial rule by democratic institutions.

The minority European, Chinese, and Arab populations were highly concentrated within Surabaya municipality and its immediate hinterland of Surabaya residency. Although Indonesians dominated the population of Surabaya, these urban inhabitants were only 2 percent of the Indonesian population of East Java. Conversely, 25 percent of East Java's population of Chinese and Other

TABLE 3.5
Eligible municipal voters by ethnic group, Surabaya, 1930

	Dutch	Other Foreign	Other Native	Town
Number	5,693	2,518	2,501	10,712
% of voters	53	23.5	23.5	100
% of male pop.	43	9	2	6

Sources: SGS 1930 (21); Census 1930.

Foreign Orientals and 41 percent of the European population were to be found in the municipality (table 3.6). The city, together with its immediate hinterland, accounted for one-third of the Chinese population and half the European population. Apart from Malang (7,463), Madiun (1,681) and Kediri (1,028), no other town in East Java contained more than one thousand Europeans (Census 1930, vol. 6). The political and economic power of the Dutch was thus not only urban based but also concentrated in the port cities and their immediate hinterlands. In East Java, Surabaya was the cornerstone of Dutch power.

Later censuses have not distinguished ethnic groups but some trends can be identified. First, with the expulsion of Dutch nationals in 1958 the European community of Surabaya all but disappeared. Compared with the twenty-six thousand Europeans counted in 1930, in 1991 just 149 Dutch were registered, along with 94 Japanese and presumably a handful of other Europeans submerged among the 143 persons in the category "other" (KMS, SDA 1991, 84). It is therefore hardly surprising that the city's European veneer quickly disintegrated. The built environment retained the faded signs of its European origins but European society had been banished from all but the privacy of a few expatriate homes.

The trend in the size of the Chinese community is more difficult to determine because ethnic Chinese are now enumerated only if they have retained Chinese nationality. Since 1965 most ethnic Chinese have taken Indonesian names and nationality and are therefore no longer distinguished in official figures. Those who stubbornly endure the additional discrimination and harassment involved in alien registration are an older and diminishing group. In 1985 the Chinese community numbered 38,400, virtually the same as the entire Chinese population in 1930 (KMS, SDA 1985, 41); by 1996 the entire foreign population was only 27,000 (KS 1997, 41). Figures on religious affiliation may, however, give some insight (table 3.7). Since few Chinese have converted to Islam but a significant number of Javanese have become Christian, it may be presumed that the 84 percent of people who adhere to Islam are almost entirely Javanese and Madurese while the 12 percent who adhere to Christianity (Catholic and Protestant sects) plus the 1.5 percent who are Buddhists constitute the notional upper limit for ethnic Chinese. Allowing for Christian groups from East Nusa Tenggara, Ambon, and North Sulawesi and some Javanese converts, it is

TABLE 3.6
Ethnic composition of East Java, 1930

Location	European	Chinese	Other Asians	Indonesians	Total
1.Surabaya (city)	25,900	38,900	5,600	271,300	341,700
2.Surabaya (res.)	30,700	55,800	8,400	2,081,500	2,176,400
3.East Java	63,300	158,500	22,200	14,812,000	15,055,700
1:3 (%)	41	25	25	2	2
2:3 (%)	49	35	38	14	14

Source: Census 1930.

TABLE 3.7
Religion in Surabaya (urban), 1998

Religion	%
Islam	84
Christianity	12
Hinduism	2.5
Buddhism	1.5
Total	100

Source: KMS, SDA 1998 (195).

therefore unlikely that ethnic Chinese constituted more than the 11 percent of the population in 1930.

From the social viewpoint, of course, what matters is not official classification or skin color but cultural identity. Despite adoption of Indonesian citizenship, an Indonesian name, and an official religion, Indonesian-Chinese have still not been accepted as equal citizens by the majority Indonesian community. As witnessed on Java between 1996 and 1998, anti-Chinese riots still occur. While educated Chinese were gradually merging into a fairly amorphous middle class, the obvious wealth of many Chinese, their distinctive features, and non-Islamic culture and religion remain a barrier to integration and make them vulnerable as a political scapegoat.

A good insight into the continuing ethnic fragmentation of Surabaya is the use of language. The 1980 census and 1995 Supas included a question on the language of daily household use (table 3.8). In Jakarta by 1995 nearly 97 percent of the population claimed that the national language, Bahasa Indonesia, was their vernacular language and almost 100 percent claimed to be able to speak it. In Surabaya, by contrast, only 17 percent of people claimed to use Indonesian as their daily language, although most were still able to speak the national language. The proportion admitting to being unable to speak it fell from 20 percent in 1980 to just 3 percent in 1995, mainly because of the death of older people who had never been so schooled. Yet the proportion speaking Indonesian at home

TABLE 3.8
Language of daily use, Surabaya and Jakarta, 1980, 1995 (%)

	Surabaya		Jakarta	
	1980	1995	1980	1995
Bahasa Indonesia	20	17	92	96.5
Other	80	83	8	3.5
speak Bahasa	60	80	—	—
no Bahasa	20	3	—	—
Total	100	100	100	100

Source: Census 1980; BPS, Supas 1995a,c.

did not increase over the decade. In fact there had been almost no change since a 1970 survey that found that in Surabaya 84 percent of Indonesians usually spoke regional dialects at home (Weldon 1974, 45). That most people in Surabaya continued to use regional languages at home despite the increasing ability to speak Indonesian shows that in this respect local culture still overrides national education.

In Surabaya, ethnic identities remain strong. Except in the north of the city, where Madurese people constitute the majority of the population, Javanese is the language of daily use, both at home and in public. Indonesian has replaced Dutch as the language of government but even there Javanese is pervasive, for civil servants in Surabaya are almost entirely Javanese. In secondary schools Indonesian is the language of instruction but Javanese is the language of the playground. Though still used in private conversation, Chinese languages have all but ceased to be used in public and it may be presumed that a majority of the population for whom Indonesian is the language of daily use are in fact ethnic Chinese. Many Chinese, however, are also fluent in Javanese.

This view of Surabaya as an essentially Javanese city is supported by evidence on place of birth. The 1985 intercensal survey (Supas) confirmed that, as in 1930, the great majority of people were born within the province of East Java (table 3.9). In 1930 almost half the *Indonesian* population had been born within the municipality of Surabaya and no less than 92 percent within the province of East Java. According to the 1985 survey, 91 percent of the *total* population (now including assimilated Chinese) were born within the province of East Java and 59 percent within the city of Surabaya itself.

Confirmation of the narrowness of Surabaya's migration hinterland is provided by data on the district of birth of migrants to the city. In 1985 almost four-fifths of migrants came from the city and the surrounding province of East Java (table 3.10). Of these local migrants, about 15 percent came from the island of Madura and therefore did not speak Javanese. The same proportion came from

TABLE 3.9
Place of birth, Surabaya, 1930 and 1985 (%)

Region of Origin	1930[a]	1985	All Migrants
Surabaya (municip.)	*47.7*	*59.4*	—
Madura		6.2	14.6
Gresik & West[b]		6.1	15.1
Lower Brantas[c]		9.4	23.2
Malang & Oosthoek[d]		4.6	11.8
South Coast[e]		3.2	7.9
Madiun[f]		2.1	5.3
East Java	*92.4*	*91.0*	*77.9*
Central Java		3.8	9.4
West Java/Jakarta		1.4	3.4
Java	*97.5*	*96.2*	*90.7*
East Indonesia		2.6	6.4
Sumatra		0.9	2.3
Indonesia	*99.0*	*99.7*	*99.4*
Overseas	1.0	0.3	0.6
Total	100	100	100

Source: Census 1930; BPS, Supas 1985 (data tapes).
[a]Indonesian population only.
[b]Gresik, Lamongan, Bojonegoro, Tuban.
[c]Sidoarjo, Mojokerto, Jombang, Kediri, Nganjuk.
[d]Malang, Pasuruan, Probolinggo, Bondowoso, Panarukan, Situbondo, Banyuwangi, Jember, Lumajang.
[e]Blitar, Tulungagung, Trenggalek, Ponorogo, Pacitan.
[f]Madiun, Magetan, Ngawi.

TABLE 3.10
Distance of migration, Surabaya and Jakarta, 1985 (%)

Place of Birth	Surabaya	Jakarta
City	59.4	60.0
Adjacent province	91.0	72.9
All Java/Madura	96.2	90.5
Indonesia	99.7	99.8
Overseas	0.3	0.2
Total	100	100

Source: Calculated from BPS, Supas 1985 (data tapes).

the dry lands of Gresik, Lamongan, Tuban, and Bojonegoro to the west of Surabaya, while another quarter of migrants had been born in the fertile Lower Brantas Valley (including Kediri and Nganjuk). These are all traditional sources of labor migration to Surabaya. The balance of migrants from East Java came from the rest of the province. The wide spread of these sources of migration confirms that Surabaya is still the only major focus of rural-urban migration in the province. By contrast, in the case of Jakarta a similar proportion (60 percent) of the population were born within the city but only a third of migrants to Jakarta came from the adjacent and ethnically Sundanese province of West Java; the other two-thirds of migrants hailed from Central or East Java (17.5 percent), from Sumatra (6.7 percent), and from Kalimantan or eastern Indonesia (2.7 percent).

Notwithstanding its extensive trading links with the eastern archipelago (chap. 7), Surabaya therefore is—and has long been—a provincial rather than a national city. As the capital, Jakarta is unambiguously an Indonesian city, as yet perhaps the only one. It is actually closer to Sumatra than to the Javanese-speaking part of Java that lies east of Cirebon. Since Independence, Javanese have been the main ethnic group to flock to Jakarta but the city has become a melting pot in which the national language is spoken, not Javanese. Surabaya remains predominantly a Javanese-speaking city, notwithstanding a substantial admixture of Madurese and ethnic Chinese. Indeed, Surabaya is now a much more provincial city than it used to be in the colonial period. The repatriation of the Dutch, the partial assimilation of the Chinese, and the near total assimilation of the Arab and other Asian communities has removed most of the cosmopolitan veneer for which Surabaya once used to be known.

Occupations

The occupational distribution of a city's workforce reveals how its population is structured by needs of production. In the countryside, where production is dominated by agriculture, a large proportion of the population are classified as farmers, regardless of the many other jobs to which they may turn their hands. In the city, the occupational structure is much more complex. First, the primary sector, even including vegetable growing, poultry raising, and fishing, is very small. Second, except for the important field of housework, the nonmarket economy is also unimportant. The distinguishing feature of any city is occupational specialization in industry and services. Employment data are available to the five-digit level from censuses and expenditure surveys but for ease of interpretation have been regrouped to identify the main field of work and, where possible, to show up changing trends.

The proportion of the population engaged in the workforce seems at first glance to have remained fairly stable between 1930 and 1990. According to the 1930 census, about 42 percent of the total Indonesian population was then actively employed (table 3.11).[4] Sixty years later the aggregate participation rate was only slightly lower, at 40 percent. These figures nevertheless disguise important trends in participation rates by gender. On the one hand, the proportion of actively working males fell from 62 to 52 percent, probably mainly because of the rising rate of school enrollment. In 1980 about a quarter of the male working-age population had been at school (Census 1980). On the other hand and despite a rising trend in female school attendance, the proportion of working-age women in the workforce increased from 23 percent in 1930 to 29 percent in 1990 (table 3.11). Even so there was still a marked imbalance between the sexes. Of the population of working age (ten years or older), almost two-thirds of males but only a little over one-third of females were in the workforce. In 1980 some 43 percent of working-age women had been engaged in household duties but only 1 percent of men. Observation suggests, however, that women classified as housewives typically have some supplementary source of income. Common sources of such earnings are cooking snacks, running neighborhood stalls (warung), keeping boarders, money lending, and trade.

The earliest comprehensive breakdown of occupation is the 1930 census. The largest identified categories were manufacturing (20 percent), (household) servants (20 percent), and trade (15 percent) (table 3.12). The largest single group (22 percent), however, is "other/unknown." This seems to include unskilled Indonesian day laborers (known pejoratively as coolies) as well as various private services. Unfortunately there is no way of differentiating these laborers by industry, such as manufacturing (including the dockyards), construction, and transport (including the port).

The 1930 census also shows the marked ethnic differences in employment (table 3.12). As the most highly educated group,

TABLE 3.11
Workforce participation by gender, Surabaya 1930, 1980, 1990 (%)[a]

	1930[b]	1980	1990	>10 years
Male	62	59	52	65.7
Female	23	27	29	36.3
Total	42	42	40	50.5

Source: Censuses 1930, 1980, 1990.
[a]Excluding unemployed (not counted in 1930).
[b]Indonesian population only.

TABLE 3.12
Occupation by main ethnic group, Surabaya, 1930 (%)

	European	Chinese	Indonesian	Number	Total %
Primary production	7	1	2	2,966	2
Manufacturing	9	30	20	27,486	20
Trade	26	57	9	20,901	15
Transport & comm.	15	3	10	12,582	9
Professional	14	3	—	1,670	1
Govt. & armed forces	23	1	10	12,860	9
Servants	—	1	24	27,317	20
Other/unknown	6	4	25	30,627	23
Total	100	100	100	136,409	100

Source: Census 1930.

Europeans were disproportionately represented in the professions, public service, and the armed forces. Their main occupation, however, was trade (26 percent). This reflected not only Surabaya's importance as an international port but also the dominance of its foreign trade by Dutch import-export houses. The Chinese community showed a remarkable concentration in just two occupations, trade (57 percent) and manufacturing (30 percent). In the Indonesian community, employment was fairly widely dispersed. Apart from the large category of "other" (25 percent), the main occupations were household servants (24 percent) and manufacturing (20 percent). Another 10 percent were recorded as employed in government or the armed forces. The category of household servants is worthy of particular note, not only because it was the largest specified occupation but also because it was disproportionately female. Many of these people would have worked for European families, the women as cooks, maids, and children's nurses (*amah*), the men as gardeners and drivers.

Comparison with the next detailed census, that of 1971, suggests a degree of structural change (table 3.13). Admittedly the data are not readily comparable and any comparisons must be treated with caution. First, there is the aforementioned problem of large residual categories: the 1971 census also contained a large residual category, which by comparison with the subsequent census is likely to consist mainly of members of the civil service and armed forces. Secondly, the 1971 census included four new and predominantly rural *kecamatan* brought under the municipal boundaries in 1965, thereby accounting for a sudden increase in the share of the primary sector employment. Subject to these caveats, there appears a definite trend toward a more service-oriented economy. The share of trade and what is described loosely as community services (including household servants) both rose, while manufacturing, which in the 1930 census was understated by its share of the coolie category, had markedly fallen away. There was as yet no evidence of a trend toward industrialization (see chap. 5).

TABLE 3.13
Economically active population by sector, Surabaya, 1930–95; Jakarta, 1995 (%)

Sector	1930	1971	1980	1990	1995	Jakarta
Primary	2	7	1.5	2	1	1
Manufacturing	20	12	16	21.5	24	18.5
Service	78	81	83.5	76.5	75	80.5
Construction	—	5	5	6	4	5.5
Trade, hotels, restrnts.	15	23	23	24	34	28
Transport & comm.	9	10	10	8	8	7.5
Finance, bus. services	—	1	1	3	2	7.5
Servants	20					
Community services	—	32	32	34	27	32
Govt., armed forces	9	—	11	—	—	—
Other[a]	25	10	1.5	1.5	—	—
Total	100	100	100	100	100	100

Sources: Censuses; BPS, Supas 1995a,c.
[a]Includes coolies.

These results point to an essential feature of Surabaya's history during the long period of stagnation from about 1930 to the early 1970s. The shift to an occupational structure more dominated by the tertiary sector was certainly structural change but it was not development, if development is defined as a process whereby resources move to more highly productive sectors. On the contrary, this structural change was symptomatic of economic stagnation. Because the modern sector was so small and growing so slowly—by the 1960s it was probably contracting—the flood of migrants to the city had no choice but to seek a livelihood from already overcrowded marginal service activities (the informal sector). McGee (1967) described this process as pseudo-urbanization, though it was urbanization nonetheless.

The classification of occupations based on the standard international code does not help to identify the main components of the informal sector but some insight can be gained from the 1981 Susenas expenditure survey (table 3.14). Factory workers, manual workers (including building and construction workers), and tradesmen, who collectively may be identified as the industrial proletariat, accounted for a quarter of total employment. A third was accounted for by three identifiable informal-sector activities, namely petty trade (20 percent), household servants (11 percent) and *becak* drivers (3 percent). The share of household servants had fallen by about half since the colonial period, probably attributable to the repatriation of the wealthy European elite, but by 1981 the share of petty trade alone was much greater than the entire trade sector in 1930 (tables 3.14, 3.15). The explosive growth of petty trade was corroborated by the changed appearance of the city's streets.

Comparison of the 1971 and 1980 censuses with the 1995 Supas shows that rapid New Order growth generated marked structural change (table 3.13). The most conspicuous feature is the rise in the workforce share of manufacturing (including utilities). This was most immediately at the expense of the primary sector, which

TABLE 3.14
Economically active population by occupation, urban Surabaya and Jakarta, 1980, 1981 (%)

Occupation	Surabaya	Jakarta
Factory & manual	21	23
Transport, materials	10	8
becak	*3*	*1*
Petty trade	20	20
Other sales	6	6
Household servants	11	8
Other services	8	9
Clerical	9	12
Professional[a]	10	11
Armed forces	4	3
Total	99[b]	100

Source: BPS, Susenas 1981 (data tapes).
[a]Includes managers, supervisors, proprietors, teachers, health professionals, others.
[b]Rounding error (and in subsequent tables).

TABLE 3.15

Adult literacy by ethnic group and gender, Surabaya, 1930, 1990 (%)

	European[a]			Chinese[a]			Indonesian[a]			1990[b]		
	M	F	Tot.	M	F	Tot.	M	F	Tot.	M	F	Tot.
Dutch	50.5	62	56	8	6	7	6	1	3	—	—	—
Literate	98.5	95	97	54	23	44	25	3	14	96	87	92
Illiterate	1.5	5	3	46	77	56	75	97	86	4	13	8
Total	100	100	100	100	100	100	100	100	100	100	100	100

Sources: Censuses 1930, 1990.

[a] Adults more than twenty years old.

[b] Adults more than ten years old.

declined from almost 7 to just 1 percent, a process visible in the conversion of fields to housing, factories, and offices. Growth of the manufacturing workforce, mainly by migration of workers from elsewhere in East Java, was also at the expense of some slower-growing parts of the service sector. Interpretation is nevertheless clouded by large inconsistencies between the 1990 census and the 1995 Supas in trade and community services. The size of the large service-sector component of government and armed forces—almost 11 percent in the 1980 census but not specified thereafter—is also obscure.

Surabaya's occupational structure now looks more industrialized than that of Jakarta, though around 1980 their primary, manufacturing, and service sectors were of remarkably similar relative size. Notwithstanding the much greater amount of manufacturing employment in Jakarta, by 1990 Surabaya's industrial workforce was already proportionately larger (table 3.13). Including the adjacent kabupaten of Sidoarjo and Gresik, the 1995 figure for Greater Surabaya would rise to 30 percent, compared with 23 percent for Greater Jakarta (Jabotabek) (BPS, Supas 1995b,c). There are also some notable differences between Surabaya and Jakarta in composition of the service sector. Reflecting its provincial status, Surabaya's finance and business services sector is much smaller, as also that of community, social, and personal services (which includes government).

Education

In the colonial period, few Indonesians had yet received any form of modern education. The 1930 census figures reveal just how discriminatory was the provision of education. Among the European adult population, literacy was 97 percent, which is to say all but universal. In the Chinese population, however, literacy was only 44 percent and among the Indonesian population it was a mere 14 percent (table 3.15). These were figures for a leading metropolitan area! Moreover, they disguise another glaring form of discrimination. In any disadvantaged social group, women tend to bear the brunt of discrimination. So it was in colonial Surabaya. European women had a general literacy rate equivalent to males but Chinese women (23 percent) had less than half the literacy rate of males (54 percent). Indonesian women were almost universally illiterate: among males the literacy rate of 25 percent was bad enough but among women it was just 3 percent. Ethnic discrimination was even more extreme in terms of literacy in Dutch, the language of government and the corporate world. Because many Eurasians were not literate in Dutch, for all Europeans the rate of literacy in Dutch was only 56 percent: among Chinese it was 7 percent and among Indonesians 3 percent. The opportunities for white-collar employment in the modern and Dutch-speaking sector of the economy were correspondingly restricted.

After Independence, the abolition of illiteracy was made a national goal. Despite an acute shortage of qualified teachers, primary school enrollments increased at about ten percent per annum during the 1950s (Feith 1962, 221). School buildings were used twice each day, morning and afternoon. The Mass Education Division of the Department of Education introduced adult literacy classes in kampungs and villages throughout the country (Feith 1962, 315; Abeyasekere 1987, 179). By 1973 almost two-thirds of Surabaya's relevant age cohort were attending primary school: several percentage points above the provincial average but by no means the highest rate in the province (Heneveld 1978, 77–79). In 1974, at the start of the Second Five-Year Plan (Repelita II), the government embarked on a crash program to expand primary education, with the national goal of 85 percent participation by the end of the plan period. By 1990, across the entire urban population of East Java, only one percent of the 10–19 age cohort had never attended school (Census 1990). The achievement was all the more remarkable in view of the sheer size of the population. In Surabaya that meant that 92 percent of the adult population were now functionally literate and the disadvantage of the female population had been largely overcome. Although 13 percent of adult women were illiterate compared with only 4 percent of men, this was very much a problem of older people who had grown up before such education was widely available. In the two generations since Independence, the literacy campaign has therefore eliminated one of the great inequities of colonial rule and, at the same time, created a huge fund of human capital.

Less comprehensively but from an even smaller base, educational opportunities have also expanded at the secondary and tertiary levels. In the 1980s junior and senior high school enrollments increased sharply as a consequence of the rising participation in junior high school. By 1990 almost a quarter of women and a third of men over the age of ten had completed secondary school (table 3.16). At diploma and university level, educational opportunities were still very restricted. By 1990 just 2 percent of the population had completed any form of tertiary education. There was also still a strong gender bias, with almost twice as many men as women having graduated from university. Nevertheless, even if the number

TABLE 3.16
Educational attainment, Surabaya, 1990

	Male		Female		Total	
Level	%	Cumul.	%	Cumul.	%	Cumul.
Never attended	8	8	23	23	15.6	16
Primary (not completed)	26	34	28	51	27.2	43
Primary (completed)	27	61	24.5	75	25.7	69
Junior high[a]	18.5	80	13.2	89	15.7	84
Senior high[a]	17.5	97	10.4	99	13.8	98
Academy	1.6	98.6	0.6	99.5	1.1	99
University	1.3	99.9	0.5	100	0.9	100

Source: Census 1990.
[a]Includes vocational training.

of tertiary graduates was relatively small, it is worth noting that they were equivalent to two-thirds of Surabaya's population in 1905!

Distribution

One of society's fundamental injustices is that some families have much more income, spending power and wealth than others. In a developing country like Indonesia, without the safety net of the welfare state, these inequalities are very marked. They have little to do with how hard people work. The view that people are poor because they are lazy is untenable. Inequalities are systematic and correlate with education levels, employment rates, and occupation. These variables in turn can be traced back to production, as reflected in industrial structure and the level of economic activity. The resultant distribution of income, expenditure, and wealth translates into what may be referred to as a mode of consumption or, more loosely, the lifestyles that give society its distinctive character. Those who are well-off have a measure of control over their lives, which they can indulge and embellish according to fashion and personal whim. Collectively such families leave their mark on the city. Occupying the most space for home and grounds, vehicles, work, and entertainment, while at the same time being influential in government, they have the means and the power to determine the pattern of urban land use. The poor, by contrast, are fully exposed to the instabilities of the market and the political process. Not only do they have to put up with poor living conditions but they occupy very insecure niches in both the urban economy and the physical city. Jellinek (1991) shows that the fundamental problem for kampung dwellers in inner city Jakarta is not lack of income—which at times has been higher in informal- than in formal-sector occupations—but the chronic instability of income and consequent insecurity and vulnerability. This section first analyzes data on expenditure distribution and then explores the physical manifestations of living conditions and trends since the colonial period.

Expenditure data from the periodic national surveys of household expenditure (Susenas) are much more reliable and informative than income data. The 1981 Susenas sample of 502 households for urban Surabaya was large enough to give a good insight into the distribution of spending power in the city. If households are ranked by expenditure per capita into a top 20 percent, a middle 40 percent, and a bottom 40 percent, the distribution of expenditure shows up as unequal but not markedly skewed (table 3.17). The top quintile spent double its pro rata share of expenditure while the bottom two quintiles spent only half. By the mid-1990s the top quintile had raised its share several percentage points at the expense of the two lowest. This does not mean that the poor became poorer but that the expenditure of the well-off increased faster than that of the rest of society.

Contrary to what might have been expected, Surabaya's distribution of expenditure looked very similar to that of Jakarta (table 3.17). The obvious size and wealth of the Jakarta elite would suggest Jakarta's distribution to be much more skewed. Yet in 1981 this expected bias did not show up in the data. By the mid-1990s the top quintile of households actually held a slightly higher share and the bottom two quintiles a slightly lower share of expenditure than in Jakarta. Nevertheless, the overall pattern remained very similar.

TABLE 3.17
Distribution of expenditure, urban Surabaya and Jakarta, 1981, 1995–97 (%)

	Surabaya		Jakarta	
Expenditure Group	1981	1995–97[a]	1981	1995–97[a]
Top 20%	40.9	45.3	42.4	44.3
Mid 40%	38.6	36.0	35.2	36.2
Bottom 40%	20.5	18.7	22.4	19.5
Total	100	100	100	100

Source: BPS, Susenas 1981, 1995, 1996, 1997 (data tapes).
[a]Average.

In the absence of municipal income or expenditure data for the colonial period, trends in living standards must be deduced from physical conditions. Basic information on housing is available from the 1930 census. At that time, the average number of family members per house varied little (4.3 for European families, 5.7 for Indonesian; table 3.18). No data were collected on house size but the construction material gives some insight into quality. Of the total housing stock, 30 percent were brick, 63 percent wood or woven bamboo (*gedek*), and 7 percent unknown materials (but probably mostly wood and bamboo). These different housing types were not distributed evenly across the population. No less than 91 percent of Europeans lived in brick houses and 63 percent of Chinese, but only 16 percent of Indonesians. Admittedly, brick houses were not necessarily superior: a house with woven bamboo walls could be cool and comfortable. The reality was, however, that bamboo houses were usually much smaller, often had dirt floors, and were located in crowded kampungs with appalling sanitary conditions (chap. 4). Such figures reflect the stark visual contrast between the garden suburbs of the Europeans and the kampung housing of the mass of Indonesians.

After 1930, the availability and quality of housing must have deteriorated. The depression of the 1930s caused suspension of public

TABLE 3.18
Housing types by ethnic group, Surabaya, 1930

Group	Persons/ House	Brick (%)	Non-brick/ Tile Roof (%)	Other (%)	Unknown (%)	Total
European	4.3	91	4	—	5	100
Chinese	5.2	63	30	1	6	100
Other	5.2	77	16	1	6	100
Indonesian	5.7	16	64	13	7	100
Total	5.5	30	53	7	10	100

Source: Census 1930.

investment in housing and urban infrastructure. Subsequently, the rapid growth of population during the Japanese occupation, the destruction of many kampungs in the Battle of Surabaya, and the renewed flood of immigrants after 1946 all worked to depress the size and quality of the housing stock (see also chap. 2). Most new housing was of a temporary and inferior kind. By the 1950s squatter housing was no longer hidden away off the main streets but was highly visible in formerly open spaces, such as in parks and along riverbanks and railway lines (chap. 6). Much of this new housing had no public infrastructure.

Since the early 1970s, rising real incomes have financed not only a large increment in the housing stock but also much upgrading of existing houses. Within kampungs, the rebuilding of houses with brick walls has proceeded apace. Wood and bamboo were now regarded as inferior materials. Whereas in 1930 only 30 percent of houses were of brick, by 1995 this figure had risen to 82 percent (table 3.19). Although most houses were still one story, the number of multiple-story dwellings had risen from 6 to 11 percent between 1980 and 1995. Even in kampungs, it was becoming common for kampung dwellers to obtain more room by adding a second story.

Census data also give some insight into the ownership of housing. While houses may be small and of simple construction, they are often the major stake that people have in the material world, a

TABLE 3.19
Housing types, Surabaya 1930, 1980, 1995 (%)

	Brick	Non-brick/Tile Roof	Unknown	Other	Total
1930	30	53	7	10	100
1980	57	21[a]	21[b]	1	100[c,d]
1995	82	11[a]	3[b]	4	100[c,e]

Sources: Censuses 1930, 1980; BPS, Supas 1995c.
[a]Wood.
[b]Bamboo.
[c]Urban Surabaya, ordinary households only.
[d]One-story 94%, multistory 6%.
[e]One-story 89%, multistory 11%.

fact that helps to explain the often bitter resistance of kampung dwellers to forced relocation (see also Jellinek 1991). In the 1970s exactly half of all households owned their own dwellings, a proportion that increased marginally between 1971 and 1995 (table 3.20). Rental households tend to be occupied either by civil servants or company employees, whose housing is often provided at a subsidized rent as part of the conditions of employment, or by the very poor, who cannot afford to build or buy their own home and thereby find themselves caught in a poverty trap. Data for this category do not include the large number of students and single people who come to work in Surabaya without their families and rent a room or just a space to sleep. In the census, they are counted, like servants, as part of the extended household.

One of the best indicators of socioeconomic status is the size of house that a family occupies. As income rises, families give high priority to more space. Poorer families are unhappy to put up with kampung houses that are much smaller and more closely crowded than in the village, which is seen as perhaps the greatest disadvantage of urban living. The rich also have an insatiable demand for space. Bungalow homes that in colonial times were regarded as the height of European luxury, the envy of those who visited from Holland, are nowadays surpassed by lavish two-story mansions. In 1981, the distribution of floor area corresponded very closely to that of household expenditure per capita (table 3.21). By the mid-1990s floor area was more equitably distributed than expenditure in both Surabaya and Jakarta but—surprisingly—less so in Surabaya despite cheaper land.

Floor and land area have remained extremely small for most households (table 3.22). In 1995 over half of all households occupied a living area of less than 50 square meters (7m x 7m). In fact, 29 percent of households occupied less than 20 square meters (4.5m x 4.5m), which by Western standards is but one room (BPS, Supas 1995c). The inclusion of yard area makes little difference to the relativities because few poor households have any surrounding land except for public space.

TABLE 3.20
Home ownership, Surabaya, 1971, 1995 (%)

	1971	1995
Owner-occupied	50.5	56
Private rental	38	37
Official rental	5	0.5
Other	6.5	6.5
Total	100	100

Sources: Census 1971; BPS, Supas 1995c.

TABLE 3.21
House size by expenditure group, urban Surabaya and Jakarta, 1981, 1995–97 (%)

	Surabaya				Jakarta			
	H/H Exp.[a]		Floor Area (m^2)		H/H Exp.		Floor Area (m^2)	
Expenditure Group	1981	1995–97	1981	1995–97	1981	1995–97	1981	1995–97
Top 20%	40.9	45.3	38.8	35.4	42.4	44.3	32.2	30.23
Mid 40%	38.6	36.0	40.9	38.7	35.2	36.2	39.9	39.2
Bottom 40%	20.5	18.7	20.3	25.9	22.4	19.5	27.9	30.53
Total	100	100	100	100	100	100	100	99.9

Source: BPS, Susenas 1981, 1995, 1996, 1997 (data tapes).
[a]Household expenditure per capita.

TABLE 3.22
House and lot size, Surabaya, 1995 (m^2)

Area	<50	<100	<150	<200	Other
Floor	56	83	92	99	1
Land	47	73	85	97	3

Source: BPS, Supas 1995c.

In terms of comfort and health, access to basic amenities is as important as the type and size of house. Since the 1971 census, a good deal of information has become available on urban amenities. A comprehensive 1981 survey of household facilities revealed that in Surabaya 86 percent of households had their own kitchen—almost a definition of a household—64 percent their own laundry area, 62 percent their own bathing place (*mandi*), and 54 percent their own toilet (about the same proportion as in Jakarta) (table 3.23). Access to these amenities was highly correlated with household expenditure. By 1981 more than four-fifths of the top 20 percent of households had private access to all facilities. Among the bottom 40 percent, 82 percent had access to their own kitchen but only 51 percent to their own laundry, 46 percent to their own bathing place, and just 35 percent to their own toilet.

Census data confirm a marked improvement in living conditions under the New Order. Poor urban households were most disadvantaged in access to private toilets and in 1971 only 35 percent of households had access to their own private toilet: 42 percent shared or used public toilets and 23 percent had to make do with other facilities, mainly nearby rivers and canals (table 3.24). By 1995 the proportion with their own toilets had risen to 58 percent, and another 31 percent shared private facilities. Few households still had to use rivers and canals, whose banks had been cleared of squatters (chap. 6). Kampung improvement programs had also

TABLE 3.23
Access to own household amenities by expenditure group, urban Surabaya, 1981 (%)

	Toilet	Bath	Laundry	Kitchen
Top 20%	82	84	82	89
Mid 40%	58	67	68	90
Bottom 40%	35	46	57	82
Average	54	62	64	86

Source: BPS, Susenas 1981 (data tapes).
Note: Expenditure group based on per capita household expenditure.

improved public facilities (chap. 4). Whatever the balance of consideration between privacy, convenience, and sanitation, this trend toward own toilets is a clear welfare gain. A similar pattern applies to household bathing places.

Another indicator of improvement in basic needs is the provision of water. In 1971, 67 percent of households (table 3.25) still fetched their drinking water from wells and bores, which were usually polluted by sewage. By 1995, just one percent of households lacked access to the piped and chemically treated water supply, although this water still requires boiling (chap. 4). For nondrinking use, such as washing and bathing, for which water quality is less important, access to the reticulated supply rose only modestly, from 28 percent in 1971 to 45 percent in 1995, mainly by substitution for well or bore water. This would seem to be a matter of choice: households do not have to pay for water raised from their own wells or bores. Inhabitants of Surabaya were certainly much better off than those in Jakarta, where despite severe contamination, in 1995 almost half of all households still relied on bores or wells for drinking water and 74 percent for other uses (BPS, Supas 1995c).

Census data provide two other physical indicators of rising living standards, namely type of fuel for household lighting and cooking. In 1971, when power supplies were still erratic and few kampungs were connected to the grid, only about a third of all households used electric lighting and two-thirds, kerosene lamps (table 3.26). By 1990 the use of electricity for lighting had become almost universal, with just 1 percent of households still relying on kerosene or gas lamps. This involved a great increase in comfort because kerosene lamps not only made the small rooms of kampung houses too hot but also added to their stuffiness with unpleasant fumes.

For cooking, wood and charcoal used to be the main fuel, in urban kampungs as in rural villages. As deforestation forced up the real price of wood fuels, introduction of cheap kerosene stoves switched demand to kerosene. By 1971 some 86 percent of households used kerosene and only 12 percent, wood or charcoal. Nine

TABLE 3.24
Access to toilet facilities, urban Surabaya, 1971, 1995 (%)

Year	Own	Shared	Public	Other	Total
1971	35	26	16	23	100
1995	58	31	7	4	100

Sources: Census 1971; BPS, Supas 1995c.

TABLE 3.25
Source of water, urban Surabaya, 1971, 1995 (%)

	Drinking Water		Washing Water	
Source	1971	1995	1971	1995
Piped	77	99	28	45
Well/bore	22	1	69	55
Other[a]	1	—	3	—
Total	100	100	100	100

Sources: Census 1971; BPS, Supas 1995c.

[a]Includes river, spring, rainwater, or other.

TABLE 3.26
Source of lighting, urban Surabaya, 1971, 1995 (%)

Year	Electricity	Kero. Lamp	Other	Total
1971	37	63	—	100
1995	99	1	—	100

Sources: Census 1971; BPS, Supas 1995c.

years later kerosene usage had increased to 94 percent while that of now very expensive wood fuels was insignificant (table 3.27). Since then rising prosperity has caused gas and electric stoves to become popular among the better off. In 1971 only 1.4 percent of households used such expensive consumer durables but by 1995 the proportion had increased to 13 percent compared with 24 percent in Jakarta (BPS, Supas 1995c).

Data on ownership of selected consumer durables are available from 1980 but unfortunately cannot be correlated with household expenditure. By 1995, two-thirds of all households owned a television set and almost four-fifths a radio–cassette player (table 3.28). Households that did not own a television set could usually gain access through neighbors or community facilities. By the late 1980s any evening stroll through the kampungs confirmed that television ownership had become common and that watching the flickering

TABLE 3.27
Cooking fuel, urban Surabaya, 1971, 1980, 1995 (%)

	Kerosene	Wood, Coal, Charcoal	Electricity	Gas	Other	Total
1971	85.8	12.1	1.1	0.3	0.7	100
1980	94.0	1.1	1.4	2.6	0.9	100
1995	82.8	1.0	2.6	10.6	3.0	100

Sources: Censuses; BPS, Supas 1995c.

TABLE 3.28
Ownership of consumer durables, Surabaya and Jakarta, 1980, 1995 (% of households)

	Surabaya		Jakarta	
Item	1980	1995	1980	1995
Radio-cassette	58	81	81	91
Television	44	68	67	83
Motorcycle	43	41	37	28
Automobile	—	10	20	16

Sources: Censuses; BPS, Supas 1995a,c.

screen was probably the main leisure activity. Meanwhile, well-off households were buying videocassette recorders and supporting the new retailing activity of video rental.

As might be expected, the penetration of consumer durables in Surabaya lagged about five years behind Jakarta (table 3.28). The most striking difference was in vehicle ownership. By 1995 only 10 percent of households owned a car in Surabaya, compared with 27.5 percent in Jakarta. Conversely, Surabaya had a higher rate of motorcycle and bicycle ownership. In both cities, the more widespread ownership of consumer durables by households of only modest means was consistent with the evidence of improvements in kampung infrastructure and housing. While the middle class obviously fared best out of New Order economic growth, the population at large also clearly benefited in material terms. To what extent better material welfare translated into an improved quality of life is a larger question.

Beyond a Colonial Society

Surabaya in the late 1990s was not a scaled-up version of Surabaya in 1900. Economic boom, depression, war, revolution and decolonization, political turmoil and prolonged economic stagnation, followed by the boom of the New Order and the recent bust, together upset any established order or "natural" path of development. Over the course of the twentieth century, change has been much more apparent than continuity.

The most obvious change is that in the latter half of the twentieth century Surabaya has outgrown the social structure of a colonial society. Under Dutch rule, the city had been dominated by Europeans, who held power, income, and wealth out of all proportion to their small number. They alone enjoyed unrestricted access to secondary education, to high-paying jobs in the formal sector, and to all the security and comforts of a suburban lifestyle, with servants to do most of the work. In mode of consumption, they were unambiguously middle class, spending heavily on prestige items such as motor cars and lesser consumer durables while restricting the enjoyment of them to members of the immediate nuclear family. They also controlled all the levers of power and made most of the decisions that mattered in government, business, and the professions. They were the unchallenged elite of Surabaya, even if they did co-opt a few better-educated and wealthy members of the Chinese community and the Indonesian aristocracy. The locus of Indonesian society, by contrast, was the other, invisible city of the kampungs. Tucked away behind the main streets and on the urban fringe, the kampungs were overcrowded, unsanitary, and without even token political power but they were nonetheless vibrant communities, the root of the identity of the arek Suroboyo (Frederick 1989). As seen in chapter 2, this dual social structure was overturned by the Japanese occupation, shakily restored in 1946, and then gradually eroded after Independence.

What kind of society emerged from this social revolution? The 1981 survey of household expenditure showed a clear nexus between expenditure and education. Only 12 percent of heads of households in the bottom two quintiles had completed more than primary schooling, compared with 39 percent in the top quintile (table 3.29). In this top quintile the proportion of household heads with tertiary training was only 6 percent but these householders nevertheless made up 70 percent of those with any form of tertiary education. By the mid-1990s there had been a dramatic overall rise in educational standards but the top quintile continued to dominate tertiary education.

Surabaya lagged behind Jakarta in level of education. In the mid-1990s Surabaya had a higher proportion of both rich and poor household heads who were unschooled or had completed only primary education (table 3.29). Conversely, in Jakarta both rich and poor households enjoyed much better access to tertiary education. This situation is readily explained by the greater educational and white-collar employment opportunities in Jakarta and migration to the capital of those holding tertiary qualifications.

TABLE 3.29
Educational attainment by expenditure group, Surabaya and Jakarta, 1981, 1995–97 (%)

	Surabaya				Jakarta			
	1981		1995–97 average		1981		1995–97 average	
Education	Top 20%	Bottom 40%	Top 20%	Bottom 40%	Top 20%	Bottom 40%	Top 20%	Bottom 40%
Attending	22.0	19.1	30.4	29.2	21.7	20.8	27.6	34.2
No schooling	14.3	34.5	5.0	13.4	13.9	35.4	3.1	7.2
Primary	24.6	34.6	14.1	22.9	22.2	33.7	12.4	20.7
Lower Second.	15.9	7.4	10.7	14.7	11.2	6.2	11.1	14.0
Upper Second.	17.3	4.3	25.4	18.7	23.4	3.6	26.3	21.5
Tertiary	5.9	0.1	14.2	1.2	7.5	0.2	19.5	2.4
Total	100	100	99.8	100.1	99.9	99.9	100	100

Source: BPS, Susenas 1981 (data tapes).

Note: Expenditure group based on per capita household expenditure.

Educational qualifications were reflected in job status. White-collar employment was the preserve of those with secondary or tertiary education, whereas those with little or no formal education had to be satisfied as manual workers, typically with less job security and lower pay. For Surabaya a precise occupational breakdown by socioeconomic status is impossible because the standard employment categories are so broad. Nevertheless, after exclusion of the large category of household servants (11 percent of the sample), who were counted as belonging to the household in which they are employed, a clear pattern emerged for 1981 (table 3.30). In the poorest two quintiles, half of the workforce was employed as manual workers (mainly in manufacturing and construction) or in transport and materials handling; in the richest quintile, by contrast, these two categories accounted for only 13 percent. If petty trade (stall owners and hawkers) were included, the proportions rose to three-quarters and one-third respectively. Conversely, the

TABLE 3.30
Occupation by expenditure group, Surabaya, 1981 (%)

Occupation	Bottom 40%	Middle 40%	Top 20%	Total
Manual Work[a]	32	24	9.5	24
Transport Work[b]	19	9	3.5	12
Petty Trade	25	22	22	23
Subtotal	*76*	*55*	*35*	*59*
Other Sales	4	5	16.5	7
Clerical	4.5	12.5	13.5	10
Professional[c]	8	18.5	24	16
Other Services	7.5	9	11	9
Subtotal	*24*	*45*	*65*	*42*
Total	100	100	100	101

Source: BPS, Susenas 1981 (data tapes).
Note: Expenditure group based on per capita household expenditure; household servants excluded from workforce.
[a]Process workers, building workers, artisans, farmers.
[b]Includes materials handling.
[c]Managers, supervisors, proprietors, teachers, health workers, professionals, armed forces.

white-collar categories of clerical and professional (including managers, supervisors, and proprietors, the professionals in education, health, and law and the armed forces) accounted for less than 13 percent of the poorest two quintiles but more than 37 percent of the highest.

Such correlations suggest that the repatriation of the Dutch had less of an impact on social structure than might have been expected. Although the ethnic basis of discrimination was broken down, education, occupation, and income have remained the fundamentals of the social structure. This is confirmed by observation. While the formerly Dutch-owned bungalows have been modernized with new façades, extensions, low ceilings, and air-conditioning—and often garish modern furnishings seemingly inappropriate for such a hot climate—the material aspects of the suburban lifestyle seem to have changed remarkably little. Better-off Indonesians can now afford cars, not to mention weekend bungalows in the hills and overseas trips. Their homes are still well staffed by servants. Indeed, the Westernized Indonesian elite of today is probably just as middle class as the Dutch elite of the late-colonial period.

It would be helpful if the size of the middle class could be quantified and its characteristics compared with those of the rest of the population. Unfortunately, this turns out to be extremely difficult. An obvious starting point would be occupation. Those classified loosely in table 3.30 as professionals and who constituted 16 percent of all workers (excluding servants) might be regarded as quintessentially middle class. Yet, according to expenditure, only a third fell in the top quintile of households. Conversely, the category of petty trade, which could be identified as part of the informal sector, constituted 25 percent of workers in the bottom 40 percent but not much less (22 percent) in the top quintile. Some petty traders seemed to enjoy quite high incomes. Neither broad occupational categories nor household expenditure are therefore reliable guides to membership of the middle class.

An alternative approach would be to distinguish the very different modes of consumption of the middle class in their suburban bungalows from the rest of the population living in the kampungs. I have argued (Dick 1985, 1990) that there is a fundamental distinction in mode of consumption between those living in kampungs, who share the means of consumption, and those living in suburban bungalows with exclusive control of their means of consumption. Kampung households, living in close proximity along the narrow pathways (*gang*), rely on their neighbors for security and are careful not to antagonize them by conspicuous consumption. Suburban households, by contrast, living in detached houses facing onto the street, have no social check upon conspicuous consumption and attempt to maintain their privacy and security by high fences, locked doors, and barred windows. Here the physical signs of social alienation are readily apparent. A high correlation may also be observed in the use of motor vehicles, the ultimate status symbol of the middle class. Nowadays, suburban dwellers can typically afford to own a car—or use one as a perquisite of employment—and have a large enough yard to be able to garage it under lock and key. In the kampung, by contrast, motor vehicles are impractical because they cannot negotiate the narrow pathways. Motorcycles are therefore the preferred form of private transport for those who can afford to own more than a bicycle. In the absence of better data, the 10 percent of car-owning households in 1995 is therefore probably the best approximation of the size of Surabaya's middle class (table 3.28).

The difficulties of quantifying social class point to an important conclusion. While those who live in suburban bungalows tend to be better off than those in the kampung, the economic distinction is not at all sharp. On the one hand, many families occupy their bungalows at low rents as a perquisite of employment, especially in the public service, without necessarily enjoying high money incomes. On the other hand, some families living in the kampung are quite well off: they own their own house and can afford to give their children a good education yet continue to enjoy the social security provided by kampung society. There is certainly a clear distinction in lifestyle between those who live in the kampung and take part in kampung life and those who isolate themselves from their neighbors both physically and socially, but this does not necessarily correlate with household expenditure, occupation, and education.

Observation confirms that kampung society is indeed very scrambled in terms of conventional socioeconomic variables. Teachers, for example, are people of high education but modest incomes who often play a prominent role as kampung leaders. Petty traders are typically people of little education who may nevertheless enjoy fairly high incomes by kampung standards, albeit unstable and insecure. Transport drivers may also earn fairly high incomes by working very long hours. Reflecting the diversity of household incomes, kampung houses are also a jumble of sizes. People add to their houses and possessions as they can afford—and sell off when they fall on hard times. This diversity, underpinned by social mores and religion, is the part of the secret of the vitality and resilience of kampung society.

Kampung society is therefore a conscious lifestyle based on a shared set of values, not just a backwater for those who cannot afford a suburban, middle-class lifestyle. In fact in Surabaya, as elsewhere in urban Java, kampungs often exclude the very poor, who have no territorial stake within the kampung and cannot afford to maintain the reciprocity that legitimizes and sustains kampung society (see Jellinek 1991; Sullivan 1994). People such as squatters, scavengers (*gelandangan*), and beggars tend to be fringe dwellers, regarded with as much suspicion by kampung dwellers as they in turn are regarded by suburbanites along the main streets (Guinness 1986).[5] Individual poor families may nevertheless be admitted to the kampung by renting a room and accepting the obligations of kampung life. Better-off kampung dwellers may opt out in favor of a suburban lifestyle if their urge for conspicuous private consumption can no longer be contained and the background criticism of kampung neighbors becomes too annoying. Membership in kampung society is therefore always permeable on the upper and lower margins.

At the end of the New Order boom the shape of Surabaya society was therefore still hard to discern. Economic growth had enhanced social mobility, enabling many to move out of the cramped and socially regulated kampung environment into suburban, middle-class society. The new towns and luxury suburbs attested to that trend. While ethnic Chinese were prominent, there were enough Indonesian businessmen, professionals, and civil servants to suggest that the emerging middle-class society was becoming multiracial. Meanwhile, kampung society was pulled by conflicting forces. On the one hand, rising incomes and pervasive consumerist propaganda diffused by billboards, television, and the print media, were encouraging privatization of the means of consumption and a breakdown in the shared values that had held together the social fabric. At the same time, the moral force of resurgent Islam, emphasizing the nexus between religious beliefs and social responsibility, was reinforcing the kampung community. The lower middle class therefore remained torn between a set of values arising from how they lived and another set arising from where they lived. This dilemma has carried over into the era of Reformasi and party politics.

Chapter 4

GOVERNMENT

The growing involvement of government in the routine aspects of social and economic life has been a persistent trend since the end of the nineteenth century. This has been most apparent in cities, whose rapid growth in area, population, and density meant that public welfare could not be safeguarded by benign neglect and market forces. Potable water, sewage disposal and garbage collection, public transport, and eventually modern town planning, became practical needs that transcended ideology. Yet until establishment of the Municipality in 1906 (chap. 2), Surabaya had no specifically urban government. The city and its rural hinterland were encompassed within the regency of Surabaya and administered very loosely by the Dutch assistant resident and his Javanese counterpart, the regent (bupati).[1] All matters of government were the responsibility of the omnipotent Binnenlands Bestuur (Colonial Civil Service). In reality this bureaucracy was so undermanned and so technically underqualified that it sought to do very little and achieved even less. Its role was essentially one of attempting to maintain law and order (*rust en orde*), raising taxes, and providing the basic public infrastructure of roads, canals, and bridges. In the nineteenth century this minimalist role differed little between rural and urban areas.

Several reasons can be adduced for the trend toward more active government. First, the rapidly growing Dutch population, with a long tradition of responsible municipal government in the Netherlands, was demanding more of government in the Indies, at least in meeting its own needs for comfort and amenities. The burghers of Surabaya, the Rotterdam of the East, were embarrassed by unfavorable comparisons with the Netherlands, Batavia, or neighboring British colonies like Singapore. A vocal Dutch-language press articulated the local point of view. Second, proclamation in 1901 of the Ethical Policy marked not only a new concern for the welfare of the indigenous population but also a commitment to government intervention to bring about necessary improvements. The formation of the municipalities was part of this new approach. Third, growth in the population and area of the city meant that some planning of public services and land use could no longer be postponed. Colonial rule provided a direct channel for the transfer of best practice European policy and technology.

Colonial governments were nevertheless very slow to act. Administrators were under pressure to economize on expenditures and, by the nature of colonial rule, not at all responsive to—or even aware of—the needs of the "native" population. As a general rule, the willingness to intervene was in direct proportion to how much problems impinged upon the small European population. The maintenance of law and order therefore had priority. Outlays were made for public health only when it became apparent through plague, cholera, or typhoid that there was a serious threat to the health of Europeans. Schooling was minimal. The outcome was a highly privileged European community relying on its elected council to serve its needs and protect it against contamination from the local populace. Kampung dwellers perceived that the Municipality had little regard for their own needs and resented its high-handed interventions.

At Independence and in the aftermath of war and revolution, there was an acute crisis of public infrastructure but almost no resources to tackle the many problems. As in other soon-to-be Third

World cities, rapid rural-urban migration meant that problems actually worsened. Not until the New Order did the good fortune of the oil boom provide the resources for steady progress to be made at last in the infrastructure of public health, education, and housing. Yet the outcome was not perceived to be a fairer society. As in the late-colonial period, government seemed to spend in ways that made the city more safe and comfortable for the expanding middle class. Under Sukarno there had been a sense of shared deprivation. Kampung dwellers now felt themselves to be marginalized in a postcolonial version of a dualistic society.

This chapter looks at the evolution of government policy in the fields of public health, kampung improvement, public housing, and education, leaving town planning to be covered in chapter 6. Because of marked discontinuities in policy, it is helpful to distinguish three main periods: colonial, post-Independence, and the New Order. The late-colonial period is dealt with at some length because that is when the foundations were laid for policies that would be followed after Independence. After 1949 the goals were more ambitious but the state ceased to be an effective instrument for achieving them, even in the capital of Jakarta. This period of inflated rhetoric and meager achievement is dealt with fairly briefly. The systematic development and implementation of policy under the New Order is examined more carefully to draw out continuities and discontinuities with the colonial period.

Colonial Government

LAW AND ORDER

Nothing more epitomized the fragility of the colonial state around the start of the twentieth century than the parlous state of the police force. While Dutch forces waged war to extend colonial authority in the Outer Islands, in the largest city of the Indies the responsibility for good order rested in the hands of a small band of

European sheriffs (*schout*) and deputy sheriffs assisted by teams of Indonesian runners (*oppasser*) (Faber 1931, 93). In practice this unruly port city was virtually unpatrolled. People had perforce to look out for themselves. In the event of thievery or assault, the only resort was to the time-honored institution of hue and cry. Not that the state was powerless. As an occupied territory, the Netherlands Indies were an armed camp and any overt challenge to colonial authority was met with force. Fernando (1995) describes one such incident just south of Surabaya in May 1904. However, military intervention was clumsy and of no use against random acts of petty crime.

Responsibility for nighttime security devolved upon the kampung heads. The night watch (*ronda malam*) was maintained not by police but by the non-European population in discharge of their labor service obligations (Faber 1936, 107) (fig. 4.1). Those who did not wish to put in time paid others to serve in their place. Motiva-

Figure 4.1. Kampung watch and guardhouse, Gubeng, ca. 1900. KIT Alb. 340, bl. 30, neg. 149/34.

tion was hardly to be expected. In the event of a disturbance, the alarm would be sounded by striking a hollow bamboo cylinder or wooden block (*kentongan* or *tongtong*) suspended beside the little guardhouse at the entrance to the kampung. A somewhat different warning would be sounded in case of fire, which in kampung houses built of highly combustible material was a common hazard. A fire brigade had existed since Daendels's time but prompt mutual aid was usually more efficacious.

The one significant gain in law and order before 1900 was attributable not to the police but to modern technology. Until the late nineteenth century Surabaya at night had been as pitch-black as any village. Being a rough port city, however, it was a great deal more dangerous. During the twelve dark hours it was foolhardy to venture onto the streets except for urgent or clandestine business. In the European quarter, around what is now the old central business district, men who set out in the evening for the club (*societeit,* or *soos*), and perhaps on the way home dallied with one of the ladies of the night, would bring a servant to bear a lamp before him. Faber (1931, 103–4) mentions that until 1864 "natives" were obliged to carry a lamp at night, a marvelously unenforceable regulation. Early attempts to pay contractors to pierce the gloom with coconut oil lamps and then, after 1864, with kerosene lamps proved disappointing. Modern street lighting was finally achieved in 1881, when the new gas factory introduced gas mantles—electric street lighting did not take over until after 1919 (Faber 1931, 105; SGS 1919). Street lighting brought a sense of security that allowed the city's European and Chinese communities to develop a much more vigorous nightlife. And as more people came onto the streets at night it also became safer, even if caution still had to be exercised against pickpockets and other petty thieves.

A modern police force dates back no earlier than 1914, when colonial rule was being consolidated after conquest of the Outer Islands. Following the appointment in 1911 of the first police commissioners, who replaced the sheriffs in the three main cities (Batavia, Semarang, and Surabaya), new police regulations were drafted that introduced a completely new form of organization and method of operation (Faber 1931, 107–13). Surabaya was divided into six precincts under a central administration, which also contained specialist sections to deal with such matters as criminal investigation, vice, forgery, firearms, opium, and alien registration (supervision of foreign nationals). As the number of motorized vehicles began to soar, the traffic section became more and more important. Faber (1931, 113) points out that by about 1930 the traffic section alone, with twelve Europeans and 120 constables, was larger than the entire police force twenty years earlier. Another modern and very secretive section was the Political Information Service (Politieke Inlichtingendienst, PID), whose prime task was to monitor the activities of Indonesian nationalists and suspected foreign subversives such as Japanese (Frederick 1989, 5–6; Poeze 1994). The police force grew so rapidly that by 1919 it numbered in all some 1,300, which after budgetary cuts during the Depression reduced to about 950 in 1933 (Frederick 1989, 5). Officially this force was known as the Town Police (Stadspolitie), to distinguish it from the Veldspolitie, which had responsibility for rural or village areas, but it remained under the firm control of the central government, not the Municipality. That centralization carried over to post-Independence Indonesia, in which police were until 1999 part of the armed forces.

PUBLIC HEALTH

Despite being the leading city in the Indies, at the beginning of the twentieth century Surabaya was still a most unhealthy place, even if Jakarta was worse. A survey of the period 1903–11 yielded a death rate of 36 per thousand for Surabaya compared with 57.8 for Jakarta (Abeyasekere 1987, 205). In both cities the main causes of death and morbidity were the same, namely malaria and intestinal diseases. As had always been typical of life in the tropics, everyone suffered illness. Some recovered, others died. Life was a lottery.

Many Europeans believed that strong drink would improve their chances and, even if it did not, at least they would have fewer regrets. Chinese and those Indonesians who could afford it likewise had their opium. Fatalism sapped the demand for modern preventive medicine.

Malaria was rife. Like the old town of Batavia and Semarang, Surabaya was built just a few feet above sea level, its sluggish natural drainage being dependent on the tides. The situation had been made a great deal worse after the 1830s by the ill-conceived fortifications (chap. 6). The growing population was now crowded within the walls and encircling moats, which soon became clogged with refuse and fecal matter. After the fortifications were abandoned in 1880 the moats were gradually filled in but sections long remained as stagnant backwaters. Along the prograding shoreline of Madura Strait lay swamps and ponds (*tambak*) used for fish breeding and salt making. Because the land had consolidated around what were originally islands, kampungs in lower-lying parts of the town were also prone to flooding in the west monsoon, sometimes for weeks at a time (Heida 1939, 49). As the dry season gained hold, standing water would contract into brackish, stagnant pools, ideal breeding places for the anopheles mosquito. Hence the incidence of malaria peaked in the middle of the year (Faber 1936, 310–11). The worst outbreak in the late-colonial period was in 1907 but, despite greatly improved knowledge of the disease, it remained a serious problem until the late 1920s. The harbor works begun in 1911 (see chap. 2) provided ideal breeding grounds amid the reclaimed but still unoccupied terrain. In 1916 the nearby naval base reported 1,000 malaria cases out of a workforce of around 3,000; in 1923 there were 1,240 cases among a rather larger workforce (MES 1916, 1923).

Cholera, the worldwide scourge of the nineteenth century, had also become endemic. The first pandemic broke out in Java in 1821 (Boomgaard 1987, 53–55). In 1864 the fourth pandemic, apparently brought to Java by pilgrims returning from Mecca, was estimated to have caused at least six thousand deaths in the city (Faber

1931, 239). The cycle of disease could not be broken because absence of a sewerage system ensured contaminated groundwater and canals, which were also the source of drinking water. Outbreaks typically occurred in the dry season, when rains no longer flushed out the drainage system, the water table fell, and people drew scarce water from polluted wells. In the twentieth century serious outbreaks occurred in 1900, 1902, and 1908, with a last mild epidemic in 1918, allegedly imported from nearby Sidoarjo (Faber 1936, 299–300). Although somewhat less virulent, typhoid was another consequence of poor sanitary conditions, while dysentery and other intestinal illnesses contributed to very high rates of infant mortality. Other prevalent diseases were tuberculosis, eye infections (including trachoma), skin infections, and, among some population groups, syphilis and other venereal diseases.

Despite very high levels of morbidity, the infrastructure of public health remained premodern until well into the 1900s. Advances in medical science that were transforming hospital practice and urban sanitation in Europe barely influenced conditions in Indonesia. A well-informed medical historian, D. Schoute (1935, 75:1467), maintained that around 1900 hospitals in Indonesia were little improved over their sorry state three decades earlier. Given the Europeanization of the commerce and urban society of the Indies that followed the opening of the Suez Canal, it is curious that the public health system should have lagged so badly. Various reasons can be adduced: the small size of the European population, a parsimonious administration, fatalistic attitudes, and so on. The starting point, however, must be the peculiar origins of public health services in Indonesia.

In the nineteenth century the government's main concern with public health had been to maintain the effective strength of the army and navy, the bulwark of colonial power. In the musty, crowded barracks of unsanitary and malarial coastal towns, death rates were appallingly high. As part of his "crash program" for the defense of Surabaya, in 1808 Governor-General Daendels had ordered the construction of what was for the time a model military hospital at

Simpang, isolated from the then small town but with ready access by the river. By 1867 it had over four hundred beds (Schoute 1935, 75:825–28). The purpose was not so much to treat the sick as to isolate them, presuming that nature could take its course without risk of continuing infection. The most serious cases were sent to convalesce or to die in the highland resort of Malang and, after 1873, to the hill station of Tosari (Schoute 1935, 75:905–6).

From 1828 to 1873, the Civil Health Service (Burgelijke Geneeskundige Dienst, BGD) was under the control of the Military Health Service. After stringent cutbacks, only in the three main cities did it retain its own doctors and buildings (Schoute 1935, 75:733, 907–8). In Surabaya the entire staff comprised in 1864 just two doctors, an apothecary, a midwife, and the hospital superintendent (Faber 1931, 228–29). The miserable public hospital (*stadsverband*) was located inside the prison walls. A medical report of 1872 described the old buildings as "poorly ventilated, damp, stuffy and of rundown appearance" and condemned the outbuildings as "veritable pigsties" (*ware hokken*). Toilet facilities were unsanitary, drinking water was drawn from the polluted Kali Mas, and there were no usable surgical instruments (Schoute 1935, 75:916–17). In 1906 this embarrassment of a public hospital was relocated from the prison to buildings adjacent to the military hospital (Faber 1936, 293). Nevertheless, as late as 1911 the staff of the Civil Health Service was no larger than fifty years earlier. Responsibility for all matters of public health still devolved upon two salaried medical superintendents, who had almost no staff or resources and besides administration had also in alternate days to do hospital rounds (Faber 1936, 288).

As the most prosperous community, Europeans enjoyed health options not available to the Indonesian population. First, there were a few doctors who retired from the Military Health Service into private practice (Faber 1931, 229). If hospitalization became a last resort, European patients would be treated in segregated wards in the Military Hospital. After 1898 they could also be admitted to the private nursing hospital across the river at Ngemplak. Probably just as efficacious was retreat to one of the many rest homes in the cooler and more pleasant surroundings of the highlands. For those unable any longer to cope with the rigors of the tropics, there was the option of repatriation to the Netherlands.

The only preventive public health program in the nineteenth century was vaccination against smallpox. This had begun in the 1800s but for lack of vaccine and manpower proceeded spasmodically, with bursts of activity following serious outbreaks. By 1860 about half the population may have been treated (Boomgaard 1987, 62–63), and probably a higher proportion in the main cities. Meanwhile, to relieve the problem of manpower, in 1851 a government school had been opened in Jakarta to train Indonesian paramedics-cum-vaccinators known as *Dokter Jawa* (Abeyasekere 1987, 198). The first of these graduates was posted to Surabaya in 1857 (Faber 1931, 229).

Government was called upon insistently to provide funds for a safe drinking water supply. People relied mainly on polluted wells. Especially in the dry season, this source was supplemented by water drawn at low tide (when the salt content was lowest) from the filthy Kali Mas, which doubled as a sewer. Carried in pails to each house by coolies bearing shoulder poles, the water was then allowed to settle in vats before being drawn off for purification (Faber 1931, 231–33). After years of discussion, in 1900 tenders were let for construction of a reticulated system that was opened three years later, drawing on water piped from natural springs at Kasri in the foothills. On its formation in 1906, the Municipality took over from the Department of Public Works the management of the water supply, which for some years was its only involvement in public health.

Official complacency finally succumbed to the outbreak of plague in 1910. This disease, caught from fleas that were carried by host rats, was said to have been introduced to Java by a ship unloading Burmese rice in Surabaya, but the first outbreak occurred in the highlands near Malang in November 1910 (Hull 1987). Not until March 1911 were cases reported in Surabaya and for some reason the city was spared the worst ravages. Peak mortality did not occur until 1914, with about one thousand deaths, making about fifteen hundred between 1911 and 1914 (Faber 1936, 300; Hull 1987, 232). The citizenry responded promptly to the threat by forming a Plague Control Committee, which raised funds for various hygienic measures. Responsibility was soon taken over by the government, which was bestirred into setting up a plague control section with its headquarters in Malang. Posts were set up just outside the city on the main highways and at Gunungsari, on the edge of the Brantas River, to inspect incoming passengers and goods, especially those carried by oxcart and prahu, and to fumigate those suspected of carrying infected rats or fleas. Within the town some twelve thousand kampung houses were subject to weekly sanitary inspection by plague officers (Faber 1936, 297). Besides the clearance of household refuse, tiled roofs were mandated to prevent rats from nesting in the usual thatch ceilings.[2] Although these sanitary measures were relaxed when the plague had been brought under control, they foreshadowed the revival in the late 1920s of public concern with kampung living conditions.

The outbreak of plague was decisive not so much for its severity—the influenza epidemic of 1918 was far more virulent (Brown 1987)—as because it reoriented expectations and policy. The terrible fear induced by the plague obliged the government to act. Within the existing minimalist system it had little scope, which led in turn to reorganization of the public health service. As more professionals became involved and government officials saw for themselves the appalling conditions in the kampungs, the problems began to be tackled on a broad front that applied basic principles of preventive medicine derived from scientific research. All this took many years to work itself through but, once begun, the trend was irreversible. This can be seen both in the course of institutional reforms and in the development of health policy.

One sign of changing attitudes was the reorganization in 1911 of the languishing Civil Health Service, which at last was separated from and elevated in status above the older Military Health

Service. Like the Police and the Department of Public Works, it remained under control of the central government, with regional inspectorates for West, Central, and East Java (Faber 1936, 288–89). In November 1916, three years after Jakarta, a Local Health Service (Gezondheidsdienst) was established under the new inspectorate with specific responsibility for the city of Surabaya (SGS 1917). Its task was not patient care but preventive hygiene, with a heavy emphasis on data collection and research, what would now be called epidemiology. At around the same time, the Department of Public Works established a special division of Irrigation and Sanitation Works, of which the latter part was in 1925 merged into a restructured Public Health Service (Dienst der Volksgezondheid) (Balen 1987; Jonkers 1948, chap. 10). The change of name from the implicitly exclusive term *Burger* (citizen, with the nuance of the Dutch freeburgher; as in Burgelijke Geneeskundige Dienst) to the inclusive and racially neutral term *Volk* (people) suggested more commitment to the common welfare.

These administrative changes did not, however, bring much improvement in the public hospital system. The immediate benefit was that the medical superintendent gained the assistance of two private physicians to take over his hospital rounds, freeing him for administrative tasks while improving patient care (Faber 1936, 288–89). In 1915 the Public Hospital (*Stadsverband*) was officially upgraded to the more impressively sounding Central Public Hospital (*Centrale Burgerlijke Ziekeninrichting*) but conditions remained very basic, with minimal medical attention for ordinary "natives" (Faber 1931, 139–41; 1936, 291–92). There was such gross overcrowding that beds had to be laid in double rows along the narrow verandahs that faced onto the courtyard (Faber 1936, 291, 293). This situation persisted until 1923, when the military hospital was at last closed. Over the next six years the whole Simpang complex was renovated and reorganized as a single unit of seven hundred to seven hundred fifty beds (Faber 1936, 292). This long overdue upgrading of the Public Hospital established it as a proper teaching hospital for the new medical school.

The physical constraints of the venerable hospital buildings soon became apparent. The time-honored layout of a large interior courtyard with banyan tree, surrounded by low buildings with verandahs, much like any large hotel, had sufficed when the main aim of the hospital was to isolate infected troops from their barracks. It was not conducive to a sterile environment and modern medical care, the more so because the once spacious layout had become cluttered with additional buildings. Tiedeman (1939) mentions that nursing wards were spread over a hundred locations—also that the complex was overrun with rats. In 1917 the Municipality sold the central government a twenty-five-hectare tract of former rice fields to the east at Karang Menjangan, not only for the new medical school but apparently also for a new public hospital and regional laboratory (Faber 1936, 171). It is likely that the budgetary cutbacks that accompanied the recession of the early 1920s caused the new hospital to be canceled and refurbishment of the old Simpang hospital to be taken in hand as a much cheaper alternative. Since the life of the Simpang hospital was thereby extended another fifty years, it was probably a good investment, but needed to be complemented by a more modern facility. The contrast with Jakarta's modern public hospital at Salemba must have been a continuing embarrassment, not least to the medical school.

In 1930 a government committee appointed to study the future of the Public Hospital recommended in favor of a new complex (Tiedeman 1939). When the depression of the 1930s had passed, the project was revived, albeit with no great haste. One of the most pressing reasons for expansion was the explosion in the use of polyclinic facilities by day patients. The old public hospital had been viewed with horror as a last resort for the desperately ill. For most ills, non-Europeans relied on traditional remedies. When cheap polyclinic services were made available in the refurbished Simpang hospital, outpatient visits soared from just 11,000 in 1921 to 112,000 in 1929 and by 1937 had doubled again to 222,000, a rate of 600 to 800 patients each day, which the old hospital could scarcely accommodate. This new pattern of demand called for a different kind of hospital, one that separated polyclinics from nursing wards. The new central teaching hospital, designed as an integrated complex and located just across the road from the medical school finally opened in January 1940. Now known as Rumah Sakit Dr. Sutomo and with more recent extensions, it is still the city's main public hospital.[3] Together with the medical faculty and the regional laboratory of the Public Health Service, it also established the city as a center of research in tropical medicine.

During the interwar years the private hospital system also greatly expanded. Three new hospitals were opened in the new garden suburb of Darmo. In 1922 the Surabaya Nursing Hospital moved from Ngemplak to Darmo Boulevard, followed in 1925 by the opening of the William Booth (Salvation Army) Women and Children's Hospital and in 1934 the transfer from Undaan of the Roman Catholic St. Vincentius à Paulo Hospital (Faber 1936, 288–91). The Surabaya Eye Surgery Clinic (now Dr. Yap Eye Hospital) occupied its current premises in Undaan in 1933, and there was also a very small Chinese hospital in Kaliondo, near the Chinese quarter. In total, by 1940–41 there were around fifteen hundred hospital beds—about a thousand in the public and naval hospitals and another five hundred in the various private institutions (AGS 1945, 219). Before 1920 Surabaya had been a place to flee when one became ill. Now it was firmly established as a medical center with facilities of European standard. Nevertheless, there was a wide range in the quality of care. While the public hospital provided free basic care to all, private hospitals were primarily for those who could afford to pay.

The plague scare of 1911 also highlighted the importance of garbage collection. After a decade of private contracting, the task was taken over by the Municipality about 1916. A fleet of oxcarts was used to collect household garbage and market refuse, which was dumped as landfill in salt ponds (*tambak*) on the northwest fringe of the city. Under municipal control, the area served grew steadily. Until the 1920s, collection was more or less confined to the European and Chinese districts. In 1919 the Municipality began a regular garbage collection from kampungs on a trial basis but this lapsed when funding was not forthcoming from the central government. A formal Garbage Ordinance (Vuilnisverordening) was proclaimed in 1922 that required households to place all waste in a bin for daily collection (Faber 1936, 148). After 1929 it was progressively introduced to kampungs as well (SGS 1929–31). In the meantime, kampung dwellers were left to follow their traditional methods of burning and burying garbage (more difficult as the density of housing increased), throwing it in the river or canal, or leaving it to rot. In those days before plastic, kampung garbage was almost entirely organic but, as recognized by the plague control teams, it provided an excellent food supply for the city's large rat population. Whereas in 1914 the contractor had collected only 360 cubic meters of refuse, by 1930 the volume had reached 283,000 cubic meters (SGS 1930). At the end of 1929 the main dump was relocated to Karang Menjangan, east of Gubeng station; rice fields were gradually reclaimed for sports fields and eventually sites for the new public hospital and the campus of Airlangga University.

Better drainage was needed both to reduce the severity of wet season flooding and to eliminate the breeding grounds of malarial mosquitoes. This involved major projects by the reorganized Department of Public Works. In 1915 a separate division of Irrigation and Sanitation Works had been set up, which led a year later to the establishment of a local office to work in with the municipal engineers. As in irrigation, primary works were the responsibility of the central government, secondary works of local government. The first initiative was to dredge and widen the Wonokromo Canal, built in 1856 as a single straight section to carry the floodwaters of the Surabaya River (Brantas) past the city into Madura Strait. These original works no longer protected the city from annual flooding, probably because the clearing of upland forest had increased runoff and peak flows. Completed in 1920, the new works included the massive Jagir barrage and floodgates (fig. 4.2) opposite Wonokromo, which still isolate the Kali Mas from the main river (Faber 1936, 144–45). The next major task, on which

Figure 4.2. Flood control: the Jagir barrage (1920) near Wonokromo, 1996. Photo by author.

work began in 1925, was to dredge out the northwest flood basin (*boezem*) at Morokrembangan, which collected floodwaters in that sector and discharged them at low tide into Madura Strait. This shallow basin had become a vast breeding ground for mosquitoes. Meanwhile, associated with the harbor works, swamps on both sides of the Kali Mas, including around the naval base, were progressively filled in with sand to eliminate surface water and provide terrain for housing or commercial activity. On a smaller scale, such infilling was carried on under the kampung improvement scheme (see below). These works, which should have been carried out years earlier, brought about a dramatic decline in the incidence of malaria in the older part of Surabaya, though as explained below, the disease recurred during the Japanese occupation, when these flood control systems were not maintained. In the newer southern part of the city, canal systems had been designed to tap the Surabaya River at Gunungsari and bring dry-season irrigation water into the former rice fields, not to carry off wet-season floodwater. Because of the great costs of changing the levels and direction of flow, in the new garden suburb of Darmo giant pumps were installed to lift water from the street drains into the adjacent canals.

Dutch engineering skills were not so well utilized in tackling the sewerage problem. Houses used pits that were either periodically cleaned out or simply discharged into open drains and flushed into the river. As in rural villages, kampung households used waterways or pit latrines. With growth in urban population and area, the disease hazard escalated, especially after the cholera outbreak. Ironically the provision of a reticulated water supply in 1903 reduced the pressure for a modern sewerage system. In 1916 an expert study of the soil structure and groundwater of Surabaya concluded that septic tanks would be suitable (Faber 1936, 146–47). Accordingly the new European suburbs, such as Darmo, were provided not with a reticulated sewerage system but with household septic tanks. This was also the case with public toilets and washhouses that were built by the Municipality to serve kampung dwellers. In 1927 a resurgence of typhoid led to appointment at the request of the Municipality of a Sewerage Commission. Its report in 1930 recommended a reticulated scheme for the whole city at an estimated cost of nine million guilders (Faber 1936, 147). Because the Depression was then tightening its grip, the central government refused to countenance such a large outlay. In 1937 sewage contamination was identified as a major cause of the seasonally recurring wave of stomach illnesses but again government recoiled from the huge costs (DBOW 1937, 64). With urban growth the real cost has continued to escalate ever since. In the 1990s Surabaya still lacked a modern sewerage system and intestinal diseases were as rife as ever.

As for the water supply, the problem was to keep up with the rapid growth of demand. Between 1906, when the Municipality took over production and distribution, and 1931 consumption grew at a rate of almost 10 percent per annum. Household consumption was the main component, 61.5 percent in 1919 compared with only 11.5 percent for industry and commerce (SGS 1919). To increase the flow pumping stations were installed south of the city at Wonocolo in 1916 and at Sidoarjo in 1920 but supply still lagged behind demand (Faber 1936, 329–32). In 1920 the Municipality was forced to supplement the insufficient natural water supply by drawing again on the waters of the Kali Mas. The filtration plant at Ngagel, just below the Wonokromo bridge, was opened two years later. Household use continued to grow quickly—hardly surprising when the widening reticulated network delivered cheap water at the turn of a tap. The problem with taps, however, was that they could be left running. Especially in the kampungs, tampering with the public hydrants led to much waste (Cobban 1971, 189–92). The Municipality battled to stem the waste of water, experimenting with different types of meters and tariff schedules (see below). As late as 1930 a quarter of the flow was estimated to be "lost" (SGS 1930). However, with the addition of the springwater from Umbulan (above Pasuruan) in January 1933 and the halving of consumption during the Depression, the town at last had a large margin of excess capacity, which allowed the Ngagel plant to be placed in reserve (Faber 1936, 294n, 332; SGS 1932).

The more active roles of both central and municipal governments caused problems of jurisdiction and funding. After May 1929 the local public health service—the main operational side of public health—became the responsibility of the Municipality (SGS 1930). By 1934 its tasks were fourfold (SGS 1934, 131). First came hygiene control. Following the eradication of plague and cholera, this role had focused on the fight against malaria. By 1934 malaria had in turn practically disappeared, except in the marshy northeast, and hygiene control was broadened to more general preventive medicine. Second, after 1913 in response to the plague threat, there began veterinary supervision of dairies, bakeries, and slaughterhouses—all vital to the health of Europeans—and livery stables, which hired the thousands of ponies needed for the town's fleet of dokar (Faber 1936, 321–28). Third was the operation of the new school medical service and, after June 1933, three new baby health centers. Finally, there was the operation of the town hearse and part of the ambulance service. All this was done by a staff of one full-time and one part-time physician, four nurses, three malaria officers (*mantri*), one dairy superintendent and his assistant, and three workmen (SGS 1933, 1934). The Public Hospital remained under central government control.

Declining death rates attested to the benefits of these belated improvements in local health infrastructure. Between the late 1900s and the census year 1930 the death rate for the Indonesian population roughly halved, while that for Europeans fell by two-thirds (Faber 1936, 318). This reflected the declining incidence of most of the main infectious diseases. By the late 1920s Surabaya was no longer the most unhealthy of the north-coast port cities. Its death rate was well below that of Jakarta and somewhat better even than the highlands town of Malang (table 4.1). International comparisons were less favorable. Surabaya's death rate was over three times that of the equivalent Dutch cities of Amsterdam and Rotterdam. As far as can be judged, there seems to have been no significant reduction in death rates during the 1930s for any ethnic group, although a weak trend may have been disguised by an increasing underestimate of population after the 1930 census.

Aggregate figures, however, disguise the markedly different mortality rates between ethnic groups. In the late 1900s death rates for the Indonesian community were about double those for the European. By the late 1930s the death rate among the thirty thousand

TABLE 4.1
Death rates by municipality, Java and Netherlands, 1928–29 (per thousand)

Municipality	Death Rate	Other	Death Rate
Pasuruan (E. Java)	40	East Java	18
Jakarta	39		
Malang (E. Java)	33	Amsterdam	9
Semarang (W. Java)	32	Rotterdam	8
Surabaya	29		
Bandung (W. Java)	21		

Source: Stam 1930.

Europeans in Surabaya had been reduced to around the level in Holland. Death rates for the Indonesian population, however, were now about two and a half times higher (table 4.2). Even allowing for some underestimate of the Indonesian population, the differential had certainly not narrowed since the 1900s and probably widened. In the case of infant mortality, it was dramatic. In 1938 infant mortality accounted for nearly 35 percent of reported Indonesian births but a mere 2.4 percent of European births. Of course it would have been remarkable had it been otherwise. The European community was much smaller, much better off, much better educated, lived in less crowded and more hygienic surroundings and controlled all the levers of government. Today the Indonesian middle class enjoys similar advantages.

In sickness as in health, the ethnic divide therefore distinguished people as sharply as does wealth today. Access to health services was very unequal. Faber (1936, 289) mentions revealingly that in the public hospital the two European physicians treated only Europeans, leaving to Indonesian doctors the treatment of everyone else. Nevertheless, by the eve of the Pacific War the Indonesian community enjoyed much better access to Western medicine than a generation before. This is shown very clearly by the above-mentioned explosion in outpatient visits to the Public Hospital. It can be seen also in the growth of clinics outside the hospital system, often run by religious or other charitable bodies. In the

TABLE 4.2
Death rates by ethnic group, Surabaya, 1938 (per thousand)

Ethnic Group	Number	Death Rate	Infant Mortality
Indonesian	298,400	23.7	34.8
Chinese	46,200	15.5	14.2
European	29,800	9.3	2.4
Total	380,400[a]	21.5	28.1

Source: SGS 1938.
[a]Includes 6,000 "other orientals."

1920s the Islamic movement Muhammadiyah opened its own clinics, staffed by Indonesian doctors (including the young Dr. Sutomo), who in 1929 treated almost seventeen thousand patients, or about fifty per day (Faber 1936, 48, 292). In the mid-1930s, when the Municipality decided to concentrate resources on infant health care, it transferred its two child health centers to Muhammadiyah and the Chinese hospital association, Soe Swie Tiong Hwa Ie Wan (SGS 1935, 146–47). The combination of well-trained Indonesian doctors emerging from the new medical schools and increasing organizational sophistication gave rise to a practical, grassroots nationalism that was also manifest in education (see below).

VENEREAL DISEASE

The issue of venereal disease deserves separate treatment for several reasons. First, as a port city and naval base, Surabaya has always supported a thriving business in prostitution, causing venereal disease to be a prime public health issue. Second, after 1913 venereal disease was the only one that was treated as a matter for the police rather than the medical system. Whereas application of the new scientific approach to treatment and prevention brought much improvement in public health in the late-colonial period, enforcement of public morality laws prevented such progress in the case of sexually transmitted diseases. Of this, female prostitutes as social outcasts were the main victims. Third, although all diseases have some social as well as environmental causes, venereal disease more than any other throws into relief the relations between the various groups in the plural society of the East Indies and the peculiar mind-set by which it was governed.

In the nineteenth century, when most Europeans in Java were unmarried men and one might still speak of a garrison society, government policy was pragmatic. Brothels were tolerated as a necessary amenity for frustrated soldiers and sailors and informal prostitution was practised throughout the city.[4] Alarm at the spread of syphilis, especially in the army and navy, led in the 1830s to the beginnings of a system of periodic examination of prostitutes by government medical officers (Schoute 1935, 75:737–42). Regulation was formalized in 1852 when the home government approved a Law for the Prevention of Harmful Consequences Arising from Prostitution. Modeled on the French system, the law required prostitutes to register with the police and to undergo regular medical examination. To facilitate medical supervision and maintain a level of social decorum, prostitutes were to work as much as possible in licensed brothels, for which the brothel keeper was held legally responsible. Although in Surabaya the law did not come into effect until 1858, after 1852 prostitution was already confined to three "bordello kampungs" on the urban fringe: Bandaran, Sawahan, and Nyamplungan.

By virtue of its strategic location, the main site was Bandaran, on the east bank of the Kali Mas, just north of the military barracks of Fort Prins Hendrik and within walking distance of the naval base (map 6.4). By 1867 it had 351 registered prostitutes (Schoute 1935, 75:740). A road led through a swamp to a fenced enclosure that three years earlier had been described as a mosquito-ridden place of bamboo shacks amid stinking, rubbish-strewn pools of green, stagnant water.[5] After 1864 any brothels remaining in the Chinese and Malay kampungs were required to move to Kapasan, on the eastern fringe, where a new site was prepared, surrounded by a moat and fence with entrances to the main road (Faber 1931, 243). The original locations and the new site just south of the Chinese quarter suggest that it may have been intended to serve the Chinese, but it is unclear how much attention the authorities paid to this still more or less self-governing community.

The effectiveness of the localization policy was open to challenge. In 1867 a senior naval office complained that the incidence of syphilis was still rising and that if the trend continued Surabaya would become "a second Yokohama" (Schoute 1935, 75:740). In the previous year 196 Europeans and sixty-two local crew members had been admitted to the military hospital at Simpang, these figures apparently excluding soldiers and civilians. Reasons for the worsening problem are not hard to identify. Even in the bordello kampungs, medical examination of the hundreds of registered prostitutes was much more lax than the weekly visit insisted upon in the new local bordello regulation of 1874 (Faber 1931, 244). Under revisions to the penal code, responsibility for supervision was decentralized to the residencies but, without matching resources. One overworked physician had to do that whole task and other things beside. Moreover, as could be expected, the police had little success in suppressing informal prostitution in other parts of the town and outlying places. No doubt many had their own reasons not to patronize the official brothel kampungs.

Regulation was therefore an unhappy compromise that satisfied no one. With more resources, the system could probably have worked much better. The welfare of both the women and their clients would have been improved directly but a lower rate of transmission of syphilis and gonorrhea would have benefited all communities. Instead, human irrationality led to political pressure to do away with supervision altogether. In Singapore, where supervision was abandoned in 1887 under pressure on the home government from would-be keepers of public morals, the entirely predictable consequence was an explosion in the incidence of venereal disease (Warren 1993). In Indonesia the Dutch colonial government held much longer to the status quo but the result was the same. After the Netherlands government had in 1910 passed the Public Morality Laws, the governor-general was obliged to order medical inspection of prostitutes to be terminated from 1 March 1911. On 1 September 1913 new morality laws came into force that made organized prostitution a criminal offense (Hesselink 1987; Hull, Sulistyaningsih, and Jones 1998).

The morality laws gave the colony a veneer of middle-class morality. They did not, of course, bring about any reduction in the trade of prostitution. Indeed, as concubinage ceased to be socially acceptable and the city's population was swelled by Javanese, Madurese, Chinese, and European immigrants, the demand by men for sexual services must have supported a growing number of prostitutes (Ming 1983; Ingleson 1986). Suppression of legalized brothels must also have brought more women onto the streets, for how else were they to find customers? Under pressure not only from European but also Indonesian nationalist lobbies, in 1920 Surabaya joined other municipalities in tightening the laws against soliciting in public places. As Ingleson observes, "it was street soliciting that really offended European (and probably middle-class Indonesian) sensibilities" (1986, 132). Out of sight was to be out of mind. Though it was not actually illegal for a woman to support herself by prostitution, streetwalkers who were regarded as too conspicuous or offensive could be subject to arrest and fines (Heselink 1987, 207).

Streetwalking was only one sector of a large, clandestine industry. A rare insight into its structure was provided by Simons (1939), formerly head of the venereal disease unit in Leiden, who made a survey of local conditions during a short visit to Surabaya. His main informant seems to have been the inspector of the local vice squad. Aside from the numerous evening streetwalkers and their touts, the two main centers of prostitution were in the far north and south of the city. In the north, just outside the harbor of Tanjung Perak, were many small cafe-bars offering alcohol and dancing to visiting sailors and where the hostesses would often make themselves available after hours. A more sophisticated variant were some European nightclubs in the main town. In the south, along the Banyu Urip Canal, lay an informal brothel kampung. By the light of a kerosene lamp, women waited in groups beside little bamboo bridges that led to huts on the other side of the canal. Simons was escorted there by the head of the vice squad, who evidently tolerated the kampung as a lesser evil. Because no "respectable" person would have reason to go at night beyond the suburbs and along that dark track, there was no affront to public decency. In the old lower town, a few restaurants and hotels still operated as brothels for an exclusively Chinese or Japanese clientele. These seem to have been accepted as a fact of life, whereas brothels catering to Europeans or providing European or Eurasian women to an Asian clientele had a more precarious existence. Where the full force of the law came to bear was upon homosexual and child prostitution. In this case the client himself was liable to arrest.

Simons identified one other category of prostitution that now seems curious, namely Indonesian maids having liaisons with their European householder. That it should be a category at all is probably recognition that until the twentieth century it was acceptable in European society for an unmarried man to cohabit with and even have children by an Indonesian concubine (*nyai*), whose nominal status was that of housekeeper. That the category should survive into the late 1930s reveals a glimpse of the racial angst that haunted colonial society, the counterpoint to the racial segmentation. Nyai existed in the first place because Indonesian women were rarely accepted as wives in respectable European society. By the twentieth century, as more Dutch women settled in the Netherlands Indies and the nuclear family became the building block of European society, Indonesian women were relegated to the status of household servants. But for all the care that went into the architecture of this plural society as a functional unit, at a personal and household level it was impossible to prevent emotional engagement across racial lines, either genuine or exploitative. Social pressures forced such liaisons into the marketplace, which the morality laws then sought to control. From this perspective, Simons's category of household prostitution, presumably derived from his police informants, was entirely logical.

The medical consequence of such diverse and unregulated prostitution was perpetuation of high rates of venereal disease among all groups of the population to the end of the colonial period. The army, one of the most vulnerable groups, showed a very high rate of infection. Simons (1939, 5690) states that across the whole colonial army the combined incidence of syphilis, gonorrhea, and venereal sores reached peaks of 241 per thousand in 1911 (the year compulsory examination of prostitutes was abolished) and 263 in 1920 before falling gradually to 92 per thousand in 1935. The eventual improvement was attributable to the provision of condoms to soldiers (Simons 1939, 5692). The only other organizations to supply prophylactics were the navy and the private shipping companies. For the population at large, Simons (1941, 1635–36) estimated that in the main cities of Java some 15 percent of the population was infected. In terms of hospital admissions and sick leave, it was one of the colony's major diseases. Moreover, the incidence of venereal disease appears to have been increasing, in marked contrast to the declining morbidity rates for other diseases including malaria (Ingleson 1986, 134).

KAMPUNG IMPROVEMENT

Until the mid-1920s the Municipality followed a policy of nonintervention in kampung affairs except under extraordinary circumstances such as the antiplague measures of the 1910s and mass inoculations against cholera in 1918. Such measures lapsed, however, once the crisis had passed. It was a matter of financial pragmatism. The institution of kampung autonomy, however illogical and threadbare, was a convenient legal excuse for government to evade the heavy liability that would be incurred along with responsibility for popular welfare. Nevertheless, the kampung question (*kampongvraagstuk*) haunted both the welfare-minded central government and the rationalizing Municipality like a bad conscience. In February 1918 the central government passed a constitutional amendment that allowed municipalities to incorporate kampungs by ordinance but pledged no funding to support such an initiative. Semarang's socially progressive council set up a committee that reported in 1920 (Cobban 1988, 281). Surabaya was more tardy. The resident of Surabaya from 1922 to 1924 reported at the end of his term that the kampungs in Surabaya were "disorganised" and that the heads "no longer had any influence" (ARA, MK, V.7–3–25/6: 7). In 1924 the Municipality formed the Kampongcommissie Faubel, which inter alia recommended appointment of an Indonesian as native adviser with responsibility for kampung affairs (SGS 1928, 108–10). In July 1927 the Municipal Council of Surabaya passed a carefully worded resolution that requested the central government to abolish kampung autonomy but on the proviso that it speedily reconsider its decision not to offer financial compensation (SGS, *GB* 1927, no. 166: 109). In December 1927, R. Soeparto, hitherto chairman of the Native Court at Meester Cornelis (Jakarta), was appointed Adviser for Native Affairs.[6] However, when it had become apparent that the central government would not budge on financial compensation, the position was terminated on 1 January 1930, after only two years (SGS 1929, 102).

Without waiting for the matter to be settled, in 1924 the Municipality had taken its own initiative on kampung improvement (*kampongverbetering*). Plans were drawn up for a Fl 600,000 program spread over six years for improving kampung drainage, sewerage, and bathing and toilet facilities (Faber 1936, 156).[7] Implementation began in 1925. Canals were filled in and replaced by underground sewers, open kampung drains were covered over as pathways, and public bathing places and toilets provided with metered fresh water supplies (SGS 1929, 170–71) (fig. 4.3). Eventually the central government relented somewhat. The Housing Congress of 1925 and the Kampongcommissie report (1926) paved the way for agreement to in May 1927 to allocate a subsidy for improvement of those kampungs to be incorporated into the municipalities. A meeting in February 1928 between the Adviser on Decentralisation, mayors, and heads of Public Works from all over Indonesia yielded no unanimity as to what kampung improvement might mean, but in February 1929 the government agreed to subsidize municipalities for half the cost of improvements, without regard to the legal status of the kampungs (KVC 1939, 16–18). In Surabaya by the end of 1931, out of 590 hectares of kampungs on government land (excluding about 100 hectares on private estates), some 200 hectares had been improved—135 hectares only partially—for an outlay of Fl 513,000. Of the Fl 3 million estimated to complete the balance of work, in 1932 a sum of Fl 313,000 was allocated to

Figure 4.3a. Prewar kampung improvement: before. KIT 628.2/4 no.47, neg.711 (Surabaya) N.47/48.

Figure 4.3b. Prewar kampung improvement: after. KIT 628.2/4 no.47, neg.711 (Surabaya) N.47/48.

improve 65 hectares (SGS 1932). These works were carried out without central government subsidy. In the following year, however, municipal finances felt the full force of the world depression and for the next few years expenditures on kampung improvement were minimal.

The revival of kampung improvement in the late 1930s was a product of central government initiative. In 1937 the government announced a Fl 25 million Welfare Fund, part of which was earmarked for kampung improvement and Fl 80,000 allocated to Surabaya. From 1938 the government allocated Fl 500,000 per annum to municipalities for kampung improvement and in May appointed a Kampung Improvement Commission (Kampongverbeteringscommissie) to determine how the funds should be allocated (KVC 1939). In its first report (April 1939), the commission was scathing, in terms that hardly sound outdated, about the past neglect of kampungs:

> Repeatedly the Commission was amazed and disagreeably surprised by prevailing views, by the slight interest shown in previous years, by the fact that numerous other less urgent needs were given preference above the improvement of kampung conditions. . . . Apparently the desire to achieve a complete and outwardly visible result frequently deceived the municipality, which time after time placed the demands of heavy traffic and various other interests ahead of the modest and not easy to obtain results in the kampong environment. (KVC 1939, 21)

The commission also observed that the consequences of years of neglect was compounded by a refusal to introduce even elementary building controls, maintenance or garbage collection until kampungs had been improved—what these days would be known as a catch-22. In this Surabaya was less at fault than other cities.

Kampung improvement was not necessarily altruistic. From the viewpoint of a more enlightened age we can easily share the indignation of the commission at the grossly inequitable distribution of civic amenities. Yet the matter was not quite so straightforward.

Even at a time when municipalities and the central government were defending the virtues of kampung autonomy while resisting mild pressures to allocate funds to kampung infrastructure, there was no hesitation to intervene on a massive scale when kampungs were perceived to be a health hazard to the European population, as during the plague scare of the 1910s. The opening up of new European suburbs brought about an ongoing fear of the spread of disease from nearby kampungs. It was no coincidence that the original elements of kampung improvement—drainage, sewerage, garbage disposal—were closely associated with sanitary conditions. Moreover, intervention was not free of the attitude that Furnivall recognized in the Ethical Policy: "to emphasize the development of material wealth rather than of human welfare, and to consider what can be done *for* the Javan rather than what can be done *with* the Javan, without noticing that the real problem was to discover what the Javan would do for himself. Their standpoint was individualist, and the problem was regarded as mechanical rather than as social" (1944, 235; emphasis in original).

While kampung improvement was admirable in its concern for what is now known as basic needs, the fact remains that the basic needs were defined by Dutch administrators. Kampung dwellers got what they were told they needed. And the Municipality was most put out when they were not grateful and did not use the new facilities in the proper way, such as keeping the new pathways and gutters clean.

A good example of the gulf between well-intentioned administrators and independent kampung dwellers was the issue of garbage disposal. In 1929 the Garbage By-law was declared applicable to kampungs and over the next two years gradually enforced. Street refuse, which had been dumped in bins placed symbolically at entrances to kampungs, was now to be deposited in closed carts, which were emptied twice a day and taken away at night, so that no refuse was left in the evening and there was "no unaesthetic sight of large garbage bins" (SGS 1929, 242). In 1930 the municipality noted that the population was cooperating but, ironically, much less so in improved kampungs, where it was more convenient to throw household refuse into the fine open drains (SGS, 1930, 262). A year later the Municipal Report observed with frustration: "When the By-law has just been introduced to a kampung complex, all goes well, apparently because it is something new and long awaited. After some time, one sees the number of bins gradually diminish and be replaced by baskets [*kranjang*], which then also disappear and the garbage is placed in a pile in front of the house or in a drain" (SGS 1931, 205).

The report then observed with bemusement that the problem was greatest not in the poorest kampungs but in the well-founded ones, such as Peneleh, Plampitan, and Undaan (fig. 4.4). The Council's response was to introduce an inspection service: households that failed to restore a bin a week after being warned were issued with a summons. By contrast, the Council expressed satisfaction with the response in the European suburbs, though noting that only the poorer households used the regulation bin instead of more impressive models. At the same time it was noted that, in the

Figure 4.4. Kampung Plampitan, a well-founded kampung and prewar home of prominent Indonesian nationalists, 1987. Photo by author.

exclusive European suburbs of Darmo and Kupang, householders threw everything conceivable over the back fence into the fire access lanes. The analogy with the apparently inexplicable behavior of better-off kampung dwellers went begging.

Another conflict arose with the introduction of water meters. To reduce fecal pollution and control the spread of infectious diseases such as typhoid and cholera, as part of kampung improvement the Municipality sought to install a block of septic toilets and public bathing places in every kampung. By 1931 there were sixty-eight such units across the city (SGS 1931). However, this exacerbated the long-standing problem of controlling water consumption from the public hydrants. Kampung dwellers, who had been used to drawing water freely from the river and from wells, regarded it as an inexhaustible, God-given resource. For them it was logical to leave water flowing from the new taps. Water Authority engineers devised the technical solution of coin-fed meters, introduced in 1926 (Faber 1936, 331), but thereby provoked passive resistance. Kampung dwellers objected to paying for what previously had been a free resource and applied great ingenuity to sabotaging this new instrument of government control (Cobban 1971, 189–91; Balen 1987, 21–22). Despite many attempts at improving the meters to prevent tampering, the authority never managed for long to restrict water consumption or to force kampung dwellers to pay for it.[8]

Though hardly outstanding, Surabaya's record on kampung improvement was still much better than the national average. By the beginning of 1938 only about a fifth of all urban kampungs were estimated to have been improved, with an estimated Fl 8 million required to improve the remainder (KVC 1939, 22). In Surabaya by the end of 1939 a total of 361 hectares of kampungs had been either fully or largely improved at a cost of Fl 1 million, of which about 30 percent had been provided by the central government (Heida 1939, 49). Including kampungs on private estates, that represented not quite half the total area. Nevertheless, as the commission recognized, the more kampungs were improved the more pressing became the problem of maintenance. Four causes of deterioration were identified: inadequate drainage, rising density of population, lack of cooperation from kampung dwellers, and lack of supervision by the Municipality (KVC 1939, 33–36). The solution to the lack of cooperation was, not surprisingly, perceived to be education: "the native urban mass must be educated to order, neatness, and social responsibility" (KVC 1939, 35). Though the commission was not explicit, the implication was clear: if education was ineffective, then the municipalities should resort to sanctions, as in the case of garbage collection.

The trend toward increasing interference with the minutiae of kampung life was indicated by the responsibilities that the commission set for the municipalities, including the monitoring of building density and the application of building controls (KVC 1939, 52–53). With more and more sources of conflict it is not surprising, as Frederick (1989) argues so well, that kampung improvement did not so much make "the natives" grateful as exacerbate their hatred of an authoritarian colonial bureaucracy, a hatred that exploded when the Dutch sought to return in 1945. Kampung dwellers would have much preferred to have been left alone.

MARKETS AND STREET SELLERS

Because cities do not provide their own subsistence, markets are the fundamental economic institution of urban life. They function both to provision the city and as clearing stations in wider networks of commerce. Traditionally all markets were actual places where goods were displayed for sale as buyers and sellers met face to face to haggle over prices and quantities. In the precolonial period foreign trade also passed through such marketplaces, which Reid describes as "the central organizing principle of trade" (1993, 91). The subsequent disintegration of this primitive market economy was brought about by the state monopolies imposed first by the East India Company (VOC) and then more recently, after 1830, by the Nederlandsche Handel Maatschappij (NHM; Netherlands Trading Company). By the twentieth century foreign trade was organized by European and Chinese firms under contractual arrangements that completely bypassed local markets. What remained of the old market economy was the lower circuit of the urban economy, the realm of indigenous traders, many of whom were women. For all these reasons it also had close links with kampung society.

Government became involved with markets at an early stage as a means of raising revenue. Until the mid-nineteenth century, the colonial government farmed out the management of markets, invariably to Chinese, thereby enjoying the tax revenues while avoiding the burden of administration. Market levies evolved into a de facto transit tax, and harassment and overcharging of traders became so rife that in 1851 the governor-general used emergency powers to abolish the market farms in favor of direct administration (Diehl 1993, 220–21). Except for those on the private estates, markets then became the responsibility of regional government. However, the concern was still to collect revenue more efficiently, not to outlay funds on improvements (Faber 1936, 178). Where facilities such as covered sheds were provided, they were usually owned by private interests, who were allowed to charge additional fees for their use. Hygiene seems to have been virtually unsupervised.

The administration of markets is logically a municipal matter. Yet although the Municipality was established in 1906, not until April 1914 did the central government pass a general decree to transfer responsibility for local markets. Like other municipalities, Surabaya formed a Market Authority (Pasarbedrijf), which formally began operations on 1 February 1915 and during the first year took control of eleven markets of varying size and function (Neyndorff 1939).[9] The authority set about its task with great thoroughness. Bare earth that turned into quagmire in the rainy season was paved with hard surface. Privately owned sheds were taken over and as necessary replaced with more substantial structures. Tap water was supplied free of charge. Laborers were hired to sweep up and carry out the rubbish. The veterinary service that had begun in 1913 supervised the sale of meat, for which special stalls were built with tiled floors and with gauze screens to keep out the flies. Since European households through their Indonesian servants also drew their food from these markets, such measures were not without self-interest.

After this initial phase of consolidation, in the mid-1920s the Pasarbedrijf began to build more permanent structures. When the town of Wonokromo on the far side of the Surabaya River was incorporated into the municipality in 1925, the big Pasar Wonokromo was taken over from the residency of Surabaya and completely rebuilt (SGS 1929, 364). The next large project in the late 1920s was the relocation and rebuilding of Pasar Turi (SGS 1927, 245). These buildings were still constructed in traditional style, with wooden frames and tiled roofs. When the middle section of Pasar Genteng, the main market in the Tunjungan shopping district, was rebuilt in 1932, it was to a new design of reinforced concrete (fig. 4.5). This led on to the grand art deco façades and vaulted halls of Pasar

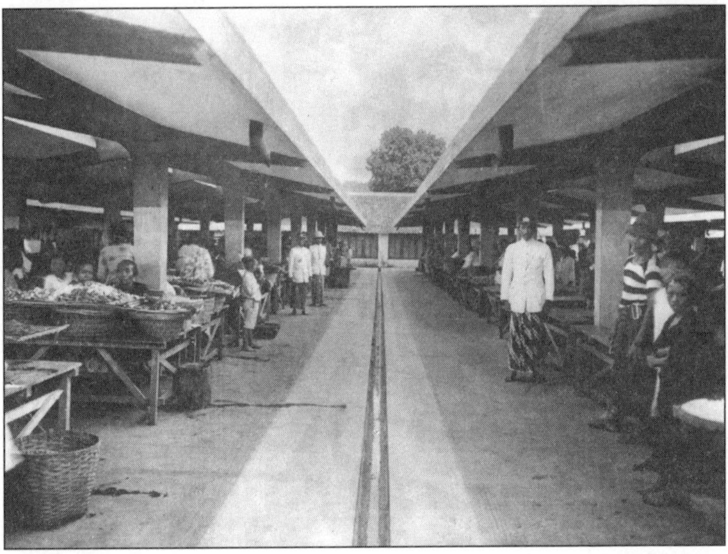

Figure 4.5. Pasar Genteng after reconstruction in 1932. KIT, 381.13 N.254.

Blauran (1934) and Pasar Pabean (1938–39), which were not only works of architecture in their own right but also for the first time integrated—or disguised?—indigenous markets with the façade of the modern city.

The empire of the Pasarbedrijf steadily expanded. In November 1926 new market bylaws (*pasarverordeningen*) were passed to extend licensing, hygiene controls, and inspection to the remaining private markets (SGS 1927, 245; Faber 1936, 179). When these improved standards proved unenforceable, the Pasarbedrijf began to take them over. The next step, evidently on hygienic grounds, was to forbid markets in the kampungs. To this end former private markets were rebuilt on a larger scale and, where these were too far away, small neighborhood markets (*buurtpasar*) were established on the edge of kampung districts. Addition of another twenty-five markets from 1928 onward brought the total to forty-one administered markets by the end of 1938 (Neyndorff 1939, 57). The authority also took on responsibility for erection and supervision of icehouses, which were set in strategic locations as distribution points for this now essential commodity.

In the 1930s a threat to the well-ordered market system and public order was perceived in the emergence of unregulated street sellers (*straatverkoopers*) (fig. 4.6). Along with other informal-sector activities, such as prostitution and small-scale urban public transport, the growth of street selling reflected the search for alternative income-earning opportunities during the Depression, as again in the late 1990s. This evil—as so uncompromisingly defined by Put (1939, 111), head of the Pasarbedrijf in Bandung—seems to have been a general concern among the municipalities of Java. In 1939, Surabaya was host to a local government conference on street selling. Foremost among the concerns of officials was loss of revenue from the erosion of market turnover. Declining standards of public hygiene control were also cited. The weight of the public interest, however, seems to have been placed upon price rises and instability that were expected to flow from some catastrophic disruption of the market network. With little regard to economic

Figure 4.6. Unregulated street selling, 1987. Photo by author.

logic, it seems to have been believed simultaneously that street sellers would overcharge and that the turnover of markets would be seriously eroded, causing prices to become more volatile. Logic, however, was probably not to be expected. A cynic might observe that the natural inclination of any gathering of the heads of local market authorities would be to defend their monopoly and revenues, and to that end could be expected to deploy whatever arguments would generate the greatest fear of change. In Surabaya the dense network of neighborhood markets seems to have kept street selling in check. (Put 1939, 111) observed that street selling was much less widespread in Surabaya than in other Indonesian cities.

The administration of markets, like that of kampung improvement, was pervaded by a colonial attitude that progress was to be measured by the improvement in the built environment. A bizarre but illuminating view was that of the leading town planner, Ir. Karsten. He submitted that the Indies city was the center of order (*ordening*) and that the market was "a necessary element in the ordering of economic life" to transform the "primitive agrarian" mentality of the population to an "urban-ordered" mentality (Put 1939: 110). Here without equivocation speaks the confident voice of the social engineer. Although the context is slightly different, the planners and the people are the same as in the case of kampung improvement. However desirable the better living environment brought about by kampung improvement, these remarks show the raw edge. It becomes more obvious why there was such a bitter politico-cultural clash between enlightened but arrogant bureaucrats and the proud arek Suroboyo, who did not wish their mentalities to be upgraded to "urban-ordered" at the decree of their Dutch rulers.

PUBLIC HOUSING

Until about 1915 housing was not a matter to which either central or the municipal government had given much thought. The assumption was that sufficient housing would be built by private enterprise. There was a good deal of private construction of European bungalow housing but demand was growing faster, the result being an acute housing shortage that affected both Europeans and Indonesians (SMNA 1917; MES 1919). To relieve the shortage of land for suburban housing, in 1916 the Municipality took the initiative of buying two private estates at Ketabang (1.2 square kilometers), in the vicinity of what became the municipal precinct, for development as a housing project. A year later the Grond- en Woningbedrijf (Land and Housing Authority) was set up to manage this and other developments (see chap. 6). To provide finance to owner-occupants, a mortgage enterprise was set up in October 1918 (Ruckert 1930, 165). This venture lapsed because of failure to raise the necessary municipal loan (SGS 1919), but in 1925 the Municipal Savings Bank (Gemeente Spaarbank) was created by takeover of an illiquid private savings and mortgage bank (GS 1925).

The Land and Housing Authority provided for the needs of middle-class Europeans. At Gubeng and Ketabang, wide tree-lined streets were laid out for modern bungalows set back behind neat front gardens. Only on the edge of the development beside the railway line was there some construction of kampung housing: 163 one- and two-room dwellings for displaced kampung dwellers (Ambengan and Jimerto) (Faber 1936, 164–65). This bias reflected the market. Because Europeans had much greater capacity to pay and were more creditworthy, it was more profitable to build bungalows than a much larger number of very small houses. Although in 1916 the Municipality had relaxed the building regulations in an attempt to make the construction of kampung housing profitable to private enterprise, this seems, as in more recent years, to have had almost no effect (Faber 1936, 164). At this stage the only official concern with kampung housing was construction and sanitation under the Plague Ordinance.

The growth of government awareness of the urban housing problem owed much to the initiative of the town planner Thomas Karsten (Bogaers and Ruijter 1986). In 1915, at the age of thirty-one, he had arrived in the Indies to work in an architectural bureau in Semarang that at the time stood out among Indonesian cities for its concern with social conditions. In 1911, Alderman Tillema had carried out a survey of kampung living conditions, and in 1916 the Municipality had begun to construct small-scale housing. Karsten set up a local chapter of the Social Technical Society of Democratic Engineers and Architects, which had been in the forefront of the development of municipal housing in the Netherlands. Through the society, in April 1922 Karsten organized in Semarang the first Housing Congress, which placed public housing firmly on the political agenda. The congress agreed that housing was essentially a matter for local government but that central government would have to assist, not only financially but also in legislative revisions to facilitate the sale and transfer of land, to establish conditions for the loan of funds, and to abolish kampung autonomy (ARA, MK 2.10.36.02: MR 2351/22). A second Public Housing Congress followed in 1925, with more attention to the needs of non-Europeans.

Between these two congresses, the central government decided to assist with public housing. The vehicle was to be public housing corporations (NV voor Volkshuisvesting), three-quarters of whose capital would be held by the central government and the balance by the respective municipality (Stam 1930, 134–36). The first corporation was established at Semarang in December 1925. Surabaya followed in January 1927 with paid-up capital of Fl 100,000 supplemented by a Fl 275,000 issue of bonds. The corporation began construction at the beginning of 1928 with contracts for 336 "coolie huts" of one or two rooms at kampung Sidodadi, near the naval base, and 110 houses for Indonesians and 12 for Eurasians at Ketabang East (SGS 1927, 124–27). By the beginning of 1933, when the last two dwellings were handed over, the corporation had built 933 houses and 332 huts, while the Land and Housing Authority had built 521 houses and 10 huts (fig. 4.7). By then the Depression had caused the bottom to fall out of the housing market. In mid-1933 about nine hundred houses (private and public) with rental above Fl 50 per month were unoccupied (SGS 1933, 95). Rents for public housing began to be lowered cautiously in response to the general deflation but despite a steady decline in rents until 1937, many houses stood wastefully empty until demand recovered in 1937. By the end of 1938 almost no public housing was still unoccupied (SGS 1938) and in 1940 the corporation resumed construction with a few houses.

Although the corporation and the Land and Housing Authority were meant to provide low-cost housing, both programs were heavily biased toward housing for Europeans. In 1930, Europeans had constituted only 7.6 percent of the city's population (table 3.4), yet excluding the coolie huts they occupied almost half of this public housing and dominated all but the two cheapest categories (SGS 1933). Indonesians occupied half the corporation's coolie huts—the balance were Chinese—but only a quarter of its houses. These housing ventures certainly helped to ease the housing shortage in Surabaya but the rate of construction was too slow to make much of an impact on overcrowding in the kampungs. A thorough housing

Figure 4.7. *Top:* Municipal housing, ca. 1929; *bottom:* NV Volkshuisvesting low-cost housing. From Kerchman 1930.

survey carried out by the Municipality in 1928–29 had estimated a total shortage of twenty-two thousand homes, equal to half the existing housing stock (SGS 1929, 176–89). Thus the combined interwar housing construction of the Municipality and the corporation, including huts, was equivalent to just 8 percent of this shortage. The fundamental problem, which much later was also to bedevil public housing under the New Order, was how to build low-cost housing cheaply enough to be affordable to kampung dwellers and in an acceptable style. The barracks-like rows of accommodation provided by the municipal housing corporations was satisfactory neither in cost nor design (Cobban 1993).

EDUCATION

At the close of the nineteenth century formal education was still primarily for children of the Dutch community, including a large proportion of Eurasians. In 1896, Surabaya had only twelve primary schools: six boys' and two girls' government schools, one boys' and one girls' private school, and one boys' and one girls' Catholic school (Faber 1931, 251). Secondary schooling was confined to the Public High School (Hoogere Burgerschool, HBS) founded in 1875, the second such school in the Indies, which in 1923 moved to its present location in Ketabang (Faber 1931, 268–70; Sutherland 1979, 46). At the end of 1900 the high school had an enrollment of 225 students, of whom all but one were European (KV 1901). Through this system Dutch children could qualify for employment in the civil service or private trading houses. All teaching was in Dutch and aimed at standards equivalent to schools in the Netherlands (Penders 1968b). The greater mobility that had followed the opening of the Suez Canal made it important that children could readily transfer from one system to the other.

Educational opportunities for Indonesian children were extended slowly and begrudgingly as an almost wasted expense. The process nevertheless began before the Ethical Policy made education a

Good Thing. As early as 1853 the Maatschappij tot Nut van het Algemeen (Society for the General Welfare) had opened in Surabaya a primary school to teach Javanese children the rudiments (Faber 1931, 330). It closed after only seven years, reportedly for lack of interest, but in the same year the government itself had opened a school in kampung Krambangan to educate the sons of Indonesian heads for low-level administrative positions (Faber 1931, 254). After 1864 a few sons of the aristocracy had been accommodated in Dutch-language schools (Sutherland 1979, 46). For the population at large, however, formal education was nonexistent. Here the only access to education was limited rote learning through Islamic teachers in the kampungs. After the formation of the Department of Education and Religion in 1867, the government began more purposefully to extend vernacular primary schools (Brugmans 1961, 154–55). Nevertheless, these schools offered just a three-year course, which hardly equipped students to work in the modern sector of colonial society.

To fill the great gap between the Dutch and the vernacular systems, in 1892 the government established a new stream of "first-class" primary schools with a five-year curriculum that included Western subjects such as history, geography, natural history, and surveying (Brugmans 1961, 160–61). Second-class popular schools (*volksscholen*) remained as before, with just a very basic three-year curriculum for six- to eight-year-olds. The new schools were a marked improvement but the aristocracy quite rightly continued to regard them as inferior to the Dutch-language system. This pressure of expectations, combined with the rising demand for competent Indonesian officials, led in 1914 to the first-class schools being upgraded to a full seven-year course, with final-year instruction mainly in Dutch (Penders 1968b, 129). These Hollandsch-Inlandsche (HIS) and Hollandsch-Chineesche (HCS) schools, according to the vernacular language in the lower grades, enabled brighter students to proceed on to the new junior high school (Meer Uitgebreid Lager Onderwijs, MULO) and then, after three years, to senior high school (Middelbare School). For the brightest students from the second-class schools, access to Dutch-language secondary school was later provided through establishment from 1921 of several "link" schools (*schakelscholen*). Furthermore, the HIS diploma was also graded as equivalent to a minor official's (*kleinambtenaars*) diploma, which at last established a general pathway into the prestigious civil service.[10] Indonesians thereby became strong competitors for positions formerly dominated by Dutch-speaking Eurasians.

Comparison of figures for the years 1918 and 1929 gives some idea of educational progress during the interwar period. Table 4.3 applies only to government or government-subsidized schools, and thereby understates vernacular education, but gives a good picture of the "formal" education system. Clearly the system did expand, albeit from a very low base, but secondary education remained very restricted, not least because the colonial government feared that Dutch-educated Indonesians would become an "intellectual proletariat" (Penders 1968b). Most resources went into the Dutch-language system, and almost half of all Dutch-language primary school students were in the European schools. This translated into a huge difference in attendance rates. Virtually all Dutch

TABLE 4.3
Enrollment by type of school, Surabaya, 1918, 1929

	January 1918		November 1929		
School Type	Number of Schools	Students	Number of Schools	Students	%
Vernacular	9	1,144	15	2,087	17
Indonesian (HIS)	2	407	9	1,857	15
Chinese (HCS)	4	830	6	1,823	15
European	18	3,864	22	4,581	38
Total Primary	*33*	*6,245*	*52*	*10,348*	*85*
Lower secondary (MULO)	—	—	4	977	8
Upper secondary	—	—	4	808	7
Total Secondary	—	—	*8*	*1,785*	*15*
Total	—	—	60	12,133	100

Source: SGS 1918, 1919, 1930.

children went to school, but very few Indonesians. Brugmans (1961, 158) claims that by 1940 about 40 percent of Indonesian children aged six to eight were attending primary school. However, those Indonesian children who did attend school in most cases reached only the three-year *volksschool* (vernacular primary school), barely achieving functional literacy in the vernacular. Despite Brugman's apologia, the 1930 census starkly revealed that the literacy rate in Surabaya among adult Indonesians was only 14 percent, compared with 97 percent for adult Europeans (table 3.15; Penders 1968b, 144–46).

For students who failed to gain one of the few high school places, the options were few. The Mulo-level Dutch-language Koningin Emma School offered vocational training. Founded in 1912 as a development of the long-standing Citizens' Evening School (Burgeravondschool),[11] it was managed by the Municipality. When demand rose during the 1920s, day classes were introduced and the school became the Citizens' Trades School (retaining the same acronym in Dutch). Girls also had access to the Household and Industry School, which taught applied skills (Faber 1936, 338). For Indonesians who could not follow the Dutch-language streams of secondary education, the options were limited indeed. Apart from one school sponsored by the Taman Siswa nationalist education movement, there seems to have been no secondary schooling in the vernacular. The main option after 1909 was the Natives Trades School (Ambachtsschool), which in Malay taught metalwork and woodwork as well as automobile and electrical mechanics: by 1937–38 it had about 350 students (Faber 1936, 336). Such skills were in high demand and could earn good premiums over unskilled work but, as blue-collar jobs, had no appeal to children of the priyayi.

Opportunities for tertiary training were even more limited than in Jakarta, the sole options being medicine and dentistry. The pioneer tertiary institute in Indonesia had been the medical school (School for the Training of Native Doctors; School tot Opleiding van Inlandsche Artsen, STOVIA), founded in Jakarta in 1898 by raising to faculty status the long-established Dokter Jawa school

(Abeyasekere 1987, 198). The increased demand for local doctors resulting from the plague epidemic of 1911 seems to have been the main factor behind the decision two years later to establish a medical school (Nederlandsch-Indische Artsenschool, NIAS) in Surabaya. Classes began in 1916 in temporary premises while new buildings were constructed at Karang Menjangan, on the eastern fringe of the city, just beyond the Gubeng railway station. Occupied in 1924, the new complex, including a very fine auditorium, would eventually become the core of the campus of Airlangga University. In 1928 there was added an adjacent dental school (School tot Opleiding van Inlandsche Tandarts, STOVIT). By the end of the decade about three hundred students were engaged in the seven-year medical course and another fifty in the five-year dental course (Faber 1936, 294). Unlike the equivalent institutions in Jakarta, however, neither school was raised to faculty status. Despite its established position as the industrial center of Indonesia, Surabaya missed out on becoming the site of the Technical College (Technische Hogeschool; later, Institut Teknologi Bandung, ITB), which opened at Bandung in 1920; the Law College (1924) and Faculty of Arts (Faculteit der Letteren) (1940) were both established in Jakarta. By the eve of the Pacific War, Jakarta therefore had a university in all but name, which after Independence became Universitas Indonesia. Except in medicine and dentistry, Surabaya's best high school graduates had either to move to Jakarta or to seek a place in the Netherlands. Insofar as Surabaya served as an educational center, it was only for secondary education.

The public bias against Indonesian, and especially Indonesian secondary education, worsened during the 1930s. Policy was driven by the determination of the central government to cut back expenditure of all kinds in order to balance the budget. In education this was achieved in three main ways. First, greater responsibility for basic primary schooling was devolved to a rather unenthusiastic local government, which hitherto had played much less of a role than in the Netherlands. In August 1936 the Municipality was allocated another sixteen volksscholen in addition to the six it already operated (SGS 1936, 143; 1937, 132). Inspection and the training of teachers for the higher grades were allocated to the provincial government (POJ 1939, 126), while the central government continued to control Dutch-language education. Second, the central government ruthlessly closed schools, including one of the two lower secondary (Mulo) schools in Surabaya, and all but suspended teacher training, which led to closure of the European Teacher Training School (Faber 1936, 335–36). Third, the government heavily cut subsidies to nongovernment schools, which particularly disadvantaged financially weak Indonesian schools.

With the demand for education higher than ever, this assault on government schools and subsidies stimulated an unexpectedly vigorous response from the private sector, not least among the Indonesian community. As early as 1914 the political movement Sarekat Islam had established in Surabaya a school for young girls (named after the pioneering woman writer Raden Adjeng Kartini, 1879–1904), which in 1918 had gained official recognition and subsidy and eventually evolved into a proper Hollandsch-Inlandsche school (Faber 1936, 47). There ensued a proliferation of what the Dutch authorities called wild schools, implying that they were spontaneous, unofficial, and, by extension, dubious. They were organized by a wide range of religious, communal, and nationalist organizations, only a few with any expertise in education, like Taman Siswa and the modernist Islamic Muhammadiyah, which in 1939 also opened its own Mulo school to replace that closed by the government (Penders 1968b, 380; Siauw 1982, 14). Nevertheless, despite official concerns about the quality of teaching in these schools, there was a pool of unemployed and dedicated young people who had received some modern education and were enthusiastic about teaching in schools free of government control. Frederick (1989, 58, 76–77n) estimates that in Surabaya by the late 1930s there were about seventy-five wild schools with some two hundred teachers and perhaps as many as seventy-five hundred students. Heida (1939) quotes a higher contemporary estimate of around a hundred such schools. Since in the 1938–39 academic year the number of children attending second-class government schools (including *vervolgscholen,* the last three grades of primary school) was only forty-seven hundred (SGS 1938), the unofficial schools had clearly become the dominant sector.

Education was therefore a field in which government raised expectations but did not impose its authority. Certainly it retained firm control over prestigious Dutch-language education for the elite with access to white-collar employment, but it forfeited control over popular primary school education. Just as Indonesian doctors had brought modern medicine to kampung families, nationalist organizations also brought modern education to kampung children, hitherto dependent on religious catechists (Frederick 1989, 58–63). As youths many of these children would become prominent in 1945 in the fight for independence. The educated elite who led the movement for independence thereby helped to sow the seeds of popular revolt.

Beyond Independence

Good government is a matter of routine as much as policy. In the late-colonial period the battle had been over policy, leading eventually to the struggle for control of government itself. This heroic drama still seizes the attention fifty years after Independence. However, regardless of whether government was under Dutch, Japanese, or Indonesian control, the basic functions of government still had to be performed. By 1941, Surabaya had become a city of around four hundred thousand people (chap. 3), whose management was a complex task involving three levels of bureaucracy. Flood control and drainage, public health, and education, for example, were now technically sophisticated and called for professional expertise. The city was looked after by a middle to senior management of Dutch officials who organized a mainly Indonesian workforce to do the actual work. The tragedy of the Japanese occupation and the subsequent Revolution was that the government whose sovereignty was finally taken over in December 1949 was so much less effective than that which had existed at the end of 1941, not least because the cadre of senior Dutch bureaucrats had been removed before their Indonesian successors had been properly trained. Moreover, much of what was patiently achieved during the 1950s was squandered in the debacle of Guided Democracy.

The period between 1942 and 1966 can therefore be seen as a losing struggle to restore an ideal of good government that had been inherited from the colonial era, which people began to look back to more wistfully as the *zaman normal* (normal time). Catapulted into top positions, senior Indonesian bureaucrats were often very committed and aware of the deficiencies. They tried to restore normality but lacked experience and expertise and, above all, were rarely provided with the necessary funds. While bureaucratic structures and habits proved amazingly resilient,[12] government gradually ceased to deliver results. As politics came more and more to dominate the bureaucracy, the outcome was crisis management, whose meager results were covered up in a bluster of rhetoric. As was the case with the colonial government before 1900, it was in theory omni-competent but in practice achieved very little. The difference was that the bureaucracy itself turned into a vast, self-generating, self-serving, welfare organization (Feith 1967).

In Surabaya the new republic inherited a modern city in decay. This was most visible in the widespread physical destruction (chap. 2). Although the Dutch had cleared away most of the rubble and restored basic utilities, parts of the city where the fighting of November 1945 had been most fierce, such as Pasar Besar, Tunjungan, and Kaliasin, still showed gutted buildings (fig. 1.9). Burned-out kampungs had been resettled spontaneously but almost no attention had been given to restoration of pathways, drains, or water supply. Less apparent but more urgent for the population at large was the breakdown of public health. This could be attributed in the first instance to prolonged neglect of infrastructure but the underlying cause was the weakening of the bureaucracy that had responsibility for such mundane affairs. What funds became available tended still to be applied to law and order, communications, and European-style housing, while the kampungs as ever languished out of sight. Meanwhile, all around the city, squatters had begun to occupy niches where they were little bothered by a city administration preoccupied with more immediate problems. The flood of people eventually overwhelmed the modest efforts being made to improve the situation.

The first efforts of the new republican government were directed toward mass programs, most notably in public health and education. Top priority in public health was the scourge of malaria, which had flared up again during the Japanese occupation. As flood control and drainage systems were neglected, as fish ponds were abandoned, and as public inspectors ceased to harry the populace, standing water soon began to accumulate and mosquitoes to thrive, especially in the north of the city. The worst problem was the northwest flood basin, which had silted so badly that at high tide the saltwater flowed back into kampung drains, creating brackish conditions ideal for breeding the anopheles mosquito. In 1950 the Department of Public Works began the rehabilitation of drainage systems (KP 1953, 588), but funds were not forthcoming for urgent major works such as the dredging of the flood basin (*SP,* 31/12/53). The city government recognized the problems but for want of central government funds little was done. Meanwhile Indonesia joined the World Health Organization's global malaria eradication program, which relied on mass spraying of DDT (Hugo et al. 1987, 110). The Malaria Control Office (Djawatan Pemberantas Malaria) in Surabaya took delivery early in 1952 of a hundred sprayers and fifty tonnes of DDT from the United States and began spraying around the edge of the city in the districts of Sukolilo, Tandes, and Cermee (*SP,* 19/2/52). This achieved good results. In kampungs where in 1948 death rates from malaria had been as high as 80 percent, by 1953 the corresponding figures had fallen to less than 5 percent (*SP,* 31/12/53). Nevertheless, as late as January 1956 in kampung Bangunrejo, on the edge of the northwestern flood basin, three people were dying every day from malaria and 60 percent of the inhabitants were found to be infected (*SP,* 28/1/56).

The availability of hospital beds showed no improvement. The new public hospital at Karang Menjangan, which had opened in 1940, was not returned by the navy until September 1953 in exchange for a new twenty-hectare site beyond Wonokromo (*SP,* 28/9/53, 24/10/53). In the interim a much larger urban population was forced to rely on the very limited services of the old hospital at Simpang. Basic health services had begun to be provided through clinics during the interwar years, both as outpatient clinics in public hospitals and as independent and sometimes nongovernmental facilities. After Independence the central government saw clinics as a low-cost means of delivering community health programs. Besides standard medical clinics (Balai Pengobatan), priority was given to establishing mother and child health clinics (Balai Kesehatan Ibu dan Anak, BKIA) (KP 1953, 600). Polyclinics (Balai Kesehatan) combined these two functions; there were six in Surabaya by mid-1958 (*SP,* 9/6/58).

Despite shortage of funds and personnel, efforts were made to rehabilitate kampung infrastructure. Kampung improvement had been resumed in 1949 by the Dutch with work on about twenty-eight hundred hectares. At the end of 1953 it was claimed that almost four hundred thousand hectares of kampungs, about a quarter of the area of the city, had been rehabilitated, although the nature and quality of the work was not specified (*SP,* 8/12/53). However, the magnitude of the task continued to increase, as immigrants flooded into the city, establishing new kampungs and increasing the density of existing ones. Squatters were also seen to be a problem: by 1953 some three thousand illegal dwellings had been identified. About a third of them, located in new settlements on the site of former rubbish dumps, were given the legal status of kampungs and earmarked for kampung improvement (*SP,* 31/12/53). Police were called in to remove others, with temporary buildings being erected in the new fringe kampungs for those displaced (chap. 6). Such measures did not stem the tide of immigration. As the Communist Party (PKI) began to support the rights of squatters in sometimes violent demonstrations, the political cost of forced clearances eventually became too high.

EDUCATION

Education had been a prime concern of the nationalist movement in late-colonial times. A right of universal education was enshrined in the Constitution of 1945 and on Independence there was a clear goal of universal literacy. The expansion of formal education, however, was limited by public revenue and the lag involved in teacher training. Heavy emphasis was therefore placed on mass adult education to combat illiteracy in the villages and kampungs. This was a logical development of the former wild schools set up by nationalist organizations in the 1930s and drew on the enthusiasm and idealism of the time. The official ten-year Campaign against Illiteracy (Pemberantasan Buta Huruf, PBH) commenced early in 1951 and by the end of the following year had mobilized over seventeen thousand teachers across East Java with enrollment in the six-monthly courses of around six hundred thousand students (KP 1953, 693–95). Although pass rates were only around 20 percent, by 1958 over a tenth of the national population had gained certificates of literacy (BPS, SPI 1958).

Formal education involved more students than before the war but standards had fallen badly. The Japanese had quickly abolished all teaching in Dutch and moved to unify the two streams with a standard Indonesian- and Japanese-language curriculum (Frederick 1989, 105–7). Volksscholen, which had offered only three-year courses, were to be upgraded to a full six years. This reform improved the prospects of second-stream students but eroded the standard of the first stream, which hitherto had been pegged to equivalent levels in the Netherlands. There were simply not enough trained teachers to raise everyone to the higher standard—in 1951 almost one-third of the city's seventy-eight primary schools were still offering only a three-year curriculum (KP 1953, 698). Besides, few teachers from the Dutch-language stream were comfortable teaching in Indonesian, which was not a vernacular language in Surabaya, let alone in Japanese. Students also found it hard to adjust to the more regimented discipline and the greater emphasis on rote learning (Frederick 1989, 107). Apart from being the Japanese style, this probably also reflected a lack of acceptable textbooks. By 1950 there was a cohort of students whose proper education had been cut short by the war and another that had been educated entirely outside the Dutch system. The newest cohort of teachers was also less qualified than their elders. This was a poor base from which to launch a huge expansion of the primary education system. Besides the technical difficulty of setting standards, there was an ideological clash. Attempts to restore prewar standards for select schools were regarded as a product of colonial thinking. Revolutionary virtue involved bringing enlightenment to the masses. The outcome was a de facto dual system, in which all schools nominally followed the same curriculum but some schools adhered to a much higher standard than others. As a big city, Surabaya naturally attracted the better primary school teachers and remained one of the few centers of secondary education.

In the case of tertiary education, hitherto very circumscribed, a dramatic initiative was the realization in Surabaya of a full university. The significance of the event was underlined by its foundations on Heroes' Day (Hari Pahlawan), 10 November 1954, the annual commemoration of the Battle of Surabaya. Named Airlangga after an early warrior king of eastern Java, the university was constituted by the old medical and dental schools and the recently founded law school (1950). An economics faculty was added in 1961, and later those of pharmacy and veterinary science. At first there was no campus and faculties were scattered around the city wherever room could be found. In the early 1960s, the long-awaited main building was opened at Karang Menjangan, close to the medical faculty and the public hospital. What could not so readily be achieved was international standing. Universities were vulnerable to the decline in the standard of secondary teaching. Until the crisis of 1958, Dutch lecturers were employed and thereafter several English-speaking lecturers, but fewer and fewer students were any longer fluent in either language. In time low standards became entrenched, at Airlangga as elsewhere. By the mid-1960s Indonesia was all but isolated from the western world and it hardly seemed to matter. Only later did it become apparent that this was one of the most deplorable and intractable legacies of revolutionary nationalism. What had in the 1940s begun as Japanese xenophobia and democratic idealism for mass education ultimately cast a very long shadow, stunting the intellectual development of perhaps two generations of the nation's elite.

HOUSING

Independence began with an urban housing crisis. In Surabaya the destruction of whole residential districts during the fighting of November 1945 had made it all the more difficult to accommodate the explosion of population after the late 1940s (chaps. 2, 3). When the city reverted to Dutch administration during 1946, one of the priorities had been to regain control over the European housing stock. A housing office (Stichting Bevolkingshuisvesting) was set up to allocate and administer vacant houses, to which rights of occupancy were granted by way of a *vestiging besluit* (VB), later *surat izin penempatan* (SIP). Centralized allocation of housing and rent control was consistent with controls over most of the rest of the formal economy, including the distribution of food and clothing. After Independence, the housing office was taken over by the newly formed Department of Public Housing (Djawatan Perumahan Rakjat) of the central Ministry of Social Affairs. The Municipality protested such centralization, but without effect. A separate municipal housing office (Dinas Rumah) took over the housing stock of the former NV Volkshuisvesting (KMS, Dinas Tanah and Rumah, interview, 3/11/87).

Measures were also taken to boost the supply of urban public housing. In July 1950, Mayor Doel Arnowo introduced a monthly municipal lottery to generate revenues for kampung improvement and public housing, which enabled work to begin on twenty-five kampung houses at Tambaksari, in the northeast, to replace dwellings destroyed during the fighting (*NC,* 7/6/50, 29/7/50). By early 1952, when he completed his term of office, about seventy such houses had been built at Tambaksari and nearby Kampung Wonosari (*JP,* 17/1/52). At the same time it was estimated that twenty-five hundred houses were needed in Surabaya just for public servants (*pegawai negeri*) (*JP,* 17/3/52). Even with the lottery, the Municipality did not have the funds to tackle a housing crisis of this magnitude.

A socialist central government could hardly ignore this crisis. There were models in the interventionist housing programs of European governments busy with postwar reconstruction. In August 1950 the national government convened in Bandung a Healthy Public Housing Congress, which helped to redefine a role for the central government in the provision of public housing (Sardjono 1986). The resultant Department of Public Housing began activities in July 1951 and one of its first initiatives was to distribute grants to all kabupaten and municipalities (KP 1953, 581–3). Surabaya received a twenty-five-year loan of Rp 2.26 million, which was to be allocated to people whose houses had been damaged or destroyed during the fighting, or who owned land on which they wanted to build. The funds could also be used to build houses on municipal land. This ad hoc program achieved modest results, including some small-scale housing for its own employees at Tambaksari, for the Post Office Savings Bank at Karang Menjangan, and for several hundred harbor workers at Tanjung Perak (*SP,* 31/12/53). However, the first houses built in 1951/52 were criticized as being "mini villas," not cheap housing for the poor (KP 1953, 581). This contradiction was never resolved in subsequent programs.

In 1952 the central government sought to formalize the funding of housing by decreeing that each local government might set up a municipal Development Fund (Yayasan Kas Pembangunan, YKP). Organized as a savings cooperative, the YKP would issue home loans and administer repayments, which could then be recycled for new construction (Sardjono 1986). The concept seems to have originated with Sumitro Djojohadikusumo, who based it on the German Bausparkasse, with which he was familiar from his study in Europe; he adopted it when he became Minister for Trade and Industry.[13] As initial capital, Surabaya contributed the houses built under the original loan. In effect, the YKP took over the role of the prewar Public Housing Corporation (NV Volkshuisvesting). Given the flow of rural-urban migration (chap. 3), the rate of construction hardly made a dent in the overall housing shortage but it eased the housing crisis for an expanding government bureaucracy and the armed forces. For all intents it was public housing for public servants.

Meanwhile, the energetic new mayor, Moestadjab, had already taken his own initiative to begin rebuilding the city. Because municipal funds were minimal, he came to an agreement with the private contractor Ong Kie Tjay to set up the joint venture Opera (Oesaha Perumahan Rakyat, Public Housing Venture). Although as the name suggests the emphasis was to have been on public housing, this role was soon overtaken by the national strategy of the YKP. Accordingly the first big project with which Opera became associated was the construction of a row of shops and offices and what became the Olympic Hotel at the beginning of Darmo Boulevard (not far from what is now the Hyatt Hotel). Rumor has it that President Sukarno himself suggested the construction of a modern hotel where he could stay on his periodic visits to his home town. Although nowadays only the curious architectural feature of the glass tower and flagpole above the corner might attract a passing glance to the eastern side of the boulevard, when it opened in the mid-1950s the hotel would have commanded the entrance to Surabaya from the airport.

Since public housing and YKP funds were available only to public servants, the private sector had to cope with the housing shortage with its own resources. After Independence, the national housing office ceased to assist Dutch companies in the provision of rental housing, obliging them to buy their own land for new construction. The pressure increased in June 1953 when the Ministry of Social Affairs determined that public rental dwellings (*huurinstantiewoningen*) would revert to the government when vacated by existing tenants. Dutch companies would thereby lose their postwar entitlement to government-owned housing and be forced entirely into the open market. They had no choice but to build or lease company housing if they were to attract expatriate staff to work in Indonesia. Domestic firms also built their own housing complexes (*SP,* 22/9/53; *JP,* 15/7/55).

In 1958 the entire private Dutch housing stock, mainly in garden suburbs such as Darmo, also came under public control. Houses were seized along with business assets. Because the number of administered dwellings thereby increased so greatly, responsibility for housing was passed back to the provincial level. The provincial Housing (Affairs) Office (Kantor Urusan Perumahan) took over management of these houses on behalf of the Dutch Assets Control Committee (Panitia Pelaksanaan Penguasaan Hak Milik Belanda) of the Lands Department (Dinas Agraria). By way of rationalization, in 1963 the Department of Internal Affairs approved the local operations of the national housing office to be transferred to the Municipality, although it was another five years before the provincial government implemented the decision. These administrative changes nevertheless made little difference in the way the housing stock was administered.[14]

After the seizure of Dutch housing in 1958, the government dominated the market for bungalow-style housing in Surabaya. The significance of this controlled housing stock was not just its size but also its allocation. Since Independence, one of the fringe benefits of working at a low salary in the civil service has been the provision of good housing at a highly subsidized rent. This fringe benefit was particularly important for senior officials and officers in the armed forces who were posted to the local offices of central government departments on tours of duty. Under a 1987 decree, however, the local housing office (Dinas Perumahan Daerah) was gradually to contract to an information office as houses were gradually sold to the their existing occupants. In 1986 it was estimated that the city had about two hundred fifty thousand "permanent" houses, including better kampung housing, of which seventy thousand were still managed by the housing office (*SP,* 4/11/86). In the 1960s, before the resumption of new housing construction, the proportion would have been considerably higher.

Meanwhile, Indonesian firms, both private and public and including banks, factories, shipping companies, and the airline Garuda, had continued to build their own housing complexes for white-collar staff, partly as payment of wages in kind and partly as a means of exercising some control over their workforce. Because these new housing complexes were not always well served by public transport and only senior executives would enjoy access to a company vehicle, it became common for firms to arrange company transport for the journey to and from work, thereby maintaining some discipline over working hours. Clerical staff, cleaners, and drivers, however, as in the colonial period, continued to live mainly in the kampungs, in smaller and less permanent dwellings but with a high rate of home ownership. Aside from company housing, there was little interest in private real estate development. Official rent control and the problems of gaining title to land made such investment uneconomic.

GUIDED DEMOCRACY

These early initiatives—little more than emergency measures—were not followed through with more comprehensive programs that would have made up for the lost decade of the 1940s and begun to redress the gross inequities inherited from the colonial period. The problems were diagnosed, sensible proposals were brought forward, but the necessary resources were seldom made available to do anything. Across the various welfare sectors, the impression is of abundant good intentions but few results. Especially after President Sukarno's declaration in 1958 of Guided Democracy, the national government was too remote, too preoccupied with national and international politics, and ever more chronically short of funds, to do much that was constructive at a local level or indeed, as Abeyasekere (1987) suggests, even in Jakarta itself.

In Surabaya, the Municipality was well aware of the problems but its revenue was minimal. As immigrants continued to flock into an already overcrowded city, problems that in the early 1950s had been tackled with optimism began to seem intractable. Local government, which was becoming more politicized and less professional, gradually ceased to be a functional, goal-oriented bureaucracy. As at the provincial and national levels, the main achievement of the public sector was to reproduce itself. In a situation of accelerating inflation and a worsening housing shortage, public sector employment offered the security of wages in kind (rice and other basic commodities, transport, and housing) combined with opportunities for petty graft and the flexibility to engage in other employment for supplementary cash income. While failing to mobilize resources to rehabilitate and extend the city's decaying infrastructure, the bureaucracy nevertheless created an entirely artificial demand for its services, in terms of multiple permits and a multiplicity of signatures. Floating above all this, the elected Municipal Assembly acted out a burlesque of party politics, the vigor of the rhetoric being in inverse proportion to the capacity to achieve anything.

The New Order

In the late 1960s, when political and economic stability had been restored, the New Order government began to tackle the massive problems of public health and education. Some of the first initiatives were taken at a local level. Cooperation in the Master Plan Project between the Surabaya Institute of Technology (ITS) and the Municipality also gave rise in 1969 to a pilot kampung improvement scheme (later known as the W. R. Supratman Project), whereby the municipal government donated materials in kind, such as concrete blocks, to communities willing to build or repair drains and paths. The desperate lack of funds precluded any major programs. Even the provincial government had few independent sources of revenue. The history of local welfare measures is therefore very much that of central government programs. Within the framework of five-year plans, priorities and guidelines were set in Jakarta and funds were provided to provincial and local government to meet targets. Local initiative was restricted to adaptation of programs and choice of locations. Not until the 1980s did local government begin implementing public health programs in its own right. This initiative owed much to the appointment in 1984 of a new mayor, Dr. Poernomo Kasidi, a former army doctor with a strong personal commitment to public health. The rest of this chapter will examine the evolution under the New Order of programs in the fields of education, public health, kampung improvement, and housing, with attention to some of the similarities with and differences from policies of the colonial era.

EDUCATION

One of the most impressive achievements of the New Order was realization of the national goal of universal primary school education. In 1969, at the outset of the First Five-Year Development Plan (Repelita I), national primary school enrollments were about two-thirds that of the seven-to-twelve age group (DOI 1969, 2c/16). For Surabaya, ten new primary schools were to be constructed in this first year, 1969–70 (*Kompas,* 1/4/70). During the 1970s construction of new primary schools and teacher training became priorities in the disbursement of oil tax revenues, so that by the mid-1980s primary school enrollments had reached almost 95 percent of that age group (Jones 1994, 163). In Surabaya, the number of children attending primary school increased from over two hundred thousand in 1973 to a peak of almost three hundred thousand in the mid-1980s, translating into an enrollment rate of just over 90 percent among the seven-to-twelve age group—even higher if Islamic primary schools (*madrasah ibtidaiyah*) were included (table 4.4). Thereafter smaller family size led to gradual decline in numbers, though not enrollment rates.

Rapid expansion of primary education soon generated demand for more places in secondary education, which hitherto had been very restricted. Nationally the percentage completing senior high school rose from 11 percent for males (5 percent for females) in 1971 to 35 percent (26 percent) in 1990 (Jones 1994, 163). In Surabaya enrollments in both junior and senior high school soared from almost 70,000 in 1974 to 242,000 in 1998/99 (table 4.4). The large majority of primary school students now continue their education. The participation rate was much higher than the national average, reflecting both Surabaya's early lead in secondary education and the logic of continuing to centralize large high schools in urban centers.

In secondary education, the government played a much less direct role. Whereas primary schooling was dominated by state schools, with two-thirds of all pupils, the rapid expansion of secondary schooling was led by the private sector. Well-established government schools continued to enjoy high status and entry was fiercely competitive, but by 1998–99 just over one-third of junior high and only one-quarter of senior high students were in government schools (table 4.5). The role of government was to monitor standards rather than to invest directly in services. Nevertheless, schools that were organized on a nonprofit basis and met specified standards became eligible for state subsidies, including payment of teachers' salaries. Only part of costs needed therefore to be covered by the levy of fees and community contributions, which was consistent with the mix of private and social benefits that flow from advanced education. This policy approach was similar to that of the colonial period, the original subsidy ordinance dating from 1895 (Penders 1968b, 29).

TABLE 4.4
Enrollment by level of education, Surabaya

Level	1974	%	1984–85	%	1993–94	%	1998–99	%
Primary	223,702	77	295,700	58	270,800	56	224,300	48
Lower secondary	44,049	15	126,400	25	116,400	24	115,700	25
Upper secondary	24,467	8	88,400	17	94,900	20	126,300	27
Total	292,218	100	510,500	100	482,100	100	466,300	100

Sources: KMS, Statistik Kodya Surabaya 1978; KMS, SDA (annual).

TABLE 4.5
Enrollment by type of school, Surabaya, 1998–99 (%)

Level	Government	Private	Total
Primary	66	34	100
Lower secondary	37	63	100
Upper secondary	25	75	100

Source: KMS, SDA 1998.

TABLE 4.6
Enrollment in tertiary education, Surabaya, 1995–96

University	Number of Students
Airlangga	14,334
Institut Teknologi Surabaya	9,430
IKIP (Teachers' College)	8,422
IAIN Sunan Ampel (Islamic)	5,064
Open University	20,156
All public universities	57,406
All private universities	104,141
All universities	161,547
Institutes, colleges, academies	41,270
Total	202,817

Source: KMS, SDA 1995

Increasing retention rate in secondary education led in turn to a demand for more places in tertiary education. Here again the government relied mainly on the private sector. Established government tertiary institutions such as Airlangga University, Surabaya Institute of Technology, and the Teachers' College (Institut Keguruan dan Ilmu Pendidikan, IKIP) saw a modest expansion, supplemented by foundation of the Open University. Otherwise the government left the expansion of tertiary education to the private sector. By 1993, Surabaya boasted no fewer than twenty-three private universities with some seventeen thousand enrolled students (KMS, SDA 1993) (table 4.6). Some of these universities, such as

Widya Mandala (Catholic) and Petra (Protestant), were founded during the Old Order, but until the 1980s private universities had an inferior reputation. This was less a matter of quality of teaching than of status, for many lecturers were hired after hours from state institutions. However, the increasing demand for tertiary education and competition between campuses has led to a steady improvement in both the quality of private universities and the status of their degrees, to the point where private firms are now preferring to employ graduates from private universities. Airlangga and ITS continued to enjoy prestige and to command high entry premiums but are more oriented toward public sector employment and the professions.

For Surabaya this rapid expansion of secondary and tertiary education had two notable consequences. First, especially in tertiary education, Surabaya has reinforced its role as the main educational center in East Java, drawing students not just from the rest of the province but also from parts of the Outer Islands, where there are fewer tertiary institutions and standards tend to be lower. Education is therefore an important part of the economic base. In 1993 about thirty thousand teachers were employed in primary and secondary education and another seventy-five hundred to ten thousand in the tertiary sector, depending on the extent of double counting (KMS, SDA 1993). According to a different set of figures, about 40 percent of all central government civil servants in Surabaya were employed in the Department of Education and most of these would have been teachers.

The second consequence was the unemployment of graduates from secondary and tertiary education. Although Surabaya offered more white-collar jobs than elsewhere in the province, it also had an abundance of people seeking those jobs. Unsuccessful job seekers were reluctant to return to their towns or villages to take lower-status jobs, and their numbers were swelled by frustrated secondary graduates from rural areas. By the mid-1980s it was therefore becoming common for secondary school graduates, who a decade or so earlier would have been assured of a white-collar job, to have to find work in the informal sector, especially driving public transport vehicles, selling goods, manning photocopy kiosks, and engaging in jobs that were on the margins of the law. The same situation applied to other main cities of Indonesia and was the modern equivalent of the colonial government's intellectual proletariat.

PUBLIC HEALTH

In a city located in such an unhealthy location and with overburdened infrastructure, widespread poverty, and much low-grade housing, public health continued to be a vital concern. As in the colonial period, control of dysentery and mosquito-borne diseases such as dengue fever,[15] which can be traced back to problems of water supply, drainage, and garbage disposal, required heavy investment in public works. Provision of hospitals and supervision of prostitution are also traditional public health policies. However, the New Order government went much further, by giving high priority to development of a national network of clinic-based health services, including family planning. In rural areas, community health centers (Pusat Kesehatan Masyarakat, Puskesmas) for the first time made available personalized health services; in urban areas like Surabaya these clinics have improved the coverage of health services and brought them within the range of poorer kampung dwellers, who previously relied on traditional medicine.

Water Supply

With demand growing at around 8 percent per annum (*SP,* 15/7/95), the shortage of clean water has remained an intractable problem. The reticulated supply is now drawn almost entirely from the heavily polluted Surabaya River.[16] Three water purification plants at Ngagel and the new plant upstream at Karang Pilang (opened in 1989) remove impurities by the addition of calcium chloride and aluminum sulfate to the point where the water, after boiling, is meant to be safe for drinking. However, because the pipes that reticulate the water are so old and leak so badly, and because, as explained above, sewage is disposed of into septic tanks, the water becomes contaminated the before it reaches the consumer.[17] The cost of installing a reticulated sewerage and treatment system is now exorbitant. In consequence, the drinking water supply is permanently contaminated and dysentery is endemic. Inadequate boiling of drinking water or use of unboiled water for washing food can cause outbreaks of infection. Use of contaminated well water for bathing and laundry is another source of infection. Outbreaks become more serious in the dry season, because there is no flushing of groundwater, and peak at the end of the dry season. Though rarely fatal to adults, the disease results in considerable mortality among infants.

In the 1980s industry emerged as another source of drinking-water pollution. Attracted by the advantages of cheap land outside the city, good road access, and ready waste disposal, factories had located along both banks of the Surabaya River. An environmental audit in 1985 determined that 80 percent of the pollution load was of industrial origin and identified forty factories as likely to be causing serious industrial pollution along the forty kilometers from Mojokerto downstream to Surabaya (Encona 1985, 1986). As early as 1977 the governor of East Java had issued a decree requiring all factories along the Brantas River to install waste treatment plants but the decree was not enforced. During the dry season of 1982 there was a marked deterioration in water quality. Despite a trial flush of the Surabaya River, the problem recurred in subsequent dry seasons and was clearly traced to worsening industrial pollution and, to a lesser extent, to household organic wastes. By the end of the dry season, even after purification, the water was again turbid, yellowish, and gave off a noticeable odor. People also complained of itchy skin after washing. To allay public disquiet, in 1986 the provincial government set up an anti-pollution team under the deputy governor and secured agreement from the worst polluters to install treatment plants (*JP*, 12/11/87). Reinforcing provincial decrees on water quality, in May 1989 the central government's Clean Rivers (Prokasih) Program was proclaimed in East Java (*SP,* 21/10/89; Koffel 1994).

Yet for all this bureaucratic activity, at the end of 1994 it had to be admitted that almost nothing had changed (*SP,* 28/12/94). The worst industrial polluters identified in the mid-1980s had still not installed the required waste treatment plants, nor had they yet been charged for any offenses, though a couple of attempts at legal action had failed on legal technicalities (Koffel 1994). Despite periodic flushing of the Surabaya River, water quality had worsened to the point where it was declared by one expert as unfit to drink even after purification (*SP,* 4/10/95). In response to media demands for stern action against polluters, in April 1995 the Indonesia Environment Lobby (Wahana Lingkungan Hidup Indonesia, Walhi) took unsuccessful legal action against three paper companies identified as the most serious polluters (*SP,* 11/4/95, 9/5/98). Meanwhile the assistant governor, Masdoeki, maintained psychological pressure against the offending factories and backed the formation of a provincial-level Environmental Impact Control Board (Badan Pengendali Dampak Lingkungan, Bapedal) in accordance with Presidential Authority (Keppres) no. 7 of 1994 (*SP,* 17/10/95). The power of the provincial government to impose sanctions nevertheless remained extremely weak, especially against large corporations with good political connections in Jakarta (Koffel 1994). Here, as in colonial times, was exposed the difference between the central government's rhetoric of decentralization and its failure to delegate to local government the financial and legal powers to deal with matters of urgent local concern.

Drainage and Flood Control

Despite a degree of fatalism about the city's rundown infrastructure, Surabayans never ceased to demand a solution to the perennial problem of flooding. Each year around January roads would become impassable, houses would be flooded, and everyone would fret at the disruption to their daily lives and curse the government for its inaction. The root of the problem was the siltation of the canal system designed by the Dutch to drain the low-lying city. The big Morokrembangan flood basin had become so shallow as to no longer function. The Kali Mas, which before the war had been a wide river negotiable by laden prahus, was barely half its official width and so shallow that it could be waded across at low tide (compare figs 4.8, 4.9). Around Simpang and Kayun the banks had been turned into rice fields and vegetable gardens. In the heart of the business district, at the Red Bridge, squatters had built shacks and were actually growing maize and cassava (fig. 4.9). From there to Wonokromo the river was lined with illegal extensions and squatter shacks, all of whose families threw their garbage into the river. Drains leading into the canals were blocked. The pumps meant to raise storm water from low-lying areas had long since broken down. The once elaborate flood control system had thus long since ceased to function.

Figure 4.8. Busy river traffic on the Kali Mas, ca. 1907. From author's collection.

Figure 4.9. Siltation and farming: the Kali Mas at Jembatan Merah, 1974. Photo by author.

In 1975, at the outset of the Second Five-Year Plan, the central government finally responded to the flood problem by setting up the Lower Brantas Project (Proyek Brantas Hilir). This major public works scheme, which in Surabaya primarily involved dredging the ten kilometers of the Kali Mas, from the Brantas River at Wonokromo to its mouth at Madura Strait, was to be funded primarily by a Japanese aid loan of $4.5 million, supplemented by rupiah funds through the Development Budget (*Kompas,* 27/3/76). However, before work could begin on dredging the river, buildings had first to be cleared from its banks. This proved to be a protracted process (chap. 6). In March 1976 the project began dredging in a middle section of the river around Kayun, where there were few riverbank inhabitants. During the year clearance of the riverbanks began at Wonokromo and proceeded northward. As the banks were cleared, the river was dredged back to the long-buried brick retaining walls constructed by the Dutch; behind them the spoil was dumped to form levees, parts of which were landscaped. As late as 1984 there were still disputes with businessmen over the release of land along Jalan Karet in the central business district but the project terminated about 1986 with the completion of new stone retaining walls. The improvement in flood control and sanitation was marked, though maintenance dredging was still required, as were controls against the reinfiltration of squatters.[18]

As the Kali Mas works neared completion, a similar project was begun to rehabilitate the Kali Pegirian, which branches from the Kali Mas in the middle of the city at Undaan and then follows a parallel course to its mouth at Semampir, just to the east of the former naval base. The Kali Pegirian was also built out with squatter shacks and illegal extensions but even more narrow and shallow. World Bank funds were made available for the public works but the Municipality had to fund compensation of displaced riverbank dwellers. In 1984 both banks of the river were cleared simultaneously from Undaan to Semampir (chap. 6), which enabled work to proceed expeditiously and be completed by 1987, except for construction of the retaining wall at Semampir.

Nevertheless, the Municipality could not rest on its laurels. Without dredging, the Kali Mas was estimated to shallow by more than a meter per year through siltation and accumulation of rubbish (*SP,* 18/11/86). If there were not frequent police raids, squatters reoccupied riverbanks (fig. 1.13). In the dry season water hyacinth clogged minor canals and accelerated siltation. All these problems were exemplified by the perpetual crisis of the crucial Morokrembangan flood basin: dredging began in 1976 and was completed in August 1985 yet barely a year later it was again shallow and clogged by water hyacinth; almost a thousand squatter huts had been cleared in 1979–80 but were rapidly reappearing (*SP,* 7/11/86).

Flood control was complicated by the southward spread of the city: canals such as Banyu Urip, Gubeng, and Kalibokor that were designed to bring irrigation water to the rice fields were higher than the surrounding land and therefore unsuitable for drainage (*SP,* 8/10/87). Moreover, as irrigation canals they came under the jurisdiction of the provincial government, whereas the main drainage channels, including the Kali Mas and Pegirian, were the responsibility of the central government's Department of Public

Works (*SP,* 7/2/95). Although the Municipality drew on central government and World Bank funds to maintain and upgrade the expanding urban network of gutters and drains, the return was modest because in many areas there was still no drainage system that could actually carry away the floodwaters. And new housing projects, which increased the rate of runoff, had been allowed to be built to the south and west without main drainage channels to connect with flood control systems (*SP,* 17/11/95).

Despite considerable efforts at rehabilitation, the flood problem had therefore spread over a wider area. In May 2000 discussions over a drainage master plan reported that 15 percent of the municipality was affected by wet-season flooding (*SP,* 15/5/00). When the rains came early in November 1997, there ensued a general fourteen-hour electricity blackout (*Kompas,* 25/11/97). The local press pointed out that in some flood-prone area residents had given up waiting for government action and taken their own initiative to raise the floor level of their houses (*SP,* 17/11/95). They have also raised the level of roadways and pathways. And this has some logic. In view of the high infrastructure costs involved in providing a functional drainage system over a low-lying urban area of ever-increasing size, it may actually be cheaper to modify the design of housing. The more intractable problem is to modify the design of cars and roadways. One way or another, this tax must be paid if the city is to survive in its awkward location.

Garbage Disposal

An important aspect of flood control, as well as an issue of public health in its own right, garbage disposal is one of the mundane but essential tasks of local government. Public garbage collection was carefully organized in the colonial period but after Independence became haphazard. One of the initiatives of mayor Poernomo Kasidi (1984–94), formerly an army medical officer, was involvement in the Clean City (Kota Adipura) campaign. An annual competition, instituted in 1986 by President Soeharto, gave the Municipality an incentive to improve the state of public sanitation. Criteria for the award were public participation, project management, public health, and physical conditions (*SP,* 7/6/95). A separate Sanitary Department had been set up in 1984 to organize garbage disposal and cleaning of markets, streets, parks, and drains, but the results had been disappointing. In mid-1987 the mayor appointed a new head, who applied some lateral thinking. Since there was little scope to expand the budget, the neighborhood community was made responsible for collecting its own garbage and delivering it to the adjacent council depot, from where council trucks would take it to the landfill site. A levy was imposed on each household, Rp 1,000 per month for better-off households and Rp 500 for kampung households, to finance purchase of rubbish carts and the wages of a small army of some ten thousand local rubbish collectors and street sweepers, known after the color of their uniform as the Yellow Force (Pasukan Kuning). As part of their increased status, members of the Yellow Force were also given bylaw powers to fine people for littering offenses. As its contribution, the Municipality increased the workforce of street sweepers from 400 to 650. It worked. Surabaya won Clean City awards every year from 1988 to 1995, including gold awards in 1992, 1993, and 1995 (*SP,* 7/6/95). Along the way, the city gained a new sense of civic pride and, across the country, a much more positive image (Silas 1996; E. Indrayana, interview, 14/11/87).

Clinical Health Services

The New Order government took over the system of polyclinics and sought to bring as many public health services as possible together in a polyclinic staffed by a medical team under the direction of a qualified doctor. These community health clinics (Puskesmas) combined existing mother and child health clinics (BKIA) with an out-patient clinic, dentistry, family planning services, health education, and other preventive and curative services (Hugo et al. 1987, 110). Although the program was conceived primarily to meet the health needs of people in rural areas, who had no access to hospital services, much the same concept was applied to cities such as Surabaya. The number of Puskesmas clinics in the municipality increased from 27 in 1984 to 48 in 1995, besides which there were 57 subsidiary clinics; these were staffed by 99 doctors, 68 dentists, 169 midwives, and 145 nurses and in 1995 recorded 2.1 million visits, plus another 2.2 million visits to child health centers (KMS, SDA 1984, 1995). These clinics have filled the huge gap between the overcrowded emergency rooms of public hospitals and the fee-charging, after-hours services of doctors and dentists, who typically work in the public health system during the day and operate private practice at home in the evening (usually between 5 and 7 P.M.).

Another specific form of clinic was the family planning clinic, of which Surabaya had 147 by 1995 (KMS, SDA 1995). After two decades in which governments had consistently refused official support to family planning initiatives, in 1970 the New Order government embraced a national family planning program with the establishment by presidential decree of the National Family Planning Coordinating Board (BKKBN) (Hugo et al. 1987, 140–42). The decision was made to provide services through clinics by full-time professional staff. On grounds of economy, existing Department of Health clinics were used at first, but later specialist family planning clinics were set up. In Surabaya, as in East Java generally, the family planning has had a dramatic impact on birth rates and family size (Hull 1993).

The hospital system also expanded. In the 1950s there had still been only the one public hospital plus a new naval hospital at Wonokromo; by 1995 there were twenty-three general hospitals with forty-six hundred beds (KMS, SDA 1995). Of these, four were public, eight military, and eleven private. There was increasing differentiation between the very basic subsidized care that is available to ordinary people in public wards and the technologically sophisticated services for those who can afford to pay. With the expansion of niche private hospitals for the well-to-do, a selling point for luxury housing projects, the rich had less need to travel overseas or to Jakarta for such specialist services such as heart or cancer treatment. Kampung dwellers, however, often could not afford prescribed treatment, the high price of pharmaceuticals giving rise to agonizing decisions. Increasingly the issue was not the availability but the cost of health care. The two-tier system of public and private health care began to look more and more like the dualistic colonial health system.

Prostitution and Venereal Disease

In view of the continuing high incidence of venereal disease, one of the first decisions taken after Independence was to build a Venereal Diseases Research Institute and Hospital (Institut Penyelidikan dan Pemberantasan Penyakit Kelamin). The foundation stone was laid by the health minister in November 1951 and the official opening took place in August 1953 (KP 1953, 611–3; *SP,* 28/8/53). With medical expertise, proper diagnosis, and the availability of penicillin, the means were now at hand greatly to reduce the incidence of venereal disease. To facilitate medical supervision, the government reverted to the nineteenth-century policy of allowing brothels in specific localities (*lokalisasi*). By November 1958 almost forty-five hundred prostitutes (and about seven hundred pimps) were registered with the police (*SP,* 5/11/58). Brothel kampungs were located on the periphery and physical conditions were often primitive. Press reports in 1958 gave some insight into conditions in the main kampung of Bangunrejo, a squatter settlement in the southeast of the Morokrembangan flood basin. There were some six hundred houses, almost half of which served as rooms for a small army of almost two thousand registered prostitutes, most from the poor southern districts of East Java. Reminiscent of the nineteenth-century brothel kampung of Bandaran, Bangunrejo had access to neither drinking water nor electricity and had the highest incidence of malaria of any kampung in the city, all in all a less than ideal nocturnal rendezvous (*SP,* 28/1/56, 14/6/58, 5/11/58). Medical supervision was lax. In mid-1958 about 85 percent of registered prostitutes were infected. The response was a one-week emergency campaign to treat the city's 4,242 registered prostitutes with penicillin (SP 9/6, 18/6/58).

In the 1960s and 1970s more salubrious brothel kampung were granted status under the localization policy, the best-known being the almost respectable Dolly/Jarak complex in what had been the very poor hillside kampung of Dukuh Kupang among the graveyards behind the Banyu Urip canal. Sulistyaningsih and Swasono (1993; cited in Hull, Sulistyaningsih, and Jones 1998, 68–77) estimated the complex to employ around twenty-five hundred women, most under thirty years of age and recent immigrants from rural villages. By the standards of unskilled women, they enjoyed high earnings. In 1993 it was estimated that almost fifteen hundred prostitutes in and around Dolly generated an income of at least Rp 3.6 billion ($1.5 million) per annum and provided direct and indirect employment for many thousands more as pimps, housekeepers, bartenders and bar girls, staff in shops, pharmacies, and cinemas, stallholders, parking attendants, and so forth (*SP,* 8/5/95).

The Indonesian government has been no more successful than the Dutch in controlling the illegal fringe of prostitution. In 1958 it was estimated that there were almost as many unregistered as registered prostitutes (*SP,* 5/11/58). Despite growth of the city, the number of registered prostitutes barely changed between 1958 and 1993, suggesting a proliferation of unregistered sex workers. Hull, Sulistyaningsih, and Jones (1998, 69) estimated a total of at least 10,000 workers, made up of 7,500 in brothels, 1,000 in nightclubs, 400 in massage parlors, 450 call girls, and an indeterminate number of streetwalkers. The last category is of lowest status. Known as "night butterflies" (*kupu-kupu malam*), they are visible of necessity but mobile enough to flee occasional police raids. The cheapest offer their services to the city's floating population of poor single men en plein air in the night's dark places, such as graveyards and riverbanks, where no overhead is incurred; the more respectable take their clients to rented rooms in poor kampungs. Nightclubs and steambaths had been closed down as immoral in the early 1970s, giving rise to clandestine activity in beauty salons, massage parlors, and unlicensed brothels, while call girls operated discreetly through hotels, often entertaining out-of-town visitors. With more knowledge of the trade than most clients, taxi and becak drivers willingly procured as a sideline. Rising disposable incomes led to the opening of many new bars and restaurants, the growing popularity of discotheques, especially among middle-class youth, a boom in construction of luxury hotels, and a new wave of nightclubs.

Proliferation of the commercial sex industry made proper medical supervision all but impossible. The initiatives of the 1950s had brought the then most dangerous sexually transmitted disease, syphilis, under control, even if gonorrhea remained virulent because of the unevenness of treatment and the emergence of resistant strains. However, the new epidemic of AIDS was as fatal as syphilis and incurable. Medical logic demanded urgent intervention to minimize its spread but, despite evidence of increasing incidence among sex workers, official policy remained insouciant. A pretense of police control was no more than petty harassment to extract pocket money. Much of the initiative in public education, especially among young people, was taken by nongovernmental organizations.

MARKETS

Although the system of market administration has changed little since Dutch times, policy has swung from strict regulation to virtual laissez-faire and back again. With regard to administration, the Pasarbedrijf was Indonesianized into PD Pasar [Perusahaan Dareah, regional government enterprise] but its functions remained the same. New buildings were constructed to replace those damaged during the Battle of Surabaya: Wonokromo in 1950,

Keputran in 1952, Turi in 1953, and (New) Wonokromo in 1958. New markets were established in newly settled fringe areas. The main difference from the colonial period was that market bylaws were now barely enforced. Hygiene control all but lapsed, rubbish collection became erratic, squatters built shacks around the perimeter of markets, and traders set up illegal stalls outside in parking lots and side streets. Apart from occasional police raids, street sellers were allowed to do business more or less where they pleased, winning the battle with authority by sheer weight of numbers. This collapse of regulatory control, also observed in the intrusion of squatter housing and the explosion in the number of becak, was part of a general trend in the 1960s toward a triumph of the informal sector.

Early in the New Order the pendulum began to swing back toward regulation, though less dramatically in Surabaya than in Jakarta under reformist mayor Ali Sadikin (1966–77) (Abeyasekere 1987). One trend was toward multistory markets, with the subsidiary aim of reducing the number of street sellers. The wholesale center of Pasar Turi was the first in Surabaya, opening in mid-1968 (*SP,* 24/8/68). It burned down almost immediately and in 1970 was rebuilt as a three-story structure with around three thousand stalls (*Kompas,* 1/4/70).[19] Pasar Atom, on the edge of the Chinese business district, was similarly rebuilt. These two very large markets both came under provincial government control. PD Pasar, however, continued to be held back by an acute lack of capital until 1974 under the Second Five-Year Plan. Central government grants for local infrastructure (Inpres, Instruksi Presiden) were then earmarked inter alia for improvement of local markets (Wit 1973). These annual grants allowed gradual rehabilitation and modernization of the entire market infrastructure, much of which still dated from the colonial period. In a few cases, such as Pasar Genteng and Pasar Tunjungan, private investors funded the redevelopment (PD Pasar, interview, 11/87). The number of markets and licensed traders remained fairly static despite the growth of population. In the mid-1980s PD Pasar counted around thirty thousand market traders, which may be compared with an estimated forty-five to sixty thousand street sellers (KMS, SDA annual; Bijlmer 1987, 178).

Surabaya's administration was more cautious than Jakarta's in moving against street traders. Around the mid-1970s, street traders began to be cleared away from the main arterial roads, the so-called *jalan protokol.* This measure accompanied the banning of becak from these roads and the extension of one-way traffic flow. Unlike in Jakarta, however, traders were not pushed out of the central city. As in the case of becak drivers, they were recognized as having some right to a livelihood, provided they did not intrude onto the main roads or otherwise disrupt the smooth flow of traffic. If they did intrude illegally, they risked being arrested by the police and losing their cart with all its stock. Places were designated where street traders could set up their carts, especially at night. In the 1990s there has been some success along Malaysian lines with open-air markets for cheap hawker food. How such measures affected the number as opposed to the spatial distribution of street sellers is unknown.

Despite the apparent continuities, the long-run trend has been toward the marginalization of official markets. While markets still fill an important niche in the urban economy, the lack of growth in trader numbers at a time of rapid growth in real income per capita shows that the expansion of wholesale and retail trade has been in other directions, notably toward supermarkets and shopping plazas, which have the advantages of comfort and fixed prices (see also chap. 6). Middle-class people no longer shop in traditional markets, which are regarded disdainfully as hot, dirty, unsafe, and socially disreputable. A popular recreation even of poor people is to go window-shopping in the new air-conditioned shopping palaces, which also feature numerous cheap eating places, cinemas, and children's game parlors. These new complexes are privately owned and managed. Government still sets the regulations and collects its taxes but it is no longer the entrepreneur. The continued public administration of traditional markets is the heritage of another era.

In the early years of the New Order, construction of public housing all but ceased. The central government had provided no more funds after 1962. Repayments on existing mortgages had enabled the municipal Development Fund (YKP) to maintain construction, so that by the end of 1965 it had completed just over a thousand bungalows and a number of small houses (KMS, YKP 1983). However, its capital base was destroyed in 1966 by introduction of the new rupiah at one-thousandth of the former value. Remaining funds were used to pay off the original central government loan, now much devalued by inflation, but that left almost nothing for new construction. To restore the YKP's financial base, in 1969 the municipal government appointed it to manage the lottery to finance the city's hosting of the Seventh National Sports Competition (PON VII) (YKP, interview, 21/11/87). With a commission of Rp 15 million, the YKP was able to increase construction from just fourteen units in 1970 to a total of twelve hundred units by 1976. An economic environment of low inflation enabled the YKP to be reestablished on a sound base as a kind of building society, whereby applicants could open savings accounts to accumulate a minimum qualifying deposit and establish creditworthiness for subsequent mortgage repayments. This was so successful that by 1996 the YKP had during the New Order built almost nine thousand houses with a combined land area of five hundred hectares (KMS, YKP 1996).

At the outset of the Second Five-Year Plan (Repelita II) in 1974, the central government also began to play a more active role in the provision of low-cost public housing. As part of a more systematic approach to equity, it reentered the housing market with the formation of the National Housing Corporation (Pembangunan Perumahan Nasional, Perumnas). Unlike the earlier ventures NV Volkshuisvesting and YKP, Perumnas was owned and managed entirely by the central government. Flush with oil tax revenues, the central government could now pursue its own priorities without reference to local governments. In Surabaya, Perumnas began construction around 1980 with a project of seventeen hundred single-room "core" units to house people displaced by the Lower Brantas scheme. Construction accelerated in the early 1980s with a much larger project to build almost seven thousand mainly low-cost units at Tandes in the northwest. By 1984, at the end of the Third Five-Year Plan, Perumnas had already completed almost ten thousand units, compared with just thirty-three hundred built by the municipal YKP between 1972 and 1984 (Perumnas, interview, 15/10/87; KMS ca. 1984a).

As the local economy began to strengthen in the early 1970s, private real estate ventures emerged to cater to the upper end of the market (chap. 6). Emergence of a private market for middle-class housing was facilitated by institutional reform. In 1974 the establishment of Perumnas had been accompanied by introduction of a Home Ownership Credit Scheme (Kredit Pemilikan Rumah) to provide mortgage finance for owner occupancy, using as a vehicle the National Savings Bank (Bank Tabungan Negara). With rapid growth in savings, demand for housing soon outran the modest capacity of Perumnas and the government realized that there was no need to retain a nexus with public sector construction, even for civil servants. In the late 1970s National Savings Bank financing also became available for homes built by the private sector, which soon came to assume the major share of its loans (Lewis 1993). Bungalow or villa housing for the middle class was taken over by the private sector. This marked a return to the situation in the colonial period, when housing for the Dutch community was for the most part built by the private sector under bank mortgages financed by private savings. Indeed, the 1980s was probably the first decade since the 1920s when the rate of private formal-sector housing construction exceeded that of public housing.

In this more dynamic housing market, the role of the public sector was redefined as the provision of low-cost housing. This comprised mostly small houses (*rumah sederhana,* RS) and very small houses (*rumah sangat sederhana,* RSS) which, to economize on the cost of land, were built in rows like tenements (fig. 4.10). Such

Figure 4.10. Low-cost housing (uncompleted), Driyorejo, 1999. Photo by author.

housing was at best only marginally profitable for the private sector. The Department of Housing sought to achieve a cross-subsidy by imposing on developers a requirement to build in the ratio of 1:3:6, which is to say for every "luxury" house, three "average" (*sedang*) and six "basic" (*sederhana*) houses. However, developers regarded such a mix as compromising the marketing and profitability of their middle-class and elite projects. One solution was to build low-cost housing elsewhere, on cheaper land. The other was to pay a fine to the Municipality—in 1995, Rp 1.6 million per unit in default—which enabled the Municipality to subsidize other private contractors to built low-cost projects (*SP,* 7/2/95). Nevertheless, by the mid-1990s the price of land within the municipality was so high that genuine low-cost housing was economic only across the border in adjacent kabupaten. Only residual projects were being completed in Surabaya, such as fifteen hundred very small houses at Benowo for the city's street sweepers and garbage collectors (*SP,* 4/5/95).

The largest public low-cost housing project was a "new town" development of one thousand hectares southeast of the municipality at Driyorejo. Planning began around 1980 but not until 1995 did building commence. By then there was a waiting list of thirty-two thousand applicants (*SP,* 6/11/95). For the six thousand units in the first stage of two hundred hectares, 75 percent were to be allocated to government employees, both civilian and military, 10 percent to kampung dwellers displaced by government projects, and 15 percent to others (*SP,* 14/6/95). The same proportions applied to a smaller complex of a thousand units on Madura (*SP,* 10/11/95). Thus, as ever, public housing was really housing for the public sector. The low salaries earned by civil servants restricted their access to the private housing market and the threat of losing public housing remained a powerful control over their loyalty. Ordinary people, by contrast, were discouraged by the relatively high cost, the standardized grid pattern of the project, and the lack of the many informal services that proliferate in the more spontaneous kampung.

The other growth area in public housing was high-rise flats for the poor, a segment not yet perceived as profitable by the private sector. In Jakarta, Perumnas had early in 1981 completed a large project of a thousand flats at Tanah Abang, a crowded market district in central Jakarta, followed by another large project just west of the main thoroughfare of Jalan Thamrin (Jellinek 1991). Hitherto the only flats in Surabaya for low-income families had been a small emergency project of 120 units in Urip Sumiharjo built in 1985 for the municipal Housing Office (Dinas Rumah) after the kampung had been destroyed by fire (KMS, Dinas Rumah, interview, 3/11/87). The first planned rehousing project was carried out in the late 1980s in the densely settled kampung of Dupak Bangunrejo. A survey in 1987–88 by the Institute of Technology had found almost eighteen hundred persons per hectare in very poor housing. Single-story wooden houses were subdivided into tiny compartments, each occupied by a family of four or five persons, in all perhaps more than twenty people per dwelling. In this case upgrading infrastructure through kampung improvement was thought unlikely to be of much benefit. The alternative was a slum clearance project to demolish the shacks and build multistory flats.

To initiate flat construction in Surabaya, the central government provided funds on a shared basis with the Municipality. The pilot project involved two three-story blocks of flats; each block comprised twenty-five nearly identical units with a single main room measuring about three by six meters with attached kitchen and bathroom. The 250 people who had occupied the seventeen former dwellings were to be rehoused at a monthly rent of Rp 2,500 per unit, the same as previously paid for a wooden compartment. With similar funding another four blocks (100 units) were completed in May 1990 to rehouse 366 people who had occupied forty former kampung houses (*SP,* 17/3/89, 6/7/89, 25/5/90). The apparent success of this project led to further schemes in the Dupak area and another large project to rehouse some three thousand people on almost two hectares at Sombo, the first stage of which was opened in December 1990 (*SP,* 19/12/90) (fig. 4.11).

Whether as claimed these schemes actually benefited kampung dwellers is a matter for research. Jellinek (1991) identifies the

Figure 4.11. Low-income flats, Sombo, 1995. Photo by author.

weaknesses of the Kebon Kacang rehousing project in Jakarta: the difficulty and cost of securing temporary accommodation between demolition and rehousing, the disruption to informal-sector employment, the proliferation of illegal levies by low-level government officials, and the difficulties of meeting fixed repayments on mortgages, water, and electricity from fluctuating incomes. The kampung ceased to exist as an urban community and the former kampung dwellers were dispersed. In Jakarta the people whose houses were demolished were not always the ones who secured the new flats and some of those who did were soon forced to sell and move to the city fringe. Incidental newspaper reports suggest that at least some of these problems had emerged in Surabaya (see *SP,* 5/12/91). On the other hand, the design of these flats appeared to be an improvement on early blocks in Jakarta and rents were set at a more affordable level, though the housing shortage made it impossible to prevent resale for windfall gain.

Within the bureaucracy the view gained strength that these model projects should be developed into a program of general slum clearance and flat rehousing, as in Singapore. In the 1990s the word *kumuh* (slum) became part of the discourse. From a bureaucratic and town-planning perspective such programs looked very attractive. Rehousing the poor met equity goals, gave the city a more modern appearance, and impressed foreign visitors. A further unspoken consideration was that such large projects would generate official and unofficial income for both bureaucrats and contractors.

The end of the New Order brought about a more critical view of public housing. Although low-cost housing did not suffer the same speculative collapse as the private real estate sector, there was still excess capacity. Of the approximately four thousand units completed in the Driyorejo new town project, only a few hundred were occupied (Silas 1999; my fieldwork, 24/7/99) (fig. 4.10). Even at discounted prices, they were still too expensive for ordinary people. The best prospect was sale to shrewd middle-class buyers, who could buy two adjacent dwellings, add another story, and convert them into a cheap but very acceptable villa. Thus even "low-cost" housing continued to be lower-middle-class housing. Bureaucratic inefficiencies and endemic corruption made it unlikely this would ever change. Reflecting on the experience of several decades, Surabaya architect and town planner Johan Silas (interview, 23/7/99) concluded that the best way to improve housing for the poor would be to give them title to small parcels of land and let them use their own ingenuity and resources to build appropriate housing.

KAMPUNG IMPROVEMENT

Kampung improvement was revived in 1969, on the initiative of the Municipality, to demonstrate that development was beginning to bring tangible benefits to ordinary people (Silas, interview, 3/10/87). Since the Municipality had such limited funds, this first scheme relied heavily on self-help, with the Municipality providing concrete slabs to be laid as paths and drains by voluntary labor. Although modest, this scheme known as the W. R. Supratman Project was significant politically because it marked a recognition by the Municipality, then drawing up an urban master plan, that the kampungs were not some temporary slum but a viable living environment with a great human potential for improvement. In 1973 the Faculty of Architecture at the Institute of Technology (ITS) put forward a model of the ideal kampung as a realistic goal of city planning. That led in 1974 to a pilot project of a more elaborate kampung improvement scheme. Adoption on any scale, however, awaited funding.

The key to extension of the kampung improvement scheme was the World Bank. In 1975, at the outset of the Second Five-Year Plan, the bank launched in Jakarta a pilot kampung improvement project, Urban I, which was grafted onto the city's own local scheme, the M. H. Thamrin Project, which had been introduced in 1969. Success of the World Bank's initial project led in 1977 to a better-funded project, Urban II (1976–79), which was extended to

Surabaya. With the funds available at 6 percent, repayable over twenty years, the Municipality was now able to move beyond self-help schemes to the provision of a range of public facilities: paths, drains, water hydrants, bathing, laundry and toilet blocks, health clinics, and primary schools. The Urban II project in Surabaya was not a copy of Jakarta's Urban I scheme. Officials had gained some experience from the W. R. Supratman Project, sought advice from the Institute of Technology, and were less authoritarian than in Jakarta, thereby avoiding some of the problems described by Jellinek (1991, 110–12). Because World Bank and rupiah development funds could not cover all kampungs, the W. R. Supratman Project was not entirely superseded.

The experience gained from the Urban II project led to further refinements. Under Urban III, which began in 1979 and was contemporary with the Third Five-Year Plan, supplementary schemes were introduced in the form of a Drainage Improvement Project (DRIP) to rehabilitate main drains and of a Solid Waste Improvement Project (SWIP) to provide trucks for garbage collection. Funds from provincial and municipal budgets were also used to fund the positions of 250 community health workers to staff new health clinics. Up to this point improvement was concentrated in better-established kampungs, which were densely populated. By the 1980s, however, urban sprawl had given rise to poorly serviced kampungs on the urban fringe. In 1984, at the start of the Urban V project but with bank officials turning a blind eye, the Municipality brought two fringe kampungs into the kampung improvement scheme. Two years later, when it had been demonstrated that it would be cheaper in the long run to provide kampung infrastructure before kampungs became densely settled, fringe kampungs were brought officially into the scheme.

Thus kampung improvement was gradually able to benefit a larger and larger proportion of the city's kampung population. At the same time, what had begun as a simple project to lay concrete paths and drains had come to focus on the provision of all forms of infrastructure needed to meet the basic needs of kampung dwellers.

Kampungs initially favored by the W. R. Supratman Project therefore needed further investment to bring them to the standard of other Urban III and Urban V kampungs. Not all this investment, however, depended on foreign involvement. Competitions across the whole city for the best-presented kampungs were an incentive for kampung leaders to call upon voluntary labor to upgrade kampungs even when public funds were not provided.

The modest public investment in kampung infrastructure was well and truly exceeded by the funds that kampung dwellers spent on their own dwellings. The returning inhabitants and new migrants who established themselves in Surabaya from 1946 onward built with whatever materials were cheap and at hand, typically woven bamboo matting (*atap*) nailed to wooden beams. During the 1970s households invested part of their rising real incomes in rebuilding, typically in brick, plaster, and whitewash and sometimes adding a second story as the only way of obtaining extra space—a similar process was observed in Jakarta (Jellinek 1991). As neighbors sought first to emulate and then to avoid the embarrassment of being seen still to be living in a shack, these small, piecemeal renovations gradually changed the appearance of entire kampungs. Even squatter settlements were gradually transformed into physically substantial communities. Formal kampung improvement, voluntary projects, and spontaneous private investment were thus part of a single process.

By the late 1980s, almost twenty years of kampung improvement and the sustained involvement of international agencies had therefore registered impressive gains. First, most kampungs had been "improved" to some extent, the upgrading of public facilities matching the increasing private investment in the kampung housing stock. Not only were the living standards of kampung dwellers greatly improved, as witnessed by the socioeconomic statistics quoted in chapter 3, but also kampungs gained recognition from government officials as respectable places to live, instead of being seen merely as slums. Second, whereas in 1969 the provision of infrastructure to kampungs had been seen as marginal to the main aims of government, by the late 1980s the principle had gained acceptance that the provision of infrastructure should be coordinated across the whole city, including kampungs. This changing perception among government officials coincided with a shift by international agencies back toward investment in urban infrastructure. The emphasis of the 1970s on investment in rural development seemed unsustainable in the light of rapid urbanization and the appalling living conditions of the mass of urban dwellers.

Whether kampungs will in fact survive in their present form is nevertheless still an open question. By the late 1980s the view had gained official acceptance that improvement of the poorest and most densely settled inner city communities would bring only marginal benefits. In Jakarta, where land prices were much higher, kampungs were rapidly being squeezed out of the inner city to make way for office blocks, shopping malls, and apartment towers. Driven by the private sector, the process involved outright clearance rather than rehousing. Having been paid their meager compensation, the former inhabitants were left to fend for themselves on the outskirts. In Surabaya so-called slum clearance was more incidental. The Kampung Improvement Program enjoyed broad support and seemed to give kampungs better prospects of surviving as independent communities. Nevertheless, by the mid-1990s, as inner city land became ever more valuable, there were signs of increasing pressure on those kampungs from opportunistic developers. Had the boom continued, it is likely that municipal officials would have given way to market forces and promoted rehousing schemes. Instead the sudden collapse of the land market in 1997 gave inner-city kampungs a new lease on life.

Conclusion

Despite conquest, revolution, domestic turmoil, and virtual civil war, the role of government has grown inexorably over the course of the twentieth century. This trend stands in marked contrast to the great fluctuations in the size of the economy and associated living standards. Nevertheless, the phenomenon has not been self-evident to those observing politics at the national level. The literature emphasizes the growing weakness of the central government between 1942 and the mid-1960s, while at the same time noting the explosion in the size of the bureaucracy. Partly it is a confusion of terminology. Feith (1967, 396–97) maintains that after the suspension of parliamentary democracy, the bureaucracy, intertwined with the armed forces and Sukarno's Nationalist Party (PNI), came to dominate the political arena. No longer, however, was the bureaucracy the instrument of a single will. Under the ideology of nationalism, the state had been infiltrated, fragmented, and exploited by popular interests (Anderson 1983). Scale translated not into power but into inertia. Policy was more rhetoric than substance, a moral claim rather than a performance objective. And yet, in the long run, that set of moral claims, emerging inchoately in the late-colonial period and crystallized by revolution, came to redefine the task of the state and the future role of government. If in the Sukarno era there was little progress beyond rhetoric, under the New Order much was at last achieved with the help of better resources.

The experience of Surabaya suggests a good deal of continuity between the welfare programs introduced by the late-colonial government and the more broadly based programs of the New Order. In the fields of public health, education, markets, kampung improvement, and public housing the colonial government laid the foundations for New Order programs. That is not to say that New Order programs replicated those of the colonial administration, although parallels can be identified. It is rather that the New Order commitment to development led it to identify a similar functional role for government, as opposed to the essentially political and symbolic orientation of the Old Order. Large cities give rise to functional demands that have to be met within technological and financial constraints. The number of polyclinics, the number of schools and the proportion of children enrolled in them, the rate of construction of public housing, the length of kampung guttering, and the cleanliness of city streets now became objective criteria by which to assess the performance of the various levels of government. Government encouraged such assessment by announcing goals and publishing a flood of statistics on their implementation.

The New Order state was nevertheless much more highly centralized than the late-colonial state. The elite of the colonial period, albeit Dutch, enjoyed a good deal of autonomy in local government through an elected council. Although the Gemeente had been heavily dependent on the central government for funding, local government was the one level of government at which elected representatives held decision-making, as opposed to merely advisory, powers. Local democracy was taken away by the Japanese, reinstated in the 1950s in the era of party politics, and again suppressed in the mid-1960s under martial law. Meanwhile the local revenue base had also atrophied. Power thus gravitated back to the center, where it had resided before the Decentralization Law of 1903. Decision making was again entirely bureaucratic. Local government was now much larger but its bureaucracy was still an organic part of the state bureaucracy.

Unlike Jakarta, which as the national capital enjoyed the status of a special province (Daerah Khusus Ibukota), the Municipality of Surabaya still belonged to the third tier of government. Although the second largest city in the country, its administrative status was that of any other rural district (kabupaten). The mayor was subordinate to both the provincial governor and the Department of Internal Affairs. The consequent lack of power and resources undoubtedly held back development of the city. For the crucial first decade of the New Order, Jakarta was fortunate to have both a dynamic mayor in Ali Sadikin (1966–77) and the benefit of the revenues he generated, not always by orthodox means (Abeyasekere 1987, 220). Meanwhile Surabaya languished. Some benefit may, however, have accrued to the province. Surabaya's lack of autonomy made it easier to spread the fruits of development across the rest of the province and thereby to avoid extreme concentration of economic activity and wealth (Dick, Fox, and Mackie 1993).

During the 1980s, local government became a more effective instrument. In Surabaya the origins of this new professionalism can be traced back to the work of the master plan team over the 1970s (chap. 6). The establishment nationally in 1979 of the second-level Regional Development Planning Boards, or Bappeda (Badan Perencanaan Pembangunan Daerah) gave form and legitimacy to local initiative (MacAndrews, Sibero, and Fisher 1982). With the appointment as mayor of Dr. Poernomo Kasidi in 1984, the city finally obtained a leader committed to practical improvements. The Kota Adipura campaign exemplified this functional orientation and professionalism, as well as sound strategic thinking. More generous central government subsidies plus a growth tax in the form of the revised Land and Buildings Tax (Pajak Bangunan dan Bumi) provided funds to support enlarged programs. Responsibility and funding between central and local government became somewhat more balanced.

As in the late-colonial period, however, the benefits and costs of intervention were very inequitably distributed. The New Order government paid much more attention than the former colonial government to raising popular welfare through programs of education, health, and housing. A disproportionate share of benefits still flowed to the middle class, but now the bulk of the population also enjoyed a dividend from rapid economic growth. According to statistics, kampung dwellers enjoyed much better access to education, health, and housing. The problem was that in practice they could afford only basic services. They could enjoy "free" public education if they could finance the unofficial costs and living expenses. They could attend clinics but not necessarily afford the medicines. Most "low-cost" public housing was beyond their means and in any case not suited to kampung communities. Moreover, the expanding market economy and associated state intervention generated powerful backwash effects, especially the suppression of informal-sector jobs and the restructuring of urban land use (chap. 6). While government ministers and officials spoke confidently of development and social indicators, the talk of the common people was more and more eloquent with frustration and anger over their marginalization. In a society dominated by money, the conspicuous consumption of the elite assaulted their dignity. These discourses belonged to different social and political worlds. With the downfall of Soeharto, the people's voices began once more to be heard in the corridors of power. At least for a while, even middle-class society was ashamed.

At the end of the twentieth century and from a functional instead of an ideological perspective, the relationship between the late-colonial and New Order states can be reinterpreted. This involves reassessment of both periods. According to conventional historiography, the Ethical Policy of 1901 was a turning point in colonial policy but subsequent budgetary stringency and political repression restricted policy and ultimately caused the high ideals themselves to be abandoned. The Indonesian Revolution thus became a moral imperative. This is a good story, but from a functional perspective it could be portrayed quite differently. By the interwar years the expanding colonial state was belatedly taking on the form and role of a modern state, thereby outgrowing itself. Because of self-imposed ethnic constraints, the late-colonial state could not buy off enough people to maintain control without repression, but in the 1930s mild repression was sufficient to achieve the purpose. Had the Japanese invasion not occurred, colonial rule would have survived at least into the 1950s. If the late-colonial period is dated from 1901, it actually lasted just a decade longer than the New Order.

When the colonial state of the interwar period is compared with the New Order of the 1980s and 1990s, intriguing similarities are revealed in the functional role of government and the class interests. From a moral perspective, this could be read as an indictment of New Order policy, which fell well below the high ideals of the Revolution, just as colonial policy fell short of its Ethical ideals. From a functional perspective, both states can be seen to be grappling with the complex technical and organizational demands of a modern society. Not surprisingly, this challenge first became apparent in the main cities, the frontiers of the modern world. Late-colonial European society was quite highly urbanized, even though the overall level of urbanization was very low. In the New Order period, with renewed economic growth and rapid urbanization, Indonesian society evolved toward the pattern set precociously by hothouse colonial urban society. The crucial difference was that power and wealth were no longer monopolized by one privileged ethnic group. In the 1930s the Municipality had responded to the needs of European middle-class society. By the 1990s that middle-class society was Indonesian, including Indonesian-Chinese. The Revolution and Independence had reallocated power within middle-class society but, not so obviously, had also changed the fundamental nature of the state itself.

Chapter 5

INDUSTRY

Surabaya has a long industrial history. Despite a widespread view that industrialization is a recent phenomenon in the Third World, after the mid-nineteenth century the technology of the Industrial Revolution was introduced quite rapidly to the main port cities of Asia. The question is why this early technology transfer failed to generate a cumulative process of industrialization. At the end of the nineteenth century, Surabaya ranked alongside Calcutta, Singapore, Hong Kong, and Shanghai in the application of steam power to modern industry. Surabaya was the workshop of the Netherlands Indies with a heavy industry base supporting sugar milling, railways, and shipping. There was also a limited range of consumer goods industries serving mainly the small European community. Had the colonial government been committed to industrial development, this would have been a good starting point for industrialization. However, government saw industry as merely ancillary—to support the plantation economy and communications and to provide the few consumer necessities that were either too perishable (bread, ice, ice cream) or too bulky (tiles, bricks) to be shipped from the Netherlands. All other goods could be imported. Isolation during World War I led to a brief spurt of industrial expansion but no effort was made to sustain it. Not until the

1930s was there a change of policy, when the emergency of the Depression and the threat from cheap Japanese manufactures led to a new regime of protectionism. For the first time the colonial government actively sought to stimulate industrial development and with some success.

From the outbreak of the Pacific War to the early years of the New Order, governments maintained a policy of industrial development but without the resources to give it substance. The boom of 1939–41 ended abruptly with the Japanese occupation and the turmoil of revolution. After Independence, the new Indonesian government embraced the goal of industrialization but despite various pilot industrial projects could neither mobilize sufficient public investment nor sustain a stable economic environment conducive to private investment. What development did occur was heavily biased toward Jakarta, which since the 1930s had taken over industrial leadership. In Surabaya, industrial expansion was not renewed until the mid-1970s, at first by import substitution. After the mid-1980s the non-oil export drive greatly widened the market and appeared at last to have generated a self-sustaining process of industrialization. Surabaya's export base consists no longer of agricultural products but of manufactures (chap. 7). What is surprising about Surabaya's emergence as an industrial center is not that it occurred but that it took so long.

This chapter is partly chronological and partly thematic. The chronological narrative begins with an extended account of the city's early industrialization up to the 1930s and seeks to identify the stimuli to and constraints upon industrial development in an open, export-oriented economy. It then reviews the protectionist policies of the 1930s, the impact of the Japanese occupation and subsequent rehabilitation, the reformulation of policy after Independence, the nationalizations of 1958–65, and the changes in industrial policy and industrial structure under the New Order. Greater weight is given to the period before 1970, about which least is known. Because of the availability for the first time of good statistics, the New Order is treated fairly succinctly but particular attention is given to the emergence of Greater Surabaya as an industrial agglomeration, to structural change, and to the role of the small-scale sector.

Proto-Industrialization

In the mid-nineteenth century, Surabaya's economy was as yet little differentiated from the rural hinterland. An occupational breakdown for 1857 shows that employment in the city itself was still dominated by the primary sector: farming and fishing (Hageman 1859). The urban boundaries are not identified but it may be presumed that most kampungs still retained a rural character, especially those on the surrounding private estates. Most of the non-primary employment, almost another third of the total, was associated with the service sector, especially household servants, "coolie" laborers, traders, and sailors. Industrial activities accounted for less than 10 percent.[1]

In the mid-nineteenth century industry still meant manufacturing in the literal sense of articles made by hand. Except for a few large government establishments, production was by artisans in small workshops. Since ships, carriages, and other machines and furniture were then still made almost entirely of wood, the largest industrial category was woodworking, including sawmilling (table 5.1). Next was metalworking. Here the Industrial Revolution was beginning to have an impact, but iron casting and fabrication, work with copper and brass, and finer gold- and silverwork were for the most part traditional Javanese crafts. Textiles and clothing (including weaving, batik, tailoring, and sail making) accounted for another fifth, including several hundred female workers. Leather work involved the tanning of hides and the manufacture of both footwear and saddles and harness, horses and ponies being the main form of private and public transport. The final specified category was the manufacture for local construction and household use of bricks and earthenware. Except for bakers, no other

TABLE 5.1
Occupation of adult males, Surabaya, 1857

Occupation	Employees	%
Primary	*23,200*	*59*
Farming	21,700	
Fishing	1,500	
Secondary	*3,142*	*8*
Woodworking[a]	1,090	
Metalworking[b]	873	
Textiles/clothing[c]	664	
Leather[d]	180	
Bricks, earthenware	330	
Bakers	5	
Tertiary	*12,233*	*31.5*
Servants	3,920	
Coolies	3,550	
Traders	1,351	
Sailors	1,150	
Priests	770	
Prostitutes	610	
Other[e]	882	
Unemployed	*600*	*1.5*
Total[f]	39,175	100
All adult males	44,825	

Source: Hageman 1859.
[a]Includes sawmillers.
[b]Includes gold/silversmiths.
[c]Includes batik workers, weavers, sail makers, tailors.
[d]Includes cobblers, saddle makers.
[e]Includes grooms, musicians, launderers, restaurateurs.
[f]Includes 455 females in batik, weaving, and trade.

occupations are specified but there would certainly have been some printing and, on private lands, the manufacture of sugar and perhaps also rum (*arak*). Farmers and fishermen and much of the female population would also have been active in cottage industries, making items for their own consumption and sale in the town.

Most of this "industrial" workforce was Indonesian. According to the enumeration, there were about three thousand full-time Indonesian workers, 114 Europeans (including Eurasians), and just 33 Chinese (Hageman 1859, 138). The involvement of the Indonesian population is confirmed by an 1872 address list that identifies activities by the specific kampung in which they clustered: watchmakers, furniture makers, copper founders, brass founders, turners, ivory and horn workers, ferry builders, batikers, shoemakers, clothing makers, saddlemakers, vehicle builders, goldsmiths, rattan workers, lime burners, potters and brick makers, and tanners (Faber 1931, 185). As yet there was no marked difference between the technology and scale of European, Chinese, and Indonesian workshops. All three communities shared a common artisanal tradition. Dualism became apparent only with the application of steam power. However, as late as 1853 the first official tally counted only seventy steam engines throughout the Netherlands Indies (KV 1859, 143).

Establishment of large manufacturing plants using the new technology of the Industrial Revolution was at first dependent on state enterprise. In 1808, during the Napoleonic Wars and British blockade, Governor-General Daendels decided on Surabaya as the site of an arsenal (*Constructie-Winkel*), which developed into the main industrial undertaking in the colony. In 1849 the arsenal was split into an ordnance shop (*Artillerie Constructie-Winkel*) for the army and a boiler shop (*Fabriek voor de Marine, het Stoomwezen en Nijverheid*), primarily for the navy, which took over its management at the beginning of 1851. By then construction was well under way at the mouth of the Kali Mas of a modern naval base to be fitted out with shipbuilding and repair facilities—the shipyard (*timmerwerf*) was transferred there in 1851. In the late 1850s the boiler shop employed about 600 men, the naval dockyard about 650 (KV 1858–60), and the arsenal another 1,600 (Hageman 1859, 140), making a total workforce in these defense industries of almost 3,000 men. The trend toward composite and later iron- and steel-hulled warships soon made it desirable to transfer the boiler shop to the naval dockyard. After many bureaucratic delays, the shift was finally completed in 1893, coinciding with closure of the outmoded naval base on Onrust Island, in the Bay of Jakarta.

Concentration of naval facilities in Surabaya made it one of the largest defense installations in Southeast Asia with a daily workforce of around twenty-three hundred men. The naval base also served as training ground for the managers and skilled employees of a nascent private sector. Men like F. J. H. Bayer, A. W. Remmert, and F. Willems who set up the first private engineering shops in Surabaya had formerly held high positions in the arsenal, the boiler shop, or the naval base (Faber 1931, 170–5). Master craftsmen from Europe also trained local Javanese labor in the latest Western metalworking techniques. Reflecting a long tradition of metalworking, the skills of the Javanese tradesmen were highly praised and recognized in the precision of their handiwork as the equal of European workmen (KV 1859, 43). The boiler shop also ran a training school for Eurasian children, about forty in 1860 out of a total workforce of about six hundred per day (KV 1860, 43).

Spearheading the Industrial Revolution in the Netherlands Indies was the sugar industry, which was concentrated in eastern Java. The sugar industry had become a leading sector after introduction of the Cultivation System in the 1830s. The original mills were simple, cattle-powered mills using grindstones; the European-owned mills soon switched to water power. Steam boilers were first applied to a vacuum pan in 1836 and by the 1850s were widely used in the boiling up process (Gorkom 1879, 304). By the mid-1850s eighteen mills had been established in the immediate hinterland of Surabaya, of which almost two-thirds used some form of steam power for vacuum pans or centrifuges (Umbgrove 1862–63). By 1859, the first year for which a statistical breakdown is available, no less than 89 percent of all private, nonmarine steam engines were accounted for by the sugar industry (KV 1859). Liberalization of the industry around 1870 gave rise to another surge in investment: during the 1870s the number of boilers used in the sugar industry increased almost threefold, from 342 in 1871 to about 1,000 in 1881 (Segers 1987, 46–47). As late as 1900 the industry still accounted for 90 percent of the *capacity* of steam boilers used in private manufacturing (KV 1901, app. 10). However, the dispersal of mills meant that this first wave of the Industrial Revolution transformed neither town nor countryside (Dick 1993c).

The most direct impact of the sugar mills on Surabaya was rapid growth of a private engineering industry. Cattle- and water-powered mills, whose machinery consisted almost entirely of wooden parts, had required the services of carpenters rather than metalworkers. Boilers, vacuum pans, centrifuges, and steam engines were imported, mainly from Britain, but maintenance and repair had to be done locally. A mill could not be left idle for a season while a new piece of equipment or part was shipped out to the colony. The high cost of the new machinery made it essential that skilled engineering services were locally available and able to respond to almost any emergency. By the mid-1850s both private and public enterprise was able to build machinery as complex as entire mills (KV 1854, 147; 1857, 152). The sugar industry also induced a demand for metal sluices and gates and drawing mechanisms for irrigation works. By 1863, Surabaya had six engineering works and steam-powered sawmills with a combined capacity of 94 horsepower. By contrast, Jakarta had three such firms and Semarang only two (KV 1863, 218–19).

The engineering industry also benefited from rapid growth in steam shipping. Although most ships still had wooden hulls, their engines, boilers, and driving mechanisms required careful maintenance. Naval ships were slipped at the dockyard, while the boiler shop on the Kali Mas refitted the machinery. The syndicate that in 1852 had inaugurated regular interisland steamship lines, in 1859 opened a drydock and repair shop in Surabaya for maintenance of the fleet (KV 1860, 157). By 1863 it boasted a forge, turning shop, and boiler shop and by 1866 also a brass and iron foundry (KV 1863, 219; 1866, 199). In 1878 the yard was incorporated into NV Nederlandsch-Indische Industrie ("de Industrie"), its output by then redirected toward the sugar industry (fig. 5.1). Meanwhile, the Netherlands Indies Steam Navigation Company, which in 1865 had taken over the interisland mail contract, had opened its own works on the opposite bank of the Kali Mas. These early repair yards foreshadowed the twentieth-century Droogdok Maatschappij Soerabaja, with its large floating docks and slipways.

The third new industry underpinning the expansion of metalworking was railways. In East Java the first railway opened in 1878, being the state-owned line from Surabaya to the adjacent port of Pasuruan, soon extended to Malang, in the highlands (chap. 7). The East Java Steam Tram Company (Oost Java Stoomtram Maatschappij, OJS) opened the first tram line between Surabaya and its hinterland in 1891. This was the start of a mania for railway building, not least by the sugar mills to handle the transport of

Figure 5.1. The old engineering workshop "de Industrie" on the east bank of the Kali Mas in 1987, shortly before demolition. Note the heavy crane. Photo by author.

cane from the field to the mill. Surabaya became the location for the main workshops of the State Railways (Staatsspoorwegen) and the OJS. Local engineering firms also did a good deal of work for the private tramway companies.

In the latter half of the nineteenth century Europeans also began to invest in consumer goods industries. In 1853 a small sugar refinery was opened on the river just south of the town, the by-product of which was manufactured into rum (Faber 1931, 177). By the end of 1867 there were three ice factories, which in turn promoted the consumption of mineral waters and soft drinks (KV 1867). By 1873 there was a steam printery (KV 1873, 156).

By 1870, Surabaya had therefore already become an outpost of industrial Europe. In this it played a role very similar to other port cities such as Calcutta, Singapore, Hong Kong, and Shanghai and the logic was the same. The needs of defense and the modern steam age, combined with the slowness and unreliability of shipping links with Europe via the Cape of Good Hope, meant that some manufacturing and engineering capability was essential. As already noted, a mill owner could not afford to miss a whole sugar harvest while a vital spare part was ordered and delivered from Holland. Shipowners could not afford a steamer to be laid up for a year. Having the best harbor, the best river links with the interior, and a prosperous sugar industry in its hinterland, Surabaya was the logical place in Java to concentrate such heavy industry.

Opening of the Suez Canal in 1869 and introduction of regular steamship links with Europe brought to an end this first easy phase of industrialization. With faster and more reliable transit times, the degree of natural protection markedly diminished. Nevertheless, driven by buoyant export demand, the growth of sugar manufacture, railways, and steam shipping was so rapid that there was enough work to keep several large engineering workshops in steady work, even if the emphasis was now more on repair than manufacture. Light manufacturing also became more diverse, though the number of establishments was too small to constitute another leading sector.

The modest size and scope of the private modern manufacturing sector around 1900 is apparent from the listing by locality in the annual Colonial Report (*Koloniaal Verslag*). Modern sector employment of around 2,500, corresponding to enterprises using steam power, was dominated by metalworking (despite omission of the drydock company; see table 5.2). The second and third most important activities were ice and mineral water (excluding ten small, nonmechanized enterprises). The balance is made up of individual plants, of which the most notable was the oil refinery at Wonokromo (opened in 1889) and the gasworks (1879).[2] A concession for electricity supply had been let in 1893 but in 1900 was not yet in operation—here Surabaya lagged behind Jakarta (1897) and Medan (1899) (KV 1901). Omitted from table 5.2 are several very large modern public sector enterprises: around 1900 the naval dockyard employed around two thousand workers, the arsenal probably at least one thousand, and the railway workshops perhaps another five hundred. An estimate of three thousand for the three establishments would give a combined private and public modern-sector employment of fifty-five hundred workers, mainly in metalworking and ship repair. On the basis of the city's 1905 population (150,000) and assuming that the male participation rate was about the same as that in 1930 (62 percent), the small modern industrial sector by itself would have represented around 10 percent of the male workforce.

The size of the nonmechanized sector of manufacturing is more problematic. The annual listing in the Colonial Report accounts for around a thousand workers, in fields as diverse as furniture, carriage works, piano repair, cigars, soap, and mineral waters (table 5.2). Omitted, however, is the entire textile, clothing, and footwear industry, most food processing, and all cottage industry (including small-scale metalworking). These probably accounted for several thousand more full- and part-time workers. Indeed, the nonmechanized sector of manufacturing may have employed as many as the

TABLE 5.2
Private manufacturing establishments and employees, Surabaya city, 1899; Surabaya residency, 1914

Industry	1899 Establ.	1899 Employees	1914 Establ.	1914 Employees
Mechanized	*39*	*2,498*	*152*	*6,352*
Metalworking[a]	11	1,323	89	4,104
Printing	7	440	17	1,270
Oil refinery	1	300	1	60
Ice, mineral water	16	219	25	400
Gasworks	1	100	1	143
Bakeries	1	25	15	167
Other	2	91	4	208
Unmechanized	*48*	*1,044*	*249*	*2,782*
Woodworking	37	418	139	1,427
Carriageworks	5	271	3	119
Cigars	1	200	—	—
Soap	3	59	15	111
Other FDT	—	—	30	225
Other TCF[b]	—	—	11	149
Other nonmetal	—	—	10	160
Other chemical	—	—	5	195
Other	2	96	36	396
Urban fringe	*25*	*409*	*38*	*865*
Brick and tile	19	282	12	163
Lime	6	127	26	702
Total	112	3,951	439	9,999
(Naval base)	1	2,000	1	3,400

Source: Koloniaal Verslag 1901, 1915.
[a]Excludes naval dockyard, railway workshops.
[b]Excludes tailoring.

mechanized sector, implying an industry share of the workforce of around 20 percent, about the same as in 1930 (chap. 3).

A more comprehensive overview of the manufacturing sector on the eve of World War I can be gained from the 1915 Colonial Report, which enumerated 439 industrial establishments and ten thousand workers across the whole of the Surabaya residency, excluding plantation enterprises such as sugar mills (table 5.2). Interpretation is a bit tricky. Perhaps 2,500 of these workers were employed in the rural hinterland in activities or establishments such as lime burning, brick and tile making, sawpits, small forges for the shoeing of horses, and carpentry shops for the repair of carriages. Conversely, the survey underenumerates manufacturing in the city of Surabaya, such as food preparation (other than bread and biscuits), cigarettes and cigars, tailoring and dressmaking, and the further processing of agricultural commodities. Public-sector manufacturing is also again omitted: in 1914 the naval base alone employed thirty-four hundred men, to which should be added the railway workshops, for a total of at least four thousand workers. A complete census might therefore have reckoned at least twelve thousand industrial workers within the immediate environs of the city.

The above rough figures suggest fairly rapid growth in industrial employment between 1900 and 1914 but they are too incomplete to reveal any trend. Apart from the problem of distinguishing the city of Surabaya from the surrounding residency, it is impossible to know how much of the increase in recorded employment is due to improved coverage and how much to economic growth. Nevertheless, the performance of a couple of leading industries seems to confirm that the industrial sector had been growing quite rapidly. In metalworking and printing, firms seem to have been fairly well enumerated in the 1901 Colonial Report. Over the fourteen years, recorded employment in private sector metalworking doubled, from 1,300 to at least 3,000, while employment in printing almost tripled, from 440 to 1,270.

World War I set off a new spurt of industrial development based on import substitution. The shift of the European economy from civilian to war production and the redeployment of shipping brought about a reorientation of imports toward the United States and Japan. At the same time, the surge in ocean freight rates restored a high level of natural protection. During 1917–18, the Netherlands Indies came under Allied blockade and foreign trade all but ceased (chap. 2). In these circumstances, the colony had to become more self-reliant. Growth was most spectacular in heavy industry and in vegetable oil. The engineering industry, which for several decades had concentrated mainly on repair work, now turned increasingly toward fabrication and many new firms entered the industry (ARA, NHM 1944). Wooden shipbuilding again flourished. The processing of vegetable (mainly coconut) oil and the manufacture of soap and margarine was boosted by the withdrawal from the world market of German factories, which on the eve of the war had pressed between 80 and 90 percent of the copra imported to Europe (Kamerling 1982, 37). Exports from Java rose from 1.3 million liters in 1914 to a peak of 77 million liters in 1920 (ARA, NHM 1944, 49). By the end of the war the pressing of coconut oil from copra had become one of the main manufacturing industries in the Netherlands Indies. Other new industries were chemicals, rubber, packaging materials, cement, and cigarettes. The main constraint was the difficulty of shipping essential raw materials and machinery from North America and Japan.

As the leading industrial center in the Netherlands Indies, Surabaya was the favored location for much of this expansion of manufacturing. In the metals and machinery sector, the number of firms in Surabaya and the workforce swelled considerably. The city also saw a marked expansion in the number of soap manufacturers, mainly Chinese (ARA, NHM 1944, 60). New industries established by Europeans during or immediately after the war included sulfuric acid (Chemische Industrie Maatschappij), rubber (Soerabaia Rubberfabriek 'Ngagel'), earthenware (NICKI), soaps and toiletries (Georg Dralle, which in 1940 became Unilever), paint (Regnault), surgical bandages (De Cock, later Eerste Nederlandsch-Indische Verbandstoffenfabriek), and industrial gases (Hoek's Machine- en

Zuurstoffabriek). The notable exception to Surabaya's role in this industrial development was the new vegetable oil industry. In this case, as in the sugar industry, the mills were located in the hinterland (in East Java at Banyuwangi, Blitar, Kediri, and Tulungagung). The role of Surabaya was confined to storage and export.

Industrial development in Surabaya was facilitated by the far-sighted decision of the Municipality in October 1916 to establish an industrial estate. Five months later purchase was concluded for a large tract of land that had been the Chinese-owned sugar estate of Ngagel (Faber 1931, 247). Its location just south of the city between the river and the national railway line was highly strategic, ensuring good transport links between the port and the hinterland (see map 6.6). The first firm to take up land was the engineering firm Braat, which privately had purchased an adjacent fifteen-hectare site and in 1919 began to transfer its plant from the old site beside the central business district (fig. 5.2). By the end of 1919 another fifty hectares had been allocated on long-term lease to sixteen firms, including four engineering firms, two chemical firms, an oil mill, a

Figure 5.2. The Braat workshops, next to the Ngagel industrial estate, from a company advertisement ca. 1934. Courtesy the late D. Schaap.

mineral water factory, a rubber factory, a battery factory, and a timber mill (SGS 1919). Like Braat and Ligtvoet (concreteware), some of these firms were relocating operations to a larger and more convenient site but others were new ventures.

A clear indicator of the strength of the boom in Surabaya were the complaints of labor shortage. In 1918–19 the naval base reported very high rates of absenteeism, said to be common in other factories (MES 1918–19). The owners of the Waroe sugar factory, which lay closest to the city, just south of Wonokromo, complained in the 1920 annual report of the lack of labor for planting, harvesting, and transport of cane because of the availability of higher-paying employment in Surabaya. These complaints were repeated in the following year, with specific reference to the attractions of well-paid day labor on the ongoing harbor construction. Recognizing the disadvantage of the mill's proximity to Surabaya, the owners made the decision to experiment with mechanized field preparation (Waroe 1920–21).

INDUSTRY STRUCTURE AROUND 1920

A good overview of the structure of industry in Surabaya at the end of the wartime boom can be gleaned from an official directory of Netherlands Indies industry for 1921. The directory is not a census and is messy to analyze, but assuming an average of about three persons per household enterprise, the directory's total recorded employment for Surabaya of almost 19,000 can be regarded as a considerable underestimate (table 5.3).[3] Including the 2,000 people employed in the brick- and tile works around the clay pits of Sepanjang (about seven kilometers southwest of the city), actual industrial employment may have been as high as 25,000. Compared with the above 1914 estimate (12–15,000), a postwar range of 20–25,000 is robust enough to suggest that during World War I manufacturing employment in Surabaya must have increased by at least 50 percent.

TABLE 5.3
Composition of manufacturing by establishments and employment, Surabaya, 1921

Industry/Sector	Establishments >5 employees	Employees	Households <5 employees
Food, Drink, Tobacco	*44*	*1,495*	*20*
Bakeries	11	127	6
Other foodstuffs	5	419 -	5
Ice, soft drinks	22	640	5
Spirits	3	171 +	2
Cigars, cigarettes	3	138 +	2
Textiles, Clothing, Footwear	*19*	*783* +	*14*
Weaving, batik	2	98 +	7
Tailoring	12	—	2
Leather	5	685	5
Wood & Products	*57*	*965* +	*65*
Furniture, etc.	42	665 +	57
Sawmills	8	300	1
Shipyards	7	—	7
Paper & Printing	*18*	*1,172* +	*11*
Chemicals & Pharmaceuticals	*35*	*243* +	*5*
Soap	12	94 +	1
Other[a]	23	149 +	4
Building Materials	*51*	*2,136*	*66*
Bricks & tiles[b]	41	1,962	26 (?)
Lime kilns[b]	5	158 -	37 (?)
Other	5	16 +	3
Metals & Machinery	*69*	*11,460*	*47*
Engineering workshops	23	10,326	—
Forges, smiths[c]	18	395	33
Vehicle repair shops	15	682	9
Jewelers	13	57 +	5
Total	293	18,254	228

Source: DLNH 1921.

Note: +/- signs indicate likely under/overallocation to Surabaya municipality.

[a]Includes vegetable oil.

[b]Urban fringe.

[c]Includes brass.

This highly disaggregated data shows an industrial profile that was hardly typical of a Third World colony: a large metals and machinery sector, a small FDT (food, drink, tobacco) sector, and an insignificant TCF (textiles, clothing, footwear) sector. Metals and machinery was boosted by wartime demands and continued to dominate the city's manufacturing base with more than half of recorded employment in 1921.[4] By contrast, high wartime urban labor costs pushed the TCF sector to its nadir. Apart from a modern surgical dressings factory opened in 1920, the only other textile manufacture was a handful of small Indonesian batikers. Tailoring, however, was much under-recorded. Leather working was better represented, with one large and several medium-size establishments, plus several household shoemakers. Main components of the FDT sector were bakeries, soft drinks, and ice plus a few small Chinese establishments making noodles, tahu, and soy sauce; the processing of Indonesian-style foods was entirely omitted. Despite some underreporting, several reasons can be adduced for this sector's small size. First, better-off households employed servants to shop and cook and therefore had little need to buy packaged foods. Second, much processing of basic foodstuffs such as rice, sugar, coffee, and tea was carried out not in Surabaya but in the rural hinterland. Third, the demand for European luxuries such as chocolates, biscuits, beer, and spirits was met by the import of well-known brands from Holland—there was also a lively grocery trade with Australia for items such as flour, jam, tinned fruit, butter, and condensed milk.

By number of establishments, wood and wood products was second only to metalworking, though average employment was only about fifteen persons.[5] The main category of furniture making was dominated by Chinese, although there were also Indonesian kampung enterprises. Independent Indonesian craftsmen were also involved alongside the several lighterage companies in the building and repair of wooden lighters and sailing prahus. The directory's listing for paper and printing seems incomplete: the actual workforce may have been as large as fifteen hundred to two thousand persons. Like Jakarta, Surabaya was well established as a publishing center. Besides some prominent European firms, Chinese and Indonesian enterprises were also active in publishing books and newspapers. Building materials was dominated by the manufacture of bricks and tiles. Demand for roofing tiles was boosted by the introduction in 1915 of new plague-control building regulations that banned thatch as a roofing material (Rothe 1938a, 5). In 1918 the Nederlandsch-Indische Chamotte- en Klei-industrie (NICKI) introduced large-scale, mechanized production of roof tiles, agricultural pipes, and sanitary earthenware (ARA, NHM 1944, 83). Household manufacturers of bricks, tiles, or lime were located in villages throughout the residency. Least prominent sector by employment was the diverse but rudimentary sector of chemicals and pharmaceuticals: besides the main activity of soap making, this included the Wonokromo oil refinery, town gas, other industrial gases, acids, paint, some simple pharmaceuticals, and five Chinese fireworks makers—several vegetable oil companies had offices in Surabaya but their factories were located further afield.

THE 1920S

Once the abnormal wartime level of natural protection was removed, industrial expansion ceased. During 1919 shipping services began to return to normal frequencies, though freight rates remained high. When the frenzied postwar boom collapsed in 1920, local manufacturers suddenly faced stiff competition from European imports, whose sharply reduced wholesale prices were reinforced by falling ocean freight rates. Soon German manufacturers were also forcing their way back into the market. These problems were by no means unique to the Netherlands Indies. However, the colonial government saw no reason to protect the local infant industrial sector at the expense of manufacturing interests in the Netherlands. Local firms were thus exposed to the full force of renewed competition. Those that had borrowed to set up plant at the height of the boom faced severe cash flow problems. Many firms had to suspend payment of dividends and various new industrial projects were canceled. Only a few large factories actually came to fruition, notably the Regnault paint factory, the Georg Dralle soap and toiletries plant (relocated from West Java), and in 1923 the huge Wonocolo leather factory, which took advantage of the supply of hides from the local abattoirs. On the Ngagel estate many leases changed hands.

Three industries suffered very badly from the recession: vegetable oil, chemicals, and metalworking. The vegetable oil industry almost collapsed. In 1922 exports all but ceased and the dominant firm, NV Oliefabrieken "Insulinde," was forced into liquidation by its bankers (Kamerling 1982). Its four factories in East Java (Blitar, Kediri, Tulungagung, and Banyuwangi) were taken over by the Maatschappij tot Exploitatie van Oliefabrieken (Mexolie), a subsidiary of the Nederlandsch-Indische Handelsbank, and operated mainly for the domestic market (Kamerling 1982, 248–49). Some recovery in exports in the mid-1920s encouraged one of the surviving firms, Oliefabrieken van Dongen (Olvado), to open a large new mill, Oliefabriek "Ngagel," in Surabaya's new industrial estate.

The chemical industry also contracted. Many of the plants set up during the war to meet urgent local needs were not cost efficient and closed down when reexposed to European competition. Production of sodium was discontinued, while the manufacture of industrial gases and sulfuric acid came to be monopolized by just two firms, Hoek's Machine- en Zuurstoffabriek (which also had factories at Jakarta and Bandung) and Chemische Industrie Maatschappij, at Sepanjang. Ambitious plans to diversify the local chemical industry were abandoned (ARA, NHM 1944). The pioneer rubber factory was also forced to close down but was succeeded in 1921 by the NV Soerabaia Rubberfabriek "Ngagel" with a larger and more modern plant.

The metals and engineering sector was also hit hard by renewed import competition and the sharp reduction of capital spending by both public and private sectors in the early 1920s. Between 1920–21 and 1922–23, the turnover of the six largest firms about halved (Vreede 1926, 4). Cutthroat competition ensued and by 1922–23 most firms were operating at a loss and could no longer pay dividends. Several well-known firms went out of business. Braat, the largest private engineering firm in Surabaya and indeed in the Netherlands Indies, went bankrupt and survived only because of the willingness of its main creditor to take over and reconstruct the company.

After 1924 the recovery in export markets for estate crops led to an upturn. In early 1926 a comprehensive inquiry into the metal industry in Surabaya enumerated twenty-nine establishments with a workforce of 11,500, plus another 750 to 1,500 "coolies" on daily hire (Vreede 1926, 8). This included the naval base, the drydock company, another fourteen private engineering firms, the electricity utility ANIEM, three railway and tramway workshops, and nine motor vehicle repair garages. Given that the arsenal had by then been fully transferred to Bandung, it can be judged that by the mid-1920s employment had recovered to a level comparable to that in 1920.

Consumer goods industries were probably more buoyant throughout the decade than either heavy industry or export processing, although here reliable data are almost entirely lacking. Examples would be foodstuffs, mineral waters and ice, paper and printing, and local building materials. One new industry that expanded rapidly was cigarettes. Small-scale factory production of hand-rolled clove-flavored cigarettes (kretek) dates back to around 1920, when Chinese immigrant Liem Seng Tee as Handel Maatschappij Sampoerna (Sampoerna Trading Company) first distributed his now famous Djie Sam Soe (2-3-4) brand across the city (Sampoerna 1995, 28) (fig. 5.3). Other small Chinese, Javanese, and Arab firms followed. Production fell sharply after 1929, first because of the Depression and then because of the imposition in 1932 of excise on cigarette paper (*banderol*), which brought about a switch to more crude cigarettes (*strootjes*) rolled in maize leaves (*klobot*) (Segers 1987, 26; Reijden 1936, 95–105).

Figure 5.3. Labor-intensive industry: female kretek rollers, PT Gelora, 1987. Photo by author.

THE DEPRESSION

Renewed industrial growth was cut short by the world depression of the 1930s. Its onset was already apparent by the end of 1929 and the situation worsened steadily until a trough about 1933–34. There are no indexes of industrial production to chart the trend but some figures are available for the large metals and machinery industry, which in Surabaya suffered acutely. Its main customer, the sugar industry, was forced drastically to cut back its output: new investment ceased and maintenance was reduced to the bare minimum by cannibalization of idle plant (HVS 1932). The situation of other plantation cultures was not much better. Maritime work was affected by the decline in shipping. For budgetary reasons, work at the naval base was cut back to a minimum. The turnover of the largest engineering firm, Braat, halved each year from Fl 6.3 million in 1929 to less than Fl 1 million in 1933; the normal workforce of about one thousand was reduced to just 268 skilled workers and most highly paid European technical staff were also laid off (Braat 1929–33). The drydock company reduced its workforce by more than two-thirds, from almost eighteen hundred in 1929 to just five hundred fifty in 1933 (DDMS 1919–33). Several large and well-established firms closed down. No steady recovery was apparent until 1936.

Overall the Depression bore more on utilization and employment than on industrial capacity. Industries like metals and machinery that relied heavily on investment spending bore the brunt.[6] The virtual cessation by 1931 of housing construction similarly affected the manufacture of bricks and tiles. The large Brantas distillery closed down. Yet comparison of Inspectorate of Safety (Dienst van Veiligheidstoezicht, DVT) figures for 1930 and 1936 suggests that in Surabaya residency—no breakdown is available for the municipality—the *number* of industrial establishments remained fairly static and the leading sectors, of metals and machinery and printing, showed almost no change (DVT 1930, 1936). Closure of firms in some industries, such as soft drinks and cigarettes, was offset by the emergence of new firms in others, such as textiles, rubber goods, and galvanizing. A few large plants opened in the early 1930s as the realization of projects that had been planned before the Depression. One huge project was the Java brewery (Nederlandsch-Indische Bierbrouwerijen), which opened at the end of 1931 and was taken over in 1937 by Heineken (its "Java" label eventually became Bir Bintang). More modest ventures were the Pelangi biscuit factory and a vermicelli factory.

The industrial sector recovered sooner from the Depression than the export industries because from 1933 the colonial government adopted a protective industry policy. This broke decisively with the orthodoxy that any measures to protect manufacturing in the Netherlands Indies would inflate wages and undermine export competitiveness. The reasons for this timing were twofold. First, the setback to the plantation cultures, hitherto seen as the backbone of the colonial economy, had led to great pessimism as to the potential for the unemployed to be reabsorbed in the densely populated agricultural sector (Oorschot 1956, 40–41). Second, a remarkable surge in Japanese imports had displaced both traditional suppliers (Netherlands and Britain) and competing local firms. Boosted by devaluation of the yen in December 1931, which reduced the rate against the guilder by 60 percent, Japan's share of imports to the Netherlands Indies rose from 10.5 percent in 1929 to 30 percent in 1933 (*IV* 1934). This trend was viewed with alarm as undermining Dutch control of the import-export economy and the distribution system (Mook 1944).

To restrict the penetration of Japanese imports, in 1933 the colonial government introduced the Crisis Import Ordinance (Crisis-invoerordonnantie) to enable import quotas to be imposed by item according to country of supply. Although the primary aim of these quotas was to protect the market for the exports of Dutch industry against cheap Japanese goods, they also protected local manufacturers. Firms in Surabaya benefited especially from quotas on beer (1933), sarongs, cooking pans, earthenware (all 1934), sanitary ware (1935), and sulfuric acid (1936) (Wirodihardjo 1951). The Crisis Import Ordinance of September 1933 was followed in 1934 by the Industry Regulation Ordinance (Bedrijfsreglementeeringsordonnantie), which provided a legal basis for capacity controls to prevent "destructive" competition. Such controls were imposed in 1935 on dairies, printeries, stevedores, cigarette manufacturers, foundries, weaving firms, and ice factories (Wirodihardjo 1951, 45).

In Surabaya, an important effect of the new protection was the development of a modern textile industry. The Textile Institute in Bandung (founded in 1919) had in 1926 produced an improved hand loom with a capacity seven times greater than existing hand looms; in 1930 there followed a simple machine loom with a capacity four times greater again (Oorschot 1956, 43). However, no interest was shown in East Java as a location until after 1934, when protection of the domestic production of sarongs led to the establishment of several mills in and around Surabaya. In all East Java in 1933 there were just 500 looms (NIF 2/36); by the end of 1936 there were 3,000 hand looms and 750 machine looms (Rothe 1938b, 27). Six months later the *Soerabaiasch Handelsblad* (10/5/37) reported that, if all applications were approved, the number of hand looms would rise to 6,811 and of machine looms to 1,457. Many mills were small, with fewer than 15 looms, but there were also some giants. The Martak mill, owned by an Indian merchant at Cermee, near Gresik, was reported in February 1938 to have installed 2,000 hand looms and 350 machine looms imported secondhand from Japan; at full capacity the mill employed four thousand workers, mainly women (Rothe 1938b, 8–9). Within about a hundred-kilometer radius of Surabaya were another half dozen large mills: Bintang Pari (Sukorejo), Kantjil Mas (Bangil), Kasri (Pandaan), Martak (Mojokerto), and later Nebritex (Pasuruan). Apart from cheaper land and a good supply of water, the main attraction of location in the hinterland of Surabaya was the supply of cheap unskilled labor brought about by the closure of sugar mills. Within Surabaya itself only three modern mills are known to have been established: Textielfabriek en Handelsmaatschappij Baswedan (1938), owned by the rich Arab businessman Ibrahim Baswedan, and at Ngagel two canvas producers, the Chinese-owned Nederlandsch-Indische Textielindustrie (1937) and the Dutch-owned Textielindustrie Java.

The reasons for intervention varied considerably from industry to industry. In the case of cigarettes, the original intent was to protect manufacturers of handmade clove cigarettes against competition from machine-made modern or white cigarettes. Entry of Faroka in 1932 with a new plant at Malang had led the established monopolist, British-American Tobacco (BAT), to slash prices, which during the Depression caused great hardship for kretek producers in East Java. In 1935 the Surabaya firm Sampoerna discovered a way to produce machine-made kretek without using paper subject to the 30 percent excise. With this price advantage Sampoerna's output soared from 30 million cigarettes in 1933 to 280 million in the first half of 1935, turning the tables on the two foreign manufacturers but also making life even more difficult for other kretek producers. By the end of 1936, Sampoerna's new factory was reported to employ more than four thousand workers, making it at that time the largest private employer in the city (NIF, 1/37). Production was maintained from dawn to dusk seven days a week as the Djie Sam Soe brand became known as far away as the Outer Islands (Sampoerna 1995, 33).

On welfare grounds, the government took measures to develop small-scale industry besides textiles and kretek. The combination of underemployment and protection was conducive to rapid diffusion of "appropriate technologies" throughout Java. In 1936 the government established small industry centers (*centrales*) to upgrade technology and management. In East Java these centers involved yarn spinning (Surabaya), copper- and ironwork (Bangil, Sidoarjo), furniture (Pasuruan), and pottery (Bojonegoro) (NIF, 9/36, 12/36). These initiatives were nevertheless too few and on too small a scale to have more than localized impacts, a problem that would persist with small-industry policy after independence.

RECOVERY

Recovery of consumer demand after the mid-1930s encouraged private investors to look at new ventures, a trend the Municipality sought to promote. Following the lead of Jakarta, in 1935 it began a campaign to promote Surabaya as an industrial location (NIF, 5/35). A pamphlet, *Soerabaia and the Oosthoek: There Lies a Future for Your Business,* was issued that highlighted the scope of the industrial base, the large trade of the port, the size of the local market, and the availability of good industrial land (SGS 1936a). Although the Ngagel industrial estate was not yet full, a much larger area of reclaimed land was made available just south of the port area. This campaign was backed up in June of the following year when the Association of Netherlands Indies Manufacturers opened a Permanent Industrial Exhibition in downtown Surabaya (NIF, 6/36, 7/37). In Surabaya new projects identified by the association in the late 1930s included:

1936 Lightbulbs (Eerste Javasche Gloeilampen Fabriek "Annoer"; neon lights (Alg. Industrie Mij); bicycles (Hima—transfer from Bandung)

1937 Glycerin (Javasche Koolzuur en Zuurstoffabriek)
1938 Vehicle assembly (Dodge—NV Velodrome); chocolate (TerWolde)
1939 Metal fittings (Borsumij); rubber sandals (Rubberfabriek Waroe)
1940 Coconut oil, soap (Philippine Manufacturing Corp.)
1941 Lightbulbs (Philips)
(NIF 1934–40)

Most of these projects drew on Dutch capital but the Philippine Manufacturing Corporation was a subsidiary of the American firm Proctor and Gamble, while the lightbulb factory and sandal factory (in the old Waroe sugar mill) were Japanese ventures (NIF, 10/38; ARA, NHM 1944, 75).

In general, however, the rate of industrial development in Surabaya and its hinterland during the 1930s was much slower than around Jakarta. Drastic contraction of the sugar industry caused purchasing power to be much more depressed in East Java than in West Java, which specialized more in rubber and tea plantations (Ziesel 1939, 54). Jakarta also benefited from proximity to Sumatra, whose economy was buoyed by strong demand for rubber. Thus not only did the textile industry develop very much faster in West Java but several new industries were established there including rubber tires (Goodyear), margarine (Unilever), batteries, and biscuits. Some industries that hitherto had been concentrated in East Java, such as paint and soap, also expanded there. The industrial center of gravity therefore shifted west, especially as far as consumer goods industries were concerned. One rough indicator is the consumption by industry of electrical power: by 1938 and 1939 the level of consumption in West Java was twice that in East Java (*EWNI,* 16/5/41, 832–33).

After the outbreak of World War II and the surrender of Holland in May 1940, the structure of demand shifted back in favor of Surabaya's heavy industry for the first time since the end of the postwar boom in 1920. The Netherlands Indies were now again thrown back upon their own resources. In expectation of war with Japan, the army and navy placed urgent local contracts for many items from basic field equipment such as helmets, flasks, and stainless steel kettles to sophisticated military vehicles (*EWNI,* 25/1/47, 63). Expenditures by the naval base had already doubled between 1935 and 1938, and by 1939 the workforce had expanded to around eight thousand, excluding another four thousand seagoing personnel and eight hundred at the naval flying base (Bisschop 1939; Sande Lacoste 1939). Orders were now placed with the naval base for minesweepers, with Braat for armored cars and tanks, with the rubber factory for gas masks, and so on. Suddenly, it was a seller's market. The problem was that much equipment and many vital raw materials were unavailable or had to be shipped from America, so that many projects were unable to be completed before the Japanese invasion. Nevertheless, for two years there was a marvelous boom in which heavy industry, especially the metal and machinery and chemical industries, were at long last able to operate at full capacity. The suddenness of the boom is evident from figures of power consumption by industry in East Java: growth jumped from 10 percent in 1939 to 28 percent in 1940, while the share of industry in the total increased from 34.4 percent to 38.6 percent (*EWNI,* 16/5/41, 832–33). Within such a short time, however, little investment was possible and, as during World War I, there was no long-term gain in industrial capability.

This late-colonial burst of industrialization had two other important features. First, a good deal of import substitution had been achieved in a short time, albeit in a fairly narrow range of goods. By 1938 near self-sufficiency had been achieved, for example, in cigarettes (92 percent) and cigars (80 percent), frying pans (90 percent), cigarette lighters (80 percent), paint (75 percent), soap and perfumes (72 percent), beer (70 percent: 1936 figure) and leather goods (excl. shoes: 70 percent). Domestic production was also significant for shoes (60 percent), confectionery (60 percent), biscuits (45 percent), margarine (40 percent), batteries (40 percent), and bicycles (35 percent). As intended by the quota system, much of these gains had been at the expense of Japanese imports. In the case of textiles (6 percent) and glass (9 percent), however, little had yet been achieved (ARA, NHM 1944, 40, 121).

Second, the entrepreneurial drive for industrialization was provided by a small number of large banks, trading houses, and management agencies. The "Factory" (NHM), Nederlandsch-Indische Handelsbank, Internatio, Geo. Wehry, and Borsumij were especially prominent in providing capital, technical advice, and, in the case of the trading houses, looking after distribution of the product (ARA, NHM 1944). Industrialization therefore did not cut across the tightly knit structure of colonial capital but rather consolidated it. The control over the colonial economy that Dutch capital had forfeited in the early 1930s through the rapid market penetration of Japanese goods and their direct distribution through Japanese networks was clawed back.

By 1942 solid institutional foundations had thus been laid for rapid industrialization. Had the Japanese invasion not eliminated Dutch political and economic power, it is plausible that in the 1940s the Netherlands Indies could have enjoyed the kind of sustained industrial expansion that eventually occurred in the 1970s. In that event Indonesia—and Java in particular—would have led Southeast Asia's industrialization, which in terms of historical preconditions would have been a more "natural" course of events than what actually transpired. The tragedy was not just that a generation of economic growth was lost but also that the institutional advantages did not survive decolonization.

War and Rehabilitation

At the beginning of March 1942 the wartime burst of industrial activity was interrupted by the Japanese invasion and occupation. Physical damage was not too serious. Japanese bombing had been concentrated on the military targets: the port, the naval base, and the airfield. Dutch sabotage, though intended as a scorched-earth policy, seems to have been neither systematic nor effective, apart from the naval base and oil refinery. After two weeks or so, most factories were therefore able to resume production under military supervision (*SH,* 19/3/42). One of the first tasks of the incoming Japanese administrators was to carry out a registration of industrial plants and foreign staff. During the course of 1942 most European personnel were interned and responsibility devolved upon senior Indonesian or Chinese employees under Japanese direction (Frederick 1989, 91–92, 99).

Production was reorganized to meet the needs of the Japanese war effort. The collapse of the Dutch colonial system also created an economic vacuum. The cessation of all normal foreign trade and banking and the marginalization of the Dutch firms meant that new institutions were required to integrate production and distribution. Japan itself had been a controlled economy since the late 1930s in which the power of the large business conglomerates (*zaibatsu*) was much circumscribed. In view of the urgency of economic rehabilitation, this was the obvious model to apply to Indonesia as well. On lines long familiar in Japan, many industries were organized into guilds (*kumiai*) subject to close government control. However, private enterprise was maintained, with much responsibility for distribution being delegated to Japanese trading houses that had established local networks. Stringent rationing was introduced over most basic consumer items to free surpluses for military use. The output of some industries such as beer was withdrawn entirely from public sale in order to satisfy the thirst of the armed forces (Heineken 1939–46, 3).

To promote local self-sufficiency, the Japanese sought to boost Java's modest industrial capability. Java and Malaya were seen as the only regions in the southern part of Southeast Asia able to meet the demand for more sophisticated manufactures (Miyamoto 1986, 237). Ambitious targets were set for a wide range of basic items. Two key local sectors were textiles and shipbuilding. In mid-1942 the four main weaving mills around Surabaya were organized into a Textiles Control Board (Kigyo Tosei Kai) and some months later a five-year plan was introduced to develop cotton cultivation in East and Central Java (Sutter 1959, 157, 160–61). However, local cotton cultivation was a failure and the worsening shipping shortage prevented imports. Military authorities relied on the huge stockpile of textiles confiscated from the Dutch, while withholding them from civilian use (Miyamoto 1986, 248–49; Frederick 1989, 127–22n. 147). The Indonesian population had perforce to make do with gunny sacks and funeral shrouds. A common recollection of the Japanese occupation is of having to dress in worn-out rags.

In mid-1942 senior Japanese administrators met in Singapore and decided to relieve the pressure on interisland shipping by an urgent program to construct small wooden-hulled motor vessels powered by locally made diesel engines (Sutter 1959, 145). Because of its teak plantations, engineering capability, and supply of skilled labor, Java was to be the main center of production (Miyamoto 1986). In Surabaya a yard was laid out beside the naval base, near the mouth of the Pegirian canal, where formerly the East Java Lighterage Company had managed a small ship repair yard for its own fleet. The first vessel was launched in May 1943 but, although timber was cut ruthlessly, the production of hulls and engines fell far below targets (Sutter 1959, 197; Miyamoto 1986). Timber ships are less amenable than steel ships to the economies of mass production and there was no doubt a shortage of all kinds of essential components that were not readily manufactured in Java. Such shortages plagued most other industries. By 1944 the Allied submarine campaign was systematically destroying the Japanese merchant fleet, not only preventing proper communication between Japan and Southeast Asia but also, by forcing the transfer to main routes of smaller and smaller ships, interrupting the flow of goods and raw materials even between adjacent islands.

Despite the declaration in 1944 of a New Economic Order, the reality was that Java was being bled by the unrealistic requirements of the Japanese war machine (Sato 1994). Results were uneven but, because of so many bottlenecks in supply, industrial production must have fallen below prewar levels, at least as far as the factory sector was concerned. Propaganda drives to meet plan targets merely highlighted the problem. In the small-scale and household sector the situation may have been somewhat better. Indonesian entrepreneurs seized opportunities to make articles such as soft drinks, soy sauce, and toothpaste that were no longer available through normal channels (Frederick 1989, 102). Although such firms also faced difficulties in obtaining raw materials, desperate administrators began to turn to small-scale plants and household industry to boost production (Sutter 1959). However, as in rural areas, if military requirements could not be met from increased production, they were squeezed from reduced civilian consumption.

When the Allied forces took control of Surabaya at the end of 1945, the task of industrial rehabilitation was formidable. As in 1942, the main problem was not physical destruction. Factories such as the Braat engineering workshops at Ngagel had been damaged by Allied bombing but the industrial estate had not been a prime military target like the port and naval base. Nor did industry suffer too badly from the fighting of November 1945, which took place mainly in the commercial and residential districts. When British troops occupied the city in September 1945, strategic industries were placed under military control. During 1946, as Dutch administration took over, factories were gradually returned to the former owners or managers as they presented themselves. They found that the Japanese had removed a good deal of machinery and equipment and what remained had seldom been properly maintained over the previous four years. Yet even the oil refinery, which had been a prime military target, resumed operation in September 1946 and its prewar capacity had been restored by 1948. The drydock company's huge fifteen-thousand-ton floating dock that had been scuttled by the Dutch, raised by the Japanese and then sunk again in by Allied bombing was refloated in July 1946 and recommissioned the following March (*EWI,* 9/8/47). Across the whole country it was estimated that industrial capacity rose from around 30 percent of the 1941 level in 1947 to 50–60 percent in 1948 (Geursen 1948, 717–18).

The vigor with which the returning Dutch administration tackled industrial rehabilitation bespoke new realities. Being for the most part located in the main cities, the modern industrial sector fell much more quickly into Dutch hands than the plantation sector, much of which remained hostage to Republican armed forces. Albeit by force of circumstance, the cities and their industrial base thus became more central to Dutch economic policy. In a situation of depressed agricultural exports and an apparently insatiable demand for imports, a strategy of import-substituting industrial development seemed sound policy. This was not altogether an improvisation. In exile during the Pacific War, Dutch policymakers had already begun to conceive of a more active industrial development policy (Hart 1942). It is likely that freedom from the immediate pressures of government not only gave them opportunity to reflect on the experience of the 1930s but also brought them in contact with new ideas about economic development then circulating in Britain and the United States (Arndt 1987, 43). Planned industrial development was now an economic objective in its own right (Jonkers 1948).

Plant and equipment could have been rehabilitated more quickly but for the emergence of structural problems on the supply side, whose severity the returning Dutch administrators could not have foreseen. First, the power shortage was desperate. Since the 1930s Surabaya had relied on hydroelectricity from the interior. The modern Kalikonto installations, with a capacity of 20,000 kilowatts (kW), had been damaged by Allied bombing but, before repairs could be undertaken, retreating Republican forces isolated the city by wrecking the intermediate transformer station at Bangil (Carriere 1948, 728–31). Repair of the substation was no solution because the hydroelectric stations remained under Republican control. The city had to rely on the obsolete coal-fired power station at Semampir, beside the naval base. Compared with a prewar power generation of 14,000 kW, Surabaya was now constrained to just 2,000 kW and, even with heavy power restrictions, industry could be provided with no more than 280 kW (*ERI,* 2/47, 23). As late as June 1948 the power supply was still described as "very precarious" (ARA, MK 2.10.29, 408: 6/48). Installation of three diesel units early in 1949 eased the situation by providing another 2,000 kilowatts of capacity to supplement the 5,800 kilowatts now obtainable from Semampir (Carriere 1948, 731).

Second, the whole economy faced a critical shortage of foreign exchange. On the one hand, the offensive against the Republic soaked up foreign exchange, a consequence the debilitated Dutch economy could ill afford. On the other, Republican control of the hinterland prevented the revival of exports. Foreign exchange had therefore to be tightly rationed and centralized control of foreign exchange became the basic lever of the new industrial policy (Jonkers 1948, 121). From mid-1947 foreign exchange was rationed by the Bureau of Industrial Rehabilitation (Bureau van Industrieel Herstel), which granted licenses mainly to large and medium enterprises in accordance with approved rehabilitation plans. However, there was never enough foreign exchange to allow industry to receive more than a fraction of what it needed for raw materials and spare parts, let alone for new plant and equipment. Factory owners had to scavenge for whatever materials were available. One Chinese entrepreneur, for example, who in 1946 had opened a new soft drink factory, managed to obtain carbon dioxide from the navy in return for deliveries of its product (Pabrik Limun Java, interview, 16/11/87). The situation gradually improved during 1947 and 1948 after seizure of Republican territory and recovery in exports, but America's suspension of Marshall Plan aid in retaliation for the second Police Action brought on a renewed crisis (Davis 1949, 1232). Only the most urgent orders could be met as foreign-exchange allocations were cut by a further 40 percent, but even so the allocation for 1949 was exhausted by the middle of the year (ARA, MK 2.10.29, 408: 1/49, 6/49). Thus tanners had to manage without tan, biscuit factories had enough flour but no bicarbonate of soda, soap factories had enough soda but little coconut oil, soft drink and confectionery factories could not obtain essences, ice factories ran out of sulfur dioxide and ammonia, and cigarette manufacturers could no longer obtain cellophane to wrap their packets (ARA, MK 2.10.29, 408: 1948–49). Export-processing plants, such as kapok presses, could not obtain raw materials from the hinterland, while the two chocolate factories were operating at only half capacity for want of cocoa beans. Cigarette and ice manufacturers could obtain some foreign exchange to import spare parts but none to import new machines. Amid the disorganization of a wartime economy, capacity utilization in 1949 was estimated to be only 50 percent (Oorschot 1956, 63).

Third, there was a serious shortage of skilled labor, especially in Surabaya, because of the flight of the large part of the Indonesian population. Despite all the problems of locating equipment and importing the necessary replacement parts or machines, firms seem to have found it easier to rehabilitate their physical plant than to reassemble their workforce. Especially in the metalworking industry, competition for machinery operators forced up wages. By one estimate machine shop wages had risen 400 to 500 percent above the prewar level, compared with just 80 percent in the Netherlands, even though productivity was estimated as only 45 percent of the prewar level, compared with 80 percent in the Netherlands (Hardon 1948, 702). Lack of motorized transport and the insecurity of the roads made it difficult to draw labor from farther afield.

Fourth, for all its good intentions government itself probably stifled as much as promoted rehabilitation. The legalities of war damage claims enmeshed firms in bureaucracy from the outset (Middelaer 1947, 64). When banks were allowed to reopen in May 1946, the government rationed loans through licenses issued by a credit commission: not until April 1948 were prewar bank deposits unfrozen and banks allowed to determine their own credit policy (Leeuwen 1948, 720–23). Besides foreign exchange and import licensing, the government organized domestic distribution through a system of rationing and price controls. And in those industries subject to the prewar Business Regulation Law, there was also licensing of operations and production quotas. In the late 1940s the Bureau of Industrial Rehabilitation exercised as much power as

Japan's postwar Ministry of International Trade and Industry (MITI) (see Johnson 1982). The result was certainly a much more active industrial policy than before the war (Oorschot 1949, 1268). However, the system was ramshackle and unwieldy and, in the absence of experienced personnel and good information, reacted to crises rather than applying a long-term strategy, as even its exponents came in time to recognize.[7]

Under these constraints it is perhaps surprising that industrial output recovered as rapidly as it did (fig. 5.4). After four years of acute scarcity there was a great hunger for goods, but because of the foreign-exchange crisis, imports could not satisfy the pent-up demand. Even though prices of local manufactures were on average 25 percent and in some cases 100 percent higher than imported goods (Davis 1949, 1232), there was a market for anyone who could obtain simple machinery and raw materials and for as much as could be produced. A soft drink manufacturer, Pabrik Limun Java (interview, 16/11/87), recalled how trucks had queued outside the factory to load crates off the production line. By April 1947 most branches of industry were back in production. In the case of food

Figure 5.4. Workers leaving the Braat engineering works, Ngagel, 1947. Arsip Nasional.

and textiles, output was distributed through the rationing system or allocated to the armed forces, including the entire output of the two chocolate factories and most of that of the Heineken brewery. Firms in metals and machinery had a good deal of work, especially in rehabilitating rice mills, though plantation orders, the mainstay of the industry before the war, continued to be held back by the insecurity of the hinterland (Hardon 1948, 702). The textile industry was slower to recover because most of the large mills were in the hinterland and did not come under Dutch control until the capture of Mojokerto in March 1947 or the first Police Action in July. The Bintang Pari and Kantjil Mas mills near Bangil were both badly damaged. At the end of April 1948 only 880 hand looms and 423 machine looms were in operation, compared with 8,200 and 2,700 respectively before the war (*EWI,* 1948, 419). Production also resumed for leather goods, electric light globes (Philips), car batteries, bicycles, rubber goods, chemicals (carbonic and sulfuric acid and oxygen), glass, and roof tiles (*EWI,* 7/6/47, 13, 23, 375). By mid-1948 the Dutch had enumerated 1,943 industrial establishments in the reoccupied part of East Java, of which 1,395 were in the city of Surabaya; by July 1949 the total had grown to 3,247, of which 1,973 were in Surabaya (ARA, MK 2.10.29, 408: 5/48, 7/49).

The controlled economy that carried over from the Japanese occupation favored larger, European firms. Without bureaucratic support, large-scale business was virtually impossible. And of course European businessmen were best placed to gain the necessary support from European civil servants. Across Indonesia between May 1946 and April 1948, European and American firms absorbed 85 percent of licensed industrial loans, Chinese firms another 13 percent, and Indonesian firms less than 1 percent (Leeuwen 1948, 722). In the first half of 1948, European firms received 62 percent of foreign-exchange allocations, Chinese firms 38 percent, and Indonesian firms just 0.33 percent (Geursen 1948, 719). These figures reveal that, after a brief period of Indonesianization under the Japanese, the Dutch were indeed reimposing economic as well as political control.

As a gesture toward nationalist concerns, in mid-1948 the prewar Small Industry Fund (Stichting "Fonds voor de Kleine Nijverheid") was reactivated, but even across the whole country the amount of loans distributed, mainly to textile enterprises, was minuscule (Davis 1949, 1233). After the occupation of Sidoarjo and Gresik early in 1947 had brought former centers of batik production under Dutch control, efforts were made to revive the manufacture of sarongs by advances of cambrics and dyes to producers under a kind of putting-out system (Davis 1949, 1234). By January 1949 ninety-two enterprises were counted throughout the Dutch controlled area of East Java with a production in the previous calendar year of almost half a million sarongs (ARA, MK 2.10.29, 408: 1/49). However, apart from a few hundred hand looms operated under factory conditions,[8] Surabaya was not prominent as a center of other recognized small-scale or household industries. Real wages were too high.

Recovery of Surabaya's manufacturing base lagged well behind that of Jakarta. Unlike Surabaya, Jakarta did not suffer bloody reoccupation by Allied forces and the Dutch were much better able to establish and maintain control over the surrounding hinterland. Demand and business expectations were therefore much more buoyant. Of foreign exchange requested for industrial raw materials in 1947–48, almost 80 percent was directed to West Java (mainly Jakarta) and only 13 percent to East Java (mainly Surabaya), the balance being accounted for by Central Java and the Outer Islands. Moreover, this national allocation of Fl 766 million excluded another Fl 435 in special funding to the textile industry and Fl 185 million for the printing industry, both of which were concentrated in West Java (Geursen 1948, 718–19). Similarly, of bank credit allocations from May 1946 to April 1948, the lion's share, 65 percent, went to West Java, compared with 24 percent to East Java, 4 percent to Central Java, and 7 percent to the Outer islands (Leeuwen 1948, 722). These allocations of foreign exchange and credit reinforced the lead that West Java's industries had built up in the 1930s by allowing faster rehabilitation and expansion.

Jakarta's ascendancy as the industrial center of Indonesia was therefore established before the recognition of Independence. Circumstances after Independence would reinforce Surabaya's subordinate status.

INDEPENDENCE

The transfer of sovereignty in December 1949 marked no obvious discontinuity in industrial policy, for the groundwork had been laid by the outgoing Dutch administration. The Industry Policy Guidelines of 1946 had already specified that industrial rehabilitation and development would be carried out on the basis of annual plans (Jonkers 1948, 121–22). In November 1949, on the eve of independence, the Industry Section of the Department of Economic Affairs finally issued a vague document entitled *Bijzonder Industrieel Welvaartsplan, 1950* (Special industrial welfare plan), which was intended as the basis for preparation of a detailed industry plan (DEZ 1949). Amid all the exigencies of Independence, there was no sense of urgency about industrial development and in fact the first Hatta cabinet (December 1949–August 1950) had no minister for industry (Feith 1962, 46–47). This was remedied with the succeeding Natsir cabinet, when the country's leading economist, Sumitro Djojohadikusumo, was appointed minister for trade and industry and began to set in place the elements of an industrial strategy.

In April 1951, Sumitro launched the country's first development plan, the Economic Urgency Program (also known as the Sumitro Plan). Fulfilling the promise of the Special Welfare Plan of 1949, it included an industrial development plan (Sutter 1959, 774–81). As in other newly independent countries such as India and China, industry was now regarded as the way of the future, the very essence of development. Whereas the Dutch had sought to develop industry to strengthen a fundamentally agrarian economy, the Indonesians foresaw its transformation into a modern industrial one. In line with policy since the 1930s and prevailing orthodoxy, the strategy took the apparently easy path of import substitution (Sutter 1959, 780). Imports were already restricted by a regime of revenue tariffs, licensing, and foreign-exchange allocations (Siahaan 1996, 174–75, 331). Large budget deficits kept pressure on the balance of payments, but governments resisted devaluing the rupiah: tighter quotas, surcharges, and prepayments were all imposed in desperate attempts to stem the flow of imports. The extent to which such measures translated into effective protection is impossible to quantify. Because of worsening corruption and smuggling, the actual impact of import restrictions was haphazard and bore little relation to official policy.

Capital being regarded as the missing factor in production, close attention was paid to industrial finance. To assist in financing the Economic Urgency Program, in April 1951 Sumitro organized the establishment of the State Industry Bank (Bank Industri Negara), successor to the Rehabilitation Bank (Herstelbank), set up in May 1948 and after 1960 known as Bapindo (Bank Pembangunan Indonesia) (Leeuwen 1948, 723; Siahaan 1996, 235–69). The new bank drew on foreign loans to finance various large import-substituting projects, some of which had their genesis in the colonial government's aborted emergency program for heavy industry announced in 1940 (ARA, NHM 1944, 139).

In East Java, construction began simultaneously in 1953 on a cement factory, a caustic soda plant, and a gunnysack mill, all located within the immediate hinterland of Surabaya (table 5.4). The cement plant, the largest industrial project of the 1950s, absorbed $14 million of the $100 million Export-Import Bank credit line that the United States had made available to Indonesia soon after Independence (Higgins 1957, 74). The site outside Gresik, an old trading port about twenty kilometers northwest of Surabaya (chap. 1), had been identified in the late 1930s for its proximity to large, high-grade limestone deposits.[9] On completion in 1957 the plant was opened by President Sukarno himself and marked the first step in the development of Gresik from a center of handicrafts to a

TABLE 5.4
State enterprises established in East Java, 1951–59

Company	Product	Company formed	Construction begun	Official opening
Semen Gresik	cement	1953	1954	1957
Soda	caustic soda	1951	1953	1956
Karung Rosella	gunnies	1952	1953	1956
Iglas	bottles	1955	1956	1959

zone of heavy industry. Caustic soda was an essential and strategic input for oil refining and the manufacture of industrial gases and explosives. A plant had been mooted during World War I and plans were revived in the late 1930s, when war again loomed; in the 1940 emergency program East Java was the favored location because of the salt works of Gresik and Madura and the availability of cheap hydroelectricity (ARA, NHM 1944, 68; ARA, MK 2.10.29.051: GV 25/4/40). Built at Wonocolo, just south of Surabaya, the plant was opened by Vice President Hatta in July 1956, though because of technical problems it had reached only half its planned capacity by 1960 (Siahaan 1996, 306). A few months earlier the gunnysack factory (PT Karung Rosella) had opened with the purpose of meeting about 10 percent of the country's requirement of jute sacks for sugar, coffee beans, rice, and other grains. The fourth major project, on the Ngagel industrial estate, was a glass factory (PN Gelas Indonesia, Iglas) to produce bottles for the adjacent brewery and soft drink companies.[10] Contracted as a turnkey project in November 1955, after many delays it came into production in March 1959 (Siahaan 1996, 253–55). Less successful was a seaweed (*agar-agar*) processing plant at Wonocolo, which had to close down for lack of fresh water.

Despite the publicity attracted by these large, state-owned projects, most new industrial plants and employment generation during the 1950s occurred within the private sector. Once peace and security were restored, consumption and investment picked up of their own accord. After mid-1950 the Korean War and the associated rubber boom gave a temporary boost to domestic demand, which was subsequently maintained by budget deficits. Some new factories were set up by foreign investors. In Surabaya the most notable project was the automobile assembly plant Borguin, a joint venture between the German firm Borgward and local partner Fritz Eman of Udatin (Usaha Dagang Teknik Indonesia), which opened at the end of 1955 opposite the port area at Tanjung Perak; this become the country's third vehicle assembler after Gaja Motor (formerly General Motors) and Indonesia Service Corporation (Dodge, Willys Jeep, and Ford) (Sutter 1959, 796; Siahaan 1996, 242–44, 268–69). The Industry Bank also assisted some indigenous (*pribumi*) entrepreneurs to set up private factories, several of which were located in and around Surabaya. Most of these men had good Nationalist Party (PNI) connections. Former mayor Doel Arnowo in August 1953 opened the NV Indos Knitting Factory (socks and undershirts); the Dasaad Musin concern rehabilitated the Kantjil Mas textile mill; and Rahman Tamin and Company in May 1958 opened the Ratatex textile mill at Krian (southwest of Surabaya). Madjid Asnoen, an importer of equipment, building materials, radios, bicycles, and motorcycles in 1953 diversified into manufacturing steel furniture (beds, tables, and chairs): in mid-1957 President Sukarno himself opened Asnoen's wire and nail factory at Waru.[11]

A notable feature of the Sumitro Plan was emphasis on the development of small-scale industry. As explained above, measures to improve small-scale industry had been taken during the 1930s and after the war as a means of raising indigenous welfare. Along similar lines, centers (*centrales*, *induk*) were now to be set up in industries such as woodworking, ironworking, bronze, ceramics, textiles, leather, and umbrellas (Higgins 1957, 68–9). What was unusual about the Sumitro Plan was that assistance to small-scale industry was seen as more important than investment in large-scale industry (Oorschot 1956, 73–74). This reflected nationalist distrust of large-scale enterprise, which was mostly foreign owned, and the belief in cooperatives as the ideal form of popular economic organization. However, these centers were so few—by the end of 1954 only eight were operation—so scattered, and in many cases so poorly managed that their impact was minimal (Djojohadikusumo 1954). Much the same could be said of the loan program for mechanization of small-scale enterprises (Paauw 1967, 216–17).

No provincial data on production or employment have been found for this period but a 1957 industrial directory points to diversification of manufacturing (IDI, 1957–58). Extraction of the 748 entries for the municipality of Surabaya yields the following distribution, ranked by number of establishments:

92	Printing
63	Textiles and clothing
48	Furniture
47	Bread (26) and biscuits (21)
43	Machinery (40) and shipbuilding (3)
37	Confectionery
32	Cigarettes (30) and tobacco drying (2)
30	Rubber goods
29	Leather (18) and tanning (11)
28	Sawmills; coffee roasting
24	Soft drinks
14	Cosmetics
12	Electrical workshops
11	Coconut oil; concreteware; frying pans; noodles; tapioca flour; weaving
10	Soap; spinning; tinplate
8	Soy sauce
7	Medicines; paints; paper products; rice mills
6	Glass
5	Engraving; jewelry; plastic goods; seaweed; vehicle assembly and repair; wine and spirits
4	Batik; bicycles; hats; ice; knitting
3	Krupuk; mosquito coils; preserved meat
2	Batteries; chemicals; gambier; jams; matches; toothpaste
1	Beer; bandages; dairy; gunnysacks; lamp wicks; light

bulbs; macaroni; margarine; dried peanuts; suitcases; toys; weighing scales.

Because no account is taken of size of establishment, this ranking does not indicate the relative importance of different branches of industry. Clothing and furniture establishments were typically small, whereas sole establishments such as state-owned factories, the brewery, the Philips light bulb factory and the Procter and Gamble (Filma) margarine plant were all large. Nevertheless, the list does at least highlight the proliferation of establishments in light industries such as bread and biscuit making, confectionery, cigarettes, rubber goods, soft drinks, coconut oil, concreteware, and frying pans. Except for bakeries and soft drinks, these industries had been represented by few establishments before the Japanese occupation. Though less spectacularly, the broadening of the industrial base is also evident in industries such as glass, paint, plastic goods, bicycles, mosquito coils, and matches.

The textile industry appears more significant if the area is widened to include the immediate hinterland of Surabaya. In mid-1952 the residencies of Surabaya and Malang together accounted for 99 percent of the small number of machine looms in East Java and 71 percent of hand looms (table 5.5). Kabupaten Surabaya (now Gresik) ranked second to Surabaya municipality and, as before the war, counted many hand looms. Sidoarjo was more specialized in batik, albeit with only thirty-two establishments. Surabaya also boasted a large number of tailors. Prewar figures are not readily comparable but suggest that there had as yet been little expansion.

Despite the great hopes with which Indonesia had embarked upon independence, the economic achievements of the 1950s were seen as disappointing and this was especially true of industrial development. The idea that government could mobilize underutilized resources by injections of capital, like the Marshall Plan in Western Europe, turned out to be wildly unrealistic. In Indonesia there was no educated labor force, no pool of would-be entrepreneurs, and

TABLE 5.5
Location and size of textile establishments, East Java, 1952

Residency	Kabupaten	No. of Establ.	Machine looms	%	Hand looms	%
Surabaya		90	1,879	64	5,614	47
	Surabaya	69	1,397	48	4,224	35.5
	Sidoarjo	19	164	5	1,374	11.5
	Mojokerto	1	230	11	—	—
	Jombang	1	—	—	16	—
Malang		40	1,027	35	2,812	24
	Pasuruan	9	967	33	1,164	10
	Malang	21	20	1	1,388	11
	Probolinggo	5	40	1	260	2
	Lumajang	5	—	—	105	1
Other		50	28	1	3,458	29
East Java		*180*	*2,934*	*100*	*11,889*	*100*

Source: KP 1953.

not much of a market. Inward-looking trade policies, though not controversial at the time, had made the task even more difficult. Budget deficits combined with defense of overvalued exchange rates created worsening macroeconomic instability (Paauw 1967, esp. 237–38). Foreign firms were reluctant to invest and domestic business sought short-term, speculative profits. Nevertheless, based on United Nations national income estimates, Suhadi (1967, 32–37), argues that the manufacturing sector may have grown on average at around 10 percent per annum from 1951 to 1957 and increased its share of national product from 9 to 12 percent. Stagnation occurred after 1958, when the focus of policy switched from development to distribution, in particular the role of Western and Chinese capital.

NATIONALIZATION

At independence the view of all main political parties was that the commanding heights of the economy, though still dominated by private Dutch firms, should ultimately be in the public domain. Private capital, including foreign investment, would be restricted to "nonessential" industries. During the 1950s economic policy was a tug-of-war between radical nationalists, who sought an immediate end to Dutch economic power, and those who on pragmatic grounds favored a more gradual approach (Feith 1962). By means of the 1949 Round Table agreements the Dutch government had sought to perpetuate favored treatment for Dutch business interests after Independence, but the business regime very soon began to tighten. In March 1950 the Foreign Exchange Certificate Regulation drove a wedge between the Dutch and Indonesian currencies: henceforth, export receipts were to be cashed at a rate of Fl 1 = Rp 2, while purchase of foreign exchange for imports and profit remittances was at the higher rate of Fl 1 = Rp 3 (HVA 1949, 12–13). This squeezed the rate of profit on Indonesian investments and discouraged the inflow of new equity capital, while making the reinvestment of accumulated profits more attractive. To encourage training and promotion of Indonesians, permits were introduced for employment of personnel from Holland. Managers and skilled employees who retired or resigned because they could see no future in Indonesia thus became more difficult to replace. Repeal of repressive colonial labor legislation allowed the organization of national trade unions, which targeted Dutch firms in vigorous campaigning for improved wages and conditions. State enterprises enjoyed government patronage, utilities were nationalized with compensation, and certain fields such as importing and stevedoring were reserved for Indonesian business. The combination of such restrictions pegged back the Dutch share of economic activity, though not enough to satisfy the radicals (Sutter 1959).

At the end of 1957 radical nationalists found a pretext for action when the motion for Dutch withdrawal from New Guinea was unexpectedly defeated in the United Nations. On 3 December 1957 communist-led trade unions, apparently with the tacit support of President Sukarno, began to take over prominent Dutch enterprises. The campaign began with seizure of the Jakarta head office of the Royal Packet Company (KPM), the much-resented Dutch-flag interisland shipping company, and immediately extended to its offices and ships in ports across the country, including Surabaya. As the movement spread, the army stepped in to prevent the communist-controlled trade union movement from gaining control of almost the entire modern sector. Henceforth takeovers were to be coordinated by local army commanders. A directive of 14 December specified that there should be joint trade union and military management but a military officer was placed in charge of each enterprise and trade unions were kept under tight rein. As Dutch managers and technical experts were relieved of their positions pending repatriation, the burden of day-to-day operations devolved upon any Indonesian personnel with technical expertise. Late in the month the central government issued a formal decree of nationalization, backdated to 3 December.

Only a few large Dutch factories, owned by multinational enterprises such as Heineken, Unilever, and Shell, were able to forestall nationalization by transfer to non-Dutch ownership. In Surabaya the local engineering firm Braat attempted to carry on.[12] Although registered since 1949 in Holland, Braat had always been a local company and during the 1950s had built up a good working relationship with the Indonesian authorities. Aware of the firm's strategic importance as the leading engineering firm in East Java, its manager continued throughout 1958 to employ twenty-eight Dutch personnel and to work under military supervision. By 1959, however, he had to admit that conditions such as the ban on remittances had made it impossible to carry on. Some of the banks and trading houses also attempted during 1958 to find a formula to carry on as Indonesian enterprises, but also without success. Nationalist pressure was irresistible.

Nationalization greatly strengthened central government control over the modern sector. As an interim measure, enterprises were placed under the formal direction of an Industry and Mining Enterprise Supervisory Board (Badan Penguasaan Perusahaan Industri dan Tambang, Bappit), whose head office in Jakarta took over the largest enterprises, leaving the rest to regional offices (see appendix). When the legal nationalization process had been completed, this division was formalized by Law 19/1960, which created separate categories of state enterprises (*perusahaan negara,* PN) and regional enterprises (*perusahaan daerah,* PD). During 1961, Surabaya's largest industrial firms, such as the engineering firm Barata (formerly Braat), Indra (formerly de Industrie), Bisma (formerly de Vulkaan), and Dok Surabaya (formerly Droogdok Maatschappij Soerabaja), were thus reconstituted as state enterprises and grouped under General Management Boards (Badan Pimpinan Umum, BPU); smaller firms were allocated to provincial governments as perusahaan daerah under supervision of Regional Enterprise Management Boards (Badan Pimpinan Perusahaan Daerah, Bapipda).

The takeovers of 1957–58 turned out to be just the first round. British ownership became untenable after Sukarno launched his campaign of Confrontation against Malaysia in September 1963. On 18 January 1964 the arrest of two Indonesian-flag ships in Hong Kong for nonpayment of dockyard repair bills became a pretext for trade union seizure of the Unilever plants in Jakarta, which led on the twenty-fourth to the takeover of the Unilever toiletries plant, the BAT cigarette factory, the F and N (Fraser and Neave) soft drink factory in Surabaya, and the Inbritex (formerly Nebritex) textile mill near Pasuruan, as well as a large number of plantations and trading houses throughout the country (*SP,* 20–24/1/64). The Shell refinery at Wonokromo, however, remained under foreign control until transferred at the end of 1965 to the state oil company PN Permina (later Pertamina) as part of the disposal of Shell's interests in Indonesia (Hunter 1967, 85).

The next target was U.S. firms. Following anti-American demonstrations in Surabaya in December–January 1965 (chap. 3), on 24 March workers took control of the cooking oil and margarine plant of PT Filma (formerly Proctor and Gamble), refusing to recognize its transfer in November 1963 from American to Swiss ownership (*SP,* 25/3/65). Finally, in a ceremony at the governor's residence in mid-May 1965, the German toothpaste company Prodenta, the

Singer Sewing Machine Company, the now Belgium-Luxemburg-owned Heineken brewery, and the Faroka cigarette plant in Malang were "voluntarily" handed over—the Heineken director refused to sign and was declared persona non grata (*SP*, 19/5/65). Unlike Dutch enterprises, however, these other foreign firms were not formally nationalized but placed under Indonesian "supervision," in effect military control.

By the end of May 1965 not a single foreign-owned factory remained in Surabaya, or indeed anywhere else in East Java. When foreign investment ceased, so also did the transfer of technology and expertise. In fact repatriation of so many foreign personnel, both technical and managerial, caused a drain of precious skills and know-how before Indonesians had been properly trained to take over. The distribution system virtually collapsed. As mentioned above, since the 1930s the trading houses had been the catalyst in industrial development. Internatio, for example, had invested in the CIHM sulfuric acid works at Sepanjang, the NICKI porcelain and firebrick works at Sepanjang and Ngandang, and the oxygen works and Morton confectionery factories in Surabaya; Borsumij had a metal press and Hima bicycle factory (Internatio 1938). These houses had also sponsored many other entrepreneurs by providing a market, making machines and raw materials available on long-term and short-term credit, controlling quality, and, as necessary, extending technical advice—in effect subcontracting the manufacturing process (ARA, NHM 1944). The textile industry was greatly disrupted for hitherto the mills had never had to bother about marketing. When the state trading houses (*niaga*) failed to maintain these services, factory managers were stranded, especially those in East Java, far from the main textile center in Bandung (West Java). They knew how to produce but not how to sell (Sumartono, interview, 11/87). Above all the link between East Java and the Outer Islands, which since the 1930s had provided a much-needed widening of the market, was all but broken under simultaneous assault from rebellions and martial law and the disappearance of regular shipping services (Dick 1987a).

Industrial development therefore received a severe check from nationalization and performance rapidly worsened (Soehoed 1967, 72–73). The fundamental problems were lack of investment, lack of maintenance, and lack of a market. These constituted a vicious circle, since lack of sales meant poor utilization, financial losses, and therefore inability to finance modernization. The main problem was poor utilization. For example, the textile industry had enough nominal weaving capacity to be self-sufficient but yarn supplies could sustain only a fraction of that capacity because of the acute shortage of foreign exchange (Palmer and Castles 1965). In East Java overall capacity utilization fell precipitously, from 60 to 70 percent in February 1963 to a mere 10 to 15 percent by October 1964 (*SP,* 5/11/64). Most hand looms were idle. At this point the Supreme Command for Economic Operations (KOTOE) set up the Clothing Team (Team Sandang) to attack the problem and take over the distribution of yarn (Palmer and Castles 1965, 43–44). In May 1965 the team made an inspection tour of East Java with vague promises to revitalize the industry (*SP,* 11/5/65). Problems of inadequate raw material supplies applied across the board. The brewery, for example, was reported in mid-1964 to be working at only half capacity because of lack of ingredients and bottles (*SP,* 18/7/64). Much machinery was immobilized by shortage of imported spare parts, though local ingenuity worked near miracles.

Nevertheless, some industrial investment was maintained. The central government led the way with several large foreign-aid projects intended to promote self-sufficiency.[13] Investment on a smaller scale came from the private sector but was really pseudo-industrialization. It would not have occurred but for the particular way in which the foreign-exchange regulations were administered. Because government gave priority to industrial firms in the allocation of foreign exchange, trading firms that imported finished or semifinished products were now compelled for survival to establish manufacturing enterprises. The aim was not, however, to set up an efficient plant of minimum efficient scale but to have a token operation that would be sufficient to qualify for a quota of raw or semifinished imports and perhaps also a quota of finished goods. The surplus could then be disposed of on the black market.[14]

Once the industrial center, Surabaya was now at a marked disadvantage. Import and foreign-exchange licensing had been centralized in Jakarta in the early 1950s (*SP*, 9/12/53). Companies with their main office in Surabaya found that they needed a full-time representative in Jakarta just to deal with the bureaucracy. Apart from the slower growth of population and purchasing power in East Java, foreign investors were thus further discouraged. Nationalization exacerbated the situation, since commercial decision making became even more centralized. Physical plant was probably in almost as poor a condition as at the end of the Japanese occupation but the shortage of capital and foreign exchange was even more chronic. Far from industrializing, the local economy had turned full circle. Steady progress in the decade or so after 1946 had been squandered in the next by political adventures. In the late 1960s the manufacturing sector (including utilities) accounted for less than 10 percent of national GDP (Booth and McCawley 1981, 5). When private manufacturing investment resumed in the late 1960s, it flowed not to Surabaya but to Jakarta.

New Order Industrialization

NATIONAL TRENDS

Renewed industrial development awaited an injection of capital. Since the public sector was bankrupt, the initiative had to be private. The new Foreign Investment Law (1967) and the Domestic Investment Law (1968) showed that private and even foreign capital was again welcome and provided generous concessions (Hill 1988). These new laws were accompanied by political and macroeconomic stability for the first time in many years. In 1969 inflation was held down to just 10 percent (Grenville 1981). Foreign-exchange convertibility was restored (Rosendale 1981). These achievements gave confidence that the economy was now well managed and that investments could be planned with some degree of certainty. The inflow of foreign investment was modest compared with the mobilization of domestic resources but it was the catalyst in revitalizing the large and medium (L and M) manufacturing sector. Apart from oil and banking, between 1967 and 1974 approved foreign investment flowed predominantly into manufacturing, $2 billion out of $3.5 billion (World Bank 1981, annex 5:19).

These circumstances gave rise to very different outlooks for new and existing firms. It was much easier for a new firm to establish itself with access to investment "facilities" than for an existing firm to claw its way back from insolvency. Liquidity problems affected the public sector with particular severity and at the beginning of the New Order almost the entire L and M manufacturing sector was in public hands. When seized in 1958, the plant of most former Dutch enterprises was already dated, of interwar scale and technology. After a decade of disinvestment, poor maintenance and inexperienced management under military supervision, the plant and equipment were badly run down but no funds were available for rehabilitation. As a last resort, many regional enterprises were leased out to private entrepreneurs who merely exploited the plant and left it in a worse state than before. Not until the 1970s did public-sector funds become available for rehabilitation. By then many public enterprises were no longer capable of being resuscitated, especially regional government enterprises.[15] Many private establishments were not much better off. In fact the credit squeeze after October 1966 to suppress inflation had exacerbated their liquidity crisis. Domestic demand contracted, while import liberalization increased competition. Some firms managed to survive by earning foreign exchange through exports, having funds salted away in foreign bank accounts, or through foreign associates, such as in Singapore, who were willing to remit funds or provide lines of credit. Those without such recourse in many cases just went bankrupt.

New Order industrialization divided into two periods, an early period of import substitution that perpetuated protectionist industrial policy since the 1930s and a second period from the 1980s characterized by the non-oil export drive (Hill 2000). Import substitution behind a rising tariff wall involved the usual distortions of resource allocation. For many import-competing industries the tariff rate was more than 100 percent of domestic value added, implying a net loss to the national economy—the highest effective rates applied to durable consumer goods including motor vehicles (World Bank 1981, annex 2, table 4). A regime of high effective protection combined with rapid growth of real incomes, especially among the urban middle class, helps explain why so much private investment was concentrated in the final stages of consumer good production while basic industry remained in public hands—"upstream socialism, downstream capitalism," in the famous phrase of Kunio Yoshihara (1988).

The Third Five-Year Plan (1979–84) marked a determined push for industrialization based on continuing import substitution (Hill 1988; McCawley 1981). Much of the industrial development during the first two plans had involved the establishment of consumer goods industries but often just the final stages of production. Whether in the case of soft drinks, pharmaceuticals, or motor vehicles, local manufacturing was merely an assembly operation, sustained by very high rates of effective protection. Now the aim was to invest oil revenues to consolidate an industrial base that would provide the inputs such as iron and steel, aluminum, chemicals, and plastics for downstream processing. As in the previous plan, much of the investment was to be funded by the central government from oil tax revenues.

After collapse of oil prices in the early 1980s, industrialization strategy of necessity became more outward looking. With Indonesia again in balance of payments crisis, a non-oil export drive was declared a national priority. Accompanying large exchange rate devaluations in 1983 and 1986, a series of deregulation packages were introduced to streamline customs procedures, simplify licensing, ease foreign investment guidelines, and reform the financial system (Hill 2000). Tariffs were reduced and many nontariff barriers phased out. By the mid-1980s such measures had begun to achieve rapid and sustained growth in manufactured exports. In 1987 manufactured exports for the first time surpassed agricultural exports and by 1991 were over half of merchandise exports (Hill 2000, 82).

TRENDS IN SURABAYA AND EAST JAVA

Because of its port and good transport links with the rest of the province, Surabaya was as ever the favored place in East Java to locate manufacturing plant. However, the boom did not begin to spill over from Jakarta–West Java to Surabaya–East Java until the early 1970s. By then, East Java was enjoying steady growth in real incomes, underpinned by the success of the Green Revolution rice intensification program. Growth of the rural economy was reinforced by small-scale infrastructure projects under the Kabupaten and Inpres schemes, which brought rapid improvement in rural-urban communications ("Economic Survey" 1971, 30). With a population at the 1971 census of 25.5 million, East Java was thereby more closely integrated as a growing and potentially large mass market for locally manufactured consumer goods (Dick, Fox, and Mackie 1993).

Surabaya's industrial expansion accelerated during the 1970s. In 1970 the Industry Statistics for L and M plants enumerated a manufacturing workforce of 31,700, about 5,000 more than in the Industry Census of 1964 (BPS, *Statistik industri* 1970). By 1976, L and M employment had increased 10 percent to almost 35,000 (table 5.6). Another 22,000 employees, however, were located in the adjacent kabupaten of Sidoarjo and Gresik. In 1976 some 60 percent of L and M employment was still located within the municipality, but subsequent expansion was twice as fast on the urban fringe. By 1995 there were actually more industrial workers in Sidoarjo than

TABLE 5.6
Manufacturing employment, Greater Surabaya, 1976, 1996

	1976	%	1996	%
Surabaya	34,800	60	159,300	40
Sidoarjo	16,600	28	180,550	44
Gresik	7,200	12	67,350	16
Greater Surabaya	58,600	100	407,200	100

Source: BPS, Statistik industri (annual).
Note: Large and medium (L&M) establishments, excluding oil and gas.

in the municipality. As the unit of analysis, it is therefore appropriate to refer to Greater Surabaya (including Sidoarjo and Gresik) rather than the municipality alone. Between 1976 and 1995, Greater Surabaya achieved a sustained rate of growth of 10 percent per annum in employment and 27 percent in value-added (without adjustment for inflation).[16]

The early phase of import substitution (to the mid-1980s) was epitomized by development of the new Surabaya Industrial Estate Rungkut (SIER), which opened in 1975. A joint venture of the three levels of government to overcome the shortage of good industrial sites, the 245 hectares of former rice land at Rungkut, in the southeast of the municipality, were made available as serviced sites.[17] By 1985 the estate was nearing full occupancy with 221 establishments, mostly new ventures, and about twenty-six thousand workers (table 5.7). The largest sector in terms of employment was food, drink, and tobacco (FDT), but over five thousand workers were accounted for by the Sampoerna Group's two nonmechanized kretek factories. The leading sector was chemicals. Because of zoning restrictions that required polluting industries such as petrochemicals to locate outside the city, activities at Rungkut were mainly assembly or extruding operations, but the range of products testified to the growth in consumer income and an associated shift in tastes. The largest single subgroup was plastics, an industry that had barely existed before the New Order, but now involved a wide range of consumer goods, from household items to cassettes;

TABLE 5.7
Establishments and employment by sector, Rungkut Industrial Estate, February 1985

Sector	No. of Establ.	%	Employees[a]	%
Food, drink, tobacco	34	15	7,993	31
Chemicals	62	28	6,400	25
Metals & machinery	53	24	5,337	20
Textiles, clothing, footwear	17	8	1,987	8
Nonmetals	13	6	1,563	6
Wood & furniture	16	7	1,410	5
Paper & printing	14	6	823	3
Other/unknown	12	6	649	2
Total	221	100	26,162	100

Source: Based on listing of PT Surabaya Industrial Estate Rungkut (SIER).
[a]Some establishments under construction or no employment cited.

next came pharmaceuticals, toiletries, and cosmetics, including a new Unilever plant with six hundred fifty workers, and then other chemical operations including paints, pesticides (mosquito coils), adhesives, batteries, and film laboratories. Metals and machinery was still low-tech, mainly fabrication and general engineering; another half dozen firms were involved in the component manufacture or assembly of bicycles, an activity dating back to the 1930s; about the same number again in making vehicle bodies; and a manufacturer of pressure lamps employed almost a thousand. Notable gaps in the range of enterprises were electrical and electronic goods and textiles and footwear. A leading export industry in some developing countries such as Malaysia, electrical and electronic goods accounted for a mere five hundred employees at SIER. Textiles, clothing, and footwear (TCF) was represented by just seventeen firms, with a total of two thousand employees, of which about half manufactured footwear and leather goods.

Between the early phase of import substitution and the later phase (after 1985) of the non-oil export drive, there was no significant difference in the rate of growth but a very marked shift toward light industry. The hitherto minor TCF sector, especially footwear, grew rapidly in response to export opportunities, offsetting a relative decline of the traditionally large FDT sector (table 5.8). Other expanding light-industry sectors were wood and wood products and paper and printing. Domestic demand was a significant but wood and wood products—especially plywood and furniture—was boosted by a 1980 ban on the export of timber logs and, eight years later, on the export of raw rattan (Schwarz 1990). By contrast, the city's historical bias toward heavy industry was weakened. This was particularly marked in terms of value added: heavy industry's share fell from 67 percent in 1976 to 49 percent in 1995. The corresponding share of employment fell from 56 percent to 43 percent. These broad categories nevertheless give only a very general impression and disguise considerable variation. For example, the export drive greatly boosted electrical machinery (including electronics) and fabricated metals such as metal furniture.

TABLE 5.8
Employment and value added by sector, Greater Surabaya and Greater Jakarta, 1986, 1996

	Employment		Value Added	
Sector	SBY	JKT	SBY	JKT
Light Industry	*55.7%*	*57.0%*	*50.5%*	*33.5%*
FDT	18.1	5.5	28.2	5.0
TCF	19.8	41.7	8.5	19.9
Wood, etc.	11.6	5.4	4.2	3.6
Paper & printing	4.2	4.4	9.6	5.0
Heavy Industry	*43.2%*	*39.1%*	*49.1%*	*64.8%*
Chemicals	17.8	13.0	14.5	13.6
Nonmetals	6.5	4.8	4.5	3.6
Metals & machinery	20.9	21.3	30.1	47.6
Other	*1.1*	*4.1*	*0.4*	*1.7*
Total	100%	100%	100%	100%
Number (thousands)	407	1,259		
Value (Rp trillions)			8.5	27.4

Source: Based on BPS, Statistik industri (annual).
Note: Large and medium (L&M) establishments.

The spillover of large-scale industry beyond the municipality began as early as the 1930s, when textile mills located in the foothills to tap the abundant supply of cheap labor released by the declining sugar industry and to enjoy access to cheap land and good fresh water. During the 1950s several large factories were built in rice fields along the highway south of Wonokromo, where hitherto there had been only the Wonocolo leather works and the complex of the former Waroe sugar mill. As the industrial boom gathered strength in the 1970s, a rush ensued for good highway sites, giving rise to a clear pattern of ribbon development (map 5.1). The main

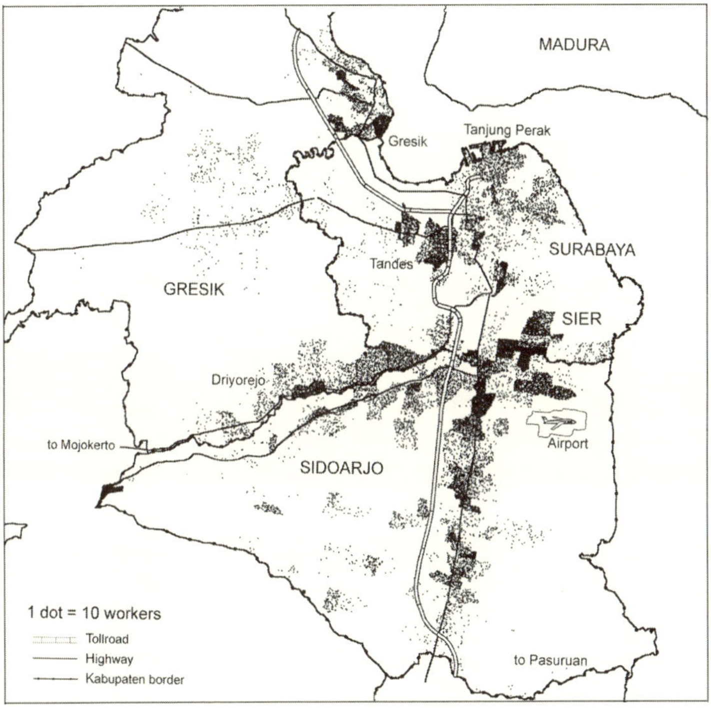

Map 5.1. Greater Surabaya: Distribution of employment in L and M manufacturing, 1990. Source: Courtesy of Peter Gardiner; based on 1990 census.

branch ran southward through Sidoarjo, toward Pasuruan and Malang; the other ran southwest, toward Mojokerto, along both banks of the Brantas River—some of these plants later caused bad water pollution (chap. 4). These ribbons were nevertheless quite thin: few factories located any distance back from the main highways. Despite the attractions of cheap land and village labor, proximity by road to the city, port, and airport was still a prerequisite of location, one enhanced in 1987 by completion of the toll road between Gempol, Waru, and the port of Tanjung Perak.

To the northwest, the opening of the Gresik cement plant in 1957 began a transformation of Gresik from a sleepy backwater surrounded by salt ponds to a cluster of heavy, power-consuming industries with bulk-handling port facilities. In the 1970s there followed completion of the state-owned petrochemical complex (Petrokimia), a power station, and plywood plants. The trend was encouraged by the Surabaya Master Plan, which zoned heavy and polluting factories outside the municipality (chap. 6). In the 1990s extension of the toll road to Gresik helped to attract other large plants, including a copper refinery.

By the mid-1990s the three districts of Greater Surabaya had grown into an industrial agglomeration with a total manufacturing workforce of over 550,000 people (table 5.9). Of these, 150,000 worked in small and household enterprises and 400,000 in the L and M sector. The L and M workforce was distributed across all two-digit sectors (table 5.9). Within East Java the degree of spatial concentration increased markedly between 1985 and 1995 in response to the opportunities of the non-oil export drive. By 1996, Greater Surabaya accounted for almost half of both employment and value added in L and M manufacturing (table 5.10). If allowance is made for the industrial ribbons extending as far as Pasuruan, Malang, and Mojokerto, the shares of this whole corridor rise to almost two-thirds. By the measure of value added, the only other substantial industrial cluster is the kretek industry, represented by the firm Gudang Garam in Kediri, to the west (Young 1993).[18]

TABLE 5.9
Employment by size of establishment, Greater Surabaya, 1986, 1996

	L&M		Small[a]		Household[b]		Total
Year	No.	%	No.	%	No.	%	No.
1986	140,500	65	35,500	17	39,000	18	215,000
1996	407,000	73	14,000	2.5	137,000	24.5	558,000

Sources: BPS, Sensus ekonomi 1986, 1996 (data tapes); BPS 1998a,b.
[a]1996 read as <20 employees (incorporated).
[b]1996 read as <20 employees (unincorporated).

TABLE 5.10
Industrial activity by location, East Java, 1986, 1996

	Employment		Value-added	
	1986	1996	1986	1996
Location	%	%	%	%
1. Surabaya	18	17	18	27
2. Sidoarjo & Gresik	16	26	21	22
3. Greater Surabaya (1+2)	34	43	39	49
4. Malang-Pasuruan-Mojokerto	18	19	18	15
5. Corridor (3+4)	52	62	57	64
6. Kediri	12	6	29	32
7. Other	36	32	14	4
East Java	100	100	100	100

Source: Calculated from BPS, Statistik industri (annual).
Note: Large and medium (L&M) establishments, excluding oil and gas.

Greater Surabaya is nevertheless much overshadowed as an industrial agglomeration by Greater Jakarta. Just as manufacturing has spread from Surabaya into the adjacent districts of Gresik and Sidoarjo, so it has spread from the capital city province of Jakarta into the adjacent kabupaten of Bogor, Tangerang and Bekasi, now known as the planning region Jabotabek. In terms of aggregate L and M–sector employment, in 1996 Greater Surabaya (0.4 million) was only about one-third the size of Jabotabek (1.25 million). Though still the country's second main industrial region, it was therefore a rather distant second.

Despite the marked difference in size, the profiles of these two agglomerations look quite similar (table 5.8). Both display a wide spread of activity across all two-digit sectors, very different from the high degree of specialization observed in the case of the next largest industrial areas around Bandung (mainly TCF) and Semarang (mainly FDT and TCF) (Kuncoro and Dick 1998). In terms of employment the salient difference between Surabaya and Jakarta is the former's much smaller TCF sector and much larger FDT sector. Value added shows a more complex pattern. Here Jakarta's higher productivity in the technologically sophisticated metals and machinery sector gives a strong bias to heavy industry and reduces the relative difference in size of the labor-intensive TCF sector. Nevertheless, Surabaya and Jakarta still more closely resemble each other than any smaller industrial areas in Indonesia. After the non-oil export drive began in the mid-1980s, Surabaya's industrial sector also grew just as fast as that of Jakarta. It may be concluded that Surabaya's industrial sector has matured into a viable industrial agglomeration of at least minimum efficient size.

The bias against Surabaya during the early phase of import substitution showed up in both foreign investment and public investment. Private capital inflow was heavily biased toward Jakarta–West Java, which over the period 1967–78 absorbed 43 percent of approved non-oil foreign investment, followed by North Sumatra, with another 15 percent (mainly the Asahan aluminum smelter) (World Bank 1981, annex 5:28). East Java ranked fourth by province but accounted for only 5 percent of the total. Foreign investors often visited Surabaya, attracted by its good port and low cost of land, but most decided to locate around Jakarta, which provided modern amenities, economies of agglomeration, and ready access to the bureaucracy. By the end of 1970 some $32 million had been approved for thirty-two projects, all in manufacturing, but only thirteen were new establishments ("Economic Survey" 1971, 34–35). Some of these early foreign investments were for rehabilitation of factories such as BAT, Heineken, and Unilever that had been taken under government control in the mid-1960s and been handed back at the beginning of the New Order in poor condition. New foreign investments were highly diverse: food processing (including the Nestlé milk factory and a South Korean monosodium glutamate plant), three cassava pelletizing factories for the export of cattle fodder, packaging materials, chemicals (paint, plastics), pharmaceuticals, and metal products (including vehicle assembly [Mitsubishi], steel pipes and wire). Unlike West Java, there was no foreign investment in textiles.

In Greater Surabaya industrialization was therefore driven by domestic investment. In 1986 just thirty-seven L and M establishments, a mere 3 percent of the total, had foreign-investment status, although their contribution to value added was rather higher, at 15 percent (BPS, *Sensus ekonomi* 1986). In no manufacturing group was foreign investment a leading sector. Over the next ten years, with the export boom and investment liberalization, the number of foreign investments increased but the role of foreign investment remained marginal. Even extending the industrial region to include the districts of Pasuruan and Mojokerto, the 134 projects enumerated in 1996 were only 5 percent of a much larger total, compared with around 12 percent in Greater Jakarta (BPS, *Sensus ekonomi* 1996). Nevertheless, these figures probably understate the role of foreign capital. Because domestic investments enjoyed simpler bureaucratic procedures, there was a tendency to seek access to foreign capital through borrowing rather than equity and to import technology through contractual agreements (Hill 1988, 45–47).

Surabaya and East Java also gained only a small share of public investment. Under the First Five-Year Plan (Repelita I; 1969–74), priority was given to raising the production of industries supporting the agricultural sector, notably fertilizer, cement, and chemicals, which together were allocated about half of planned investment; other priority industries were textiles, paper, pharmaceuticals, metals and machinery, and light and cottage industries (DOI 1969, vol. 2b: 1–47). In line with the socialist approach of the Old Order, public enterprise was to play the leading role in all but the pharmaceutical and light and cottage industries. Within the vicinity of

Surabaya, the main project was completion in July 1972 of the Petrokimia fertilizer plant at Gresik, on which construction had begun as long ago as August 1964 (Petrokimia Gresik ca.1987). There was a also a 33 percent expansion in the capacity of the Gresik cement plant and rehabilitation of the nationalized heavy-engineering firms (Barata and the merged Boma-Bisma-Indra) (Semen Gresik 1980, 65). Major public industrial projects elsewhere in East Java were expansion of the prewar paper mill at Leces (near Probolinggo) and completion of a new mill at Banyuwangi (DOI 1969, 3:80).

Public investment in heavy industry accelerated under the Second Five-Year Plan (1974–79) but no big projects were located in East Java. The government used part of its now abundant oil tax revenues to fund completion of the Krakatau steel mill in West Java, build new cement and fertilizer plants, share part of the cost of the Asahan smelter, expand oil refining capacity, and develop liquefied natural gas (LNG) facilities (World Bank 1981, 1:20). However, East Java and Surabaya in particular did benefit from expansion of the Tanjung Perak thermal power station's capacity from 50 to 150 megawatts (Husin 1993, 259), a tripling in capacity of the Gresik cement plant to 1.5 million tonnes per annum, and the opening in August 1979 of a superphosphate plant as part of the Petrokimia works (Semen Gresik 1980; Petrokimia Gresik ca. 1987). There was also some central government investment in rehabilitation and expansion of the large state-owned engineering firms. In April 1977 a new plant to manufacture diesel generators was inaugurated on the Bisma (formerly de Vulkaan) site on the Ngagel industrial estate and the capability of the heavy engineering firm Barata (formerly Braat) was upgraded (Barata, interviews, 22/10, 25/11/87).

In the 1980s Surabaya was more fortunate in gaining a huge hi-tech strategic enterprise of the Ministry for Research and Technology. This involved incorporation and complete modernization of the former naval base as PT PAL (Pangkalan Angkutan Laut [Naval base]).[19] Here the wheel had come full circle because the dockyard had led the city's early industrialization and until 1942 had been the major shipyard in the Netherlands Indies, even though most of its work was on government account. It also contributed greatly to the private sector in training large numbers of local tradesmen in metalworking and outfitting. After Independence it still employed thousands of workmen but was downgraded to naval refit and repair work. For want of new investment, by 1980 it was inefficient and technologically outmoded. The aim of the new minister, Dr. Habibie, was to transform it into a hi-tech shipyard and technological design center for both naval and commercial work that would be a spearhead of Indonesia's industrialization effort (Dick 1987a, 114). Under a ten-year program the site was progressively cleared of old buildings and workplaces, redesigned along modern lines with construction under cover inside huge sheds, and fitted out with modern plant and computer design equipment (fig. 5.5). President Soeharto commissioned the first stage in April 1985 and the yard geared up to produce both inter-island freighters and fast naval patrol boats (*IDN,* 9–10/88). With a workforce of around six thousand people, it had a massive direct

Figure 5.5. The modern PT PAL shipyard, formerly the naval dockyard, early 1990s. Photo by author.

impact on the local economy, but also important spillover effects through supply linkages and training, boosting the technological capability of the fairly large but still unsophisticated private metals and machinery sector.

In the mid-1990s, Surabaya's heavy industry was given further impetus by discovery of large offshore gas fields off the eastern tip of Madura. Because the original field was too small for LNG export, the National Gas Corporation (Perum Gas Negara) decided to use it for domestic consumption by constructing a 370-kilometer undersea pipeline to Gempol, just south of Surabaya, and from there connecting to Surabaya and other main towns in East Java, allowing distribution to both industry and households as a substitute for more expensive oil fuels (*SP,* 10/1/95). Large industrial consumers were connected in 1995 and the distribution network was to be linked up during 1996–97. Then in August 1995 the announcement was made of discovery of a much larger field that would justify construction of export-processing refineries (*SP,* 3/8/95). By the end of 1995 no fewer than three refineries were projected for East Java, one at Probolinggo and two at the northeastern tip, around Situbondo (*SP,* 16/11/95). Availability of abundant cheap energy, from offshore oil and gas, as well as East Kalimantan coal, sustain hopes that East Java may yet become a base for upstream petrochemicals industries.

During the 1990s these heavy-industrial projects underpinned a surge in foreign investment (table 5.11). The underlying factor, however, was the success of Indonesia's non-oil export drive combined with liberalization of foreign-investment rules. Unlike the 1970s, East Java was now well positioned to attract foreign firms and joint ventures. On the basis of new approvals, in 1994 East Java became for the first time Indonesia's leading province for foreign investment (*SP,* 23/12/94). More significant was the trend in realization, which in mid-1996 was only 45 percent of approved investment (BIS 1997). The currency crisis after mid-1997 almost halted new foreign investment but depreciation of the rupiah was so great that export industries remain a potentially attractive field.

TABLE 5.11
Value of foreign investment approvals, East Java, 1990–98 ($ millions/Rp trillions)

Year	1990	1991	1992	1993	1994	1995	1996	1997	1998
$ Value	—	—	—	—	6.8	10.7	2.8	4.9	0.7
Rp Value	2.6	4.4	3.6	4.0	9.6	5.8	12.7	12.0	—

Sources: BIS 1997; KSP (annual).

INFORMAL-SECTOR ENTERPRISE

Despite the dominance of L and M establishments by value added, the small (five to nineteen workers) and household (less than five) sectors make an important contribution to employment. This informal sector is nevertheless elusive because of the huge number of enterprises and the paucity of data. Unincorporated enterprises are not captured by standard registration and statistical reporting. The only comprehensive source is the ten-yearly economic census (BPS, *Sensus ekonomi*) by household of all *nonagricultural* enterprises, but the reliability of even this data is suspect. For want of clear definition or close questioning, many household or streetside income-earning activities are almost certainly overlooked. Nevertheless, in 1996 all enumerated informal-sector enterprises accounted for employment of over half a million in Surabaya municipality and almost one million in Greater Surabaya (BPS 1998b). This section begins with an overview of the distribution of unincorporated enterprises across all sectors according to the most recent 1996 census and then focuses on their specific contribution to manufacturing.

Most unincorporated enterprises are minute. Of the 326,336 unincorporated enterprises identified for Surabaya municipality in the 1996 census, two-thirds were owner operated and the average size of establishment was just 1.7 persons (BPS 1998b). Barely 10 percent of owner-operators actually paid a wage for supplementary labor. In terms of activity, the main components by size of workforce were, not surprisingly, retail trade (mainly small stalls), restaurants and warung (food stalls), manufacturing, and transport and communications. Manufacturing enterprises were larger than average (3.7 persons), which raised this sector's share in unincorporated-sector employment to 9 percent (table 5.12).

For Greater Surabaya in 1996 informal-sector manufacturing nevertheless provided almost 150,000 jobs, more than the entire L and M sector in 1986 (table 5.8). Compared with the diversity of the city's L and M manufacturing base, the unincorporated sector was quite narrowly specialized. According to the size of wages and salaries in 1996, only two subsectors stood out in the municipality and across Greater Surabaya, namely textiles, clothing, and footwear (TCF) and wood and wood products (table 5.13). The TCF sector comprised mainly tailors or dressmakers and leather workers making shoes or bags (fig. 5.6); wood and wood products was mainly furniture making and bamboo and rattan weaving. Food, drink, and tobacco (FDT) enterprises were concentrated in the manufacture of *tempe* (soybean cake), *krupuk* (prawn crackers)

Figure 5.6. Small-scale industry: sandalmakers, Chinese quarter, 1987. Photo by author.

TABLE 5.12
Employment in unincorporated enterprises by sector, Surabaya, 1996

Sector	Employment (thousands)	%
Manufacturing	52	9
Construction	7	1
Retail	226	40
Restaurants/warungs	105	19
Transport & comm.	44	8
Other	130	23
Total	564	100

Source: BPS 1998b.

TABLE 5.13
Sectoral distribution of unincorporated enterprises by wage bill, Greater Surabaya, 1996 (Rp. billions)

Sector	Surabaya	Sidoarjo	Gresik	Total	%
FDT	5.5	3.8	2.3	11.6	11.3
TCF	17.1	13.3	4.6	35.0	34.2
Wood & products	15.0	4.2	0.9	20.1	19.6
Paper & printing	5.2	0.9	0.2	6.3	6.3
Chemical	2.5	0.7	0.2	3.4	3.3
Nonmetals	1.4	0.7	1.8	3.9	3.8
Metals & machinery	5.5	6.5	1.6	13.6	13.3
Other	5.6	1.5	1.3	8.4	8.2
Total	57.8	31.6	12.9	102.3	100

Source: BPS 1998b.

(fig. 5.7), and low-grade salt from natural saltwater pans along the northwest coast. Metals and machinery consisted mainly of simple metal products, vehicle repairs, and welding.

The switch in the mid-1980s to outward-looking industrialization did not obviously boost informal-sector manufacturing beyond what might have been expected from the trend of rising real incomes. According to census figures, between 1986 and 1996 employment growth in labor-intensive small and unincorporated enterprises lagged somewhat behind that of the L and M sector (table 5.9). The notable exception was the TCF sector, which dramatically increased its share of informal manufacturing employment to take over from FDT as the leading unincorporated sector. This reflected the proliferation of opportunities for subcontracting

Figure 5.7. Cottage industry: krupuk drying, Kenjeran, 1997. Photo by author.

garment making from large firms. However, wood and wood products, which might have been expected to benefit similarly from export expansion, grew no faster than the overall trend in informal-sector manufacturing. This performance was rather disappointing, for after the 1988 ban on export of raw rattan, Surabaya had been designated a center for labor-intensive manufacture of furniture and other wood and rattan products. Also disappointing was the metals and machinery sector. Since the mid-1980s state enterprises had been required to subcontract work to small-scale firms and to submit monthly and annual reports of progress (Bisma, interview, 22/10/87). Circumstantial evidence suggests that subcontracting was becoming more widespread, especially in component manufacture, but from a very small base and involving incorporated rather than unincorporated small firms.

Conclusion

Surabaya's rapid industrial development under the New Order was the culmination of an industrial revolution in slow motion. In the second half of the nineteenth century industrial revolution technologies were applied vigorously to manufacturing and communications in East Java as part of the transition to a capitalist plantation economy. However, the logical next step of developing a local, machine-powered textile industry did not occur because the industry was developed in the Netherlands in order to supply the Indonesian market (Dick 1993c). The powerful plantation interest found common cause with the rising Dutch manufacturing interest in keeping Java under a regime of free trade and cheap labor. Although only a minor part of Java's land and labor was involved in estate production, the institutions of high capitalism, the state, and the island's sophisticated infrastructure were attuned to the needs of this plantation sector. The colonial government's indifference to industrial development and the ineffectiveness of Indonesian governments prior to the New Order were fateful for

Surabaya. Had industrial development been carried to the next stage around the turn of the century, the industrial center of Java would almost certainly have been Surabaya, not Jakarta. At that time Surabaya enjoyed the benefits of a strong leading sector in the sugar industry and growth in mass purchasing power and showed signs of becoming a significant industrial agglomeration. By the 1930s, when industrial development was at last embraced as a policy goal, the sugar industry was in a state of collapse and purchasing power in East Java was weak. West Java and Sumatra were sustained by the more buoyant rubber industry, to the benefit of Jakarta. After Independence, as the capital of a centralized state, Jakarta experienced faster population growth and attracted the lion's share of what import substitution did occur. Industrial leadership thereby passed decisively to Jakarta.

The industrial development that resumed in Surabaya in the 1970s involved rapid industrialization of the municipality and its immediate hinterland. From 1985 to 1992 this was masked by defective estimates of gross regional domestic product (GRDP) which showed the share of the manufacturing sector (including the utilities: power, gas, and water) as fairly constant at around 20 percent (KMS, SDA 1993). Reworking of the estimates from 1993 onward, however, have shown the share of manufacturing as increasing to 37 percent in 1997 (table 5.14). The most spectacular gains, however, have been in the adjacent kabupaten of Gresik and Sidoarjo, where by 1997 manufacturing accounted for no less than 52 and 58 percent of GRDP respectively. These formerly rural districts are now heavily industrialized. Given the scarcity of industrial land within the municipality, and the impact of zoning restrictions, it is hardly surprising that industry should have been attracted to cheaper land and labor in the rural hinterland.

In Surabaya the broad service sector is nevertheless more important than manufacturing, being just over half of GRDP, compared with only one-third in Gresik and Sidoarjo (table 5.14). If Gresik and Sidoarjo are now primarily industrial districts, Surabaya is still primarily a service center. Just as in the nineteenth and early

TABLE 5.14
Composition of gross regional domestic product, Greater Surabaya, 1985, 1997 (current prices)

	Surabaya		Gresik	Sidoarjo
Sector	1985	1997	1997	1997
Agriculture & mining	1	—	12	5
Manufacturing[a]	22	37	52	58
Construction	6.5	11	5.5	3
Trade, hotels, restaurants	28	26.5	20	20
Transport & communication	13.5	10	2.5	7
Banking & finance	9	9.5	5	3
Other services	20	6	3	4
Total	100	100	100	100

Sources: KMS, SDA 1991, 1998; KS, KSDA 1999; KG, KGDA 1998.
[a]Includes utilities (power, gas, and water).

twentieth centuries Surabaya developed as a service center for East Java's plantation economy, so its latest boom has strengthened its position as a service center to a rapidly industrializing hinterland. Historically the main component of the service sector was trade (including hotels and restaurants) but its share has gradually been declining. The boom of the 1990s stimulated the growth of construction and an increasingly deregulated banking and financial services sector, both around 10 percent of GRDP in 1997, together with transport and communications. The evidence could be seen in the city's rapidly changing skyline, the proliferation of grand new bank and insurance buildings, the new stock exchange, as well as shopping malls and luxury housing projects.

The importance to Surabaya of the service sector may suggest that this chapter has been looking in the wrong direction. Nevertheless, many of these services are linked to industrialization. In the nineteenth and early twentieth centuries, it was the dominant agricultural sector that gave Surabaya its particular character as a plantation town. Modern Surabaya draws its dynamism from the manufacturing sector. In both cases the process of engagement with the international economy has not only given the opportunity for sustained expansion of output and employment but also generated the capital to rebuild the city in a new guise (chap. 6). Chapter 7 will explore the pattern of engagement, disengagement, and re-engagement with the international economy that has set the underlying rhythm of Surabaya's twentieth-century economic history.

Chapter 6

LAND

Land use, the evolving compromise between human ambition and the natural and built environment, is a physical manifestation of economic and social change. Urban growth involves continual but highly uneven adjustment of land use both within the existing city and on the urban-rural fringe. These processes and the resultant conflicts are mediated by markets and by planning and regulation. Spatial form (morphology) and the built environment therefore resemble a living fossil. Streets, buildings, and place names speak eloquently of the past, especially in dialogue with written sources, maps, photos, oral recollections, and, in this case, the personal experience of walking around and observing over almost thirty years. This chapter has two main themes, first the uneasy relationship between the formal or modern city of the elite and the unstructured kampungs of the people and, second, the impact of the irregular economic cycle of boom and bust. Those unfamiliar with the city may skim lightly over the detail of place names and focus on these themes.

Surabaya's land use history can be divided into four main phases. In the first phase, which begins with the Dutch intrusion in 1677 and lasts until the 1830s, the original and spacious Javanese city and the new walled Dutch settlement uneasily coexisted. Despite the remoteness of this period, a brief review identifies the key elements that coalesced to form the modern city. The second phase, from the 1830s until the Japanese conquest in 1942, sees an inexorable formalization of the city under Dutch control. This process is explored thematically, looking first at the enclosure of the "formal" city by fortifications, then at the trend toward suburbanization, which was facilitated by the development of public transport and eventually gave rise to decentralization of employment away from the central business district. The conflict between the spreading, land-extensive colonial city and the indigenous kampungs is examined in terms of land rights. A third phase of political turmoil and economic stagnation begins with the Japanese occupation and sees the colonial city in decay, caught in a time warp like postwar Calcutta, Rangoon, or Hanoi. This allows a resurgence of indigenous urban forms and is marked by rapid population growth and the spread of kampung settlement. The fourth phase starts in the early 1970s as the development boom of the New Order spills over from Jakarta. Here attention focuses on the reintroduction of town planning, the revival of the real estate market, and renewed land rights conflict. The conclusion argues that there are compelling similarities between the physical transformation of the city during the New Order and that which occurred in the late-colonial period.

Origins

Like the coastal cities of Holland, Surabaya is built in an alluvial delta. The land rises no more than three to six meters above sea level, except for the wedge of dry and barren ground in the southeast quarter (KMS, SDA 1993, 1). The fertility and accessibility of this rice-growing plain was the key to Surabaya's early prominence in the maritime trading world. The first geographic marker, the grave of Sunan Ampel (Ngampel), revered as one of the nine founding Muslim saints (wali), can be identified from the late fifteenth century (Graaf and Pigeaud, 1974). By this time Majapahit had collapsed and Surabaya was emerging as a city-state in its own right (chap. 2).

The first known map is a sketch dating from 1677, when the city had become the seat of the rebel leader Trunajaya and was being besieged by Dutch troops in support of the ruler of Mataram (Ricklefs 1993; map 6.1). Since the population must have been much smaller than the estimated fifty to sixty thousand before the city was sacked in 1625, the map is no guide to the extent of the port city in its early heyday. However, one can detect features that survive in the modern city, probably from that time. The main waterways of the Kali Mas and the adjacent Kali Pegirian traced

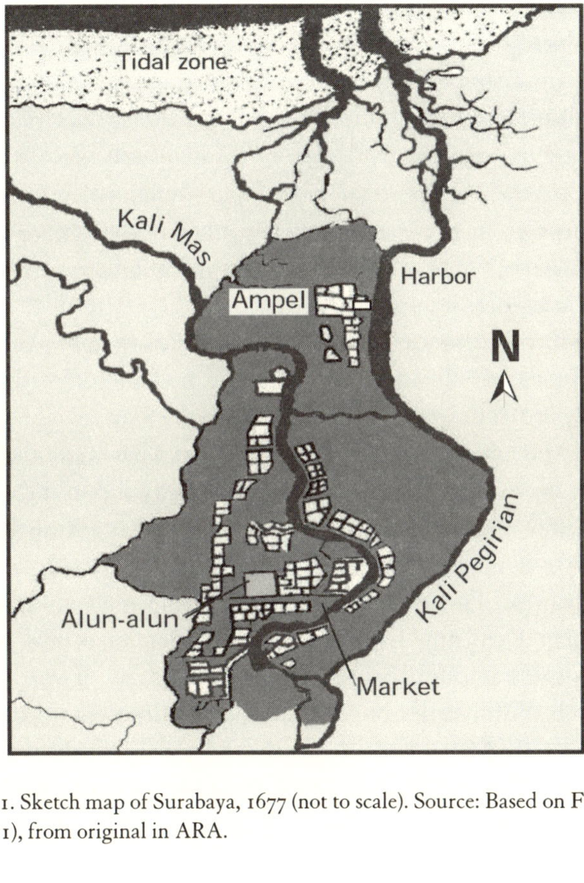

Map 6.1. Sketch map of Surabaya, 1677 (not to scale). Source: Based on Faber 1931 (11), from original in ARA.

more or less their present course, forming the backbone around which the city would coalesce. To the north, around Ampel, was the harbor and presumably the foreign traders' quarters. To the south lay the Javanese core around the characteristic large open square (*alun-alun*) that was sited near where the Heroes' Monument (Tugu Pahlawan) stands today. Between the alun-alun and the river was the Evening Market, later better known as the Great Market (Pasar Besar), which in 1905 moved to its present site of Pasar Turi.

These core Javanese elements reappear more clearly in another sketch map of 1787, some forty years after cession of the city to the Dutch (map 6.2). The alun-alun is here shown in detail with the mosque to the west and the palace compounds (*dalem*) of the first and second Javanese regents to the east and north, leaving the square open to the south, toward the towering volcano of Mount Arjuno. In the mid-nineteenth century the northern part of Surabaya's alun-alun was sacrificed to the defense works (see below) but as late as 1905 the road passing through that place was still known as Aloen-Aloenstraat (now Jalan Pahlawan). The official importance of the site was revived at the end of the 1920s with the construction of the new provincial government offices.

The 1787 map shows for the first time the extent of the kampungs which surrounded the palaces and the alun-alun. Although the map may be only a very rough guide, the kampungs stretched in a wide arc from west of the alun-alun to the long island between the Kali Mas and the Kali Pegirian, taking in what is still the kampung quarter of Peneleh and extending northward to the Ampel mosque (not shown). Kampungs also straggled southward along the river to Simpang and on to Keputran. Most of these kampungs were Javanese. However, to the north of the road to Kenjeran (now Jalan Kembang Jepun) and in the vicinity of the Ampel mosque the kampungs were identified as Malay. These would have been communities of seafaring peoples, traders, and craftsmen, not only Malay but also Madurese and probably Buginese and Arab. This ethnic distinction still persists, with the Malay communities being much more strict in their practice of Islam.

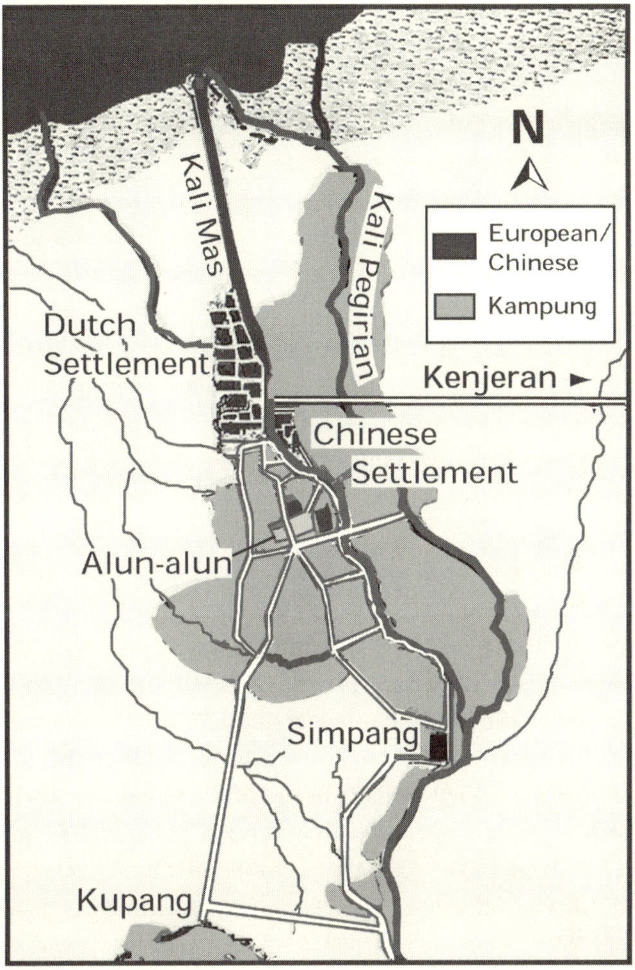

Map 6.2. Sketch map of Surabaya, 1787 (not to scale). Source: Based on Faber 1931 (25), from original in ARA.

The 1787 map also shows how the Dutch had imposed themselves upon—or rather beside—the original Javanese town. The first fortification, laid out in 1678 after the Dutch had put Trunajaya to flight, was little more than a fenced enclosure (*pagar*) beside the river just north of the alun-alun and in the vicinity of what later became Jembatan Merah (Red Bridge) (Faber 1931, 20). By the time of Valentijn's visit in 1708 there was a more substantial citadel, walled and moated, to protect the small Dutch encampment. After Governor-General van Imhoff's tour of inspection of the company's new domains in 1746, efforts were made to set the establishment in Surabaya on a proper footing.[1] This included not only rebuilding the citadel—which despite the swampy terrain was given the impressive name of Fort Belvedere—but also enclosing the whole adjacent Dutch settlement, or "factory," within a wall and moat (Faber 1931, 27). As in other factories around Asia, the Dutch like other Europeans lived and did their business within a very small, secure area.

Another new element identified in the 1787 map is the Chinese settlement. Historically the center of Chinese trade had been Gresik, but just as the Dutch settlement at Jakarta in the seventeenth century had attracted Chinese from Banten, so after the cession Surabaya also attracted Chinese from Gresik and farther afield. In a pattern reminiscent of the old port city of Malacca, they settled on the east bank of the Kali Mas opposite the Dutch factory. The original core of Surabaya's "Chinatown" was on the east bank of the Kali Mas, along the line of Jalan Karet (Rubber Street), with the three oldest clan houses: the Han, The, and Tjoa. For military reasons there was as yet no Red Bridge to link the Chinese and European settlements.

The lines of communications give a fascinating insight into the continuing insecurity of this small, isolated Dutch trading post. As had always been the case for the company's factories, its supply route and line of retreat was the sea. To improve access to the sea, the channel of the Kali Mas had been straightened, so that instead of turning northwest just below the Ampel mosque (map 6.1), it now cut through, along its modern course, in a direct line to the sea. To the north and across the old course of the river, gardens and kampungs were laid out to assist in the provisioning and manning of the settlement. However, for reasons of defense, there was only one access point to the adjacent Javanese town from the walled Dutch settlement, namely from the southeast gate.

A cartographic map of 1825 shows more accurately the pattern of land use in and around the town just before the introduction of the Cultivation System (map 6.3). Virtually every part of this entire segment of the delta has been molded by human hands into productive use. The urban core and its adjacent kampungs are surrounded in a three-quarter arc by a sea of rice fields. Even the uncultivated northwest sector is neatly divided into salt- and fishponds (*tambak*), that extend around the coast toward Gresik. Only in the terrain due north of the town, where the shoreline has rapidly prograded between the Kali Mas and the Kali Pegirian, is there any wild expanse of mangroves and palm, and even that would no doubt have been cut for firewood and atap fronds. The local people had in abundance all the means of subsistence.

The Javanese center appears around the alun-alun much as before but the Dutch and Chinese settlements have expanded and consolidated as the two ventricles of a rival urban core. They are now joined together by the first Red Bridge (Jembatan Merah), forming a strong east-west axis between the new road to Gresik (the westerly section of Daendels's post road) and the older road to Kenjeran. The city gate and most of the old walls and moat around the Dutch settlement have now been demolished and built over, allowing the highway (post road) to assume its present direct southward route along Jalan Veteran (formerly Societeitstraat) and across the alun-alun. Yet apart from a few country houses, mainly along the river, and the military hospital at Simpang, there seem to have been few permanent buildings of stone or brick anywhere beyond the European town.

Even more clearly than in the map of 1787, one now sees juxtaposed the solid, imploded elements of the formal town, part Dutch,

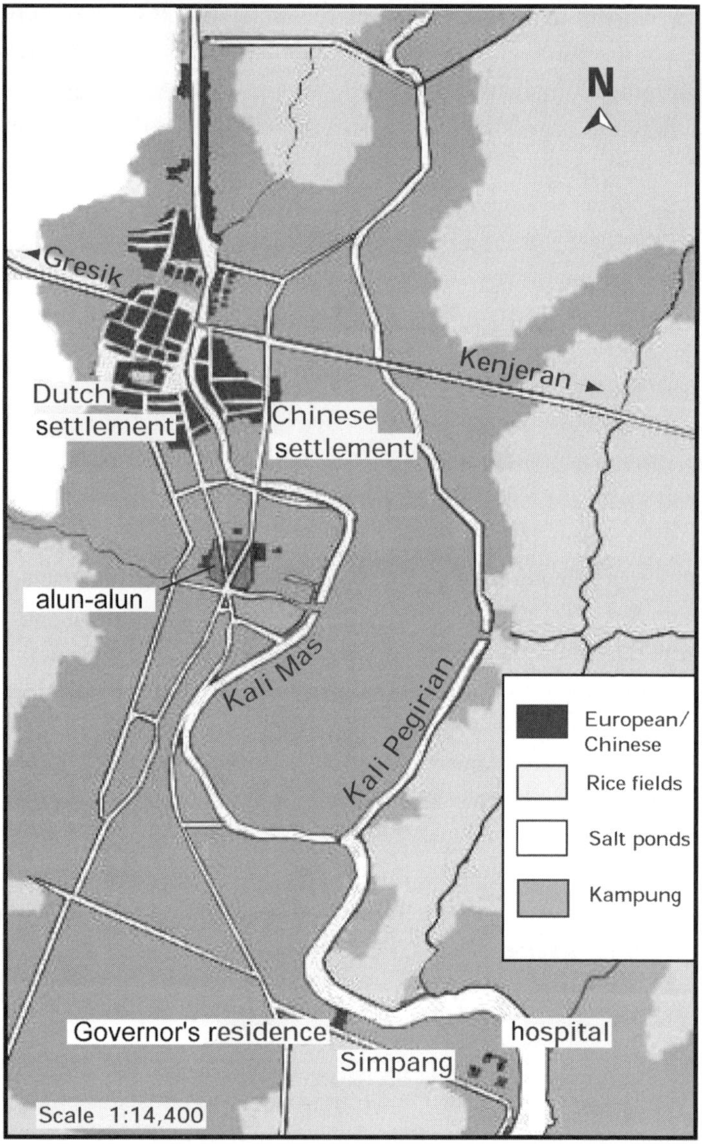

Map 6.3. Surabaya, 1825. Source: Based on original in Faber 1931.

part Chinese, and the diffuse, unstructured Javanese kampungs. The formal town is enveloped by low-density kampungs that now extend well southward beyond Simpang. Many of these kampungs, identified by name, are today part of the modern city, albeit at a much higher density of population. As portrayed on the map, they consisted not of ordered streets and blocks but of dispersed houses of woven bamboo (atap) with thatched roofs beneath a canopy of mainly fruit-bearing trees. Reid (1993, chap. 2) has argued that before the colonial era such "urban villages" were typical of even the largest of Southeast Asia's port cities, reflecting not only the absence of confining walls but also the need to provide for subsistence. He points out that under the Malay legal codes trees were the main item of property; houses could be dismantled and reassembled elsewhere.

There was no clear distinction between those kampungs that were considered urban and those that were rural. Rather there was an urban-rural continuum. The proportion of kampung dwellers engaged in nonagricultural pursuits would have been higher the closer to the core of the town. Those rice-growing kampungs closest to the city gradually became town kampungs by the influx of outsiders and the conversion of rice fields to houses and house gardens (*pekarangan*). For example, the kampungs around the alun-alun, which would have been associated with the compounds of the nobility, had no rice field (*sawah*), neither did those in the long island between the Kali Mas and Kali Pegirian. Comparison of the 1787 and 1825 maps (maps 6.2 and 6.3) also suggests the urbanization of land to the south of Embong Malang into what is still one of the great kampung districts of Surabaya. Kampungs also stretch like tentacles to the west, south, and east into the surrounding sea of sawah. Allied maps drawn up over a century later, in 1943, still show a very similar pattern of settlement to the east of the Pegirian. These kampung, typically aligning along the smaller tributaries and canals may be regarded as rural, even if their inhabitants had opportunities for trade or occasional employment in the town. In this rural domain there were no paved roads, just earthen pathways beside the waterways, for in that wet-rice plain most communication was indeed by water. Surabaya, as much as Amsterdam or Venice, was once a water-based city that merged almost imperceptibly into its hinterland, a characteristic shared with other great Southeast Asian cities (see Reid 1993, 88).

Had the land use pattern of the city and its hinterland remained so fluid, the growth of the formal town and of the total urban population could have been accommodated by displacement and denser settlement of kampungs on one margin and the conversion of rice field on the other. Such "natural" expansion of the town was inhibited by the ring of private estates alienated in the first two decades of the nineteenth century (chap. 2). The right of the estate owner to control settlement did not prevent low-density urbanization because, on the urban margin, higher rents could be gained from lease of kampung plots than from cultivation of rice and sugar. If the private estates were a barrier to urban expansion in some directions, they were porous in others. Far more disruptive was the impact of the fortifications.

Fortifications

Until elaborate and very expensive defense works were constructed between 1837 and 1845 (Faber 1931, 236), Surabaya had never been a walled city in the European or Chinese manner. Early citadels around the Javanese *kraton* (palace) complex and later the Dutch camp involved earthworks and moats but not until the mid-nineteenth century was the city as a whole surrounded by a defensive wall. Apart from the small and crowded European and Chinese settlements, Surabaya was still an open town of a style that Reid (1993) argues was typical of precolonial Southeast Asia.

Fortification of Surabaya in a Western manner was the initiative of Governor-General van den Bosch (1830–33), founder of the Cultivation System, who brought forward a grand scheme for the defense of Java. The first stone was laid in 1837 by Prins Hendrik, after whom the fort was named, and the work was finished eight years later in the style typical of most Dutch towns and also Jakarta. Around the built-up area of the city was set a wall, from which armed bastions projected into a wide moat, which faced across a stretch of unoccupied no-man's-land (map 6.4). The focal point was the star-shaped Fort Prins Hendrik on the east bank of the Kali Mas, about halfway between the center of the city and the river mouth. Whereas the Dutch had formerly lived isolated within their own walled citadel-cum-factory, an island in an essentially Javanese townscape, now the fortifications were to encompass and define the whole town as a Dutch town. The Chinese business quarter, the Malay, and the Arab quarters, with the Ampel mosque and fairly extensive tracts of kampung to the far side of the Kali Pegirian, were all enclosed within the walls.

Symbolically the fortifications marked the conquest of the old Javanese sphere by the new, expanding European town. For over one and a half centuries, Javanese, European, and Chinese communities had coexisted, the two latter as alien encampments alongside an essentially Javanese town. Now the locus of Javanese power around the alun-alun was physically obliterated. The regent's dalem and the mosque were dismantled and reincorporated within the walls. The regent was rehoused in traditional Javanese style with an open audience hall (*pendopo*); the site later became the main post office but the street in front kept the name of Regentstraat to the end of the colonial period. Just west of the new regency a fine new mosque (Kemayoran) was built in the 1840s in traditional Javanese style and between the mosque and the regency an open space was left as a token alun-alun. The symbols of Javanese power and authority were thereby encapsulated, subordinated, marginalized. Henceforth there was no alternative center of power. By population Surabaya remained a Javanese town but all power and authority rested with the Dutch. Javanese society had been decapitated. Only the kampungs remained as a "floating mass."

Cutting through the oldest and most densely settled kampungs, the fortifications necessitated a massive relocation of the kampung

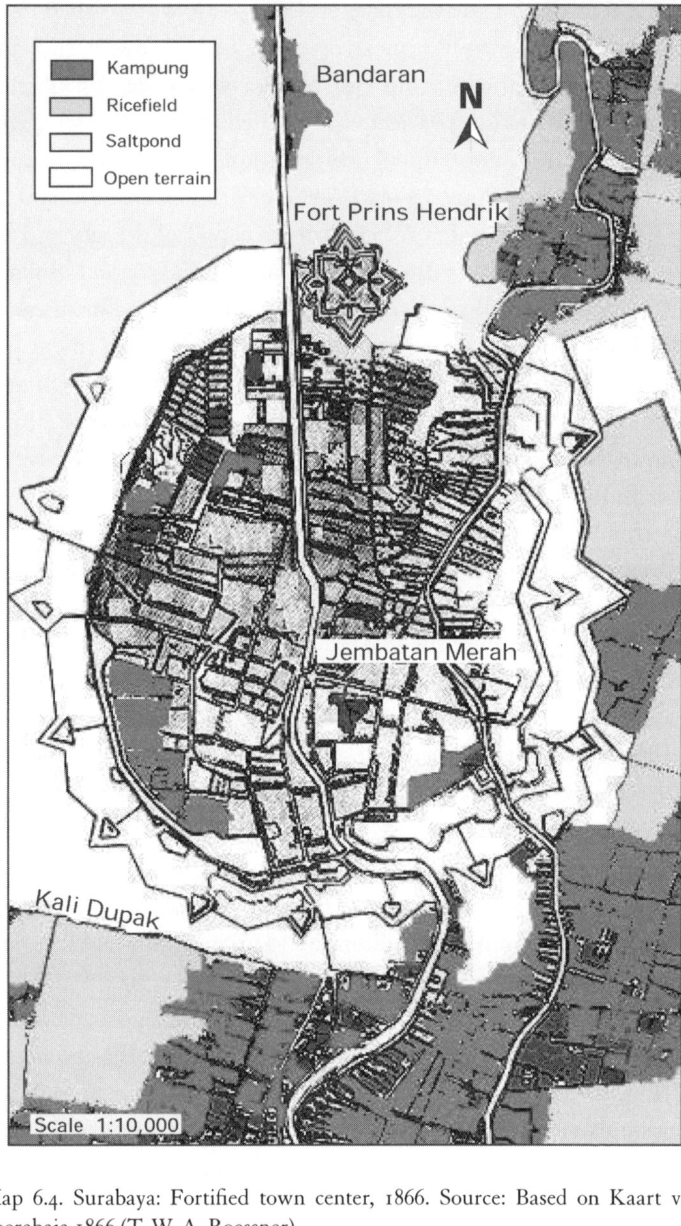

Map 6.4. Surabaya: Fortified town center, 1866. Source: Based on Kaart van Soerabaja 1866 (T. W. A. Roessner).

population. Faber (1931, 113) reports the removal of more than a quarter of the town's listed kampungs. It is doubtful that the Dutch paid any form of compensation. Displaced kampung dwellers would have dismantled their wood, bamboo, and thatch dwellings and rehoused themselves in the surviving kampungs. Rural villages were also affected because thousands of Javanese, the so-called mud-Javanese (*modderjavanen*), were brought in from the hinterland as corvée labor to dig out the moats. Their death rate was very high because of the highly unsanitary conditions and, with so much disturbed ground, the incidence of malaria.

When constructed, the fortifications were already an eighteenth-century anachronism, a ridiculous waste of money that fulfilled no useful military purpose. In terms of urban planning they were a disaster, a classic example of transferring a European model to an alien and inappropriate clime. As the experience of the old city of Jakarta should have predicted, the stagnant brackish waters of the moats became a breeding ground for disease and malaria, breaking the natural flow of waters and tides. Canals also silted up. A contemporary excerpt conveys the flavor—or rather the smell—of the problem. It refers to the Krambangan Canal, which used to flow from the Kali Mas around the western inside edge of the Dutch town and carry away to sea the sewage and garbage: "Gradually its bed silted up and it received water from the Kalimas only at very high tides. In consequence, communication between the different government establishments along the Krambangan was hindered and for a large part of the year there piled up all the filth carried into the canal by sewers and gutters, which had a terrible influence on the health of the inhabitants of the surrounding houses and establishments" (*KV* 1853, 98). By forcing the city within an enclosure, the fortifications accentuated the density of population and the health problems arising from the poor infrastructure. Although the walls enclosed a much larger area than the built-up area in 1830, the growth of population, under the stimulus of the Cultivation System and development of the sugar industry, was grossly underestimated. Both the Dutch and Chinese communities were therefore condemned to live in dark and musty houses jammed into narrow streets. In the Indonesian kampungs, which lacked even a rudimentary infrastructure to cope with high-density urban living, the situation was even worse.

In the event, the fortifications lasted only one generation. After halfhearted attempts at repair, in 1870 the decision was taken to demolish them, as also in Semarang and Jakarta, partly on grounds of public health and partly to permit urban expansion (*KV* 1871, 26). Except in the vicinity of the fort, the ban on construction within the wide expanse of no-man's-land was lifted and in January 1871 the southern half of the defense line was handed over to the civilian authorities, who proceeded to raze the walls and fill in the moat (*KV* 1872, 29). Nevertheless, after plans for modern fortifications had been overturned on grounds of cost, it was 1895 before the army could bring itself to begin dismantling the fort, part of which continued to be used as a women's prison. It survived as a substantial ruin into the mid-1930s, when it was finally demolished as a make-work project (Faber 1931, 112; SGS 1936, 1937). Today the only echo is the name Benteng (Fort), which still refers to the kampung in this area.

The one long-term benefit of the fortifications was entirely unanticipated. Their dismantling in the early 1870s conveniently preceded the decision of 1875 to build a state-owned railway from Surabaya to Pasuruan and Malang. Without having to demolish any existing buildings, the first railway station at Kota (Semut) and marshaling yards were laid out just south of the Chinese quarter along the line of the former moat. In 1884 work began to extend the line across the Kali Mas, through what had been the center of the alun-alun, and around the edge of the old moat to the sugar warehouses on the western bank of the Kali Mas (*RANI* 1900, 339). On the eastern side of the town, however, the opening of the gasworks in 1880 blocked the use of the rest of that right of way, so that when work began in 1899 on the railway extension to the eastern bank of the Kali Mas, the line had to be laid well to the east of the then built-up part of the town (map 6.5).

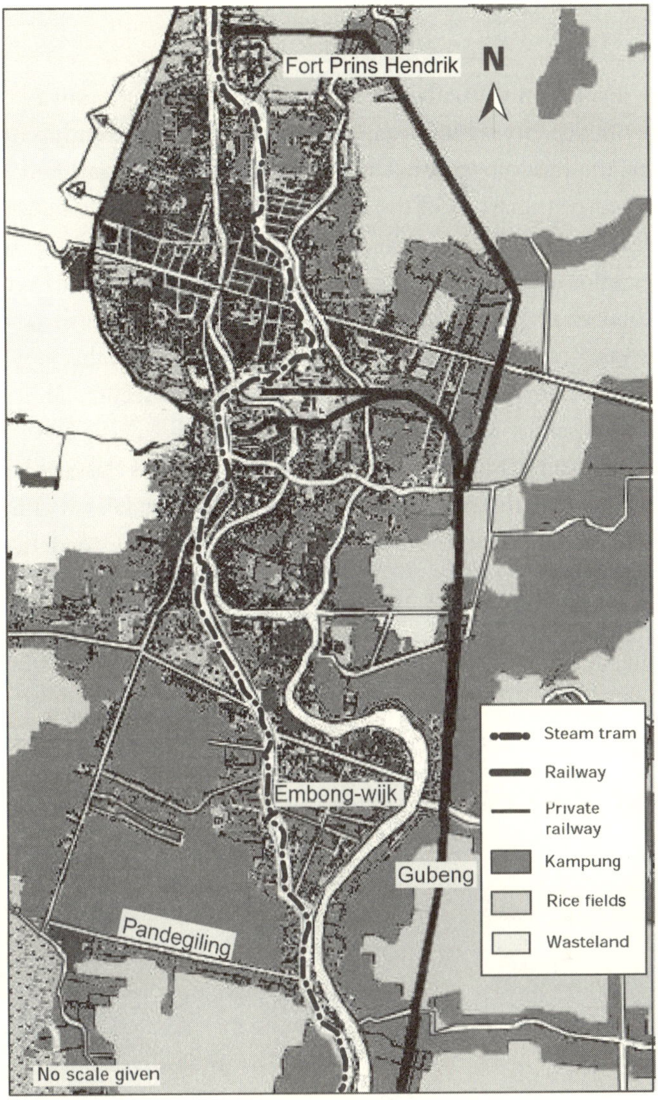

Map 6.5. Surabaya: Rail and steam tram routes, 1905. Source: Based on original in Faber 1931.

The dispersion of the better-off European population away from the crowded city center began at the end of the eighteenth century, when the local governor, Dirk van Hogendorp, dissatisfied with the cramped quarters of the official residence at Jembatan Merah, built a large mansion on the banks of the river at Simpang, about three kilometers from the center of the old town. In Jakarta country houses had come into vogue early in the eighteenth century (Abeyasekere 1987, 36), but this was the first in Surabaya, where the immediate hinterland had probably been less secure. The mansion still serves as the governor's official residence—Governor-General Daendels (1808–11) added an incongruous classical façade to the rear of the building (facing what is now Jalan Pemuda), which then became the main entrance (fig. 6.1). Daendels, and later Raffles, also provided local merchants and officials with the opportunity to found estates on agricultural land beyond the town (chap. 2). Virtually all land was alienated from the edge of the tidal

Figure 6.1. The governor's residence at Simpang, interwar years. From author's collection.

zone to beyond Wonokromo and upstream toward Sepanjang. The mainly European owners of these estates proceeded to erect mansions on only a slightly smaller scale than the resident's house at Simpang. The examples of Kupang and Simo are still extant, one long derelict, the other, rather incongruously, a biscuit factory. It then became profitable to sell off blocks along the river or main roads for mansions (*heerenhuizen*) for those who could afford to escape from the insalubrious confines of the town—few of these old houses can still be recognized by their classical facades and deep verandahs with mock Grecian columns. The result was an early form of ribbon development. Migration of European residence seems to have accelerated after the 1860s, by which time there was an acute housing shortage within the walls (Faber 1931, 43). The movement southward to marginally higher but much more healthy ground was now undertaken not just by the wealthy but also by those who might be described as middle class. The most popular location for modern town houses was along Pasar Besar, the main road south. Now occupied mainly by ethnic Chinese, most of these houses still stand in not greatly altered form. Constructed to individual designs like Victorian terraces, the larger of them two-story with wrought iron verandahs, they connect in rows facing onto paved lanes.

After the turn of the century, and rather later than Jakarta and Semarang (KPM 1903, 81), the once compact European town began to bifurcate into a central business district around Jembatan Merah and newer residential suburbs, giving rise to a clearer distinction between the lower town (*benedenstad*), embracing the port and central business district, and the upper town (*bovenstad*) of new suburbs. Although encirclement by private estates had slowed the emergence of a private housing market, this was in the long run no disadvantage, since it ensued that development would be carried out on a large scale and to some degree be planned.

The first large-scale suburban redevelopment was the initiative of the Bouwmaatschappij Kepoetran,[2] a Dutch firm incorporated in Surabaya in 1888 to subdivide the Keputran Lor estate, a triangle located just south of the governor's mansion (*JC,* 8/6/88). In 1825 the land had been mainly rice fields and ponds (map 6.3) but had since been transformed into urban kampung. The so-called Embong-wijk was laid out as a garden suburb. A boulevard (Palmenlaan, now Sudirman) was laid out through the middle of the development, which was intersected by streets with regular back-to-back blocks. At the center was a square park, which has survived. Houses were single-story bungalows that evolved into a fairly standard design: a verandah opened from a front garden onto a central living area, giving access to the main bedrooms; bathrooms and kitchen were laid out around a rear courtyard that included servants' quarters (figs. 6.2, 6.3). Thirty years later Faber (1936, 18) judged the Embong-wijk still to be one of the best-planned suburbs.

As in Jakarta and Semarang, the demand for detached bungalow housing quickened during the 1900s, and by 1905 the Chamber of Commerce could report that house construction was booming in the upper town (KKNS 1905, 23). The demand of the growing European population for modern suburban housing gave rise to a more sophisticated residential market, in which aspiring homeowners could obtain mortgage finance from specialist building societies (*hypotheekbanken*). New bouwmaatschappij began to proliferate, companies that varied considerably in size and modus operandi: selling land by the plot, building rows of houses on speculation for rental or sale, or subcontracting whole streets to specialist builders. The bottleneck was the supply of urban land. Developers followed the lead of BM Kepoetran in buying up private estates on the fringe of the built-up area—some still mainly agricultural, others mainly kampung—clearing the population, providing basic infrastructure, and then subdividing for European housing. By 1916 over fifteen hundred hectares were in the process of conversion (table 6.1; map 6.6). BM Keputran remained the leading developer, but rich Chinese and Arab families also joined in the boom. Around 1910 the prominent The family began to develop the Sawahan estate on the western fringe, while after 1913 the Arab

Figure 6.2. Classical portico of a turn-of-the-century bungalow. Photo by author.

Figure 6.3. Bungalow of the 1920s, Tegalsari. Photo by author.

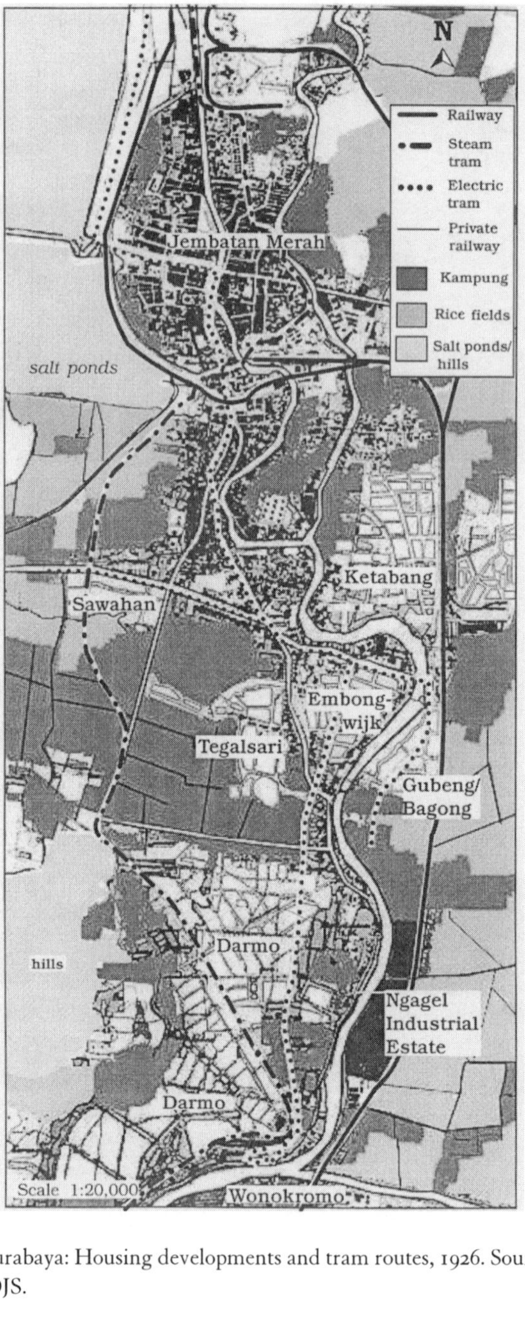

Map 6.6. Surabaya: Housing developments and tram routes, 1926. Source: Based on ARA, OJS.

merchant Ibrahim Baswedan began to develop the Bagong estate just south of Gubeng Station. Registration of new bouwmaatschappij peaked in 1911–12, by which time the market had become markedly speculative.

Shortly after its formation, the Municipality also began to play a role (table 6.1; also chap. 4). In 1909 it bought the Gubeng Jepit estate, about 130 hectares, across the river from Simpang, with the original intention of using it for a new European cemetery (Faber 1936, 171). To help overcome the housing shortage, it was soon decided to develop the part to the east of the railway as European housing. Then in late 1916 the Municipality bought up two more large estates, the 138 hectares of Ketabang North and Ketabang South, which lay north of the governor's mansion, and the 550-hectare Ngagel (or Jagir) estate much further south. Both estates lay on the eastern side of the Kali Mas, which hitherto had remained a fairly sharp dividing line between the town and its rural fringe of kampungs. Now bridges and roads were built to allow Ketabang to be redeveloped for European housing, the new town hall and municipal offices and the European high school, while

TABLE 6.1
Acquisition of main private estates for urban development, Surabaya, 1888–1916

Estate	Area 1/1/09	Population 1/1/99	Population 1/1/14	Owner (date of purchase)
Keputran North	91	3,649	—	BM Kepoetran (1888)
Embong Malang	39	3,633	142	"
Sawahan	96	2,061	—	The Family
Darmo[a]	336	4,010	3,878	BM Sawahan
Bagong	170	1,627	2,496	OJS (1912)
Gubeng	127	1,416	1,240	Baswedan (1913)
Ketabang	138	1,828	—	Municipality (1909)
Ngagel	576	5,063	4,896	Municipality (1916)
Total	1,573	23,387	—	

Source: RANI (annual).
[a]Includes Darmo, Ketampon Tengah, Kupang Gede, Grudo West.

Ngagel, or at least the minor part to the west of the railway, was earmarked for development as an industrial estate (chap. 5).

The biggest land development of all was carried out by the tramway company. Needing to purchase rights of way for an electric network, the Oost Java Stoomtram Maatschappij (OJS, East Java Steam Tram Company) decided to deal simultaneously in real estate, thereby avoiding extortionate claims and reaping the benefit of higher land prices bought about by the improved public transport. In 1912, after protracted negotiations, the company managed to consolidate several estates into a 336-hectare area extending from the edge of the town at Pandegiling (Tamarindelaan) to the riverbank opposite the market center of Wonokromo (ARA, OJS 2.20.16.20: 328). Hitherto Surabaya and Wonokromo had been separated by this extensive tract of irrigated fields, leaving the highway and tramway to follow a leisurely route along the Kali Mas. In a single development, the OJS would now close the gap. The wide Darmo boulevard with double tram tracks along the center was laid out in a straight line from Kaliasin to a terminus opposite Wonokromo. On either side the OJS would lay out a model garden suburb designed for the automobile age, with large blocks fronting onto wide and eventually tree-lined streets and backed by fire access lanes. After complicated legal problems had been sorted out, the building plan for the first stage was submitted to the Municipality in mid-1917 and approved several months later.

Despite the purchase of so many large tracts of land for urban development, lead times of several years before construction meant that the housing shortage continued to worsen during the 1910s. In the early years of World War I the rental market was already very tight. By 1917 there was comment on "the ever more pressing housing crisis" (SMNA 1917, 15). Strong demand pushed up land prices and combined with the restricted supply of materials to drive new-construction prices to hitherto unimagined levels, despite which buyers were able to borrow up to three-quarters of the value under a 6 percent mortgage (SMNA 1918, 15). As in every real estate boom, the lure of capital gain proved irresistible. Contrary to all common sense, the belief took root that land and housing were sound long-term investments, and for a brief, joyous period this did seem to be the case. However, if asset inflation was a boon to those with access to capital, it was a curse to those without. In 1917 it was observed that there was no more prospect of cheap housing or cheap rents (SMNA 1917, 17–18). This burden fell most heavily on the Indonesian population, who had been driven from their kampungs in thousands to make way for the new garden suburbs (see also below). The city's largest employer, the naval base, in 1918 identified the housing problem as the main cause of its 30 percent rate of absenteeism (MES 1918). The following year's report was more explicit: notwithstanding the increasing demand for labor in the city center, "the native" had gradually been driven right out of the city to the remote outer districts (MES 1919, 1). In the early 1920s the naval base took the initiative of laying out a nearby workers' kampung, as also on a limited scale did some private companies.

The real estate bubble deflated quickly after 1920 with the onset of the postwar recession. Development of the new garden suburbs, like construction of the new harbor, had been predicated on the hopeful assumption that general prosperity would be sustained after the end of the world war. In mid-1920 the Municipality approved plans for the second stage of the Darmo estate, but three years later few blocks had yet been sold, construction was almost at a standstill, and many finished houses were still unoccupied. Local building societies that were heavily exposed to property loans had to restructure their finances (SMNA 1921–24). Building approvals for brick houses, which had peaked at 444 in 1920, recovered to no higher than 290, and that was in 1929 (SGS, 1921, 1930). Abundant serviced land was available to meet this more modest demand. The OJS in particular had trouble selling off its land, being fortunate that the Municipality itself in 1927 bought most of the undeveloped land southwest of what is now Jalan Diponegoro (then Reyniersz Boulevard), part of which became the site for the municipal zoo. After 1930, the world depression caused the housing market to collapse again, with mild recovery only after 1937 (JHS, annual). Much of the land bank of vacant urban land was therefore not built upon until the 1950s, some forty years after the clearance of the former kampungs. Not until the 1990s was there another speculative real estate boom.

Public Transport

Suburbanization required the development of a public transport system and heavy-expenditure public infrastructure, especially bridges and roads. Until the mid-nineteenth century, most journeys had been a matter of walking, for only a wealthy few could boast carriages. In 1859 a horse omnibus was introduced to carry coolies between town and the new naval base (Faber 1931, 197–98). Pony carts (*sado;* later dokar, or dogcart) were provided for hire from 1874. In urban tramways, Surabaya lagged well behind Jakarta. In September 1890 the OJS opened a twenty-kilometer steam-tram line but this was primarily a market tram between the Madura ferry and the hinterland: only the first eight kilometers passed through the town and frequency was only every half hour (map 6.5). A dedicated urban public transport system awaited the completion in 1923–24 of an electric tramway (map 6.6; fig. 1.8). In the shape of a cross, the main north-south line followed the elongated spine of the city from the Wonokromo bridge and the new Darmo Boulevard to the central business district at Jembatan Merah (Willemsplein), there connecting via another wide boulevard to the new deep-sea harbor at Tanjung Perak; the cross-line joined the new residential suburbs of Bagong and Gubeng in the east and Sawahan in the west with the shopping and entertainment district around Simpang and Tunjungan (Duparc 1972). People could now travel every ten minutes or less on trams as modern as any in the Netherlands.

Nevertheless, by the time the electric tram system was in operation, the age of the automobile had arrived, at least for Europeans.

The first auto had arrived in Surabaya in 1890 and several were in operation by 1900, when the first regulations were introduced (Faber 1931, 202). By 1911 around 500 automobiles were registered, by 1920 about 2,000, and by 1939 a total of 6,657, including 466 taxis (SGS, annual). Europeans owned almost 60 percent of private motor vehicles. Assuming an average family size of five, by 1939 there was one car for almost every European family but only one in five Chinese or Arab families and one in thirty thousand Indonesian families. Residents of the new suburbs such as Darmo, Gubeng, and Sawahan were most likely to own a car (and to employ a driver) and to have only a supplementary need for public transport, such as for children to travel to and from school. Household servants, of course, continued to use public transport. The Depression led to a new form of cheap motorized public transport in the form of small three- and four-wheeled vehicles known generically as autolettes. In 1934, OJS traffic counts revealed that autolettes were carrying as many passengers as the tram (ARA, *OJS* 2.20.16.010: 1934).

To Indonesians, vehicle ownership meant a bicycle. The earliest figure of their number is about 9,000 in 1917, doubling to 18,000 in 1925, and again to 36,000 in 1937 (SGS, annual). Growth continued during the Depression, albeit at a slower rate, because of the availability of cheap Japanese brands. Unfortunately in this case there is no ethnic breakdown of ownership. Europeans were certainly well represented, especially school children, for the Netherlands was the European home of the bicycle. However, it was Indonesians for whom the bicycle was a transport revolution, a very necessary one in that the rapid expansion of city area and the decentralization of employment to the periphery—whether to the port of Tanjung Perak, the naval base, or the Ngagel industrial estate—meant that walking had become arduous. In 1933 the OJS commented on the permanent loss of third-class passengers to bicycles, especially on the steam-tram line to and from the naval base (ARA, OJS 2.20.16.010: 1933, 2:3–7).

By the late 1930s the population of Surabaya had therefore become highly mobile, even if walking was probably still the most common means of transport. However, the growth of motorized traffic was not without costs. By the late 1930s many of the problems that would become pressing in the 1970s were already apparent. First, it was judged necessary to widen roads, in the beginning by cutting down the trees. The shady, peaceful streets of the 1900s gave way to sun-filled streets of wall-to-wall bitumen, far less pleasant for those on foot, which is to say the Indonesian population. In the main shopping street of Tunjungan even Europeans were inconvenienced by the interminable flow of traffic and the absence of safe crossing places. Traffic lights were installed in 1938 (SGS 1938). Parking on narrow city streets reduced the space available to pedestrians, cyclists, and carts, thereby compromising safety, while elsewhere open space was transformed into bitumen. As has ever been the case, the needs and preferences of the minority who could afford cars took precedence over the large majority, who must make do with other means.

Decentralization of Employment

In the nineteenth century nonagricultural employment had been concentrated in the European and Chinese quarters. There were found the offices of the merchant houses, the export-import warehouses, the large manufactories, such as the arsenal and engineering works, and various small workshops. As in any medieval town, Europeans and Chinese lived adjacent to their place of employment. Indonesian workers, however, lived in the kampungs, for the most part beyond what in the 1830s became the fortified city center, and would have walked to and from work in the early morning and late afternoon. The main exception would have been household servants, who "lived in."

The earliest trend toward decentralization was along the river. There was a busy stream of commerce along the river as larger vessels anchored in the roads for discharge into lighters, while river prahus brought down loads of export cargoes from the hinterland.

As early as 1825 a row of permanent buildings, probably warehouses, straggled along both sides of the Kali Mas (map 6.3). However, the fortifications of the 1830s interrupted this natural progression, for Fort Prins Hendrik on one side and the moat on the other blocked any further downstream movement of commercial activity. The notable exception was the establishment in the 1850s of the naval dockyard at the mouth of the Kali Mas (chap. 5). Although it would have been logical for worker kampungs to have been built in the vicinity, the unhealthy, marshy ground made this impractical. Apart from the prostitutes kampung of Bandaran just below the fort (chap. 4; map 6.4), the space between the fort and the naval base remained wasteland.

The movement of economic activity downstream awaited the demolition of the fortifications after the 1870s and the completion of railway links. After 1890 the OJS steam tram provided a regular passenger and market connection between the naval base, the fort, and the town, which may have facilitated transfer of the boiler shop to the naval base in the early 1890s (chap. 5). More important was the extension of the State Railway across to the western side of the Kali Mas in the mid-1880s, followed in the early 1900s by an extension along the eastern side. These two links provided heavy rail access from the interior to the port and encouraged construction of the long lines of warehouses that have dominated both sides of the river for most of the twentieth century. Henceforth the sugar was shipped from the mills by rail, discharged into the warehouses, and later loaded into lighters for carriage to the deep-sea ships out in the roads (chap. 2). The river trade all but ceased. Completion in the early 1920s of the new harbor of Tanjung Perak further concentrated employment at the mouth of the river. After 1910 there was also a large workforce employed by the drydock company. With thousands of people employed each day in and around the new port, the electric tramway, which opened in 1923, was essential.

Industry was slower to move away from the old town. Besides the arsenal and, until the 1890s, the naval boiler shop, the early bakeries, mineral water plants, ice works, foundries, smiths, and engineering workshops were all located within the city walls without much regard for modern town planning. Suppression of the fortifications allowed establishments to be located at a somewhat greater distance. The railway yards and repair shops were, as mentioned above, laid out in the late 1870s just south of the Chinese quarter, while the gasworks were constructed in the former no-man's-land on the far side of the Pegirian. The 1905 map (map 6.5) identifies an adjacent limekiln, another smoky and malodorous factory. Nevertheless, these were still within a small radius of the old town and would soon be enveloped by it. In most cases residents just had to live with the inconvenience of nearby industrial establishments. Neighbors of the Braat engineering works, for example, complained about the noise.

Hitherto the few factories outside the town had been outliers of rural industry. Most of them were sugar mills that crushed the cane from the adjacent private estates, with one or two surviving arak distilleries that processed the by-product, molasses. Around 1900 the Kali Mas above Simpang had been lined with the Gubeng mill, a distillery, and the Bagong mill, all three along the narrow strip backing onto what is now Jalan Sumatra; about two kilometers upstream was the larger Ngagel mill, while on the far side of the Surabaya River above Wonokromo, within about a kilometer of each other, were the Dadungan, Ketintang, and Karah mills, which also crushed the cane from the Darmo estate. These mills were all fairly small—relics of the days when each estate crushed its own cane—and had closed down by the 1920s.

Relocation of industry beyond the old town began in the 1910s, when large tracts of cheap land became available through the redevelopment of the private estates. Nowhere was this more apparent than on the eastern side of the Kali Mas, hitherto a rural expanse outside the municipal boundaries. As explained above, the land between the railway and the river was set aside for suburban housing; that on the far side of the railway was gradually taken up in large blocks for industry and public facilities. The first large industrial relocation was the State Railways workshops, whose original premises beside the main station at Semut had become too cramped for the amount of rolling stock that now had to be serviced. As part of a massive workshop investment program, in 1910 the State Railways opened just northeast of Gubeng station a huge new workshop for the repair, maintenance, and construction of carriages for the whole of the eastern Java network (*KRN* 1930, 49–50). The complex was gradually extended with staff housing to the south and a large workers' kampung (Pacar Keling) to the north. Later an industrial-gases plant and ice factory were also located nearby. This concentration of employment was enlarged by the new medical faculty (1924) and the new public hospital (1940).[3]

In 1916 the Municipality adopted a formal policy of decentralizing industry by buying the Jagir/Ngagel estate as the site for the city's first industrial estate. The land between the river and the railway below Bagong and as far south as the Wonokromo Canal was set aside for this purpose (map 6.6; fig. 5.2). A land use plan was drawn up in 1918 and during 1919 the infrastructure was set in place: a new road along the river with bridges connecting south to Wonokromo and across the river to Dinoyo, asphalted side streets, and utilities. By the end of 1919 land was being sold off on leases of up to seventy-five years. This initiative was not only a means of providing much-needed land for industry, which had boomed during World War I, but also of segregating industry from residential areas.

By the 1920s the city's spatial distribution of employment had therefore been turned inside out. Whereas before 1900 most large-scale workplaces had been located within the old town, by 1930 the largest concentrations of employment, many thousands of workers in each case, were to be found at the northern, eastern, and southern extremities of the city, with a small concentration in the west. The urban economy now extended about twelve kilometers, from the new port of Tanjung Perak and the naval base, at the mouth of the Kali Mas, almost as far as Wonokromo. Instead of commuting into the city center, workers were now being drawn to the periphery. Employment pressures therefore reinforced the trend toward suburbanization. Although there would be long time lags, residential districts would inevitably extend toward and eventually envelop the new employment districts.

Land Rights

The restructuring of land use is inherently a source of conflict. Except in the case of unoccupied land, those in possession have to yield their chosen way of life and either be incorporated into a new milieu, or be induced to leave. In a market economy, buying out the rights of existing occupants is regarded as a fair procedure. However, if the distribution of income enables a few buyers to command large capital while many small sellers are perennially short of cash, a fair outcome cannot be assumed. Moreover, the very distribution of income that makes it so easy for the rich to buy off the poor is likely to be associated with a structure of power that makes it easy for the rich to call upon the authority of government. A modest show of force by the army or police further skews the bargaining situation, lowering the take-it-or-leave-it price and quashing any attempts to mobilize countervailing power. In Surabaya, as in Jakarta, periods of rapid urban expansion, as the 1910s and since the 1980s, have therefore been associated with mounting social frustration.

Geographic constraints of shoreline and the rivers have dictated that, except by reclamation for harbor works, Surabaya has always expanded toward the south, which has meant expansion into rural land or peri-urban kampungs. The southward spread of the European town therefore displaced the kampungs in its path. However, the indirect effect was, like a ship's bow wave, to intensify the density of those who survived. By 1866 there had ceased to be any agricultural ground to the north of what is today Pandegiling (formerly Tamarindelaan), while mansions and kampungs were also pushing west from Blauran onto the estate Sawahan and east of the

Kali Mas onto the Ketabang estates (map 6.6). The main cause of this phenomenon was undoubtedly the destruction of many older kampungs by the fortification works of the 1830s and 1840s, followed by growth in urban population. Estate owners on the whole seem to have found it profitable to convert their land from sawah, which returned them half the crop but required close supervision when under cane, to house plots, which yielded a constant stream of rental payments.

Construction of European housing involved prior removal of all existing inhabitants, cutting down the trees, and leveling the land. By the twentieth century it also involved laying out streets, drains, power lines, and telephone cables in a regular grid. As more and more estates adjacent to the town were bought up by speculators eyeing the profits to be gained from European housing, the difficulty was to organize the mass removal of the kampung dwellers, who at law enjoyed the hereditary right of occupation as long as they fulfilled their traditional obligations to the estate owner in terms of tax and corvée. Less scrupulous developers, like the new owner of the Bagong estate, sharply increased rents and then evicted those who could not pay. This created great resentment, the more so because it was becoming more difficult for displaced kampung dwellers to find land elsewhere. The BM Kepoetran tackled the problem by paying compensation if the inhabitants would renounce their rights and move elsewhere. If they challenged the amount of compensation or otherwise refused to leave, the company would apply to the Landraad for an eviction order.

After 1910, when the Landraad began to protect the rights of kampung dwellers, developers were forced to abandon crude measures of eviction in favor of a formal process of documenting and buying out customary land rights (see chap. 2). Some landowners still managed through the Landraad to secure the eviction of tenants who were in arrears, but in June 1916 the Supreme Court ruled that even nonpayment of rent did not entitle a landowner to evict: he could only demand payment of the back rent against forfeiture of removable assets. As explained in chapter 2, the solution to this legal obstacle was found in mid-1917 by the OJS tramway company in the form of a lump-sum commutation of customary land rights, paving the way for a simple rental agreement. Once households had signed away perpetuity of lease, landlords could evict at their own convenience, with only one month's notice and no fear of legal complications after payment of removal costs and compensation for any unharvested crops. The timing of clearance was now within the control of the company. Nevertheless, on its Darmo estate the OJS recognized that it was in its own interests that tenants leave willingly, which was facilitated by providing land elsewhere. Resort to court action would inevitably cause delay, besides complicating the signing of agreements with the rest of the population (ARA, OJS 2.20.16.14: 312, 8/12/17). In the case of twelve families from Ketampon Tengah who refused to leave after termination and expiry of their agreements, the company did follow the latter course, applying to the resident, who ordered them to vacate within fourteen days (ARA, OJS 2.20.16.14: 312, 21/5/18). The last families, evidently those who had been reluctant to sign the new rental agreements, left the estate voluntarily in 1919 to take up land made available to them.

From October 1917 the Municipality applied a similar approach in arranging the removal from its newly purchased land at Ketabang of some twelve hundred kampung dwellers. A three-page written agreement was produced fully describing the rights and obligations of each party. The tenant agreed to yield all rights in return for the waiving of any back rent and compensation assessed according to the size and type of house and yard. The Municipality also agreed to provide in the eastern part of the estate (across the railway line) at least a hundred square meters of land with house. The *Soerabaiasch Handelsblad* (28/11/17) reported the first queue of inhabitants outside the municipal offices for payment of compensation. These tenants were probably dealt with more fairly than elsewhere, in that they received not only compensation but land and house within a short distance of their former dwelling. Private landowners paid compensation and perhaps some removal costs but former tenants were then left to their own devices. In 1918, to make way for the new industrial estate, the Municipality also began similarly to arrange the removal of the 457 families between the river and the railway, to substitute land being made available at Ngagelrejo on the other side of the line. It was noted that these kampungs were thoroughly urban: apart from their houses these families of urban artisans, servants, and coachmen owned no more land than would grow a few banana trees.

How many people were cleared from their kampungs to make way for European housing? In 1899 the relevant private estates had a recorded population of 23,300 (table 6.1). Allowing on the one hand for subsequent population growth and, on the other hand, for the exclusion of minor estates and the fact that Bagong and Ngagel estates were only partly cleared, the actual displacement was probably between 15,000 and 25,000 people. Ketabang alone, with 1,100 kampung houses (with an average of about 5.5 persons), accounted for 5,500 (SGS 1917, 135; 1918, 139). Even the minimum estimate of 15,000 people would be about 10 percent of the total Indonesian population at the 1920 census and a much higher proportion in the upper town. The consequence of this massive but almost undocumented displacement of population was a severe and long-term housing shortage. A detailed investigation into six hundred metal industry workers carried out as late as 1926 revealed that only 8 percent owned their own house (Vreede 1926, 48–63). This was attributed explicitly to inadequate compensation for the demolished kampung houses, leaving their owners unable to afford to buy alternative accommodation. Of necessity, three-quarters of these workers had to live far from their workplace, some traveling an hour each way. Despite often deplorable living conditions, rent and transport costs were much higher than other Javanese cities and half the workers in the study were judged to have insufficient means to support their families. These grievances were judged to be a major cause of the metal industry strikes of late 1925.

Open conflict over land subsided in the 1920s. This was not because the housing crisis was overcome, for public housing and kampung improvement programs made little dent overall (chap. 4). Simply, as explained above, there was no longer need to clear land for European housing. The trend of displacement was nonetheless inexorable and always to the disadvantage of kampung dwellers. Between the wars the flash point was the hundred hectares of kampungs that formed the private estate Keputran South (Kidul), which stretched from the Kali Mas west to Kedungdoro, with its southern boundary along Jalan Pandegiling. As early as 1878 the population had grown to almost two thousand people and occupied all cultivable ground (RPL 1878). By the turn of the century the population had grown to five thousand (*RANI*). When Darmo Boulevard was laid out through the new garden suburbs, this densely settled expanse of kampungs blocked the connection with Palmenlaan (Jalan Sudirman) and Simpang. The OJS acquired a small corridor to allow the new electric tram to pass through but other traffic had still to divert along the old highway beside the river. Kampungs were standing in the way of progress. Vreede (1926, 59) reports that kampung dwellers were embittered. A year later the Municipality proposed to resume sufficient land to allow the two boulevards to be joined. After two years of negotiation with the bankrupt Chinese owners and with the assistance of an interest-free loan from the central government, in the middle of 1929 the Municipality acquired not just a wider corridor but the entire estate, nominally to improve kampung living conditions (SGS 1927–29). It then quickly resumed the necessary land and the short connecting section of roadway was completed by the end of 1930. Significantly the new section was christened Palmenlaan Zuid (South Palm Lane), exemplifying the expropriation and division of the kampung by European colonial society and its alien suburban lifestyle.

The next dispute was over the payment of land tax (*landrente*). Here the Municipality proved to be a harsher and more inflexible master than the former Chinese estate owners. Soon after taking control, the Municipality apparently increased the rent (Frederick 1989, 9). During the Depression the burden became too great and by 1933 some kampung dwellers had fallen into arrears, not only in Keputran but also in Bratang and Jagir (SGS 1933). Rates were reduced a year later but disputes dragged on. The central government looked into the matter. Finally in 1938 the Municipality lost patience. Tenants who still refused to pay the land tax were taken to court and after judgment had been given in favor of the Municipality, their houses were demolished and their rights to occupancy sold at public auction (SGS 1938, 191).

Meanwhile, it continued to irk that the kampungs of Keputran were such a highly visible eyesore from both sides of the main road, the one brief section between Tanjung Perak, Jembatan Merah, and Wonokromo, where the façade of the modern, European city, was not yet complete. The Municipality's response was to resume another eighty-eight hundred square meters of kampung land along the eastern side of the new road for modern buildings. This third phase of creeping expropriation met with bitter resistance. In 1938 the Municipality again called upon the intervention of the central government to help clear away the remaining kampung dwellers who had refused compensation (SGS 1938, 193).

In a context of increasing government interference in kampung life, these cases of displacement and coercion sowed the seeds of a bitter harvest. The inhabitants of Keputran had long been regarded as troublesome (Frederick 1989, 8), perhaps because this great expanse of kampung was the most secure and impenetrable fastness of Indonesian (Javanese) society in Surabaya, an other world where the European was an intruder, a foreigner who could not be confident of enforcing his will. According to Frederick, "the municipal government was never forgiven, and the arek Surabaya of Kampung Keputran became known for their sullen, recalcitrant attitude and their refusal to obey city laws and officials" (1989, 9). In October 1945, when the beleaguered British were still trying to carry out their mandate of transferring Dutch women and children from Japanese internment camps to the port, it was the inhabitants of Keputran who in one of the first violent incidents of the Revolution poured out onto the roadway to stop the convoy, seized the vehicles, and butchered many of the passengers (Frederick 1989, 260; also chap. 2).

Surabaya on the Eve of World War II

By the late 1930s Surabaya had taken on the appearance of a modern, Western city. "Tropical Holland," as portrayed in books of nostalgia such as Hein Buitenweg's *Krokodillenstad* (1980), was a prosperous, middle-class world of whitewashed offices, garden suburbs, automobiles, luxury hotels, prestige shopping districts, and hill resorts. How dramatically the city had changed over just one generation, roughly the same period as the New Order. Around 1900 photographs suggest a still unhurried city: shady, earthen roads without footpaths or even gutters, mainly pedestrian traffic, hawkers and coolies with shoulder poles wandering along the middle of the road, a few carts and dokar weaving their way through, and every half hour or so the open-sided steam tram chuffing by sedately (Kerchman 1930, 349). By the 1930s people had been marginalized by Progress. Streets are wider, asphalted, dominated by a steady stream of black motor cars. Dokar and cyclists seem fragile and vulnerable (Kerchman 1930, 350). At peak hours people reappear, crowded onto the footpaths, but in the era of mass public transport many more whisk by unseen, borne by the quiet miracle of the electric tram.

The urban facade was now distinguished by its modern architecture in the forefront of contemporary European style. Around the turn of the century most commercial buildings were still fairly small and obviously colonial. In the central business district and along the main thoroughfares, individual buildings merged into a streetscape of verandahs and ornate parapets. Between the wars the leading business houses vied to build grand new edifices that were statements of modern design and commercial strength. The most massive were the Handelsvereeniging Amsterdam (1925) and the Internatio (1930) buildings, the latter of which still dominates the square at Jembatan Merah. With the town hall (1927) and provincial offices (1931), government also sought to reflect prestige. Some of the leading Dutch architects enjoyed commissions in the Indies, and local architects were responsive to the current fashions.[4] Typical elements were an austere and sometimes massive façade, integrated with strong vertical and horizontal lines and decorative features such as parapets and towers. In the Netherlands such buildings were fewer and less noticeable in the traditional red-brick streetscapes. In Surabaya and Jakarta, however, the interwar building boom meant that the streetscapes were predominantly in the contemporary style. Even older buildings, such as the prestigious Oranje Hotel (later Hotel Majapahit) in Tunjungan, were remodeled with new façades. The impression was all the more striking because, in the absence of verandahs, many of these buildings were whitewashed to reflect the heat. The European façade of Surabaya, which was concentrated along a very narrow corridor, therefore looked outstandingly modern, which was a great source of pride to its Dutch citizens. The governor of East Java could boast that Surabaya was "the most modern city in the Indies" (Lumkeman, 1939, 66). There was a growing self-confidence that Surabaya and Jakarta were no longer colonial backwaters but, if anything, more modern and more dynamic than the tradition-bound and rather stuffy Netherlands.

One of the manifestations of the more vibrant, confident, self-contained European world of the interwar years was the emergence of Tunjungan as the main European shopping street and center of recreation. At the turn of the century this section of the "highway" had been little more than a country lane of hardened earth, lined by whitewashed brick fences and shaded by tall, overarching trees (fig. 6.4).[5] In the 1900s redevelopment of the district around Simpang as a European garden suburb caused the center of gravity of European society to shift southward from Pasar Besar (near the old alun-alun) into Tunjungan, where land could be purchased more cheaply and in larger blocks. The opening of the magnificent Hotel Oranje in 1911 marked the emergence of the

Figure 6.4. Tunjungan at the intersection with Embong Malang, ca. 1900. "De Club" is on the left (cf. fig. 1.9). KITLV no. 6473.

northern section as the prestige hotel district. Opening of the Simpang Club, in 1907, and the move of the Concordia Soos from the old town to Tunjungan in 1916 confirmed its status as the center of European social life (Faber 1936, 354–63). In the 1920s, as the population swelled in the new garden suburbs, Tunjungan took on its recognized form as the prestige shopping street, lined on both sides with multistory department stores such as Whiteaway and Laidlaw, Adler, and Louvre, fashion boutiques, bookstores, restaurants and ice-cream parlors, illuminated at night with flashing neon signs. Upstairs were the popular dance halls, or dancings, and nightclubs. A guidebook from the 1930s refers to Surabaya as "attractively gay and active" with "many open places, restaurants and cafes in Parisian style" (Kawata 1936). This may have picked up on a local conceit because the local head of the Bureau of Public Works also cautiously drew comparison with "a boulevard in Paris on a not too busy day" (Heida 1939, 48).

The shape of the city had also changed. Most obviously, it had elongated. In 1900, except for the naval base and some warehouses, the city proper had extended no further than the abandoned Fort Prins Hendrik to the north and the settlement of Simpang to the south. The private estates that all but encircled the city were for the most part still under cultivation. By 1930 most of these lands had been bought up for redevelopment. The city now extended in a contiguous strip from the mouth of the river to Wonokromo. Simpang was but halfway between the old town and Wonokromo. Somewhat less obviously, the city had also broadened. After 1923 the electric tramway had provided a new east-west axis between Gubeng and Sawahan, making new and cheaper land accessible for housing, enterprise, and public facilities. The introduction of private automobiles, taxis, buses, and jitneys had also freed people from dependence on the river and the north-south tram line. Suburbanization and the decentralization of employment thereby accelerated, interacted with, and reinforced each other.

These general trends have of course been part of the common urban experience of the twentieth century. What is unusual in the case of Surabaya is the rhythm and timing of these changes. As explained above, most of the restructuring of land use occurred during the decade of the 1910s, when the private estates were bought out by developers, including the Municipality itself, in a speculative boom fueled by quite unrealistic expectations as to the city's long-term growth. In the 1920s and especially the 1930s, the failure to meet those expectations left the city with a considerable land bank for future development. The supply of land was no longer a constraint. Nor was the physical infrastructure. The roadway network and public transport system were capable, with only modest improvements, of carrying a much larger volume of traffic. In all these respects the potential already existed for rapid urban expansion. What was lacking was fuel to drive the process in the sense of effective demand, real purchasing power. The Japanese occupation, the turmoil of the Revolution, and the worsening economic stagnation after Independence all constrained the growth of effective demand. Rapid growth in population generated a demand for housing, but it was a demand for cheap and therefore land-intensive housing, kampung housing. What all but disappeared with the repatriation of the Dutch was a middle class with high household incomes, a high rate of private vehicle ownership, and an effective demand for land-extensive suburban housing. The demise of the middle class after Independence happened also in Rangoon and Hanoi, with similar economic and urban stagnation.

The Postcolonial Era

Urban expansion took a different form after 1942. For over a hundred years it had been the modern, Western city that had expanded and restructured land use according to its own needs and rules, supported by the power of the colonial state. As kampung land was taken up for European housing or industry, kampung dwellers had no choice but to take whatever compensation was offered and retreat to the urban fringe, where the process was often repeated. Their powerlessness was reinforced by well-intentioned but often ill-judged intervention by the colonial bureaucracy (chap. 4). The tightening of administrative control over the use of public space, down to the minutiae of street frontages, prohibition of squatting, street selling and begging, licensing of vehicles, the regulation of traffic, and the maintenance of drains, meant that in its public aspect, Surabaya had become a well-ordered and fairly tidy quasi-European city, perhaps even more so than Anglo-Chinese Singapore. From the viewpoint of the Municipality and in the eyes of European or even Japanese visitors (Frederick 1989, 85), this was good government. In the eyes of kampung dwellers, however, it had been imposed and was thereby resented, not as good government but as colonial control.

With the defeat of the Dutch in March 1942, the pressure was released. Even under the Japanese, real political power began to pass into the hands of Indonesians, who had grown up in the kampung world. The small cadre of Japanese officials in municipal government were preoccupied with more urgent tasks than arresting the gradual erosion of colonial by-laws. Indonesian officials saw no justification in rigidly imposing laws when people's livelihoods were at stake. There was no longer the same obsession with neatness, tidiness, good order. Kampung society began to claim back the city they had so long been in but not of. Frederick (1989) rightly emphasizes the emerging sense of common identity as arek Suroboyo, the people of Surabaya, but also denoting kampung dwellers.

The main pressure for the Indonesianization of the city was rural-urban migration. Between 1940 and 1945 the population of Surabaya increased by 50 percent, from about four hundred thousand to over six hundred thousand (chap. 3). Within the three and a half years of the Japanese occupation more people flooded into the city than the entire population in 1920. Such a massive influx could not but transform the land use pattern. In order to survive, people began to squat wherever they could find enough land to build a small hut, especially along canals and rail lines (figs. 6.5, 6.6). The breakdown of the modern sector of the economy forced more and more people to eke out a subsistence on the margin. Many turned to whatever informal occupations would earn them a few cents. Two activities that suddenly became popular among Indonesians were food hawking and becak driving. In the 1930s street sellers of cooked food, except for *sate* and *soto,* had been Chinese (Notonegoro, pers. comm.). As in seventeenth-century Jakarta (Abeyasekere 1987, 29–30), they still carried their minimal equipment and stock suspended on long shoulder poles (*pikulan*), handcarts only coming into use during the 1930s. Whether because of the cessation of Chinese immigration or the lower profit margins, Indonesians now began to take on these occupations, as in Jakarta (Jellinek 1991). More relaxed enforcement of the restrictions on street selling must have opened up many new market niches.

The explosion in the number of becak, or three-wheeled pedicabs, involved a revolution in urban public transport. Its origins are obscure but the first unwieldy prototype seems to appeared in Jakarta about 1936 as an adaptation of the long-familiar goods tricycle (*bakfiets*) used especially for the delivery of fresh bread

Figure 6.5. Squatter shacks along the Banyu Urip Canal, Kupang, 1987. Photo by author.

Figure 6.6. Squatter shacks beside railway, early 1990s. Photo by author.

(Robinson 1953, 98–103). After various modifications in design, by March 1940 they were numerous enough for the Council to debate their incorporation into the traffic by-laws (SGB 11/3/40). These proceedings also reveal that they were by then becoming accepted in Makassar. However, while passengers seem to have been happy to try out this new form of transport, official attitudes were guarded. European administrators had concerns as to their safety and the interference with motorized traffic. Chinese leaders disliked their affinity to the rickshaw, with its colonial associations, and Indonesian nationalists also had their reservations about human exploitation. This may help to explain hearsay that in Surabaya the Municipality banned such vehicles when they first appeared at the end of the 1930s, although according to Frederick (1989, 111), the first becak did not appear in Surabaya in late 1941, just before the Japanese occupation. They would probably have remained a curiosity but for the introduction of severe gasoline rationing for nonmilitary vehicles. Being so much cheaper than dokar in both capital and running costs, because there was no horse to be fed and tended, they were ideal to take over the role vacated by disappearance of motorized public transport. By mid-1943 some twenty-four hundred were already in service (Frederick 1989, 111).

Spontaneous migration continued after Independence. From an estimated six hundred thousand in 1949, Surabaya's population was reckoned by municipal estimates to have reached almost one million by mid-1956 (*SP,* 26/6/56). Against the tide of so many poor villagers seeking an income and a place to live, Surabaya, like so many other Third World cities, proved to be extremely porous. Those who had relatives in the city could usually by arrangement move into existing kampungs—at first as a guest, then perhaps renting a space to sleep, later with earnings buying rights to a tiny plot of land on which to build a small hut, bringing other family members from the village and gradually, as windfalls allowed, extending and improving the original hut into a proper kampung house. In this customary way, the density of existing kampungs steadily increased. As the last of the fruit trees were cut down and the open terrain was built upon, once green, shady, an almost rural kampung took on the appearance to unsympathetic eyes of an urban slum. Poor migrants squatted wherever there was vacant, unsupervised land. Anyone entering Surabaya by train would notice the continuous row of shacks crowding in on both sides of the line from Wonokromo to Gubeng (fig. 6.6). Except from bridges, the Kali Mas was hidden behind squatters huts. Public land was the most obvious place to choose: riverbanks, fire access lanes, railway yards, building sites, and even Chinese cemeteries, where graves were demolished for building materials. In furtherance of its 1955 election pledge to transfer land from landlords to tenants, the Communist Party (PKI) encouraged the occupation of private estates, which were an easy target (*SP,* 13/6/56).

The municipal administration was unsure how to tackle the problem of squatting. Colonial legislation remained on the books but infringement was so extensive that the authorities hardly knew where to begin to enforce it. Besides, with Independence there came a sense that the government ought not to cause hardship for the people whom they now represented. Vagrants could be sent back to the countryside but squatters were regarded as urban citizens whose only crime was to be living in an unauthorized place. At first the clearance of squatters was targeted at those occupying public land needed for rebuilding. Ironically, in view of prewar tensions, this included the land next to Kampung Keputran that was to be taken up for the new Keputran market, completed in 1952 (*NC,* 14/7/50; *JP,* 12/2/52). By 1953, as government became more organized under the new mayor, Moestadjab, the Municipality became more systematic. Vagrants were rounded up and held in detention pending either repatriation to the countryside or resettlement in urban kampungs. In one raid some two hundred vagrants were detained (*SP,* 5 and 16/9/53). By September 1953 it was reported that seven hundred squatter huts (*gubuk*) had already been demolished (*SP,* 21/9/53) (fig. 6.7). The land earmarked for the new campus of Airlangga University (formerly the Armenian Sports Club golf course) and Wonokromo market were two fur-

Figure 6.7. Squatter clearance near the town hall, ca. 1953. Arsip Nasional.

ther areas to be cleared. Toward the end of the year it was estimated that there were still some 3,000 illegal dwellings, 1,800 on public land and 1,200 on private land (SP 18/11/53); a month later a higher figure was cited: five thousand illegal dwellings, of which three thousand had already been demolished and two thousand were to be demolished as soon as possible (*SP,* 21/12/53). And the influx continued. In 1955 it was reported that occupation of land along and behind the Banyu Urip Canal was worsening flooding in the adjacent, low-lying suburb of Darmo (*JP,* 19/2/55). The barren hillside above the canal, much of it long used as European and Chinese cemeteries, was regarded as wasteland free of title. Poor squatters in this area were a stronghold of the Communist Party.

There is no evidence that the Municipality ever seriously attempted to clear squatters from the private estates. The colonial government had long intended to buy back all these lands but had been thwarted by budgetary constraints right up to Independence. About 1951 discussions were held between a committee of council members and estate owners over the buying out of the seven hundred residual hectares held by fourteen European, fifteen Chinese, and six Arab owners (JP 11/2/52). Most owners were quite prepared to sell out. Rents had not been paid for years. Land was being occupied by squatters while the authorities turned a blind eye. Estate owners responded by ceasing to spend on the maintenance of infrastructure such as roads and drains, which caused flooding to worsen. Nevertheless, the Municipality could not afford compensation under a legal settlement.

The tough approach to squatters lasted until 1956. The military authorities (Koordinasi Keamanan Daerah, Regional Security Coordination) announced that illegal occupancy would no longer be tolerated after 19 January 1956 and that demolition would be entrusted to the Illegal Buildings Prevention Bureau (Biro Pentjegah Bangunan Liar) (*SP,* 25/4/56). About two weeks later an attempt to demolish squatter huts at Pakis, around the big Kembang Kuning cemetery, ended in a riot. As a crowd reportedly of three thousand attempted to prevent the demolition, police were called in and shots were fired. Four people were killed and another two wounded (*SP,* 7/5/56). The military commander promptly banned unauthorized demonstrations (*SP,* 9/5/56). Subsequently it was alleged that the demonstration had been organized by the Communist Party as a step toward implementing its policy of land reform (*SP,* 13/6/56). The PKI certainly made no secret of its support for the squatters and had increased its strength in the Municipal Assembly at the 1955 elections (chap. 2). The violent Pakis incident, which coincided with the end of Moestajab's active term of office, seems to have brought about an uneasy truce. There emerged a tacit consensus as to which areas were under public control, such as roadways and markets, where police could move against illegal intrusion, and which were de facto under popular control, such as squatter kampungs on wasteland like Pakis or on private estates.

The problem of the remaining estates in Chinese and Arab hands was resolved with the passing of the Agrarian Law of 1960, which imposed a limit of two hectares on the amount of land which could be owned as freehold other than for specified purposes. The last estates were thereby effectively abolished. Kampung and cultivated ground was formally recognized to belong to the occupants, who in any case had paid no rent since the Japanese invasion. Unoccupied and uncultivated land became government land. No compensation was paid to the former estate owners but the government allowed them to retain title and collect rents from permanent buildings along main roads such as Embong Malang and Kedongdoro (Sutoro, interview, 5/10/87). By 1970 the only estate for which no settlement had been reached with the Department of Lands (Agraria) was Patemon, since the owner had died and his son was living in England.

However, even after 1958, when the PKI gained control of the Municipal Assembly, there were still periodic squatter clearances from public land. One burst of activity occurred as late as mid-1964. The campaign was launched at the beginning of April in fairly typical fashion, with the stern warning that all illegal buildings would be demolished in due course (*SP,* 2/4/64). A month later the illegal stalls on State Railways land at Pasar Turi Station were targeted for removal, followed by several hundred squatter huts along the banks of the Kali Mas at Kramat Gantung and Achmad Jais (*SP,* 8/5, 5/6/64). The justification was that they spoiled the appearance of the city. Nevertheless, the government was extremely wary of being accused of forced demolitions and emphasized that these removals were being carried out voluntarily by the people themselves. On the appointed day the mayor himself was in attendance, along with the police, city officials, and representatives of a welfare organization. Trucks were provided on which the inhabitants could load their dismantled wooden huts and be taken to a new approved site at Dupak, where they would enjoy legal rights of occupancy. After 1951 this low-lying land beside the northwest flood basin (*boezem*), which since the 1920s had gradually been reclaimed by the dumping of the city's garbage, had been taken up to rehouse illegal squatters (*SP,* 14/6/58). By the mid-1960s it had become a densely settled expanse of poor kampungs—and also one of the main centers of cheap prostitution (chap. 4).

Land was also taken up by the government and private enterprise for bungalow-style housing for military officers, public servants, and white-collar staff. As explained in chapter 4, housing was the most important component of salary in kind, compensating for very low take-home pay. Rapid growth in the size of the armed forces and bureaucracy meant continual pressure on the demand for public housing. These bungalows were fairly modest by prewar European standards but being detached, single-story dwellings with small front gardens, back yards, and vehicle access, they still took up much more land than kampung housing and required a wider street grid. Such housing complexes therefore had to be located on the urban fringe where tracts of land were still available. At first it was possible to take up excess capacity in developments laid out between the wars. The navy and the air force built on reclaimed land just south of the port of Tanjung Perak, while the army occupied most of the undeveloped southwestern part of the former Darmo estate.

Civilian housing was built in many locations around the city but particularly in the east, where there had remained the last extensive tracts of rural land within the old municipal boundaries. In the early 1940s the railway line had still marked a sharp edge to the urban area, at least to the south of Gubeng station. Beyond the medical school and the new public hospital, the rest of the Municipality's Gubeng estate was taken up by the golf course and sports fields of the Armenian Sports Club. From there as far as the Wonokromo Canal came an almost continuous expanse of rice fields intersected with a few strands of rural kampungs, a rural scene little changed since the turn of the century. In the early 1950s the horizon was still so low that there was an uninterrupted view from the hospital to the Heineken (Bir Bintang) brewery on the industrial estate at Ngagel (Soejoenoes, interview, 10/87). With the intention of opening up land for modern housing on the eastern side of the railway, the owner of the Bagong Sabrangan estate, Ibrahim Baswedan, had just before his death in 1940 opened a low-level viaduct under the railway at Jalan Sulawesi (leading into what is now Kertajaya) but the war overtook his plans. Instead the land was taken over by the Japanese as a dispersed fuel or ammunition dump and afterward, like the nearby golf course, was occupied by squatters. In 1953 the university took steps to recover the golf course for the new campus and staff housing (*SP,* 21/9/53); ten years later the municipal housing authority (YKP; see chap. 4) added the adjacent Darma Husada complex. In the early 1960s the YKP also extended southward into the former Ngagel estate with Pucang and Ngagel Jaya. At the end of the Old Order redevelopment was still patchy but all the land between the campus and the Wonokromo Canal had been parceled up for urban development with a notional street grid (Pembina, map 1963).

By the early 1960s almost no land remained unoccupied anywhere within the municipal boundaries. Comparison of a 1940 street map and wartime aerial photographs (fig. 1.1) with a 1963 map shows just how much vacant land had been taken up during the 1940s and 1950s, mainly for housing to accommodate the almost threefold increase in population. The problem was so acute that it became hard to find new landfill sites for garbage disposal. Dupak, Wonokusumo, and Jagir (Jojoran) had been in use since the interwar period and there was now little scope for further reclamation (*SP,* 20/1/59). Complaints of the growing shortage of land for industrial development were heard soon after Independence (*SP,* 31/12/53). The Ngagel industrial estate had filled up by World War II and, except at Tanjung Perak (where the Udatin automobile assembly plant was located in the 1955), no more land had been set aside for industry. Firms therefore had to use their own initiative without too much regard to planning restrictions. Medium-scale enterprises such as chocolate, soft drink, cigarette, and paint factories managed to squeeze into fringe locations, such as along the river at Dinoyo, on the road to Kenjeran and to the west around Sawahan. Large-scale and heavy-industrial plants were forced to locate beyond the municipal boundaries. However, it was not only industry that began to locate outside the city boundaries.

Constrained by the harbor to the north and lack of transport access to the west and east, the city first spilled over its boundaries to the south in ribbon development along the main highway. Expansion beyond the small outlying settlement of Wonokromo had long been blocked by private estates still under cultivation. A group of Dutch-owned private estates totaling 930 hectares, encompassing the parcels of Wonokromo, Karang Poh, Dadoengan, Ketintang, and Karah, occupied most of the land in the triangle between the Surabaya River or Kali Mas and the highway from Wonokromo south to Waru. Until the 1930s this land had been used for sugar cultivation, thereafter mainly for rice. Apart from an almost continuous strip of kampungs along the river and surrounding the old sugar mills, the land was still entirely rural. In 1953 all this was bought by the provincial government for one million rupiah, in part to provide scope for the relocation and expansion of central and provincial government offices, which could no longer all be crowded into the provincial offices on Jalan Pahlawan. The police, the Supreme Court (Kejaksaan Tinggi), units of the Department of Agriculture, state enterprises, and the Islamic university, IAIN Sunan Ampel, are among the offices, plants, and housing complexes that began to extend southward along the highway, even though parts of the interior of this triangle remained as rice field into the late 1980s. However, despite repeated pleas, none of the land was incorporated into the municipality until 1965. In the short term the only benefit to the Municipality was the opportunity to occupy some of the old buildings vacated by provincial offices.

A further encouragement to this southward shift was the decision in 1956 to relocate the naval and civil airfield from its cramped site at Morokrembangan, beside the port of Tanjung Perak, to what was then sawah and tambak in the neighboring kabupaten of Sidoarjo. Construction by a French contractor began in 1959 and the official opening as Djuanda Airport took place on 30 May 1964, allowing Morokrembangan to be redeveloped as a naval training school (*SP,* 21/5/64). With the growth in both air travel and road transport, Tanjung Perak ceased to be the main gateway to the city. The urban axis remained north-south but the orientation was now much more toward the hinterland (see chap. 7).

One of the last acts of the Old Order had been to approve the long-awaited enlargement of the 1931 municipal boundaries. They had last been adjusted in 1931, when the city's area had been increased from sixty-three to eighty-three square kilometers.[6] Since then the enumerated population had grown threefold, from almost 350,000 to over one million. Most of this increase had been accommodated by greater density of settlement within the already built-up area but, as explained above, spillover was occurring into the adjacent rural kabupaten of Gresik and Sidoarjo. Expansion of the boundaries had been called for as long ago as 1951 (*SP,* 26/4/65). When finally promulgated in April 1965, the new boundaries increased the area more than threefold, to 290 square kilometers.[7] Five kecamatan (subdistricts) were added: to the south Wonocolo (including all the private estates purchased by the provincial government in 1953), to the east all land between the old boundary and the sea (Sukolilo and Rungkut), and to the west the mainly dry land of Karang Pilang and Tandes. Although the city was still elongated along a north-south axis, the new shape of the municipality was actually wider, especially to the west. With so much room for expansion, these boundaries have remained unchanged (map 6.7).

In 1965 there was no plan as to how the enlarged area was to be utilized. After Independence the Municipal Assembly did not endorse the Dutch town plan (Stadsplan) but no other plan was drawn up to replace it (KMS, Team Master Plan, 1970).[8] There was a good deal of ad hoc decision making but nothing that could be termed town planning. Indeed, there were no qualified town planners. Jakarta alone had a master plan, drawn up between 1957 and 1960 with foreign technical assistance and intended to be a model for other cities, but even that lapsed for want of political support (Abeyasekere 1987, 200–201). In Surabaya chaos was avoided only because the worsening economy ensured that there was too little public and private investment to transform the pattern of land use.

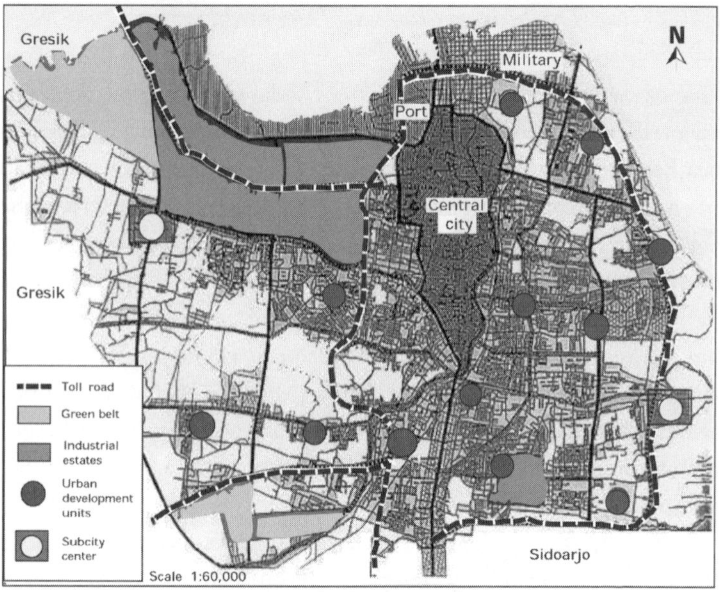

Map 6.7. Surabaya: Land use plan for 2005. Source: KMS.

Fortunately a few farsighted people realized that it would be foolish to allow such a large city to grow without any planning framework. The catalyst was the Faculty of Architecture at the Surabaya Institute of Technology (ITS), which had been established in 1960 under the auspices of the Bandung Institute of Technology (ITB) and had perpetuated its pioneering commitment to town planning. Lieutenant-Colonel Sukotjo, who at the end of October 1965 had taken over as caretaker mayor, was persuaded of this point of view and in December announced the formation of a team to draw up a master plan for the development of the city (*SP,* 9/12/65). This was to be a joint effort between the Municipality and the ITS Faculty of Architecture. The key figures were Ir. Moehtadi, a young civil engineer, who became chairman of the master plan team, and academic Ir. Johan Silas, both ITB graduates. The timing can be explained by two main factors. First, the extension of the city boundaries had created the need for urban planning. Second, clearance of squatter housing in areas known to have been sympathetic to the PKI created the opportunity to redevelop some previously settled parts of the city. Whereas the PKI's influence on urban planning had been to respect rights of occupancy, the way was now open to a more interventionist approach.

By October 1966 the master plan team had begun its task, though so much research had to be undertaken and discussed that it was January 1970 before the Outline Plan was presented (KMS, Team Master Plan, 1970). The early decision to locate the team's offices in the old Simpang Club, on the busy corner of Jalan Pemuda and Simpang, ensured that the planners did not become lost in the amorphous bureaucracy but remained in the public eye. The core of the Outline Plan were the maps outlining the intended land use by 1990 and the five-year stages by which rural land would be converted to urban use. This Outline Plan was formally accepted by the Municipal Assembly in November 1970, clearing the way for formulation of a detailed master plan. The plan for 2000 and the accompanying land use map (dated May 1977) were formally presented in July 1978, after which began the final stage, preparing detailed area plans. The long time taken to finalize the master plan was not a serious problem because the Outline Plan had already laid down the basis for land use decisions and the process of preparing the plan kept officials in regular consultation. In fact, the uncharacteristically open and informal processes of the master plan team may well in the long-run have been more important than the plan itself. Beginning when the municipal bureaucracy was still reeling from the anticommunist purge of the mid-1960s, over more than a decade the team instilled a rigorous, technocratic, and long-term approach to decision making that gradually set the tone for the rest of the administration. Several members of the team eventually rose to head municipal departments.

The core of the master plan was the land use map for 2000 (KMS, Team Master Plan, 1977).[9] Whereas much of the accompanying documentation was merely a stocktaking of the city's resources and constraints, the map was a decision-making framework. Its starting point was the assumption that the population of Surabaya would grow from almost 2 million in 1970 to around 5.5 million by 2000. Accordingly it was desirable to establish land use categories for the entire area of the municipality—and even across the borders into the neighboring kabupaten of Gresik and Sidoarjo—in some rational way before decision making was preempted by the market. In the east, almost the entire area from the edge of the city to the coastal tambak was reserved for housing. In the west, there were to be three wide new residential corridors separated by green belts, an element given much more emphasis since the Outline Plan of 1970. In the south, into Sidoarjo, development would continue to be mixed. Each corridor would be served by arterial transport routes and be linked with the rest of the city by inner and outer ring roads. Finally, in line with orthodoxy, each main "development block" of around two hundred thousand people would constitute a distinct satellite town with its own facilities.

Fortunately this framework was put in place before the urban land market began to boom. The planning team greatly overestimated the growth of population. At the 2000 census the population of the municipality was recorded as 2.6 million and the combined urban and rural population of Surabaya, Gresik, and Sidoarjo was only 5.1 million (BPS 2000a). Conversely, the growth in real income was much greater than expected in the 1970s. Because the demand for urban land increases more than proportionately with income, especially on the part of the prosperous and expanding middle class, the rate at which land was taken up for urban use was therefore roughly in line with predictions. However, the master plan guidelines were not closely followed. There was no staged release of residential land, little preservation of green belts, and until the 1990s only one genuine satellite town.

After 1992 the master plan was updated for 2005 (map 6.7). Three main changes are worthy of note. First, the existing toll road along the western side of the city was to be extended into an encircling ring road, with connection to the proposed Surabaya-Madura bridge that would open up cheap industrial and residential land in western Madura (Rachbini 1995). Second, the saltponds in the northwest were to be almost entirely reclaimed as a vast area of industrial land close by the port of Tanjung Perak. Third, to take account of population growth to the east and west, "subcity centers" and smaller "urban development units" around the urban periphery were respecified. Unlike the original master plan, however, the plan for 2005 did not attempt to plan land use across the municipal boundary into Sidoarjo kabupaten. With the rapid southward expansion of urban housing and industry this boundary, unchanged since 1965, has become an administrative absurdity.

The master plan was above all a blueprint for rapid urbanization. In a country where government has long been preoccupied with the production of rice, it remarkably had almost nothing to say about agriculture. The expectation was that agriculture that would all but disappear from the municipality. Hitherto Surabaya had always been like an island poised between the sea and the wet-rice plain. In the twentieth century the city's expansion had drawn it further southward into the rice fields. Annexation of the five kecamatan in 1965 brought the municipality a large and somewhat anomalous rural component. The master plan envisaged that by 2000 all rice fields would have been taken up for development. Being completely flat and rectangular, rice fields are ideal for urban development, needing only a layer of landfill to provide level building blocks. Figures on rural land are aggravatingly inconsistent but the trend is clear enough. Comparison of a land use map issued in 1986 with Allied aerial photos of 1944–45 suggest that by the mid-1980s to the east of the city there remained perhaps only a third of the former area of rice fields (fig. 1.1; KMS 1986, map). Between 1980 and 1993 alone, as land speculation gathered strength, the area harvested to rice, counting two to three crops per annum, fell by over 60 percent, while the physical area of irrigated rice fields shrank from 27.5 square kilometers in 1984 to 6.0 square kilometers in 1995 (SDA 1984–85, 1995). Much bunded ground was no longer under cultivation, but merely bred mosquitoes, pending reclamation as building sites. At this rate, soon no land would be left under rice.

One of the early recommendations of the master plan team was the establishment of two new industrial areas, the first since the Municipality had bought the Ngagel land in 1916. By the mid-1930s, the 45.6 hectare Ngagel estate was already full (Faber 1936, 13). Postwar industrial ventures were therefore scattered throughout the municipality wherever there was vacant land. In many cases these were plants of a type that would not have been allowed under the Nuisance Law (Hinderordonnantie) because of disturbance to adjacent residential areas. In 1976 industry was estimated to occupy 780 hectares and warehousing another 80 hectares (KMS 1978, 35). To meet the expected growth in demand, in 1975 a tract of 246 hectares at Rungkut (in the southeast of the municipality bordering on Sidoarjo) was developed as Surabaya Industrial Estate Rungkut (SIER) (chap. 5). Another 200 hectares of reclaimed tambak at Tandes, in the northeast, were made available as unserviced sites. These initiatives relieved the pressure on scarce land elsewhere in the city and provided scope for relocation of plants incompatible with residential areas.

The master plan sought as far as possible to segregate industry from residential areas. On the eastern side of the city, which was allocated for residential and educational development, no new factories were to be allowed. Industry was to be directed to the northwest (Tandes), where reclaimed fish ponds were unattractive for residential development, southwest along the river, or southward into Sidoarjo by extension of the Rungkut industrial estate. Heavy and polluting industry was to be isolated in the satellite industrial zone of Gresik, which already contained a cement plant, thermal power station, and petrochemical complex. This industrial pattern did indeed come to pass (map 5.1). Farsighted decisions in the early 1970s undoubtedly spared Surabaya from severe industrial pollution, albeit at the expense of residents of Gresik, who began to complain of the heavy dust fallout (*SP,* 16/9/87).

As the city has spread and industrial output increased, the limitations of these broad zoning restrictions have become apparent. First, until recently there has been almost no monitoring of environmental conditions. Second, residential development, both real estate and kampung, has been allowed to encroach to the edge of the Rungkut industrial estate, where a green belt would have been more appropriate. The northern part of the industrial zone at Tandes is also quite close to the new Darmo housing estate and low-cost housing projects of Perumnas. Third, although the old colonial Nuisance Law remains in force and since 1982 has been supplemented by the Environment Law, these have been little enforced and are often ignored. State enterprises like the Gresik cement plant and sugar factories, have been among the worst offenders. When state enterprises are under no pressure to comply with environmental legislation, private enterprise naturally takes its cue.

Nevertheless, Surabaya does not look like an industrial city. From the top of one of the new high-rise buildings one looks northwest across the mosaic of red roofs to the ribbon of the harbor and beyond in a broad sweep, taking in the tall, smoking chimneys of the cement works, power station, and petrochemical plant at Gresik. But that heavy industrial complex is a distant view, not even part of the municipality. Of the municipality itself, industry and warehouses together constitute only 5 percent of the total area, which is concentrated in the several enclaves of the port and naval dockyard, the old godowns along the Kali Mas, and the industrial estates at Ngagel, Rungkut, and Tandes (table 6.2). Although large generators of employment (chap. 5), none is part of the central city. Apart from offices (3 percent) and infrastructure (1 percent), the rest of the urban area is taken up by housing. These land use data reinforce the observation that Surabaya is more a service city than an industrial city. Historically it was a service center for the plantation sector. Under the New Order, with rapid industrial development within and beyond the municipal boundaries, it is increasingly becoming a service center for the manufacturing sector (chap. 5).

TABLE 6.2
Land use, Surabaya municipality, 1992 (%)

Type of Use	%	
Urban Area	50	
Housing[a]	39	
Offices	3	
Industry, warehouses	5	
Roads, rivers, drains	1	
Under development	2	
Nonurban Area	50	
Rice fields	20	
Dry fields	6	
Saltwater ponds	20	
Trees, swamps, beach	4	
Total	100	
Total area	32,100	hectares

Source: KMS, SDA 1995. Based on Final Report of the 1992 Basic Map Data Compilation Project.
[a]Includes cemeteries.

Transport Infrastructure

At the beginning of the New Order, the main limitation on the spread of the city was transport access, which still meant public transport. Despite a four- or fivefold increase in population, the electric tramway network had not been extended since 1924 and forty years later was still relying on the original rolling stock (Duparc 1972, 76). By then trams were regarded as outmoded, having been abolished in Jakarta in the early 1960s under pressure from President Sukarno in his guise as town planner (Abeyasekere 1987, 176). Besides, the State Railways—which had managed the system since 1949 and become owner, with nationalization in 1960—could not mobilize the huge sum needed to rehabilitate, let alone extend it. At the end of 1965 the Municipality decided to close it down in favor of public buses (*SP*, 11/12/65).[10]

The poorly conceived public bus system failed from the outset (Dick 1981). Instead fixed route public transport was taken over by *bemo* (*becak motor*), tiny three-wheeled Daihatsu vans powered by noisy, spluttering, and often smoky two-stroke engines and fitted in local workshops with a small rear cabin to carry six passengers. Intended to replace the becak, these cheap commercial vehicles were introduced to Jakarta in 1962 for use as public transport during the Asian Games: afterward a batch was allotted to Surabaya (*SP*, 8/11/62). In the 1970s larger four-wheeled models became common. Not until the mid-1970s did the government reformalize public transport when the state enterprise Damri introduced city buses to the twenty-two-kilometer north-south corridor from Tanjung Perak via Jembatan Merah, Tunjungan, Darmo, and Wonokromo to the Aloha roundabout, near the airport turnoff (DGLC 1977). A flat-fare structure allowed people to travel cheaply and quickly from the southern urban fringe. Displacement of bemo from the central corridor also brought cheap, fixed-route public transport to fringe areas in the east and west (Dick 1981).

The rest of the burden of public transport devolved upon the becak, which were ubiquitous and convenient but hardly a cheap means of commuting. After Independence the unlimited supply of drivers, usually rural emigrants, who were willing to work hard for modest earnings, had enabled the becak to more than hold their own despite the gradual return of motorized transport. By mid-1952 some 13,000 becak were listed with the police but about 40,000 were estimated to be in operation (*SP*, 3/9/52). A reregistration in 1967 counted 22,000 vehicles but there were an estimated 70,000 drivers (*SP*, 3/2/68), suggesting perhaps 40–50,000 vehicles. As late as 1976 a rough estimate was that becak carried over half of daily urban public transport passengers (Fouracre and Maunder 1978, 14–15). In the 1980s, however, becak bore the brunt of transport reform. They were seen as primitive, exploitative, and, above all, as the main cause of traffic congestion (Dick 1981). The Municipality banned their manufacture, denied access to main thoroughfares, and introduced motorized vehicles as replacements. The number of licensed becak was held constant at around 40,000 until 1990. By then the trend toward motorized transport was irresistible. Growth in middle-class demand was met by the licensing of several thousand taxis.

Rapid growth in private vehicle ownership meant that public transport was much less a constraint on land use than in the 1960s. At the beginning of 1940 in the whole residency of Surabaya there had been less than five thousand motor vehicles and sixteen hundred motorcycles, over half of which would have been in the city of Surabaya and most in the ownership of Europeans (*IV,* 1940, 370). After Independence, currency depreciation caused private automobiles to become very expensive and even a motorcycle was a luxury. The popular private vehicle was the bicycle. During the 1970s rising incomes and falling real prices allowed many more households to afford a motorcycle. Traffic noise became the buzz and roar of Honda and Yamaha engines. By 1982 not quite half of all trips were made by motorized transport (including motorcycles and public transport), a third by walking, and the remainder by bicycle or becak (MPW 1982, 15). Automobile numbers have been doubling every decade, but by 1997 the total of 168,600 passenger sedans, jeeps, and wagons was only a quarter of the 670,00 motorcycles (KMS, *SDA,* 1998).

The traffic explosion has imposed heavy demands on poor roads. Government saw its task unambiguously as maintaining traffic flow for the growing number of motor vehicles. One-way traffic was introduced, slow-moving vehicles like becak banned from main thoroughfares, and the narrow streets of the lower town widened. Carparks became an essential component of any new shopping or entertainment complex. The next step was to begin construction of the system of ring roads envisaged in the master plan to keep through traffic out of the inner city. The first section of toll road was opened in March 1986, followed by the extension to Tanjung Perak and to Gresik in the following year. The crisis of the late 1990s aborted the project of a high-level bridge to the island of Madura and halted work on the connecting eastern inner and outer ring roads but a raised expressway through the center of the city continues to be mooted.

Heavy investment in the road system has generated a very unequal distribution of benefits. Those rich and influential enough to obtain control of their own motor vehicle, which is to say the upper middle class, have benefited disproportionately. Except in the case of the toll road, use of road space is free, even if there are charges for parking. Middle-class breadwinners can now live in satellite towns and commute what used to be prohibitively long distances to the central business district, port, or industrial estate. Those who could not afford cars or motorcycles have probably become worse off because road investments have actually restricted the mobility of cyclists and pedestrians. Cyclists suffered the same traffic restrictions as becak and were more vulnerable to being struck by speeding vehicles. This has particularly affected students. Pedestrians have fared even worse. Road widenings usually involved loss of footpaths and footways and greater danger in crossing, except in those few places where overhead bridges are provided. Nowhere is this seen more clearly than at Wonokromo, a densely settled district that has been sliced in half by the four-lane north-south highway and its high fences. Roundabouts and even traffic lights are not designed for pedestrian traffic. And of course the process of cutting down shade trees that began in the interwar years has continued apace. Whereas in 1900 Surabaya was very much a pedestrian city, nowadays no one by choice walks more than a short distance from a carpark, if not set down at an entrance by the driver. It is just too hot, too polluted, too dangerous—and socially demeaning. The only safe and comfortable places for pedestrians are interior commercial spaces, such as shopping malls.

Real Estate

During the 1960s almost no private capital was invested in land development. From a theoretical viewpoint, this is surprising. In times of rapid inflation, land and housing is usually a good hedge, so that the hyperinflation of the mid-1960s could have been expected to have touched off a speculative boom in urban land and property. However, there were very practical reasons why this did not occur—some economic, some political. First, although there was an excess demand for housing, most of it was for very simple kampung housing, which was not attractive to the corporate sector. Second, the excess demand for modern bungalow housing was mainly from the public sector, and here private investment was discouraged by rent controls. Third, in the small private sector there was no financial intermediation to mobilize savings for home mortgages. Private housing was therefore financed almost entirely by companies for direct lease to their own employees, and even this became less common in the 1960s. Fourth, corporations that were making large profits in the 1960s were doing so mainly by manipulation of foreign exchange and parking their profits offshore. The combination of hostility to private capital and discrimination against Chinese business meant that there was almost no incentive for investment in illiquid domestic assets. Finally, speculative investment in land was made extremely difficult by the land reform of 1960 and the aggressive campaign of the Communist Party against large landholders, including the owners of the old private estates. Given the further complications of fragmented and uncertain legal title and the strong political support for squatters, any attempt to consolidate landholdings would have drawn the speculator into immediate conflict.

In the early 1970s, as the urban economy recovered, real estate projects began to proliferate, especially in the eastern and southern sectors of the city. Because land ownership was so fragmented, with complicated legal procedures for consolidating land with vacant possession, there was nevertheless a lag of some years between the initial commitment of funds and the actual release of land. One of the first projects was PT Wisma Surya at Jemur Sari (see chap. 4). In the mid-1970s there followed several modest private housing complexes on the urban fringe. State instrumentalities such as banks and large private-sector firms also bought land to build housing complexes for their staff, with locations off the main highway south of Wonokromo being most popular. In 1975, PT Sinar Galaxy began to buy up a three-hundred-hectare site to the east of the Airlangga University for the luxury Darmahusada Indah estate (Sinar Galaxy, interview, 6/11/87) (fig. 6.8). The biggest venture, probably too ambitious for the time, was the 730-hectare Darmo Grande estate on the barren, dry slopes to the west of the city. Because it was such marginal agricultural land and only lightly settled, this huge area was acquired cheaply and able to be consolidated fairly quickly. Launched in 1974 as Surabaya's first satellite town, it had a core of department stores, cinemas, and recreational facilities such as tennis courts and swimming pool, around which were laid out housing clusters with guard posts and controlled entry. Here the well-to-do and specifically the Chinese and expatriates could enjoy their wealth without fear of the urban mob. The concept was essentially that of Jakarta's elite suburb, Kebayoran Baru, which had been laid out in the late-1940s, with modern features. Yet despite the absence of direct competition, the

Figure 6.8. Modern luxury homes, Darmahusada Indah. Photo by author.

project sold badly. People were reluctant to become pioneers. The estate seemed isolated, road access was poor, the landscape looked harsh, and dry-season cracking made it difficult to build on. The developers had great difficulty persuading conservative Surabayans that the satellite town was a prestige location. Among wealthy Chinese businessmen, there may also have been a reluctance to display wealth in luxury housing. For several years the estate languished, while the syndicate split into three rival firms (Darmo Grande, Darmo Satelite Town, and Darmo Permai).

During the 1970s real estate development in Surabaya lagged well behind Jakarta. Because the modern sector was much smaller and there was much less foreign investment, the middle class was slower to emerge and the expatriate community was very small indeed. What found favor at this time were more modest but better-located housing projects in the former rice fields to the East and South of the built-up area. This shift was encouraged by the 1978 master plan, which earmarked most of the land between the city and the eastern shoreline for housing and education and proposed a set of inner and outer ring roads to facilitate this. Although these ring roads are still incomplete, existing roads were extended and widened for better access. The typical pattern of real estate development was for an area equivalent to a few suburban streets to be cleared and filled and lots advertised for sale, usually with names combining the location with words like *indah* (beautiful) or *permai* (pretty). Since the land was flat and featureless, this real estate parlance described not what was but what would become, beautiful streets of freshly painted, luxury dream homes. In splendid isolation there arose fortresslike dwellings, aggressive two-story dwellings shut off on three sides by high, gray-concrete walls and across the front by a high fence. As these lots gradually consolidated into an occupied street, an adjacent area would be reclaimed for the next stage. Such piecemeal projects relied on minimum commitment of capital and high turnover. Unlike the massive Darmo Grande development, they included no infrastructure beyond essential roads and utilities. There were no shopping centers, no entertainment complexes, no sporting facilities. For such needs people got into their cars and drove back to the city.

By the early 1980s the eastern side of Surabaya had therefore assumed a very uneven appearance. Residual plots of rice field and old rural kampungs beneath their dark green canopy of fruit trees were jumbled up with enclaves of luxury housing, new construction and tracts of grassy, partially reclaimed land alongside densely settled urban kampungs, rubbish dumps, and herds of goats, amid stagnant ponds that bred mosquitoes. Shady rural lanes along canals were crossed by dual carriageways leading into dead ends. Muddy access roads led into modern housing behind crowded kampungs. Such chaos might have been the despair of a town planner but it was typically Surabayan. Society had not yet stratified, as it would do in the satellite towns of the 1990s.

A perspective on the rapid development of the city's new outer ring can be gained from land use data for 1992 (though probably applying to the late 1980s) (table 6.2). Except for Wonocolo, where there was ribbon development along the highway, in the early 1970s these five outer kecamatan were still mainly rural with little more than village housing. Yet by the late 1980s they reportedly contained two-thirds of the city's area of permanent housing. In other words, the area of permanent housing increased threefold within about twenty years and virtually the entire increase was by way of spillover into the new kecamatan. However, it was not evenly distributed. As explained above, permanent housing was biased toward the former rice fields in the east (Sukolilo, Rungkut, and Wonocolo) with a pocket in Tandes around the Darmo satellite town. Kampung housing also spilled over into the fringe area of the new kecamatan, incorporating existing villages and establishing new settlements, some spontaneously, some by government action. In this case there was an opposite bias. Kampung housing was more concentrated in the cheap dryland zone, with an axis running northwest to southeast, from the industrial estate in Tandes via Karang Pilang along the Surabaya River to the industrial estate in Rungkut.

In the mid-1980s, as the economy recovered from the end of the oil boom, the real estate market began to pick up. On the supply side, the opening of the toll road overcame the bottleneck in access to the new housing estates on the western side of the city. The first section—from Waru, on the southern boundary of the city, to Gempol, in the direction of Malang and Pasuruan—was opened in March 1986, followed by the section from Waru to Tanjung Perak in 1987. The latter section, the first stage of the ring road proposed in the master plan, gave direct access to the Darmo Grande-Permai-Satelite development, which at last became highly desirable. This was reinforced by the opening of new high-rise hotels. On the demand side, there began to be less inhibition about indulging in luxury consumption. If in the 1970s wealthy Surabayans were still shy of public attention, by the late-1980s there were signs of open competition in luxury housing, cars, dress, and dining. People certainly had more money to spend but there was also a change of attitude, perhaps influenced by Jakarta. As more Jakarta firms began to invest in Surabaya, local businessmen did not wish to be regarded as poor provincials.

By 1990 the real estate market was entering a speculative phase. This was apparent in the proliferation of very-large-scale projects and intensifying competition for control of land. Except for Darmo Grande, housing projects had been dormitory suburbs of no more than a few hundred hectares. Now emerged competing new-town developments of more than a thousand hectares, as well as many smaller projects. The Real Estate Institute of East Java identified eight big groups of investors from Jakarta that controlled 6,300 hectares in East and West Surabaya: the Ciputra Group (2,000 hectares), Dharmala Group (1,600 hectares), Nusantara Group (1,000 hectares), and Pakuwon Group (1,100 hectares) (*SP,* 11/5/90). Several months later the mayor threatened to withdraw approval from investors who sold land without approval to earn speculative profits (*SP,* 14/8/90). However, until the 1993 deregulation package (Pakto) the vital development approvals (*izin lokasi*), which authorized investors to buy out existing landholders and consolidate tracts of land for urban development, were issued by the central government's Department of Internal Affairs on advice of the provincial governor. Jakarta-based investors could therefore make the most of their political connections to override local interests. In 1995 the Real Estate Institute complained of an oligopoly of real estate in East Java, especially in Surabaya, while a well-informed academic, Dr. Suroso Imam Zadjuli, claimed that 40 percent of Surabaya's land was controlled by ten "conglomerates" (*SP*, 27/3/95, 21/11/95). Companies that obtained development approvals were often syndicates, which through common principals were tied into larger groups. In this way very large tracts of land could be broken down into separate blocks of no more than two hundred hectares, spreading risk and deflecting public attention. Thus, in early 1995 eighteen new developers registered with the East Java Real Estate Institute in their own right from within the Ciputra Group and another ten from the Dharmala Group (*SP*, 12/1/95). Consolidation of these urban housing estates was funded by generous bank credit, including offshore borrowings, and the floating of equity on the stock exchange. For example, to finance its huge Citra Rayacomplex, the Ciputra Group was able to borrow $21 million at a prime rate of 7 percent through syndicates in Hong Kong and Singapore (*SP*, 23/3/95). With the nominal price of developed residential land rising fivefold and at a fairly steady rate between 1985 and 1994 (*PI*, 7/94, 35), and in a climate of abundant purchasing power and sustained rapid growth, the risks of such speculation did not became apparent until the currency and financial crisis of 1997–98.

Once the few remaining tracts of land within the municipality had been taken up, developers and speculators began vying for control of land in the adjacent kabupaten of Gresik and Sidoarjo—expansion northward onto Madura was impeded by the cross-harbor ferry. Especially for low-to-medium-cost housing, land prices in Surabaya were now so high as to be uneconomic. Leading developers sought to take advantage of low-interest finance to accumulate land banks while land could still be acquired at village prices. At the same time, opportunistic syndicates looked for any strategic tracts that would be likely to appreciate in value. Activity was most frenetic in Gresik, where most of the land across the border from the municipality was low, unirrigated hills of little agricultural value. Between April 1994 and May 1995 the district government issued no fewer than 184 development approvals: 100 for industry, 80 for housing projects, and 4 for warehouses and services, in all around twelve thousand hectares (*SP,* 16/9/95). However, most of these "projects" seem to have been tactical land-banking operations. As of September 1995, only six of the 184 projects had shown substantial progress, causing the district Lands Office (Badan Pertanahan Nasional) to impose a temporary freeze on development approvals (*SP,* 16/9, 3/10/95).

In the rich delta of Sidoarjo, where agricultural land was irrigated and highly productive, the pressure from developers was more piecemeal. Over the ten years from December 1984 to December 1994, development approvals were issued on twenty-eight hundred hectares for housing and three thousand hectares for industry (*SP,* 13/7/95). At a 70 percent rate of implementation for housing projects and nearly full implementation for industrial ones, this represented a transfer of about 15 percent of the district's agricultural land, primarily in a band along the main north-south highway and adjacent to the airport (*SP,* 9/6/95). These figures excluded several more speculative megaprojects that emerged in the mid-1990s as part of the chess game for control of the supply of developmental land. In August 1993 a controversial development approval was granted for reclamation of two thousand hectares of coastal mangroves to become Sidoarjo Kota Marina (Sidoarjo Marina City); two years later, when no investment had been forthcoming, the approval was scaled back to fourteen hundred hectares and allocated to another syndicate (*SP,* 22/8/95, *PI,* 6/94, 35). No physical development took place on this or various other projects before the currency crisis.

The escalating development pressures on Surabaya, Gresik, and Sidoarjo showed up the absence of any planning framework. In

1983 a Japan International Cooperation Agency study had identified an extended Surabaya metropolitan area known as Gerbang Kertosusila, a rather clumsy acronym composed of Surabaya and the surrounding kabupaten of Gresik (Gersik), Bangkalan, Mojokerto, Sidoarjo, and Lamongan (MPW 1982). However, although this encompassed most of the immediate hinterland of Surabaya, the inclusion of Bangkalan (Madura), Lamongan, and Mojokerto defined a region rather than a contiguous city and merely complicated planning and administration. Whereas Greater Jakarta (Jabotabek) has become an effective planning instrument, Gerbang Kertosusila languished as just a concept. Despite the decentralization of development approvals in 1993 and the accelerating spillover of the city from the municipality into Gresik and Sidoarjo, no steps were taken either to extend the municipal boundaries or to establish a coordinating framework. Cooperation did occur, but rivalry was the normal situation.

In Surabaya the main focus of large-scale real estate activity was the once spurned dry lands to the west of the city. This poor rural area, which had become part of the municipality as late as 1965, had little agricultural potential and lacked access roads, so that land was cheap and still in the hands of local villagers. The master plan had reserved urban corridors but until the opening of the toll road in 1987, large developers had shown little interest. The one notable exception was the Darmo Grande project of the mid-1970s, long regarded as misplaced and overambitious, but now seen to be visionary in predicting the direction in which the market would develop. By the beginning of 1995 a wide corridor of almost three thousand hectares from the toll road to the border of the municipality had been carved up in development approvals among thirteen investors (*SP,* 17/1/95). No such massive alienation of land had occurred since Daendels and Raffles had sold off the rural estates in the early nineteenth century. However, less than half of these new urban estates were actually under development, the balance constituting a land bank for future expansion. Construction was dominated by three large developers—the Jakarta-based Ciputra group and the local Dharmala and Pakuwon Jati groups—all of which began marketing in 1995 (table 6.3).

By contrast, in the east, which was mainly rice fields and readily accessible, widespread and fragmented development since the 1970s had left few tracts that could be consolidated into a large-scale projects. One exception was the coast. The master plan had classified the saltponds (tambak) and mangroves along the coast as a conservation zone to protect the fishing and prawn industry. Nevertheless, in 1989–90 the Dharmala, Pakuwon Jati, and Sac Nusantara groups managed to obtain development approvals on 3,190 hectares of this cheap land, which was located close to the city's proposed outer ring road and the campus of the Surabaya Institute of Technology (*SP,* 11/5/90). Amid continuing public controversy, in August 1995 the governor of East Java reallocated the development approvals. Citing lack of progress, he stripped Dharmala and Sac Nusantara of all but two hundred hectares in favor of seven other developers, with token concessions to environmental protection (*SP,* 30–31/8/97). By mid-1997 only the Pakuwon Group's five-hundred-hectare Laguna Indah estate, the most northerly and accessible area, was under construction. Glossy brochures foreshadowed a mega-mall, country club, international hospital, town houses and condominiums, and housing clusters such as Villa Venice, Villa Royal, Villa Riviera, Villa Westwood, Taman Mutiara (Pearl Garden), and Taman Nilam (Sapphire Garden) (fig. 6.9). By mid-1997

TABLE 6.3
Main real estate projects, Surabaya municipality, 1997

Group	Projects	Hectares	Begun
Ciputra	Citra Rayan West	2,000 [a]	1992
Pakuwon Jati	Laguna Indah (East)	500	ca.1994
	Pakuwon Indah (West)	450	1994
Dharmala	Graha Family Estate (West)	280	1993
	Bukit Darmo Golf (West)	160	1993

Source: Various.
[a]Stage I development: 1,000 hectares.

Figure 6.9. Gated community under construction, Laguna Indah, 1997. Photo by author.

some housing clusters were under construction but few facilities were yet in evidence. Surabayans had never acquired the habit of seaside living and there was much skepticism as to whether the project would be viable.

The large new estates offer mostly low-density, luxury housing to middle- and high-income households and were designed to be self-contained (figs. 6.10, 6.11). Dharmala Group's Graha Famili (originally Grande Family) Estate (280 hectares), for example, advertised in 1995 "the ultimate in comfortable family lifestyle," encompassing 1,830 houses, 14 condominium towers (1,120 units), a shopping mall, nine-hole golf course, country club, private hospital, international school, and commercial and office zones. The much larger thousand-hectare Citra Raya estate (launched as CitraLand City) consists of 635 hectares of mainly themed cluster housing, 90 hectares of commercial space, and 275 hectares of recreational space, including two eighteen-hole golf courses and country club (*PI,* 3/94, 21; brochures). It also features twenty-four-hour security, public gardens, and both a local and an international school, to which will

Figure 6.10. New apartment blocks, golf course (on left), Graha Famili, 1997. Photo by author.

Figure 6.11. New-town gated street, Pakuwon Indah, 1997. Photo by author.

be added a large shopping mall and theme park. The logic of such integration is twofold. First, the amenities establish prestige and attract homebuyers. Other facilities, such as the private hospital and international school, are necessary to attract expatriates. Second, the mall, commercial, and office zones are a means for the developer to capture and recycle as much as possible of the purchasing power of those who live in the estate.

The market in Surabaya for such luxury housing could be equated with the upper stratum of the middle class. Prime beneficiaries of the economic development of the New Order, these families earned high incomes in the booming private sector and are predominantly of Chinese extraction. Many of them were of the upwardly mobile nouveau riche, as opposed to established families in the older garden suburbs such as Darmo. They could buy into existing suburbs and renovate an old colonial bungalow but the market was thin and prices were high. Alternatively, they could buy a new site and build a modern dream home and indulge their own fantasies of being modern. What else is money for? Owning at least one private automobile, they faced no transport constraint in locating beyond the periphery. They could live among their own group in a safe and secure environment well away from the pressures and threats of the crowded kampungs and city streets. In the new estates there were no kampungs, no squatters, no street sellers, and no becak. Security kept out such intruders. The Graha Famili Estate, as a "garden city," emphasized perimeter security so that the houses themselves could, as in older parts of the city, have just low fences and hedges. In only the second year after its opening the estate already employed forty security personnel working in two shifts around the clock.

Among the oligopoly of large developers, there has been intense competition in development of these estates. The entrepreneurial skill lies in market positioning, timing, and the ability to attract early buyers and maintain the momentum of sales. Master plans are therefore promotional to the point of being fanciful. For example, apartment towers are still a new concept in Surabaya. The

Dharmala Group foreshadowed fourteen or fifteen such towers on the Graha Famili Estate, but initially only four were built to test the market. However, facilities such as the golf course (designed by Arnold Palmer) and the clubhouse were hurried to completion in the first phase of the project. Citra Raya likewise made a feature of its twin golf courses and country club, opened mid-1997, as a means of enticing members and visitors to its more far-flung estate. Indeed, the sale of club memberships is an important element of cash flow in the early phase of development. By contrast, developers held back from the expensive investment in shopping malls, doing no more by mid-1997 than lay foundations as a gesture of intent. Twelve malls had been projected to open between 1997 and 1999 (SP, 7/2/97), but few will be brought to completion.

On the eve of the Asian crisis of late 1997, the west of Surabaya in particular appeared as a vast construction site. In the midst of typical rural villages, still served only by dirt roads and relying for drinking water on daily tank trucks, were vast cleared expanses where heavy earth-moving and road-making equipment was laying drains, paving wide access roads, many of which still led nowhere, and tracing out the street pattern for new garden suburbs. In parts, rows of shops and clusters of housing had already solidified, albeit rarely occupied except for furnished display homes with exotic names (figs. 6.9, 6.10, 6.11). A few high-rise apartment towers added to the impression of development, while golf courses, country clubs, water treatment plants, and monumental gateways seemed to confirm that the city of the future was taking shape here, far from the madding crowd and with all the modern conveniences. Unquestionably, this was the new urban frontier. The force of the encroachment was seemingly irresistible. Yet were not the gardeners now decorating the landscaped terrain with lawns and beds of ornamental flowers, the same farmers who until recently had tended fields of rice and maize, groves of coconut palms, fruit trees, and bamboo? By what process had those villages been erased? As in the 1910s, the developers first had had to establish title to the land and to remove the existing inhabitants.

Land Rights

The master plan of 1978 allowed the Municipality to "regularize" the haphazard pattern of land use that had emerged over the previous three or four decades. This applied particularly to squatters on public land. Too many families and enterprises were affected for a mass eviction. The solution was to differentiate according to the degree of conflict with the master plan. Category Red meant that occupation contravened the master plan—for example, in areas reserved for open space or industry—and would have to be vacated without financial compensation but in exchange for land on the edge of the city. Yellow denoted land use that could be brought into compliance with the master plan. Green meant that occupation was in accordance with the master plan and would be legitimized by with certificates of ownership (E. Indrayana, interview, 14/11/87).

The most difficult problem was the clearance of squatters who lined the banks of the Kali Mas from Wonokromo to below Jembatan Merah. In 1975 it was estimated that around twenty thousand families, or a hundred thousand people, illegally occupied these riverbanks (*Kompas,* 27/3/76). Their occupation worsened the flood problem by weakening the banks and increasing the amount of rubbish deposited in the river. In 1973 the Municipality withdrew the temporary permits of occupancy issued in the 1960s by the Department of Public Works, declared riverbank occupation to be illegal, and advised that occupants would have to move. About a hundred hectares of land were made available at Karang Pilang to house those who would be displaced. Removal was to proceed in stages from Wonokromo northward from the beginning of 1975 as part of the Lower Brantas Project (chap. 4). Those witnessed by neighborhood heads as having occupied land before 1976 were to be paid compensation. In fact the process took longer than intended, with only two-thirds of riverbank occupants having been removed by the target date of July 1979 (*SP,* 24/3/79). For anyone familiar with the city before the mid-1970s, the change in its appearance was remarkable. The river was restored to full view, but roads along the river such as Genteng Kali, formerly a scene of jostling humanity, now seemed strangely quiet.

As the Lower Brantas Project neared completion, work began on a similar project under World Bank funding to "normalize" the parallel Kali Pegirian (chap. 4). In the light of the long delays in removing illegal occupants along the banks of the Kali Mas, the decision was taken to clear all the land at once. About six months before the official commencement of the project, kampung heads called meetings in neighborhoods along the river to explain the project and the terms of compensation. This time compensation was paid only to those who could produce a certificate of land ownership (*hak pemilikan tanah*) and had a building permit for any structure encroaching on the riverbank. Less than a hundred of the 1,336 permanent buildings met those criteria. Occupants of squatter huts received no financial compensation but were allocated land with title at Tandes on which to rebuild (*SP,* 30/4/83).

Consolidation of the large tracts needed for private real estate development was if anything more difficult than in the late-colonial period. The remaining private estates had fragmented after Independence, the last blow being the Land Reform Law of 1960, which recognized as owners those who had been living on the land, either as cultivators or householders. Developers therefore had to deal with many owners of tiny plots. For example, the Dharmala group complained that it took over three years, from 1990 to 1993, to release sufficient land to commence work on the 280-hectare Graha Famili Estate (*JP,* 11/7/97). The procedure, however, was essentially the same as that used by developers (bouwmaatschappij) and the Municipality in the late 1910s, namely payment of a lump sum to secure both ownership of the land and all rights to its disposition and use. While this could be a tedious process, skillful developers could create a snowball effect by fairly generously buying out strategic holdings, especially those of influential parties, thereby isolating and intimidating others who had no significant bargaining power. The only effective tactic to confront such well-funded developers was a united front, but that required careful organization and risked accusations of communist agitation. Some developers arranged for officers of the police or armed forces to bring pressure to bear on kampung communities, as well as to facilitate the passage of approvals through the bureaucracy. As in the 1910s, kampung dwellers could try to obtain fair compensation but the dice were loaded against them, nor did they have the choice whether to take the money or stay. Once a developer had gained approval to develop a tract of land, it was only a matter of how much he would have to pay in compensation and how long the negotiations would take.

Some of the more successful cases of resistance were against not developers but the government. Much of the "vacant" public land occupied by squatters in the 1950s was owned by the government or its instrumentalities, such as the railways, the electricity corporation (PLN), or the oil corporation (Pertamina). Over time many of these communities acquired de facto recognition as kampungs. The small kampung of Gubeng Masjid, tucked behind the railway viaduct near Gubeng station, was a good example. The squatters who had occupied this land in the 1950s had been tolerated by the State Railways on the understanding that the land remained under railway ownership and could eventually be resumed. As the original squatters sold out to newcomers, houses were rebuilt in brick and the kampung lost its temporary aspect and came to be regarded as a permanent community. It might have remained undisturbed had not a street widening in another part of the city involved the demolition of some railway offices, leading to a decision to take back the land at Gubeng as the site for a replacement building. In February 1987 the 104 families living in the kampung were given sudden notice to vacate by the end of October. Compensation was assessed according to municipal criteria from Rp 15,000 per square meter for a temporary dwelling to Rp 20,500 for a permanent one—to avoid any suggestion that kampung dwellers had acquired rights over the land, these payments were officially described as grants (*sumbangan*). At the beginning of September, when no family had yet accepted compensation or vacated the land, the State Railways appealed to the mayor, who on 2 October instructed officials to enforce the eviction by the due date. This deadline was postponed several times while kampung dwellers challenged the validity of the eviction. Gradually they accepted the inevitability of their removal, but the reality was that compensation was inadequate and few had anywhere else to go, except to move in with other poorly housed relatives. After the extended deadline of 23 November had passed with only two-fifths of the families taking compensation, the Municipality announced that land would be made available elsewhere to the displaced inhabitants. After inspecting several tracts, kampung representatives chose about two hectares of vacant land in Lakarsantri, which, although distant, at a cost of only Rp 5,000 per square meter would absorb only a third of the minimum compensation payment. Inhabitants carefully dismantled their houses, brick by brick and beam by beam (figs. 6.12, 6.13), and the railways provided trucks to transport the materials. In the end, an acceptable compromise was achieved (*JP/SP,* 10–12/87). In 1995 a very similar drama, affecting about two thousand people, was acted out over three hectares of land at the old downtown railway station.

As development pressures intensified during the 1990s, land use conflicts became a staple item in the daily press. Contrary to what might have been expected, private real estate projects were not often cited. Their expected profitability allowed firms to pay enough compensation to avoid disputes likely to cause delay. Large projects also gave scope for land swaps and community resettlement. If there were difficulties, government could act as arbiter. Most protracted disputes involved public land or public projects, or both. In the municipal budget for 1995–96, which involved a heavy public works program under the World Bank financed Surabaya Urban Development Project (SUDP), thirty-one out of thirty-six projects faced unresolved land tenure problems, about half involving road widenings (*SP,* 30/9/95). For example, the extension of Jalan Darmahusada as part of the inner ring road affected around

Figure 6.12. Kampung Gubeng Masjid, before dismantling. Photo by author.

Figure 6.13. Kampung Gubeng Masjid being "voluntarily" dismantled. Photo by author.

fifteen hundred families (*SP,* 19/9/95). Here the tendency was to invoke long-standing plans and the public interest to legitimize bad process and resort to force if necessary. The will of government should not be challenged.

The common element in all these land use conflicts was a land market in which purchasing power and information were very unevenly distributed. Kampung dwellers knew the exchange value of their small parcels but not what they were worth when consolidated into large blocks for redevelopment. It was therefore very easy for a developer to pay the going kampung price and keep the entire betterment value. After 1975 land claims were in principle to be regulated by a decree from the Minister for Internal Affairs that gave local government the power to determine the appropriate level of compensation. In 1993 a presidential decree (Keputusan Presiden [Keppres] 55/1993) transferred authority to the Minister for Lands and specified much clearer categories of landholding. There was now an explicit requirement for direct negotiation and, in the event of agreement not being reached, a mechanism for court arbitration. As the minimum basis for compensation, local government was bound to observe the most recent property valuation for the Land and Buildings Tax (Pajak Bumi dan Bangunan) (*SP,* 3/1/95). Nevertheless, the Municipality often still resorted to coercion before it initiated proper negotiations, especially with respect to its own projects. As part of the official apparatus, kampung heads were discouraged from taking the side of the people and could easily be bought off. Those who championed the rights of kampung dwellers would be branded as troublemakers, with the threat of police or army intervention if there was any disturbance. Kampung dwellers were thereby forced to bear external costs of the project through loss of home and often employment, while developers earned large profits. In the case of public projects, officials sought to minimize budgetary outlays, while skimming off unofficial payments to themselves. Without political support, it was impossible for kampung dwellers to recover more than a small fraction of the true value of their land. Instead, they ended up subsidizing the projects that displaced them.

Contributing to this powerlessness was the vagueness of land title. Postcolonial Indonesia inherited the conflict between a formal view that land belongs to whoever can establish written legal title and a popular view, rooted in custom (*adat*), that land belongs to the person who permanently occupies and tends it. As explained above, around 1910 the Dutch legal system had recognized that rights of ownership did not necessarily override rights of occupancy, obliging estate owners to buy out the rights of the inhabitants before they could legally be required to move. The approach of the State Railways at Gubeng Masjid that a grant was paid as an act of generosity was therefore a retrograde step—albeit an improvement on the past practice of bundling people into trucks at gunpoint!—because it denied that kampung dwellers had any rights at all. Since many kampung dwellers, and often entire communities, had gained occupancy in more disordered times on the basis of verbal agreements with now deceased landholders or former government officials, their formal title was difficult to establish but the moral and customary claim remained and was regarded by kampung dwellers as a right. As a major landholder and developer in its own right, the Municipality had a vested interest in not pressing ahead with regularization of land titles. Senior officials were meanwhile colluding with developers in selling off common lands set aside for the remuneration of kampung officials, a set of scandals that broke after collapse of the New Order.

Nevertheless, in Surabaya people were not cleared off their land as ruthlessly as in Jakarta. Negotiation was still preferred to arson and forced eviction, and those cases that did occur attracted unfavorable publicity. In a few cases, aggrieved communities sought redress from the local assembly (DPRD). The usual compromise was prompt resettlement, which achieved the government's or developer's objective but at a higher rate of compensation. Though in a very weak bargaining position, kampung dwellers therefore enjoyed some institutional protection. Compared with the 1910s, however, they suffered from corruption of the legal system and the absence of fair legal remedy. After 1998, when there was opportunity for redress of grievances (chap. 2), the main channel was through the DPRD rather than through the courts.

Changing Urban Form

The real estate boom since the 1970s has transformed the shape of Surabaya. In the early decades of the twentieth century the movement northward to the new port of Tanjung Perak and southward through Simpang to the new garden suburb of Darmo had followed the old axis along the Kali Mas. Some widening out to Gubeng and Sawahan along the new east-west axis did no more than maintain the proportions of this much longer city. After Independence the city continued to elongate as ribbon development extended beyond Wonokromo toward what would in 1965 become the new municipal boundary at Waru. Since the 1970s, however, the city has also burst its seams, expanding almost to the sea in the east and well into the dry lands in the west. Recent maps show a city that is becoming almost square (map 6.7). From the air a night view of the lights of Surabaya reveals no discernible shape. If all the western land taken up by developers is eventually settled, Surabaya will be wider than it is long.

These trends in the overall shape of the city have also affected its structure. The center of gravity has now moved southward to Tunjungan/Simpang. In the late-colonial period Surabaya had been schizophrenic. The central business district had remained in the old lower town around Jembatan Merah, within the line of what had been the fortifications. The retail and entertainment center, however, had shifted southward, first into Pasar Besar and then in the 1920s, drawn by the new garden suburbs, into the upper town of Tunjungan and Simpang. This pattern lasted into the 1970s amid decay at both centers. Jembatan Merah's once fine office buildings lost their paint and their façades began to crumble, the narrow streets strewn with rubbish and clogged with traffic, street sellers, and beggars. Tunjungan lost its ultramodern chic. Boutiques, bookshops, and fashionable restaurants gave way to tawdry electronic goods and furniture stores; the roadway was widened into multiple lanes of speeding, one-way traffic, forcing pedestrians to jostle with hawkers along makeshift footpaths.

Tunjungan recovered faster than Jembatan Merah. In the 1980s, as banks in particular began to build high-rise offices, the old sites at Jembatan Merah were found to be too small, besides which the area had become a bottleneck for vehicle access and parking. The main square was a crowded bus terminal, with a continual throng of people and no security. It was hardly a prestige location. The new office buildings were erected mainly along Tunjungan/Kaliasin (officially, Basuki Rahmat) and the crossroad Jalan Pemuda. While Jembatan Merah has retained some residual functions, Simpang-Tunjungan-Kaliasin can now be identified as the new central business district.

The southern end of Tunjungan extending into Kaliasin has regained its status as the city's shopping and entertainment center and as the favored location for new international hotels. There has also been investment in new shopping complexes. In December 1986, Surabaya's first enclosed, multistory shopping mall opened just opposite the Simpang intersection. Tunjungan's former renown had been as a street of department stores. Aptly named Tunjungan Plaza, the new mall exemplified the reinvention and privatization of the conventional shopping street as a vertical building. Now the private mall became the street, encompassing not only its own department store (Matahari) but also boutiques, cafes and restaurants, cinemas, video games, and so on, all contained in air-conditioned comfort with an adjacent carpark. For Surabaya it was modern, stylish, and quickly became an outstanding success. Especially on evenings and weekends, Tunjungan Plaza was as crowded as Tunjungan in its heyday. For ordinary people, the mall was cheap entertainment, a way to vicariously be part of the modern world. While most boutiques have more sales people than customers, retailers of cheap goods—like the Matahari department store, food and drink stalls, and video games parlor—did good business. Like the street itself, Tunjungan Plaza thereby became democratized. It soon annexed an adjacent project, which became Tunjungan II, and an even larger Tunjungan III opened at the end of 1995, complete with ground-floor ice-skating rink, food court, theatre district, amusement park, and trade hall. Completing the entire block of "Tunjungan City" are the Sheraton international hotel, two condominium towers, and two office towers.

The success of Tunjungan Plaza stimulated investment in other malls. In June 1988, President Soeharto himself opened Surabaya Plaza on the site of the old military hospital and in March 1995 a firm associated with his daughter Tutut opened Jembatan Merah Plaza on the site of the old arsenal. There was also a trend to build more exclusive malls in off-center, new-town locations. In January 1996 the local developer Sinar Galaxy opened the luxury Galaxy Mall, designed by American architects, in the midst of its elite Darmahusada Indah housing estate in the east of the city. Difficult to reach by public transport, its location automatically selected a high-income, car-owning clientele with a high spending propensity, which in turn attracted prestige international retailers. Three similar malls were projected at the core of new-town projects to the west of the city but construction halted after the 1997 currency crisis and is unlikely to proceed. Cheaper conventional shops and stalls then regained custom, reversing some of the more extreme social stratification apparent during the boom.

Conclusion

Over the past twenty years the built environment has changed so dramatically that Surabaya seems almost to have become another city. The obvious comparison is between the modern, bustling, functional city and the decaying, overcrowded Third World city of the 1960s. This fits easily with the familiar perspective of rapid economic development under the New Order. Another comparison, still within living memory, is with the stylish, whitewashed, well-ordered colonial city of 1941, no less modern, bustling, and functional in its own time. This perspective is more problematic because it not only suggests something in common between the late-colonial and the late New Order city but also requires explanation of why the city should have gone into eclipse between the 1930s and 1970s. It is also possible to take a very long-term perspective that views the evolution of the city over some two hundred years. This reveals an emerging dualism between an expanding formal sector and a more amorphous informal sector, which roughly equates with the kampung sector. Until the 1950s, the formal sector of business and government was associated with Dutch colonialism; under the New Order the underlying linkage can be seen as with the international capitalist economy. This chapter concludes with some reflections on the similarities and differences between late-colonial and late New Order Surabaya, leading into a history of Surabaya's relationship with the international economy (chap. 7).

Some of the similarities between the late-colonial and New Order city that appear to arise from government (chap. 4) can be traced back to the social structure within which it functions. Frederick (1989) has argued persuasively that the colonial municipality did very little to improve the welfare of the indigenous population. The facade of the well-ordered colonial city, which hid the crowded and often squalid kampungs, was the visual embodiment of the dualism of society and economy in colonial times. Policy attacked not the underlying social problems but the few unavoidable points of intersection with European society. First, the European population could not entirely be insulated from health conditions in the kampungs. Fear of disease was one of the most powerful motives for public health measures. Second, the workforce of the "modern" sector of the colonial economy was drawn from the kampungs. Some minimum spending on public health, housing, and education was needed to maintain and enhance the productivity of that workforce. Complete indifference to the kampung population was no longer possible. Yet, despite the rhetoric, what little was done tended to be to eliminate perceived threats to the minority European population rather than to improve the living standards of the mass of Indonesians. Before Independence, all this could be blamed on the fundamental inequity—and hypocrisy—of the colonial system. Once the last vestiges of colonial power had been swept away along with the entire European middle class there was no longer a foreign scapegoat for the persistence of inequality.

From the historical distance of the 1990s, the heretical question can be asked whether racial exclusivity was indeed the fundamental characteristic of the late-colonial regime. Of course it seemed to be the case, because more and more educated and upwardly mobile Indonesians kept hitting that glass ceiling. However, racial exclusivity could also be seen as defining more easily than socioeconomic status the boundaries of a privileged middle-class society in a country where most people still lived on the margin of subsistence. In other words, ethnicity helped to define the boundaries but it did not give rise to socioeconomic differentiation in the first place. This can be appreciated from two different perspectives. First, if the Dutch in the 1900s had not abandoned their noble aim of recruiting the best and the brightest of educated, young Indonesians into the colonial civil service, the governing elite could conceivably have become a Dutch-speaking meritocracy, just as a Europeanized indigenous elite emerged in the Philippines. Second, after an unusual period in the 1950s and 1960s, when a decapitated Indonesian society became fairly homogeneous in socioeconomic terms, a large and expanding middle class has reemerged—part Indonesian, part ethnic Chinese—that in many ways behaves not so differently from the former colonial elite.

By the 1990s a new social stratification had arisen that separated rich and poor as sharply as did the racial divide in colonial society. Indeed, it had reached the point where the city was beginning to disintegrate as a functional spatial unit. In the late-colonial period, suburbanization had involved the middle-class elite moving residence and recreation to garden suburbs but continuing to work in the central business district. The New Order trend went a stage further in decentralizing work as well and diminishing the importance of the central business district, an American pattern referred to as postsuburban society. As in Jakarta, most of the new-town master plans, like the shopping malls and golf courses, were a product of American designers (Dick and Rimmer 1998). That Surabaya with its dense population should be evolving toward an American pattern seems at first counterintuitive. The obvious explanation is prestige in marketing and promotion. Yet the driving force was also the same: the determination of the better-off to enjoy a comfortable, middle-class lifestyle without the intrusion of the poor, whose proximity was both a moral challenge to the ethos of conspicuous consumption and a perceived physical threat to private property. Given that the urban middle class was still disproportionately Chinese, there was also the nagging fear of the mob. Hence, as in Dutch times, kampung people were again coming to be seen as socially alien, unpredictable, uncontrollable. Glossy brochures advertising the new housing estates included reassuring pictures of uniformed security staff, conveying the subliminal message, You will be safe here.

Social stratification was facilitated by the motor vehicle and air-conditioning. The role of the automobile in causing twentieth-century urban sprawl is well recognized. Air-conditioning has been taken for granted but it has allowed Surabaya, like other prosperous cities of Southeast Asia, to turn inside out, to become a city in which people turn their back on the external environment (Dick and Rimmer 1999). Instead of improving the harsh external environment by the time-honored means of shade, water, verandahs, and gardens, developers have created artificial indoor environments. The middle class can now live in air-conditioned houses, travel in air-conditioned cars to air-conditioned offices, and enjoy recreation in air-conditioned malls. However, this artificial environment is all private space, what money can buy. The kampung dweller for the most part has to survive without air-conditioning and in public space. As the surface area of concrete, asphalt, and brick increases, so does the ambient temperature in what has always been notorious as a very hot city, especially at the end of the dry season. It is further degraded by the heat and pollution emitted by the other, air-conditioned society. Thus physical comfort is a social divide almost as sharp as skin color in the colonial period.

In late 1997, amid a worsening currency and financial crisis, the property bubble suddenly burst. The construction industry came to a halt, development companies went bankrupt, and workers were laid off. Many among the middle class no longer had the means to finance speculative investment or luxury consumption in housing. As after the previous property bubble, in the 1920s, there were again vast tracts of real estate all around Surabaya with no foreseeable prospect of finding a market. Kampung dwellers, however, were relieved of the threat of further displacement and regained opportunities for redress and restoration of their rights. Some who had been evicted without proper compensation reoccupied their land. Others sought mediation from provincial and local assemblies (DPRD). Corrupt officials were confronted with their fraudulent land deals. The outcome is as yet uncertain. After the 1920s, the property market remained slack for two decades and was then overwhelmed by political revolution. At the end of 2000 there are signs of modest economic recovery and revival of middle-class spending. The property market can be expected to remain depressed, but worsening public insecurity, including muggings and the old specter of *rampok* (looting) perpetuates the tendency toward middle-class segregation in protected new towns, especially for Sino-Indonesians. The decentralized land use pattern established during the boom is therefore unlikely to be reversed. It is too early to judge whether democratic and legal reform will better protect the rights of kampung dwellers and allow them to gain recognition as equal citizens.

Chapter 7

TRADE

As an outsider gradually discovers the complex reality of a city, from the outside looking in, previous chapters have first observed the physical aspect of Surabaya, reviewed key events in the history behind its buildings and streetscapes, introduced its people, and then looked in detail at some of the underlying structures and processes of government, economy, and land use. Such explorations have identified key pieces of the jigsaw of what is. They have also revealed a consistent pattern of change over the past century, which may be described in brief as boom-stagnation-boom-bust. The task of this final chapter is to explain this pattern. Why at the end of the nineteenth century was Surabaya the leading city of Java? Why was it overtaken and in time eclipsed by Jakarta? Why did the great bust of the early 1930s lead to a period of stagnation that lasted until the 1970s? And how has Surabaya been able to regain its economic momentum since the 1980s and to consolidate its place as Java's second industrial agglomeration and metropolitan center?

Perhaps the key puzzle is the long hiatus between the city's apparent prosperity up to 1930 and the renewal of rapid economic growth after the mid-1970s. While the slump of the 1930s is readily explained by the world depression, the reasons for the loss of commercial vitality are more complex. The political turmoil of the

Japanese occupation and the Revolution certainly disrupted the export economy, as did the seizure of Dutch-owned assets and the repatriation of Dutch citizens in 1958. The worsening inflation and overvalued exchange rates of the 1950s and 1960s also made it much harder for Surabaya and its hinterland to benefit from the boom in world trade that followed the end of World War II. Yet despite this miserable sequence of crises, the underlying problem was the failure to achieve a structural shift in the economy that would establish a basis for renewed economic growth. It was not just force of circumstance that cheated Surabaya of its prosperity. Even had there been a smooth transition to Indonesian sovereignty and had Indonesia remained an open economy, it would not have been possible to sustain the economic growth of Java by increasing the output of plantation and smallholder export crops.

The chapter begins by identifying the hinterland of Surabaya in the mid-nineteenth century and showing how it was articulated by modern means of transport between the opening of the first railways in the late-1870s and the depression of the 1930s. It then examines the hiatus in the plantation economy that can be traced back to the 1920s, when closure of the land frontier undermined the growth dynamic at the same time that world markets were tightening. The next section, based on Dick 1995, analyses foreign and interisland trade statistics to highlight the stagnation of the export base between 1930 and 1980 but also to show how the industrial development of the 1970s began to transform the composition of interisland trade and eventually, in the late 1980s, of foreign trade. This leads into consideration of the late 1980s as a new era of economic growth in which East Java at last begins to consolidate a new export base in manufacturing.

City and Hinterland

Surabaya's fluctuating fortunes cannot be explained by looking only at the city itself. We must look also at the city's changing relationship with its hinterland and the wider world. This in turn raises the issue of methodology. First, the hinterland itself is not a given. Just as the city's economy has evolved over time, so also has the extent of the hinterland, its productive base, and pattern of settlement. Second, modern modes of transport and communications have allowed a more sophisticated articulation between city and hinterland, as with Jakarta and the rest of the world.

Despite its apparent relevance, this chapter will avoid the overused category of port city, on which there is a considerable but fairly narrow literature (Broeze 1989, 1996). Nowadays, with efficient rail, road, air and telecommunications, there are not only seaports but also inland "dry ports," airports, and teleports. These multimodal possibilities can be taken into account by the terms *gateway* and *hub,* but it is not traffic per se that makes a city. All cities perform a multiplicity of functions, only some of which relate directly to trade and transport. Moreover, growth involves an accretion and diversification of functions, so that over time a progressively smaller proportion of the workforce is associated with direct port functions. Why, therefore, should port functions be elevated to primacy above government functions, industry, banking and finance, wholesaling and retailing, education, or health? Surabaya is no more obviously a port city than it is an industrial city, mall city, or education city.

Whether or not a city has a seaport, it is more helpful to envisage it as an economic system that draws in inputs and applies human energies to transform them into outputs. Conventionally this process is expressed in economic terms. The difference in value between imports and exports, which is to say the balance of trade, can also be seen as a net energy balance. If the city responds efficiently to its environment, it maintains a positive balance, which enables it to grow in size, wealth, and power. With sufficient data, the physiology of a city could be modeled in great detail. Unfortunately the data resources are extremely poor because for most purposes not cities but nations are taken as the statistical unit. Except in the case of nation-states such as Singapore, the urban economy is therefore not readily isolated as a microeconomy in its own right.

In the case of Surabaya, foreign-trade data are the only long-term series available to show the changing relationship between the city, its hinterland, and the wider world. Specified by individual port, these data cover the period 1920 to 1999. They incorporate the trade of a hinterland that corresponds as a first approximation to the province of East Java. For this region the port of Surabaya has always dominated the import trade, while its share of exports has risen from about 70 percent in the interwar years, when large tonnages of sugar were still shipped from other north-coast ports, to about 98 percent in recent years (see below). The changing volume and composition of Surabaya's foreign trade therefore tell a story about the role of city and hinterland in the world economy. Though less satisfactorily, this story can be filled out with data on domestic trade between Surabaya and the other islands of Indonesia. On the landward trade between Surabaya–East Java and the adjacent provinces of Central Java and Bali, however, the record is silent. We therefore cannot compute an overall trade balance between Surabaya–East Java and the rest of the world. At best we can assume that the landward interprovincial trade is not so large or so unbalanced as to distort the long-term trend.

Complementary data on capital flows are nonexistent at a regional level. This is frustrating because Surabaya has long been one of Java's two main financial centers. Its emergence as a capital market in the second half of the nineteenth century was closely linked with its role as the headquarters of the managing agencies for the booming plantation sector. Although no banks had their head office in Surabaya, the city's branch banks probably generated as much business as those in Jakarta. In 1925, Surabaya, like Jakarta, also gained a small stock exchange. Nevertheless, for recent years Bank Indonesia data attest to Surabaya's continuing importance as a financial center. At the beginning of 1997 the municipality plus the adjacent districts of Sidoarjo and Gresik accounted for three-quarters of East Java's bank assets, deposits, and outstanding credit (BIS 1997). This is a much higher proportion than Greater Surabaya's share of East Java's employment (43 percent) or value added (61 percent) in L and M manufacturing (BPS, *Statistik industri* 1995).

ARTICULATION OF THE HINTERLAND

In the nineteenth century, Surabaya's position as the leading port and most populous city of Java derived from its unrivaled access to a fertile and extensive hinterland. The island's only two long, navigable rivers, the Brantas and the Solo (Bengawan Solo), both flowed into the Java Sea in the vicinity of Surabaya (map 1.1). The Brantas was navigable from as far inland as Tulungagung, only a short distance from the south coast of Java. From there it flowed northward through the busy market town of Kediri and, as the valley widened into a broad plain, turned northeast to Mojokerto, where it began to form the rich Sidoarjo delta. The most northerly arm, known as the Kali Surabaya or sometimes Kali Mas, flowed northeast to Surabaya; the main southern arm, known as the Kali Porong, continued almost due east into Madura Strait. This delta and the Brantas valley, the heartland of eastern Java's wet-rice/sugar zone, constituted Surabaya's immediate hinterland.

The other main river, the Bengawan Solo, was navigable from just north of Gresik as far as the court city of Solo (Surakarta) in central Java. Although the lower two-thirds of its course lay through the dry limestone hills of Lamongan and Bojonegoro, its upper reaches tapped the lively trade not only of Solo but also by tributary the market town of Madiun. In the eighteenth century, when the trade with the court cities of the principalities was more important than that of the Brantas, Gresik had been the main commercial center. In the nineteenth century, as the delta began to be opened up for export production, Surabaya gained the ascendancy and drew to itself the trade of the Bengawan Solo.

Surabaya's other great advantage was to be a natural harbor, the only truly sheltered, all-weather anchorage along the whole north coast of Java. To the east Madura Strait widens out into a virtual inland sea, serving both the little river ports along the northeast coast and the main towns of Madura. Beyond lies the Java Sea and the greater world of the archipelago. Surabaya was therefore the natural intersection of many streams of commerce: the river trade of the interior, the coastal trade of Java and Madura, the interisland trade of Southeast Asia, and the deep-sea trade with other continents.

Java's other main coastal towns, Jakarta and Semarang, enjoyed almost none of these advantages. Though built at the mouths of rivers, the water there was so shallow that deep-sea ships had to anchor offshore, fully exposed to the monsoonal winds. Navigable for only short distances upstream, they gave access to only a very small hinterland. Before railways, the only means of access to the interior was by expensive land transport, which impeded the movement of goods, if not of people. Jakarta prospered despite few natural advantages. Without the status of being the capital city, Semarang continued to languish.

Surabaya therefore ranks with other leading port cities of Southeast Asia such as Bangkok, Rangoon, and Saigon, whose vitality and prosperity has also depended on their great rivers. At the turn of the century, when Surabaya was one of the world's great sugar ports, this was self-evident. Joseph Conrad did not need to explain to his readers where Surabaya was to be found. Yet times change and memories are short. When the geographer of Asia's port cities, Rhoads Murphey, wrote his survey in 1969, he made no mention of Surabaya. While emphasizing that most of Asia's port cities possessed "wretched harbours," he did not list Surabaya among the few exceptions (Murphey 1969, 75). Nor did he find it remarkable that a port with such outstanding natural and man-made advantages had so quickly fallen from prominence.

EMERGENCE OF THE PLANTATION ECONOMY

In the 1830s, when the Cultivation System began to stimulate the cultivation of export crops, much of East Java was still jungle or wasteland. Except for the narrow coastal plain, the eastern end of the island, the Oosthoek, was sparsely populated (Elson 1984, 26). To the west of Surabaya, settlement followed the valleys of the Brantas and, to a lesser extent, the Bengawan Solo. Labor being more scarce than land, the cultivation of export crops (primarily sugar and coffee) at first had to fit in with this distribution of population.

New sugar mills were established along two main axes of settlement. On Madura Strait, along the narrow plain of the north coast, mills were sited on the short coastal creeks and the sugar dispatched by lighter to ships anchored offshore. Along the Brantas axis, most of the early mills were located just south of Surabaya, in the densely settled delta, which was well served by waterways for movement of goods and roads for personal travel (map 1.1). From the delta, the sugar industry gradually moved upstream in a broad arc through Mojokerto toward the town of Kediri.

The location of coffee cultivation was very different. As a high-value crop with no bulky inputs, coffee was the only main export crop that could bear the cost of land transport and was therefore ideal for remote districts in the highlands. Early in the nineteenth century the colonial government had tried to enforce the planting of coffee trees in lowland villages but the environment was unsuitable (Baardweijk 1986). By the late 1850s, the delta regencies of Surabaya and Sidoardjo were no longer enumerated as having coffee trees and in Mojokerto and Kediri production had shifted into the foothills (ARA, MK: V20–10–1869/4, V20–10–1869/4).

Blessed by extensive and efficient inland waterways, eastern Java had less need of railways than central and western Java. The island's first railways connected the port of Semarang to the adjacent highlands and the court cities of Surakarta and Yogyakarta (1867–73) and Jakarta to the summer capital at Bogor (Buitenzorg) (1873), later extending to the highland town of Bandung (1884) (Weijerman 1904). Once railway construction began in East Java, however, the basic network was completed with remarkable speed. The first section of line, from Surabaya via Sidoarjo and Bangil to the sugar port of Pasuruan was completed in mid-1878 (map 7.1).

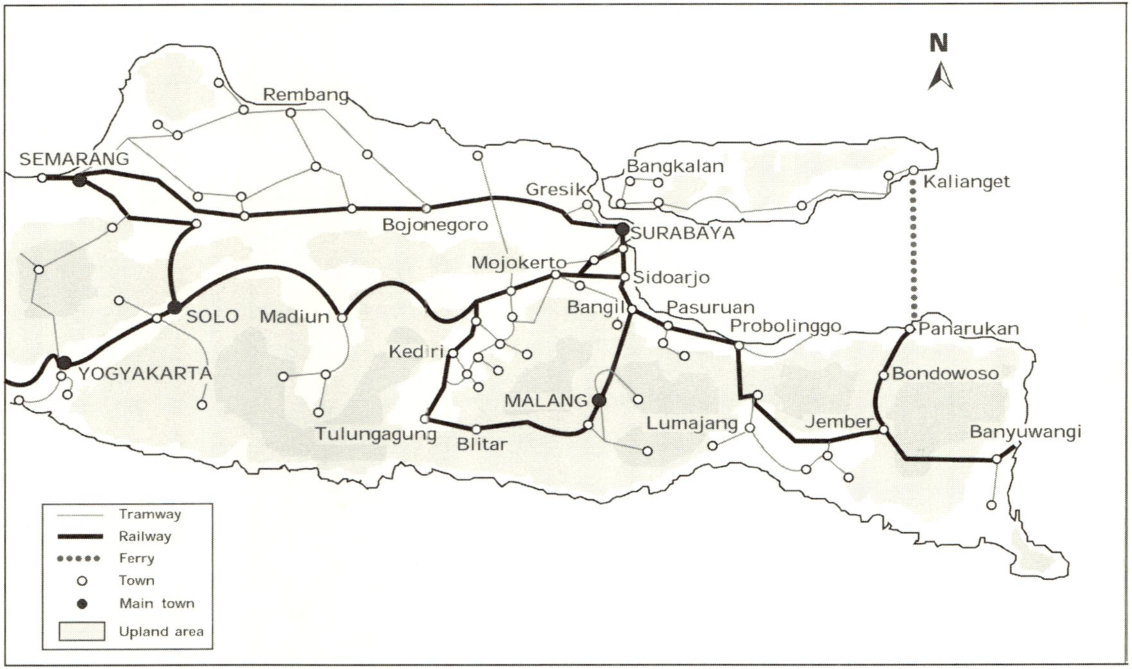

Map 7.1. Eastern Java: Rail and tram routes, 1939. Source: Based on *Officieele Reisgids, 2 November 1939–1 May 1940.*

Fourteen months later the line was extended southward from Bangil to the small highland town of Malang, after which the Pasuruan line was extended eastward along the coast to the neighboring sugar port of Probolinggo. A westward line from Surabaya up the Lower Brantas valley reached Madiun in mid-1882 and two years later connected with the central Java system at Solo. Meanwhile a branch line following the Brantas upstream to Kediri had been extended as far as Blitar in the southern hills. Thus, by 1884 the most fertile and populous regions of East Java had been linked into a single state-owned rail network focused on the port city of Surabaya.

After a ten-year pause, associated with low returns in both the coffee and sugar cultures, in the late 1890s the rail network was extended in a second construction boom. Malang and Blitar were joined by a great southern loop. The Oosthoek line was pushed south from Probolinggo to the fertile Lumajang plain and the emerging tobacco district around Jember, with extensions northeast to the outport of Panarukan and in 1903 eastward to the outport of Banyuwangi on Bali Strait. Apart from the extension of the private north-coast line from Semarang to Surabaya, the broad-gauge rail network was then virtually complete.

In the late 1890s the rail network was supplemented by a narrow-gauge network of rural tramways acting as feeder lines to the main system (map 7.1). The densest networks were in the Brantas delta below Mojokerto and around Kediri and Madiun, which allowed sugar cultivation to extend in a broader and denser band from rivers or main rail lines. The Pasuruan and Probolinggo steam tram companies performed a similar role on the north coast, the Malang steam tram company in the highlands. Upland plantations also benefited as railheads were moved closer to the point of production, reducing the need for expensive cartage by road.

Railways and tramways consolidated Surabaya's control over its hinterland at a critical time. In a common cycle of ecological decline, clearance of lowlands and hillsides, drainage of swamps, and damage to riverbanks had caused erosion and siltation, accelerated wet-season runoff and diminished dry-season flows, so that the transport arteries of the Bengawan Solo and Brantas were becoming more dangerous to navigate in the wet season and unnavigable in the dry. Then in the 1880s and 1890s the sugar industry found itself squeezed by a collapse in international prices caused by rapid growth in beet sugar output (Elson 1984, 1378). Although the crisis had not been foreseen when construction of the eastern Java rail system began, the huge investment in railways and tramways facilitated a restructuring of the sugar industry by relaxing the transport constraint. Despite running more or less parallel to the main rivers, which were also the axes of settlement, railways were a faster and more reliable mode of transport. By the early 1890s the Bengawan Solo had ceased to be a transport artery for the district of Surakarta and was of little importance to Madiun (*KV,* 1892, app. C). The Brantas river trade lingered because of high railway tariffs but by the mid-1900s it was reported that only five mills close to Surabaya still shipped their sugar harvest by river prahu (KKNS 1905, 46).

In the lowlands, railways and tramways extended the hinterland for production of export crops, especially sugar. They ensured that the Lower Brantas and the Sidoarjo delta would remain Java's main locus of sugar production. Further up the Brantas, between Mojokerto and Kediri, they permitted a greater density of mills and a wider band of cultivation across the valley. They also made mills profitable further west, in the fertile Madiun district, and drew that trade also to Surabaya—mills further west in the principalities shipped through Semarang (Osten 1930). Before the great crash of the 1930s there were almost 180 mills on Java, of which around one hundred were located in East Java: of these about sixty were located along the railway system of the Brantas valley, including six mills around Madiun and Ngawi (Segers 1987, 224).

Railways had an even more dramatic impact on the hitherto sparsely populated upland areas, which were now drawn closely into the world economy. The Agrarian Law of 1870 had created the opportunity for unoccupied land to be taken up by foreign planters on seventy-five-year heritable leases (*erfpacht*) but economic viability depended on access to the export market. The first area to be opened up was the highlands immediately south of Surabaya, with the completion of the railway to Malang in 1879. After connection to the rail network in 1884, Blitar, in the southern hills, became a boom town in a hinterland dominated by coffee estates (*KV,* 1892, app. C). At the end of the century, completion of the Malang-Blitar loop and the network of the Malang Stoomtram Mij (map 7.1) gave access to a large southern upland region that grew rapidly in population (Elson 1984, 166) and soon became Java's main locus of coffee cultivation. By the early 1920s it held a similar importance in regard to rubber (DLNH 1926). All this export moved by rail through the port of Surabaya. This was an important new axis of commerce, for hitherto the gateway to the highlands had been the nearby port of Pasuruan.

Not all of East Java was brought within the mainstream of economic life. From north-central Java through Lamongan and Gresik to Madura ran a belt of dry, infertile limestone hills that also marked the northern edge of the Lower Brantas valley. Except along the Bengawan Solo and in scattered pockets, this parched landscape could sustain only dryland agriculture, mainly rainfed or dry rice, maize, and cassava, the poor man's staples. Its only export crop was an inferior "native" tobacco. Nevertheless, this backward region still played an important role in the economy of eastern Java. The low productivity of dryland agriculture meant that strict subsistence was not a viable strategy, giving rise to a variety of supplementary, market-oriented income-earning activities (Penders 1968a). Besides tobacco, Lamongan and Madura were eastern Java's main local source of cattle for agriculture and transport, especially in the lowland wet-rice/sugar districts. Madura also supplied Surabaya and the north-coast towns of Pasuruan, Probolinggo, and Panarukan with fish, chickens, fruit, and vegetables, brought in by ferry or prahu. After Bojonegoro and Lamongan had been cleared of natural jungle, the colonial government planted the hills with teak forests, whose thinnings supplied timber yards in Gresik and Surabaya.

Because these various activities could not sustain a growing population, the dryland districts also became eastern Java's main pool of migrant labor. In the nineteenth century Bojonegoro and Lamongan already supplied much of the seasonal workforce in the sugar factories of the Lower Brantas, just as Madurese crossed to the Oosthoek to work in the sugar, tobacco, and coffee estates (*KV,* 1892). From the western part of Madura, Gresik, and Lamongan, men also flocked to Surabaya in the dry season to meet the seasonal demand for labor, especially the handling of hundreds of thousands of tonnes of bagged sugar exports. Itinerant by necessity, the Madurese were also prominent as traders, especially in tobacco, cattle, and cloth. These seasonal movements were facilitated by the building of tramways in the 1890s and 1900s.

When the province of East Java came into being on 1 January 1929, the administrative area therefore contained three fairly distinct zones, lying roughly parallel along an east-west axis:

- the densely settled, lowland wet-rice/sugar districts in a broad arc along the lower and middle Brantas River, the adjacent Madiun plain, and the northeast littoral (Oosthoek);
- the less densely settled highlands and southern hills and plains, which produced most of the upland plantation crops, most notably coffee, tobacco, and rubber;
- the dry lands of the northern limestone hills extending from Bojonegoro, Lamongan, and Gresik across to the island of Madura.

This geographical division is somewhat crude but it captures the essence of East Java's diversity and points to the complementarity of its several zones.

ZONES OF INTERDEPENDENCE

Surabaya's relationship to these three zones was manifest in different patterns for exports, imports, and business services. The city's hinterland was smallest for bulky exports like sugar, which was usually shipped through the nearest port, and most extensive for imports and business services. In the case of exports, the hinterland divided roughly along a north-south line between Surabaya and Malang. To the west of that line, as far as the border with Central Java, the railway system channeled exports to Surabaya. East of the line, exports flowed mainly through the north-coast outports of Pasuruan, Probolinggo, Panarukan, and Banyuwangi. This lopsided orientation reflected transport cost. Despite commissioning in the 1920s of Surabaya's new deep-sea harbor (chap. 2), rail tariffs were such that north-coast sugar mills could still ship more cheaply through an adjacent outport. Many of Surabaya's redundant lighters were transferred to these ports to improve their lighterage fleets (ARA, NHM, *Verslag* 1926). These ports therefore continued to be efficient in handling large seasonal tonnages of sugar, as well as tobacco and minor crops.

The plantations that exported through north-coast outports nevertheless remained heavily dependent on agency houses, banks, and trading firms in Surabaya for management, finance, shipping, and insurance. This pattern traced back to the opening up of frontier through business networks based in Surabaya. While north-coast ports had small branch offices, there was no rival center of trade. The physical movement of exports was therefore a poor indicator of actual business networks. Through the supply of banking, insurance, and other business services, the Oosthoek was tied closely to Surabaya, which also dominated the import trade.

The province of East Java can therefore be seen as a single economic unit, diverse in its parts, capable of generating a good deal of intraprovincial trade and, in its entirety, tributary to Surabaya. By virtue of its pivotal location as a safe haven between the mouth of the Brantas, the old highway to the interior, and at the gateway to Madura Strait (East Java's inland sea), Surabaya was both a port and a crossroads. However, the key to Surabaya's dynamism is that these natural highways overlapped with an intersection between wetland and dryland zones, between economic heartland and economic periphery. To be intuitive, that mix of fecundity and harshness, reflected in the coexistence between Javanese syncretism and more pure Islam, seems to lie at the root of the city's character and identity. Railways, and later highways, helped knit these wetland and dryland zones more closely together but also introduced a third dynamic element by making accessible the highland zone, the frontier where European capital could make its mark.

This perspective on Surabaya's hinterland nevertheless omits a fourth, outer zone that lies to seaward. As the legendary meeting of the shark (*sura*) and crocodile (*buaya, baya*) implies, Surabaya is an intersection between sea and shore. Historically the pattern of trade relations was determined by the direction of the monsoon winds. South and East Kalimantan were a short, easy reach across the Java Sea while, to the east, South Sulawesi, Maluku, and the island chain of Nusa Tenggara were readily accessible in season. Surabaya and Gresik began in precolonial times to serve as entrepots for the trade of eastern Indonesia, a role that in the case of the prahu trade continued into the New Order (Dick 1975). Trade networks were consolidated by migration of local traders and settlement of Chinese merchants. After the mid-nineteenth century, steamships allowed trade to be carried on year-round. In the 1900s construction of modern wharves and the monopoly policy of the KPM allowed Makassar to capture much of the trade of eastern Indonesia (Campo 1992). However, as Makassar declined as an entrepot in the 1950s, Surabaya reasserted its sway over eastern Indonesia. With industrialization, the Outer Islands of the archipelago have become an important part of the market for the manufactures of East Java, as well as a source of raw materials.

A recent overview of Surabaya's economic sphere can be gained from the network of daily air traffic. Based on February 1997 schedules, map 7.2 shows the pattern of direct, nonstop flights from Surabaya. Java accounted for half of daily domestic flights, with Jakarta the dominant connection—a shuttle service for businessmen and officials, with over thirty flights per day. Beyond Java the main connections were with Makassar (11) and Denpasar (10),

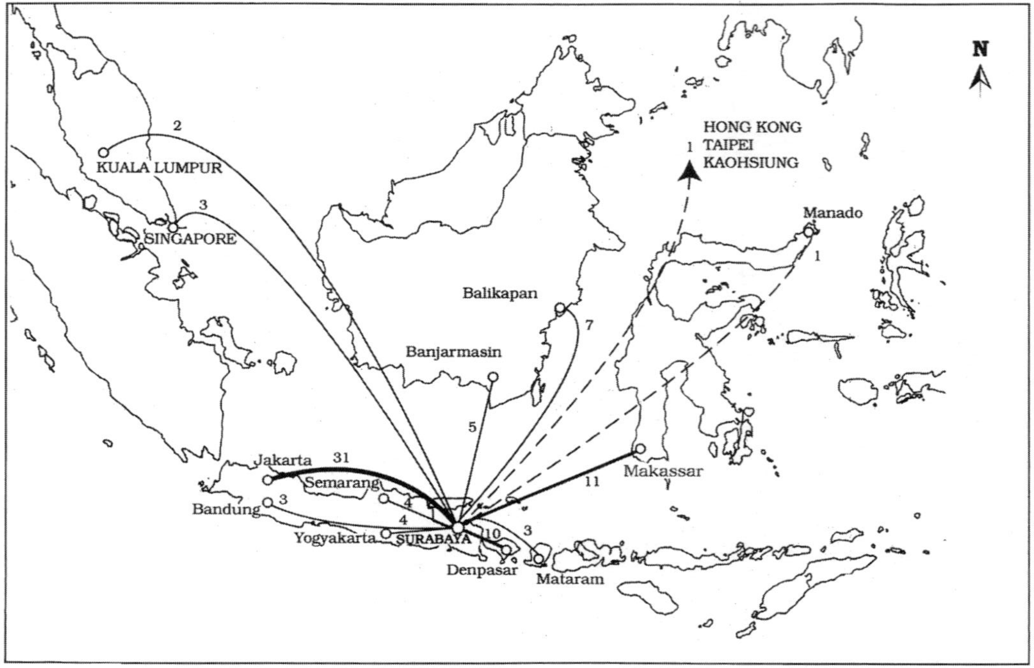

Map 7.2. Surabaya: Direct daily airline flights, February 1997. Source: OAG 1997.

followed by Balikpapan (7) and Banjarmasin (5), in East and South Kalimantan respectively. Flights to more distant locations in eastern Indonesia involved stopovers or transfers in one of these places, while those to the west of the archipelago were mediated through Jakarta. In the main this pattern of links with Kalimantan and eastern Indonesia was consistent with the historical pattern of interisland trade (see below).

The Hiatus of the Mid-Twentieth Century

In the 1920s Surabaya reached the peak of its prosperity as the capital of Java's plantation economy. This achievement was visible in the built environment of a modern, bustling city (chap. 6). Yet it was a fragile prosperity. The frenzy of the immediate postwar boom had in 1921 been succeeded by severe recession. Sugar prices made a weak recovery in 1923 before resuming their downward trend (*IV,* 1940). Rubber prices soared to a spectacular peak in 1925 before collapsing back to more normal levels (CBS 1947, 119). By 1928 sugar and rubber prices had both begun their slide into the world depression. The erratic and uncertain behavior of export revenues was reflected in the uneven growth of the city. Despite the completion of many fine new buildings and the gradual development of new suburbs, the promise of the immediate postwar years was never realized.

With the benefit of hindsight it can be seen that by the late 1920s East Java's plantation sector could no longer sustain its momentum as the leading sector in economic growth. This was most apparent in the case of sugar. In the settled lands of the Lower Brantas and the north coast, the growth in area under sugar had been achieved partly by reclamation of swampland and jungle, partly by conversion of dry land to irrigated fields, and partly by substitution for wet-rice agriculture. However, as more and more land was brought into sugar production the frontier began to close. The colonial government tightened the constraint in 1918 with new regulations to regulate the amount of land under sugar in order to maintain rice production (Elson 1984). Peak sugar acreage was not reached until 1931, but by the 1920s extensification was already a minor factor in the growth of output, which now rested on investment and technological change. Growth in harvested area accounted for half of growth in output between 1901 and 1920 but only one quarter over the subsequent decade (CEI 1975, table 7). Moreover, in the face of growing population pressure on arable land, real average land rents increased sharply after being almost static for several decades (Eng 1993a, 194–95).

Ecological evidence suggests that by the 1920s the frontier of cultivation had already been pushed beyond its natural limits. As early as the mid-nineteenth century many hillsides hastily cleared and planted with coffee trees were having to be abandoned because of erosion (Umbgrove Commissie 1862–63). Yet clearing of jungle and clean weeding of coffee estates continued to be practised, to which writers have long attributed the devastation of much of upland Java, especially in the Arjuno massif and in the southern hills around Blitar (Schaik 1986; Nibbering 1988). Coffee estates mined the soils of upland Java, just as the sugar mills had mined the forests to meet their voracious demand for firewood. The rubber boom of the 1910s was therefore the last great wave of estate plantings in East Java. There was still scope for filling in and replacement of failed plantings but the increment in output would be marginal.

Once the frontier had closed, the dynamic that had sustained the growth of the plantation sector ceased to operate. The historic endowment of abundant land and scarce labor had given way to a new endowment of abundant labor and scarce land. Javanese plantation owners were relentlessly squeezed between rising real costs of production and steadily weakening international prices as European countries rehabilitated and expanded their protected beet sugar industries. More intensive exploitation of village land and labor was no longer feasible, because of rising nationalism and a less permissive colonial government. Growth in output could be sustained only by raising productivity per unit of land. With better irrigation and improved varieties developed by the Sugar Research Station at Pasuruan, yields had already more than doubled between the 1870s and the 1910s (Eng 1993a, 191–200; Booth 1988, 223). During the 1920s, world leadership in cane breeding, combined with the application of chemical fertilizers, led to a further one-third increase in yields. Yet despite Surabaya's sugar exports doubling—from 0.5–0.6 million tonnes in the early 1920s to a peak of 1.2 million tonnes in 1928–29—falling prices meant that revenue actually declined (*IV,* 1931). The world depression of the 1930s and the international sugar agreement ensured that many mills would have to close.

In the case of perennial tree crops such as coffee and rubber, it was much harder to raise yields by scientific means because the stock of trees was fixed. Replanting involved loss of earnings over a long gestation period with an uncertain outcome. The same problem arose in switching to alternative tree crops. Although rubber prices were high in the mid-1920s, it would have been a gamble to uproot healthy coffee trees. Rubber plantings were therefore most profitable in virgin areas. East Java did increase rubber output during the 1920s—from fifteen thousand tonnes in 1920 to twenty-six thousand tonnes in 1930—but the main growth in exports was from Sumatra and Kalimantan, where vast tracts of jungle could be brought into commercial production (*IV,* 1931). In the case of tea, the other boom estate crop in West Java, East Java's production was insignificant, being barely 1 percent of that of West Java.

The export potential of smallholder agriculture was also very modest. During the 1920s East Java had shown impressive gains in the output of smallholder export crops such as tapioca, maize, and fibers. Tapioca exports through Surabaya increased from less than fifty thousand tonnes in the early 1920s to a peak of two hundred thousand tonnes in 1928, while maize exports increased from almost zero to thirty thousand tonnes by the mid-1920s (CKS, *Meerjarige jaaroverzicht*). When the sugar industry more than halved its planted area in the mid-1930s, a huge area, some one hundred thousand hectares, was released by sugar mills that closed or reneged on lease contracts with peasant landowners (CBS 1947, 40). This land was for the most part redirected to the production of other cash crops, mainly rice and secondary food crops (*palawija*). Of these, the most important was rice for local and interisland trade (see below). Tapioca exports might have been expected to increase, but in fact exports through Surabaya at their post-Depression peak of 1937 were not three-quarters of their level in 1928 (CKS, *Jaaroverzicht*). Moreover, unit values were very low. In a land-scarce economy, such land-intensive but low-yielding crops had no potential to become a leading sector.

Thus it was not merely East Java's plantation exports but its entire export economy that had collapsed. The engine had ceased to operate. Despite artificially cheap inputs of land and labor, many of East Java's plantation companies could no longer produce and sell sugar at a profit. And there was too little margin of profit for plantations to turn to the export of rice, tapioca, maize, or peanuts. Thus, for the first time in decades, many farmers were able to enjoy free disposal of their land and labor. If secondary food crops are counted along with rice, it appears that after the mid-1930s villagers were able to both produce and consume more food and thereby, despite the apparently higher incidence of taxation, to improve their standard of living (Eng 1993b; Booth 1980). From the viewpoint of rural welfare, the collapse of the export economy was probably a good thing, at least in the short term. Without new sources of growth in output and income, however, these gains would soon be swamped by population growth.

Decline of the plantation economy was accelerated by the Japanese occupation and the subsequent Revolution (chap. 2). The Japanese did little physical damage but the loss of foreign markets, lack of shipping to move even such essential wartime supplies as rubber, failure to tend plantings, and neglect of equipment caused a run-down of the capital stock. The main damage, however, was done during the Revolution. Guerrillas destroyed estate buildings and mills reoccupied by the Dutch and by a reign of terror forced many upland plantations to be evacuated. After the recognition of

Independence, Dutch capital flowed back into Java to rehabilitate mills and plantations but, despite some recovery in output, it was no longer possible to turn the clock back to 1940, let alone to 1929, and to initiate a new phase of growth in plantation exports. Seizure and nationalization of all Dutch estates in 1958 and their subordination to local army commanders ensured that the decline would be even more rapid (Mackie 1967a).

The situation observed by Clifford Geertz in the Kediri district in 1952–54 (Geertz 1967) and generalized as a historical process of "agricultural involution" (Geertz 1963, esp. 89–103) was in reality a recent and transitional phase. The plantation sector had lost the ability to generate growth and employment but no new leading sector(s) had emerged to take over that role. East Java's historically mobile and still rapidly growing population was therefore stranded in villages with very restricted employment opportunities. Migration to Surabaya had a marked impact on what was still a small city but the number of immigrants was too few to alleviate population pressure in the hinterland. Moreover, the city could not generate enough productive jobs to absorb the immigrants, who survived on their wits in a ballooning informal sector. The phenomenon of shared poverty was therefore a sign of stagnation rather than an intrinsic feature of the society itself, as came to be so widely believed.

The way out of this stagnation was understood by governments of the day, as well as by Geertz (1963): raising agricultural productivity and achieving structural change through industrialization. Ambitious goals were set, such as self-sufficiency in rice production, but the means of implementation were lacking. Instead, during the 1960s, everything was subordinated to immediate political imperatives and the economy was caught in a downward spiral of budget deficits, inflation, and balance-of-payments crises (Mackie 1967b). Renewed economic growth was delayed until the restoration of economic stability by the New Order government in the late 1960s. New leading sectors took even longer to achieve. How this transformation of comparative advantage occurred can best be seen through analysis of trade performance.

Foreign Trade

Before World War II, when Java ranked next to Cuba as the world's leading sugar exporter, sugar had been the staple of East Java's trade. Until the mid-1920s sugar had constituted over two-thirds of the value of exports through Surabaya, after which falling prices reduced the proportion to about half (table 7.1). By tonnage, however, Java's sugar exports peaked at around 3 million tonnes in 1928 and 1929: of this East Java shipped about 1.8 million tonnes, and Surabaya alone about 1.2 million tonnes. During the depression of the 1930s the Chadbourne international restriction scheme cut Java's exports severely to a temporary quota of just 1.4 million tonnes (*IV*, 1931–40). Shipments from East Java recovered to 1 million tonnes in 1939 but the respite was brief. After heavy damage to factories during the 1940s, Java's post-Independence exports never exceeded the 1954 figure of just 212,000 tonnes and ceased altogether after 1966 (BPS, *SPI*). The sugar industry survived but, apart from the by-product molasses, produced only for the domestic market. Rarely has a staple industry collapsed so dramatically.

Trends in export tonnages during the 1930s confirm that East Java's plantation sector as a whole had lost its dynamism. From the peak of the postwar boom in 1920 until 1927 the four main plantation products of sugar, coffee, rubber, and tobacco had constituted at least 80 percent of exports through the port of Surabaya (table 7.1). As prices began to weaken after 1927, this share drifted down to about 70 percent in 1930 and remained stuck at that level for the rest of the decade. The converse trend was some rise in the share of smallholder crops such as cassava, maize, and kapok and other fibers. However, this apparent diversification had little substance. These were products of low unit value and with little long-term growth potential. In fact, tonnages were no greater and in some cases much less than in the late 1920s. The export base was fragmenting rather than diversifying.

Even fifty years later, no new export staple had yet emerged. As late as 1980 the surviving "traditional" products coffee, tobacco, and rubber, plus molasses, still accounted for half the total value of East Java's exports (table 7.1). Coffee represented almost a quarter of total exports but was hardly a new leading sector. Despite much planting by smallholders (Mackie 1993), tonnage was only marginally above that in 1929 (table 7.2). Similarly, tobacco had increased its share from 1 to 13 percent, but tonnage was barely half that of 1929. The larger shares of these two products merely disguised the persistence of stagnation. Over a span of fifty years, this was a dismal trade performance.

Admittedly exports now included several nontraditional products that had formerly been insignificant or nonexistent: frozen prawns, hides, cacao, frogs' legs, and cashews, while there was also

TABLE 7.1
Main exports as share of total export value, Surabaya, selected years 1920–80 (%)

Commodity	1920	1925	1930	1939	1980 (East Java)
Sugar	71	50	53	49	5[a]
Coffee	5	10	5	5	23
Rubber	6	19	12	15	8
Tobacco	2	5	1	1	13
Subtotal	*84*	*84*	*71*	*70*	*49*
Other	16	16	29	30	51
Total	100	100	100	100	100

Sources: CKS (1921–27; 1928–40); BPS, Exports; and BPS, Imports.
[a]Molasses only.

TABLE 7.2
Tonnage of main commodity exports, East Java, 1929, 1939, 1980 (tonnes)

Commodity	1929	1939	1980
Coffee	23,823	24,017	27,065
Rubber	31,221	27,223	19,259
Tobacco	44,304	15,463	23,558

Sources: CKS (1928–40); BPS, Exports; and BPS, Imports.

an entrepot trade in rattan and timber. None of these items, however, accounted for more than 2.5 percent of export value (BPS, *Exports*). All primary products (excluding molasses) still came to just under two-thirds of the value of exports. Another fifth was taken up by an assortment of manufactured goods, of which plywood, a new industry, was the only item worth more than 2 percent of the value of exports. The emergence of a range of manufactured exports was certainly a new development but the achievement ought not to be exaggerated. An almost identical share was made up of the low-value residues of domestic food processing such as copra cake, molasses, and rice bran. As in 1939, so in 1980 the diversity of East Java's exports bore witness not to economic development but to the small size and continuing weakness of the export base.

The prolonged stagnation in East Java's export base has to be seen in the context of the trade performance of Indonesia as a whole and of the island of Java in particular (Dick 1995). As late as 1920 Java had still been the powerhouse of the Netherlands Indies, an export economy in its own right whose plantations supplied two-thirds of Netherlands Indies exports and generated huge surpluses on the balance of trade. Rapid growth in smallholder rubber and coffee in the Outer Islands caused Java's export share to fall to about half by the late-1920s. During the 1930s the crisis of the sugar industry affected Java alone, so that its share slipped further, to about a third of Netherlands Indies' exports. That downward trend continued remorselessly after Independence. By the mid-1960s Java had ceased to be a significant source of exports.

East Java's trade performance was even worse than that of Java. Despite the expansion of tea, quinine, and rubber plantations in the highlands of West Java, in 1928 East Java's share of Java's exports was still as high as 43 percent (CKS, *Jaaroverzicht*). East Java suffered most, however, from the decline of sugar exports, so that by the late-1930s its share had fallen to about one-third. This share was briefly regained in 1970 and 1971 with high coffee and tobacco prices but by the early 1980s East Java contributed only a few percent to Java's modest exports. East Java had almost no part in the

1970s oil boom, whereas Jakarta–West Java benefited heavily from offshore oil.

The contraction of East Java's export base and falling regional income was reflected in a much reduced capacity to import. As late as 1929 Surabaya was still by a good margin Java's main point of entry for import goods, with 39 percent of Java's total value of imports, compared with 31 percent for Jakarta (table 7.3).[1] Collapse of the sugar industry and deeper depression in East Java than in West Java meant that ten years later these roles were more or less reversed. After Independence, the centralization of government in Jakarta and the consequent bias of both public spending and private investment caused Jakarta's share of national imports to double, from 28 percent in 1939 to about 60 percent by 1969; during the oil boom this share fell away considerably but by 1990 had risen back to this level. Meanwhile, Surabaya had become marginalized. Its share of national imports fell from about one-fifth during the 1950s to just over one-tenth in the 1970s and was still at this dismal level twenty years later.

These trends in exports and imports come together in the balance of trade through the port of Surabaya. In the 1920s East Java

TABLE 7.3
Share of value of imports by main port, Java and Indonesia (%)

	Java[a]		Indonesia	
	Surabaya	Jakarta[b]	Surabaya	Jakarta[b]
1929	39	31	24	19
1939	33	43	22	28
1957	21	66	14	44
1969	15	87	11	60
1980	16[c]	60	12[c]	45
1990	14[c]	76	11[c]	61
1997	20[c]	66	16[c]	54

Sources: CKS (1928–40); BPS, SPI; BPS, Exports and BPS, Imports.
[a]Private trade only, excluding baggage, postal parcels, and gold and silver.
[b]To 1969 Tanjung Priok only; thereafter Special Region of Jakarta (DKI).
[c]Includes Gresik, Juanda airport and post office.

still generated a substantial trade surplus and thereby contributed, like other plantation regions of the Netherlands Indies, to colonial remittances. At the peaks of 1920 and 1924, the value of exports through Surabaya was 150 percent of the value of imports (Dick 1995, 49). Thereafter the trend was inexorably downward. The last year that the port recorded an export surplus was 1928. As the economy pulled out of the 1930s depression and import demand began to pick up, exports fell to around 60 percent of imports, the level at the transfer of sovereignty (1949). The Korean War boom brought some improvement in 1951, but thereafter the trade balance continued to worsen, for East Java as for the rest of Indonesia. Direct export taxes, worsening inflation, an overvalued exchange rate, and the lack of incentive for investment all combined to depress the export sector, while imports climbed steadily. Admittedly the trend was exaggerated by the increasing irrelevance of the official exchange rate, which in rupiah terms undervalued exports much more heavily than imports.[2] In April 1970, however, a realistic and unified exchange rate was at last restored (Arndt 1970), so that official trade figures from 1970 onward can be regarded as fairly reliable. Despite a surge in the quantity and value of coffee and tobacco, in 1970 and 1971 export earnings covered only about one-third of imports, confirming a marked downward trend since the 1950s. The sudden jump in the value of oil exports after the OPEC price increase of 1973 and associated domestic inflation caused the real exchange rate to appreciate, resulting in a flood of imports. By the mid-1970s exports covered only 15 percent of imports and by 1982, after the second OPEC oil price increase, the figure had fallen to just 13 percent.

How did Surabaya and the rest of East Java fund this huge gap between import outlays and export receipts? Until the 1980s there was no sustained inflow of private capital. After 1973 the central government drew on its abundant oil tax revenues to transfer development funds. However, East Java does not seem to have been favored over other provinces (Booth 1993). It thus seems unlikely that East Java could for so long have sustained its foreign-trade deficit without the outflow of funds squeezing the local economy to the point that deflation would have constrained the excess demand for imports. This is exactly what happened in most of Eastern Indonesia, where a similar collapse of the export base led to decline in real per capita incomes and withdrawal from the international economy. That this was not the fate of East Java, despite widespread poverty, suggests that some other factor was sustaining the foreign-trade disequilibrium.

Interisland Trade

The missing factor that explains East Java's permanent foreign-trade deficit is quite simply interregional trade. What matters to a regional economy is not the balance of *foreign* trade, as defined by national boundaries, but the balance of trade external to the region. The difficulty lies in measuring it. Even today almost no data are available on interprovincial trade by road and rail, though series have been published intermittently on interisland trade. For 1939, for example, Java as a whole shipped interisland almost twice the value of goods that it brought in, so that the foreign-trade deficit of Fl 41 million was more than offset by the surplus on interisland trade of Fl 64 million (table 7.4).

In the absence of detailed port data, an overview of the prewar interisland trade of Surabaya can be gleaned from shipping company records. The Dutch-flag KPM (Koninklijke Paketvaart Maatschappij) held a virtual monopoly on interisland shipping, so that its annual branch reports for Surabaya give a nearly complete overview of the trade except for prahu shipping (Dick 1987a,b).[3] Taking 1929 as a convenient base year, table 7.5 shows the pattern of private interisland trade. What stands out is a heavy bias toward Kalimantan. Chinese merchants in Banjarmasin and Samarinda were oriented toward Surabaya, shipping out timber and woven mats for packing sugar and tobacco (Banjarmasin) and dried fish (Samarinda), with a return trade in groceries and household items.

TABLE 7.4
Value of interisland and foreign trade by main region, Indonesia, 1939 (Fl millions)

	Kalimantan	East[a]	Sumatra	*Subtotal*	Java
Interisland					
Java outward	35	23	79	137	—
Java inward	9	9	55	73	—
Balance	*26*	*14*	*24*	*64*	—
Foreign					
Exports	93	27	353	473	272
Imports	25	20	113	158	314
Balance	*68*	*7*	*240*	*315*	*–41*

Source: CKS, Indisch verslag 1940.
[a]Sulawesi, Maluku, and Nusa Tenggara.

TABLE 7.5
KPM private interisland cargo by origin and destination, Surabaya, 1929, 1939 (lasts)

	1929		1939	
Region	Outward	Inward	Outward	Inward
1. Nusa Tenggara	14,330	15,043	9,105	17,736
2. Maluku	2,529	1,558	4,490	860
3. Sulawesi	13,293	9,513	12,336	6,854
4. Kalimantan	33,187	19,608	31,878	16,612
5. East Indonesia (1+2+3+4)	63,339	45,722	57,809	42,062
6. Java	4,543	6,682	8,503	5,429
7. Sumatra	11,913	15,120	34,076	18,891
Indonesia (5+6+7)	79,795	67,524	100,388	66,382

Source: KPM (annual).
Note: Cargo excludes coal and cattle.

Surabaya also had close links with Bali, Lombok, and Nusa Tenggara, which supplied rice, copra, onions, pigs (Bali), cattle, and horses (Sumba), though the trade of Sulawesi and Maluku flowed mainly through Makassar.

During the 1930s a trend toward import substitution was apparent in both primary products and manufactures (chap. 5). Despite the Depression, between 1929 and 1939 there was modest growth in private interisland trade between Surabaya and the rest of Indonesia, including a threefold growth in outward trade with Sumatra. Growth is understated by KPM figures, which exclude the booming prahu trade (table 7.5; Dick 1975, 1987b). There were also marked changes in composition. In 1929 outward general cargo had been dominated by sugar, while much rice was imported from Southeast Asia to meet the food deficit in East Java (table 7.6). By 1939 rice had become the main outward cargo: imports were minimal and the KPM was shipping local rice to the previously rice-importing plantation and mining districts of Sumatra. This dramatic import substitution was attributable to the switch from sugar to rice production in East Java. In 1933 the colonial government applied selective import restrictions to reserve the market of the Outer Islands for Javanese rice, which allowed idle sugar land to be switched to rice production for the interisland trade (Creutzberg 1974, 2:398–404). From a modest 30,000 tonnes in 1929, Java's exports to the Outer Islands increased to a peak of 200,000 tonnes in 1939 (CEI 1978, table 6). The increased frequency of sailings and probably cheaper freights between East Java and Sumatra facilitated trade in other products, including domestic manufactures.

The limited specification of KPM cargoes makes it hard to identify manufactured goods for which local production and interisland trade were boosted by the protectionist policies but a few noteworthy items are textiles, tobacco, beer, biscuits, and fabricated metals. With few modern textile mills and little household production in the hinterland, Surabaya probably shipped out less textiles than Jakarta, though how much was local production and

TABLE 7.6
KPM private interisland cargo by main commodity, Surabaya, 1929, 1939 (lasts)

	1929		1939	
Commodity	Outward	Inward	Outward	Inward
Sugar	34,928[a]	—	27,652	—
Rice	1,871	30,747[a]	28,474	2,207[a]
Tobacco	1,354	—	1,930	—
Coffee	1,687	3,791	2,213	—
Ironware	4,709	—	3,248	—
Textiles	4,166	—	4,278	—
Beer	—	—	4,232	—
Copra[b]	—	9,826	—	12,462
Cement[c]	—	7,706	—	7,163
Fish[d]	—	6,435	—	2,244
Shrimp Paste[e]	—	3,203	—	3,007
Wood[f]	—	4,526	—	4,878
Woven mats[f]	—	3,855	—	2,587
Onions[b]	—	—	—	1,285
Biscuits	—	—	2,630	—

Source: KPM (annual).
[a]Includes Bangkok, Saigon.
[b]From Nusa Tenggara.
[c]From Padang.
[d]From East Kalimantan.
[e]From Bagan Siapiapi.
[f]From Kalimantan.

how much reshipment of imported goods cannot be determined. According to Java's interisland trade statistics, tobacco (mainly cigarettes) was by 1939 the most valuable outbound item, ahead even of textiles (CEI 1991a, table 5; *EWNI,* 1/8/41). The tonnage of tobacco shipped from Java increased by 27 percent (cigarettes 45 percent) between 1935 and 1939, with Sumatra accounting for three-quarters of the growth in both cases. Surabaya, with the BAT and Sampoerna factories and nearby the Faroka plant in Malang, was a major point of shipment. Beer, produced in Surabaya by the new Java brewery, was separately specified in the KPM statistics in 1939 as an important item. Fabricated metals (*ijzerwerk*) probably consisted mainly of structural steel from the engineering shops in Surabaya; by the 1930s leading firms were supplying bridges, buildings, equipment, and even road rollers. These scraps of data do not bear much weight but they confirm that some specialization was at last emerging between a newly industrializing Java and the Outer Islands.

AFTER INDEPENDENCE

For 1957 it is possible for the first time to determine the pattern of interisland trade by province. The timing is fortunate because this was the last relatively normal year of interisland trade before the regional rebellions and expulsion of the Dutch. Notwithstanding its large deficit on international trade the province of East Java, like Java as a whole, as yet had no overall balance-of-payments problem. Although in domestic currency the foreign-trade deficit had swelled from 13 percent of imports in 1939 to 72 percent in 1957, this amount was covered twice over by the huge surplus in interisland trade (table 7.7). Such an outcome was possible because of the much greater rupiah quantum of interisland trade. The shrunken value of exports (just Rp 360 billion) was now dwarfed by the value of shipments to the Outer Islands (Rp 3,500 billion). Reported foreign-trade volumes had actually fallen below prewar levels, even if this was partly an illusion created by overvalued multiple exchange rates, which depressed the rupiah prices of exports and imports and encouraged smuggling.[4] At the same time, restrictions on imports such as textiles had switched demand toward domestic manufactures, whose production was located almost entirely on Java, thereby strengthening the prewar trend toward interisland specialization.

Interisland trade was dominated by East Java (Surabaya) and West Java (Jakarta) but much in favor of West Java (table 7.8) This was reflected in a marked imbalance in trade shares between the western and eastern archipelago. The more prosperous western

TABLE 7.7
Balance of foreign and interisland trade, East Java, 1957 (Rp millions)

	Foreign Trade (Surabaya)	Interisland Trade (East Java)
Outward	362	3,487
Inward	1,288	1,287
Balance	–926	2,200

Source: Calculated from BPS, SPI 1959.

TABLE 7.8
Java's interisland trade value by province, 1957 (%)

Province	Outward	Inward
East Java	37	34
Central Java	3	10
West Java	60	56
Total	100	100

Source: Calculated from BPS, SPI 1959

zone (Sumatra, Riau, and West Kalimantan) was firmly under the sway of Jakarta. Of the total trade between Java and the western zone, East Java accounted for just one-fifth and West Java almost four-fifths (table 7.9). Of East Java's small share of these interisland exports, about half went to the plantation province of North Sumatra, with which East Java had since the 1930s run a huge trade surplus. Most imports came from South Sumatra and consisted mainly of oil products from the refinery at Palembang—this was the only province with which East Java ran an interisland trade deficit. The poorer eastern zone (South and East Kalimantan, Sulawesi, Maluku, and Nusa Tenggara) was oriented toward Surabaya: East Java overall provided about two-thirds of both its exports and imports. Trade between Java and Sulawesi was shared fairly evenly both ways between West and East Java, as also were imports (mainly copra) from Maluku. However, East Java still

TABLE 7.9
East Java's share of Java's interisland trade value by zone, 1957, 1962 (%)

Zone	Outward 1957	Outward 1962	Inward 1957	Inward 1962
Western zone	20	11	21	14
Eastern zone	68	71	62	68

Source: Calculated from BPS, SPI 1959, 1963.

dominated trade with South and East Kalimantan and held a virtual monopoly on trade with Nusa Tenggara, then stretching from Bali to Timor.

The nexus between East Java and eastern Indonesia was fateful for Surabaya. While the multiplier effects of Sumatra's abundant exports, including oil, tin, and rubber, continued to benefit Jakarta—and Singapore—East Java continued to lose ground in the west. Between 1957 and 1962, when the statistical series was suspended, East Java's share of the important outward trade with the western zone fell sharply, from 20 to 11 percent (table 7.9). Instead, Surabaya remained tied to an increasingly stagnant eastern archipelago. The copra boom had long since run its course and no new export staple was emerging. Purchasing power therefore remained depressed and interisland trade was held back. After 1957 this polarization was exacerbated by the Permesta rebellion in Sulawesi and the deterioration of shipping services. Although the actual fighting was very brief, the rebellion ended the prosperity of North Sulawesi, the richest province in eastern Indonesia (Harvey 1977). Seizure of the KPM fleet in December 1957 and its subsequent expulsion most affected trade over longer distances (Dick 1987a, 18–25). Both the state-owned Pelni and private operators concentrated their services in the west of the archipelago, where they could gain a share of the lucrative import—and smuggling—trade with Singapore. It was many years before regular and efficient interisland shipping services were reestablished, especially in the eastern part of the archipelago. Much of Maluku and Nusa

Tenggara had to rely on sailing prahu for any remaining trade. Coconut oil mills on Java absorbed an increasing proportion of copra from eastern Indonesia, which in turn facilitated the outward trade. East Java was thereby able to increase its share of the textile trade with eastern Indonesia (BPS, *SPI* 1961). After production began at Gresik in 1957, cement joined sugar and cigarettes as other important items in outward trade. Nevertheless, by 1962 the tonnage of East Java's outward cargoes was about one-quarter below the level of 1957 (BPS, *SPI* 1959, 1963). The decline would have been even more marked had Surabaya not taken over entrepot functions from Makassar.

THE NEW ORDER

By 1974, when the next interisland trade value data become available, East Java no longer covered its foreign-trade deficit by the surplus on interisland trade. Compared with a foreign-trade deficit of $415 million, the surplus on interisland trade was only $157 million (table 7.10). The explanation for this turnaround lies on the import side. Although exports had been growing at a respectable rate, imports had surged by about 50 percent in 1972 and 1973 and, boosted by the oil boom, by an extraordinary 83 percent in 1974 (BPS, *Imports*).

TABLE 7.10
Balance of foreign and interisland trade, East Java, 1974

	Foreign	Interisland	
	$ millions	$ millions[a]	Rp billions
Outward	120	360	149
Inward	535	203	84
Balance	–415	157	65

Sources: Calculated from BPS, Exports; BPS, Imports; BPS ca. 1977.
[a]Converted at $1 = Rp 415.

The 1974 interisland trade statistics also show a continuing trend toward specialization in manufactures. Although the classification is haphazard, a crude categorization suggests that manufactures now constituted between two-thirds and three-quarters of Surabaya's interisland exports (table 7.11). The range of goods was fairly diverse: food, drink, and tobacco constituted the largest single

TABLE 7.11
Interisland trade by commodity, East Java, 1974

Commodity	Outward Rp millions	Outward %	Inward Rp millions	Inward %
Primary		*27.3*		*39.2*
Meat, livestock, fish	449	0.3	3,868	4.6
Rice	7,851	5.2	34	—
Sugar	29,617	20.0	72	0.1
Salt	906	0.6	4	—
Coffee, tea, spices	793	0.5	11,004	13.0
Copra	4	—	16,671	20.0
Wood	1,012	0.7	1,290	1.5
Manufactures		*66.6*		*38.2*
Tobacco	2,246	1.5	651	0.8
Flour	3,749	2.5	177	0.2
Other food & drink	33,116	22.0	3,877	4.6
Textiles[a]	9,658	6.4	947	1.1
Vegetable oils	1,791	1.2	9,185	11.0
Fertilizer	2,054	1.4	955	1.1
Chemicals	10,278	6.9	9,558	11.0
Rubber goods	1,048	0.7	168	0.2
Paper	1,328	0.9	233	0.3
Cement	3,442	2.3	316	0.4
Other nonmetals	1,452	1.0	218	0.2
Metals	8,631	5.8	914	1.1
Electronics & equipment	20,324	14.0	5,193	6.2
Miscellaneous	7,211	4.3	2161	2.6
Oil products	2,644	1.8	16,948	20.0
Total	149,600	100	84,450	100

Source: BPS ca. 1977.
[a]Includes leather.

component, followed by electronic and transport equipment, chemicals (including fertilizer), textiles, and metals (including construction materials), amounting in all to about 60 percent of the total. Although some of these manufactures would have consisted of the forwarding of imported goods, perhaps most notably in the category of electronic and transport equipment, there is no reason to doubt that there was a good proportion of local production. Interisland imports were, as ever, dominated by raw materials, which also gives some insight into the structure of the manufacturing sector. The largest single import item was crude oil and oil products, mainly from refineries in Dumai, Palembang, and Balikpapan. Almost as large was copra from eastern Indonesia to feed the coconut oil mills of Surabaya, besides which another 11 percent consisted of coconut and other vegetable oils in processed form. Another significant item—coffee, tea, and spices—consisted mainly of cloves for the manufacture of kretek. With the inclusion of the broad category of chemicals, about four-fifths of interisland imports are taken into account.

Between 1974 and 1983 a series of tonnage data shows rapid growth in interisland shipments of manufactures. Table 7.12 ranks the outward and inward trade of East Java by categories according to the average annual rate of growth over the period. In the case of the outward trade, tonnages of basic commodities such as sugar, flour, and salt grew fairly slowly, with the notable exception of rice (12 percent). East Java has always been a granary for eastern Indonesia and that role was enhanced by the Green Revolution, which began in the late 1960s (Fox 1993). Textiles and cement both grew at 8 percent, about the same as the average national rate of growth. Considerably faster rates were achieved by electrical and electronic goods and equipment, paper, metals, chemicals, and tobacco (mainly kretek), while the growth of fertilizer shipments from the Petrokimia plant at Gresik was dramatic.

Inward tonnages confirm the trend of industrialization. The spectacular growth of timber imports reflected the establishment of plywood factories oriented toward the export market; rapid

TABLE 7.12
Growth of main interisland cargoes, East Java, 1974–83 (% per annum)

Outward		Inward	
Item	Growth[a]	Item	Growth[a]
Animal feed	51	Paper	41
Fertilizer	22	Fertilizer	37
Oil products	16	Wood	30
Tobacco	16	Asphalt	18
Rubber goods	16	Other nonmetals	16
Other nonmetals	15	Other food & drink	16
Chemicals	14	Vegetable oils	13
Vegetable oils	13	Cloves, etc.	13
Metals	13	Metals	11
Rice	12	Meat, livestock	9.5
Paper	12	Copra	8.6
Electronics & equipment	10	Oil products	8.0
Wood products	10		
Textiles	8.0		
Cement	7.9		
Other food & drink	5.1		
Sugar	4.1		
Flour	3.1		
Salt	2.4		

Source: Calculated from BPS ca. 1977; 1984a.
[a]Exponential rates of growth in tonnage.

growth in vegetable oil imports was accounted for primarily by unrefined palm oil from North Sumatra (as raw material for the cooking oil industry, now diversifying away from coconut oil) (table 7.12). Yet the import pattern was becoming more complex than the import of foodstuffs and raw materials. There were also signs of cross-trade in manufactures, such as aluminum ingots and paper from North Sumatra and fertilizer (mainly urea) from Palembang.

The supply side is not of course the full story. The market in the Outer Islands would have been much smaller if the oil boom had not stimulated faster growth there as well. Until the mid-1970s the boom was more or less confined to the oil-producing areas of

Sumatra, Riau, and East Kalimantan, most of which lay in the western zone, under the sway of Jakarta. As late as 1974, when I traveled extensively in eastern Indonesia, Sulawesi, Maluku, and Nusa Tenggara were still in stagnation. Apart from East Kalimantan, which exported both oil (Balikpapan, Tarakan) and timber (Samarinda), the only bright spots were Bali (tourism) and the Minahasa district of North Sulawesi (cloves and coconut oil). Yet by about 1978 the economies of the other provinces were beginning to come to life. A clear sign was that ships sailing from Surabaya carried full deck cargoes, among which motor vehicles were particularly noticeable. As the volume of trade picked up, shipping services became more frequent and larger and more economical ships could be employed. Economic growth thereby fed upon itself. Because of its trade linkages, Surabaya was well placed to take advantage of the upswing to supply import-substituting manufactures.

Trade links were also restored with the rich plantation province of North Sumatra. Although the province had long drawn much of its sugar from East Java, after suspension of KPM services at the end of 1957 traders had had to rely mainly on the erratic and inefficient service provided by the state-owned Pelni. In the late-1960s a Surabaya entrepreneur opened a regular shipping line direct to Belawan. Assured of good bottom cargoes of sugar, he offered discounts on long-term contracts to manufacturers in Surabaya, including multinational firms such as Unilever, the Bintang brewery (Heineken), Nestlé, Philips, BAT, and Faroka, as well as domestic cigarette manufacturers (fieldwork notes, 1973–74). Market access having been secured, trade with North Sumatra grew rapidly. By the 1980s the province had become a major outlet for East Java's manufactures.

The Turning Point

The mid-1980s marked the turning point in East Java's long, disappointing foreign-trade performance. After some twenty years when the balance of trade had fluctuated without any clear trend, from 1983 the balance of trade showed a sustained improvement. By 1990 Surabaya's trade performance matched that at the height of the Korean War boom and was marginally the best outcome since 1937 (Dick 1995, 49). Three years later, with exports booming, exports and imports were at last in balance.

The new trend was apparent in the rapidly changing composition of exports. Over the previous sixty years, any rise in the value of exports had almost invariably been attributable to better prices for a quantum of traditional exports. This no longer applied. By 1999 exports of coffee, tobacco, and rubber amounted to less than 4 percent of the total (table 7.13). Their value was well exceeded by the new item of seafood, mainly frozen prawns from highly capitalized fish ponds (tambak) in Sidoarjo. The main source of better export performance, however, was the growth of manufactured exports. In 1980 manufactures were just one-fifth of East Java's exports; by the 1990s their share had increased to three-quarters.

A perspective on East Java's export performance in manufactures can be gained from comparison with Jakarta–West Java. In 1999, East Java shipped about one-quarter the value that Jakarta–West Java did and the composition was rather different (table 7.13). Unlike Jakarta–West Java, there was no dominant sector. In Jakarta–West Java, which had remained the center of the textile and clothing industry (chap. 5), textile, clothing, and footwear made up over 40 percent of exports and the value of shipments was almost twelve times that of East Java's. By contrast, East Java's exports were distributed across most sectors of manufacturing. As was the pattern in industrial production (table 5.8), they tended to be biased toward lower-value-added products. This applied, for example, to the resource-processing industries of plywood, paper, and furniture but could also be seen in machinery and equipment. In terms of percentage of exports, East Java almost matched Jakarta–West Java in metals and machinery but fell badly behind in the more sophisticated category of electronics and electrical equipment.

TABLE 7.13
Composition of exports, East Java, 1999

Commodity Group	East Java $ millions	%	Jakarta-West Java $ millions	%
Primary	*1,135*	*24.4*	*1,057*	*6.2*
Coffee, rubber, tobacco, tea	172	3.7	95	0.6
Seafoods	424	9.1	229	1.3
Other primary	539	11.6	733	4.3
Manufactures	*3,455*	*74.2*	*15,061*	*88.6*
Food, drink, tobacco	167	3.6	295	1.7
Textiles, clothing, footwear	601	12.9	7,060	41.5
Plywood	355	7.6	363	2.1
Paper & paperboard	644	13.8	870	5.1
Furniture	359	7.7	426	2.5
Chemicals, pharm., plastics	410	8.8	1,522	9.0
Metals & machinery	318	6.8	1,324	7.8
Electronics & equipment	62	1.3	1,250	7.4
Other and unspecified	539	11.7	1,951	11.5
Total non-oil	*4,590*	*98.6*	*16,118*	*94.8*
Oil	65	1.4	884	5.2
Total	4,655	100	17,002	100

Source: BPS, Exports 1999.

The emergence in the late 1980s of a new export base in manufactures was hardly spontaneous combustion. As seen in chapter 5, Surabaya had boasted a significant industrial capability since the mid-nineteenth century. Sugar factories were the first leading sector of modern industry and, along with railways and steamships, gave rise to what was for the time a significant heavy industrial base. East Java's misfortune was to be unable to sustain that industrial expansion, so that the industrial base in 1930 was only marginally more developed than fifty years earlier. When the sugar industry collapsed in the world recession, East Java's narrowly based manufacturing industry was dragged down with it, a fate quite different from that of the then much less sophisticated industrial sector in West Java.

Revitalization of East Java's modest but well-established industrial sector had begun in the 1970s, mainly in Surabaya and Malang and along the corridor between them (Dick 1993b). Supply and demand at the national level set the context. After about 1968 there was a recovery in domestic demand that received a tremendous boost from the two OPEC price increases, in 1973 and 1980. Rising real consumption was directed toward domestic industry by what became, under the Second Five-Year Plan (1974–75 to 1979–80), an aggressively protectionist strategy for import-substituting industrialization (Hill 1988, 1992). These national influences, however, did not of themselves direct industrial development to East Java in preference to any other province of Indonesia.

Although at a marked disadvantage vis-à-vis Jakarta–West Java, East Java enjoyed locational advantages over most other provinces. On the demand side, East Java had a growing mass market. The population was large—by the 1980s over 30 million in East Java itself—with a similar number in the adjacent province of Central Java. Although in the late 1960s rural people were desperately poor, discretionary purchasing power began to rise as a consequence of the Green Revolution (Booth 1988; Fox 1993). This boosted farm incomes and thereby also the demand for nonagricultural products. The impact of this stimulus was multiplied by public spending on roads and bridges, improving access from villages to market towns and from market towns to Surabaya. East Java and adjacent parts of Central Java and Bali thus became a single, well-articulated economy. Despite missing out on most of the early phase of foreign investment in manufacturing, which was concentrated in Jakarta–West Java, East Java was thereby well placed to achieve a process of bootstrap development (Dick 1993a).

The other string to East Java's economic bow was growth and diversification of interisland trade. Like the newly industrialized economies of Taiwan and South Korea, East Java began with an inward-looking phase of industrialization. Not that this was necessarily a conscious decision: with high-cost structures at the going exchange rate, ignorance of foreign markets, and lack of marketing channels, exporting seemed out of the question. The highly protected domestic market was the only market available. The advantage of Surabaya over, for example, Semarang was that the trading links with the rest of the archipelago were already established, though more so in the eastern than in the western zone.

That East Java did not experience faster manufacturing development before the mid-1980s can be attributed to the effects of "Dutch disease," namely high real exchange rates brought about by the oil boom (Warr 1992). Unlike Jakarta–West Java, East Java had minimal oil exports, was not tied to supplying the offshore oil industry, and was not privileged in the disbursement of oil tax revenues. Its industry therefore bore the brunt of a high exchange rate that cheapened imports but implicitly taxed labor-intensive exports. The large devaluation of November 1978 was intended to promote non-oil exports and boost labor absorption but was swallowed up by inflation and then overwhelmed by the second OPEC oil price increase (1980). However, the devaluations of March 1983 and October 1986 pegged back most of the oil-induced appreciation of the exchange rate (Warr 1992, fig. 5.7). This time the relative price benefits were maintained by tight money policies and reinforced by a non-oil export drive that removed many of the constraints on the export of labor-intensive manufactures (Booth 1992; Hill 1992). The initial surge in labor-intensive exports, most notably textiles and clothing, was generated in Jakarta–West Java. Relieved of the handicaps that had held it back over the previous decade, however, East Java soon followed along a similar path. Manufactured exports began to grow at a much faster rate than imports as firms reoriented themselves from the domestic to the foreign market. Access to the international economy in turn freed East Java from the constraints of the domestic market and helped accelerate economic growth.

One sign of the city's broadening horizons was the emergence of a basic network of international air links (map 7.2). Before about 1990, Surabaya had no direct international flights for international flights were restricted to Jakarta and Denpasar (Bali) to protect

Garuda's domestic market. Subsequent liberalization allowed airlines to introduce direct flights to regional destinations. Though not a tourist gateway like Medan, Surabaya was an attractive market because of rapid growth in business traffic, especially within Asia (*SP,* 28/1/95). Juanda airport was upgraded to international standards and by 1997 handled about eight international flights per day: several to Singapore and Kuala Lumpur and approximately one flight each to Hong Kong and Taipei, all transfer points for other foreign destinations (OAG 1997). Although Jakarta is still much the busiest hub in Indonesia for international traffic, followed by Denpasar, Surabaya ranks third, confirming that it has at last emerged from provincial eclipse to reclaim its status as a city of regional importance.

Conclusion

The mid-twentieth century was a crisis in Surabaya's modern economic history. During the hundred years from 1830 to 1930 the city had boomed as the headquarters, service center, and port for an expanding, plantation-based, export economy based on sugar in the lowlands and coffee and later rubber in the hills. However, the very success of that economy gradually eliminated the conditions that had made it possible. A frontier economy in which land was abundant and labor scarce was transformed into one of abundant labor and scarce land. In such circumstances, continued growth of export crops required either rising productivity of land or worsening exploitation of labor. By the early decades of the twentieth century, the frontier of the plantation economy had shifted to the less populated territory of West Java, underpinning the growth of Jakarta. The world depression of the 1930s exposed the vulnerability of East Java's plantation economy. Renewal of sustained economic growth required a structural shift from a land-intensive to a labor-intensive export base, which is to say industrialization. In the 1930s protectionist industrial policies did at last call forth investment in import-substituting manufactures, but East Java missed many of the opportunities because of the shrinking plantation sector and the consequent weakness of purchasing power. What investment did occur was heavily biased toward Jakarta, a pattern that was reinforced by the centralization of government after Independence.

The lag between East Java's initial phase of industrial development, up to the 1930s, and that which has taken place since the 1970s was so long that the latter would seem to be a fresh start rather than the revival of a much older process. The crucial inheritance of that earlier phase was not the antiquated and rundown plant and equipment, most of which had to be scrapped, nor an industrial workforce, most of which has had to be trained from scratch, but a vigorous commercial network supported by a transport system that could be rehabilitated at modest cost. In other words, at the outset of the New Order, East Java had the framework to support a much larger and more sophisticated economy than the degenerate one that then existed.

During the 1970s the domestic economy of East Java at last began to expand in response to a better macroeconomic, institutional, and policy environment and the stimulus of the Green Revolution (Dick, Fox, and Mackie 1993). The modern manufacturing sector picked up from a much smaller base than in Jakarta–West Java and took longer to achieve strong growth. Nevertheless, by the time of the oil crisis in the mid-1980s, solid foundations had been laid for new leading sectors. A large and rapidly growing market in East Java had been supplemented by "export" markets in the Outer Islands. Not until the late 1980s, however, did the transformation of comparative advantage from land-intensive plantation and smallholder exports of primary commodities to labor-intensive industrial manufactures reveal itself in *foreign*-trade performance. Adjustment of the foreign-trade regime and deregulation as part of the nonoil export drive allowed Surabaya–East Java to reap the benefits of a wider market and develop a new export base in manufactures. Having disengaged from the international market as a plantation economy, East Java now rejoined it as an industrial one. Greater Surabaya established itself as Southeast Asia's leading non-capital-city industrial area. Proof that a transformation has indeed occurred is the resilience to the crisis of the late 1990s. Whereas the depression of the 1930s destroyed the export base, by the end of 2000 the foreign-currency value of exports had exceeded their pre-crisis peak (*SP,* 12/12/00). This may give confidence that East Java's industrial expansion is at last self-sustaining.

Chapter 8

CONCLUSION

At the end of a century people look backward as well as forward, trying to gain insight into the great forces that have moved nations and peoples. Nowhere is this more true than in Indonesia, where a turbulent century reached its climax with collapse of the mighty edifice of the New Order. Once again everything is in flux: politics, economy, society, religion. It is timely to revisit Indonesia's recent history and especially to get rid of the propaganda that corrupted so much of what was written during the New Order, whether deliberately or by uncritical acceptance of New Order myths and ideology. Another intellectual challenge is to assimilate the colonial heritage and move beyond revolutionary romanticism as the basis for judging later rulers. This book has sought to meet these challenges in three complementary ways: by taking as a period the entire twentieth century, by writing about a place outside Jakarta, and by trying to go beyond the accessible middle-class experience to look into the other urban world of the kampung.

The New Order invented the Old Order as an ideological construct to embrace the entire previous period after Independence. With its fascist pedigree, the term New Order implied not only newness but also the legitimizing principles of being well-ordered (*teratur*), virtuous, and prosperous, whereas Old Order implied chaotic, dissolute, and poverty-stricken. The transitional year 1966, when the communists were slaughtered, marked the emergence from darkness into light—by a stroke of genius the acronym *repelita* for five-year development plans (*rencana pembangunan lima tahun*) invoked a light (*pelita*) that would lead the way from darkness. Terminology therefore both legitimized and delegitimized. What happened before 1966 entered the realm of myth, not the least function of which was to deny the Old Order origins of the New Order state. The power of the armed forces (ABRI) was not to be challenged, nor the 1945 constitution that sustained it, nor the unitary state and its bureaucratic structures. General Soeharto and his associates kept as much of the Old as would entrench their power while stripping away all that would constrain it. This depoliticized, desocialized state was repackaged as New and legitimized by a new national ideology of means and ends, Dual Function (Dwifungsi) and Development.

The New Order imposed itself as a new *national* culture. The reality, however, was that the so-called national culture was a Jakarta-based culture, and an elite one at that. The New Order state regulated all appointments—civil and military—through the key ministries of Internal Affairs and Defense and the State Secretariat, their offices all located within a very small radius around the presidential palace, in the heart of Jakarta. Also within this magic circle was found the Ministry of Information and state radio and television. Few programs were made in studios outside Jakarta. Folk culture was put on display from around the archipelago but, like the Mini-Indonesia theme park, these condescending, stylized gestures underlined provincial inferiority. Wives of civil servants and military were organized into the Women's Corps (Dharma Wanita) with a mission to instill "family values," discipline, and moral improvement in the lower orders of society, reinforcing the not so subliminal messages of state television and state education. These tendencies have been commented on in detail elsewhere but bear emphasis. Foreign observers looked where the official finger pointed, saw economic development, and mostly were satisfied.

Indonesians were more conscious of the pressures of social engineering, sometimes ludicrous—as in the compulsory Pancasila indoctrination courses and civil service ceremonies—but inescapable in their totality. Materialism and religion were the two great escapes. And regionalism. Because the pressure came from Jakarta, there emerged a complicit sense of provincial solidarity, perhaps most effective where it was never enunciated. East Java and Surabaya were thus an excellent vantage point.

Politically the New Order was elite-authoritarian but socially and culturally it was an urban middle-class hegemony. The middle class was denied political rights but by education and occupation could enjoy prosperity and participate in national life. By contrast, the mass of Indonesians were in but not of the New Order. General Ali Murtopo's "floating mass" strategy denied the people (*rakyat*) access to politics because they were seen as too susceptible to left-wing propaganda and organization. Stiffened by ex–military officers, the administrative control system extended down to the level of the neighborhood, just as intended by the Japanese originators of the neighborhood cell (*rukun tetangga,* RT) and without the later adaptation of local election. The rationale was that political stability would facilitate economic development. However, a people stripped of politics and voice was a people desocialized and alienated. This point was brilliantly made by the theatre troupe Gandrik in their play *Brigade Maling* (Brigade of thieves): all citizens had to surrender their hearts to the state, red rubber hearts that were duly stamped and collected, depriving people of feelings and conscience. When the state apparatus allied with market forces to destroy people's livelihoods and take away their land, there ignited a slow-burning but fierce resentment not seen since the late-colonial period. The New Order turned its own people into the enemy as surely and with as much good intent as the enlightened but clumsy administrators of the Ethical Policy. It is for your own good; later, when you have grown up, we will give you responsibility. . . .

For all its limitations and faults, this socioeconomic history of Surabaya suggests different ways of viewing Indonesia's remarkable twentieth-century experience. If the blinkers of conventional periodization are relaxed along with its lazy, habitual assumptions, there is revealed a very long-term cycle connecting the New Order back to the late-colonial period. The word *cycle* is crucial. It is not suggested that the New Order was a continuation of the late-colonial period, or any deliberate attempt to copy it. Some institutions, technologies, and habits carried over but this would be a tenuous line of argument. Rather it is argued that, despite its different origins, the New Order displayed similar features—authoritarian rule, capitalist economic development, and an expanding middle class—that in turn generated patterns resembling those in the late-colonial period. The relationship is comparative, not causal. These two periods stand in marked contrast with the intervening period of more populist government, when Indonesia was disengaging from the global economy. New light is thereby cast back on both the colonial experience and the Sukarno era (a better term than Old Order).

The resemblances between late-colonial and New Order Indonesia are remarkable only because nationalist ideology insists on conflating the prewar Netherlands Indies with colonial rule, instead of analyzing it in the context of the economic system in which colonial rule and colonial society were embedded. The argument is one of outcome, not intent or morality. If colonial rule is treated as a historical variable rather than a catchall proxy, its characteristic features stand out more clearly.

First, colonial rule involved social stratification along sharp ethnic lines. Until the mid-nineteenth century the Indies was still a mestizo society with a cleavage between a small ruling elite and the rest of the population (Taylor 1983). By 1900 capitalist economic development had given rise in the main cities to a functional middle class. The term *elite* could still be applied but *middle class* better evokes the new lifestyle: suburban, family-centered, car-owning, educated, and white-collar. And whereas *elite* implies a national phenomenon, *middle class* draws attention to commonalities with new social formations in Europe, North America, and other regions of recent European settlement. The middle class in the Indies, as elsewhere, was both modern and cosmopolitan. Its emergence was a product not of colonialism as such but of nineteenth-century economic development. The impact of colonial rule was on the composition of this class: predominantly European, secondarily Chinese, and only marginally Indonesian. Here precisely was the flash point of the nationalist movement, a vigorous group of young Indonesians, believing in knowledge, education, and merit but who found their careers and aspirations blocked by a color bar. The first two volumes of Pramoedya's tetralogy bring to life the drama that flowed from this contradiction (Pramoedya 1980a,b). Enlightened Dutchmen could dream of the Indies becoming a model, tropical, middle-class meritocracy but their own compatriots would not allow it.

Second, the colonial state was a very narrowly based, authoritarian regime whose control of society, though legitimized by an ideology of good government, ultimately relied on armed force. The Ethical Policy was introduced in the 1900s while the Outer Islands were still subject to "pacification"; as the nationalist movement gathered strength, repression intensified. When the Japanese invaded in 1942, colonial rule was still secure—unpopular but facing no effective internal challenge. Parallels with the New Order are striking: the New Order was also imposed by force, legitimized as good government (Stability and Development), supported by an Indonesianized urban middle class, and maintained by systematic repression. It stumbled sooner against the contradictions of authoritarian rule, however, because over time power was ever more concentrated in the person of Soeharto and therefore dependent on his continuing good health. Soeharto could no more liberalize the political system that entrenched the power of his family and the armed forces than the colonial government could share power with the nationalists. Neither system could evolve in any other way than becoming more repressive.

Third, colonial rule was associated with a particular form of integration with the world economy by which international capital gained access to Indonesia's resources. Economic theory posits a common transition from an agriculture-based to a manufacturing-based economy. In the case of Indonesia, economists read statistical trends of GDP and employment as locating this transition during the New Order. However the classification of primary and secondary industry is so crude that the statistics fail to capture the most significant feature of Indonesia's long-term economic transition, namely that the shift from subsistence agriculture to capitalist production took place not in the 1980s but a hundred years earlier in the form of agro-industrial plantations oriented toward the world market. Especially on Java, the industrial revolution technologies and the institutions of European capitalism were already vigorously applied in the second half of the nineteenth century in a transition to a capitalist plantation economy. Burger (1939), Boeke (1942), and Geertz (1963) rightly drew attention to the phenomenon but their insight was lost. Although only the minor part of land and labor was involved in estate production, the state, the institutions of high capitalism, and the sophisticated infrastructure were so attuned to the needs of the plantation sector that colonial Indonesia could validly be described as a plantation economy. This was very well understood by Indonesian nationalists, who in 1958 tried to settle the issue by nationalizing all Dutch enterprises. However, instead of facilitating the transition to an industrial economy, they merely transferred the plantation economy to state control at a higher level of inefficiency.

In the late-colonial period, as later under the New Order, closer integration with the world economy meant greater vulnerability to its economic cycles. Economic growth is a fitful, uneven process. Every ten years or so the business cycle generates a downturn that may worsen into recession, then confidence recovers and the economy accelerates into another boom. Underlying this and still poorly understood are much longer background cycles. Here very-long-term trends such as technological and institutional change, industrialization, global shifts of capital and labor, and the balance between productive and financial assets come into play. These cyclical patterns and their interactions can always be rationalized after the event but predicting economic trends is rather like forecasting the weather: it often rains, sometimes blows a gale, and occasionally bursts forth a hurricane. Lord Keynes acknowledged this instability by invoking his term *animal spirits.* Market forces are more a trampling herd than the fine, equilibrating mechanism usually portrayed by economists. In a downturn people become increasingly pessimistic, in an upturn increasingly optimistic. Ultimately their expectations are confounded, and they are surprised. How could everyone be so wrong? Most people are not historians and the arrogance of youth is to distrust the experience of its elders. Observation and common sense suggest that tomorrow will be much like today, that any current trend will continue. The mistake is to confuse a standpoint *in* history with history itself, like a swimmer heedless of currents and tides.

Interaction between the small local economy and the encompassing world economy had two particular consequences that show up in the economic history of Surabaya, namely retarded industrialization and the timing of real estate booms. Early industrial expansion was generated by the plantation economy, but that nexus became a hindrance after the 1930s as the plantation economy lost vitality. New protectionist industrial policies called forth investment in manufacturing of consumer goods but the weakness of local purchasing power caused East Java to miss most of the opportunities. Economic leadership passed instead to Jakarta–West Java. At the outset of the New Order, East Java still had the infrastructure and commercial networks to support a much larger and more sophisticated economy than the degenerate one then existing. Lacking was a favorable macroeconomic, institutional, and policy environment to evoke the necessary investment—and confidence in growth of the local market. The necessary stimulus was the Green Revolution of the 1970s, which boosted the domestic market in eastern Java. Large-scale manufacturing picked up from a much smaller base than in Jakarta–West Java but by the oil crisis of the mid-1980s, solid foundations had been laid for new leading sectors. The subsequent non-oil export drive and accompanying liberalization enabled Surabaya and its environs to emerge at last as a substantial industrial agglomeration oriented toward the world market. The lag between Surabaya's long initial phase of industrial development up to the 1930s and that since the 1970s was so long that the latter would seem to be a fresh start.

The other consequence that flowed from interaction with the global economy was the very long gap between real estate booms. Here most dramatically urban economic history is seen as episodic. Natural inclination is to see the evolution of a city as a fairly steady progression. Because the urban environment changes imperceptibly from day to day, events such as the demolition of a familiar landmark, the opening of a new building, or some natural disaster are abnormal and therefore newsworthy. The sequence and underlying pattern of events is seldom perceived because knowledge is incomplete and memories fallible. The real estate boom that began in the late-1980s and lasted until the collapse of 1997–98 seemed to be a unique phenomenon because nothing like it had occurred within living memory. However, a similar such boom had occurred in the 1910s. A capitalist demand for urban land had picked up in the late 1890s to meet a rising European demand for detached bungalow-style housing beyond the limits of the densely settled lower town. During the 1900s, as in the 1980s, large tracts of farmland and kampung were bought up cheaply by speculators and the Municipality. In the following decade, in the face of strong popular protest, much of this land was cleared by duress of its inhabitants and laid out for modern suburban housing. Under a paternalist Municipality, the European elite transformed the city to suit a comfortable, middle-class suburban lifestyle. When world commodity prices collapsed in 1920, the city was left with so much excess capacity that the urban property market remained sluggish to the end of the colonial period. A large part of the modern-sector housing stock was then taken into government hands, rent controls were imposed, and the institutions of the private-property market gradually atrophied. Since the plantation economy had shot its bolt, no revival of private demand was possible until manufacturing took over as the new leading sector in the 1970s. Only then did private sector developers begin to reappear. The boom, however, coincided with reintegration to the global economy.

There was no causal link between the real estate booms of the 1910s and the 1990s. The similarity lies in the phenomenon and the mechanism. Speculation is like a mold: its spores are always present in markets and are usually benign, but under favorable conditions it can very quickly become rampant and destructive. Because of the volatile nexus with bank credit, urban land markets are an ideal breeding ground. In the prior decades of the 1900s and 1980s, economic expansion had the effect of gradually raising background moisture and temperature. The necessary local condition was the emergence of a middle class with enough critical mass in terms of effective purchasing power not only to create a current demand but also—and this is the critical point—to create expectations of sharply rising future demand. This is most likely when the current stock of quality housing is small, dated, and perhaps poorly located relative to a large pent-up and anticipated demand. In the 1910s Surabaya's European community was seeking to move out of the cramped and gloomy terraces of the lower town to the new salubrious garden suburbs, an aspiration shared by new arrivals. In the late 1980s and 1990s, ethnic Chinese were relocating from downtown shop-houses to suburban villas, upwardly mobile Indonesians were moving out of the kampungs, and these twin demands were reinforced by a rising expatriate demand for luxury housing and apartments. In both periods demand was driven not just by rising real income but by shifts in lifestyle. It was underpinned by expectations that rapid economic expansion would continue, giving middle-class consumers the confidence to pledge future income to expensive current assets. The other essential element was a set of market institutions to match latent consumer demand with consolidated land banks and to generate construction. In the 1900s the key innovation was the incorporated development company (bouwmaatschappij) and the willingness of banks and friendly societies, based on Dutch experience, to lend mortgage finance. The

Municipality hastened the process by itself acting as both developer and financier. In the late 1980s the trigger was capital market liberalization, which allowed private banks to compete both in financing development companies and in offering mortgage finance and also enabled the main developers to take out syndicated offshore loans. Thus all the conditions were created for a boom, that soon became a bubble, and led inevitably to the eventual bust.

Besides these economic cycles there has also been a political cycle. The late-colonial era was typified by what would now be known as economic development combined with political repression. While the Indies were rapidly being integrated with the world economy—opening the islands to new products, new markets, new opportunities for mobility, work and lifestyle, new fashions and ideas, transforming the very nature of society, the pattern of settlement and even the physical appearance of the country—the field of political action for educated Indonesians was being more and more circumscribed. When the colonial regime disintegrated in the 1940s, Indonesians reclaimed politics and identity. Authoritarian rule gave way to mass political mobilization. After Independence failed to usher in the socialist ideal, the original nationalist equation of x = *sovereignty* was respecified as x = *political* + *economic sovereignty*. Dutch nationals were expelled, then all other foreign-owned business was taken under state control. Nationalization of the modern sector subordinated capitalist economy to a nominally socialist state and society. In the name of neocolonialism Indonesia turned not only against the white rulers but also against the faceless economic regime that was seen as having been the substance of oppression. Low wages, long hours, and poor conditions were the product of colonial exploitation, not impersonal labor markets. There was seen to be no need to maintain an economic discipline and way of thinking because that too was part of colonial oppression. However hastily conceived and clumsily applied, Guided Democracy and its associated Guided Economy (see Tan 1967) were therefore logical responses to the contradictions of the colonial order and the unresolved tensions of the 1950s. The experiment nevertheless lasted barely six years. Its weaknesses were both economic and political. Disengagement from the world economy carried a high price in terms of economic dislocation. Artificial political stability was bought for a while by huge budget deficits and soaring inflation but rested on nothing more solid than Sukarno's health. When that failed, the regime quickly disintegrated and Sukarno was toppled.

The revolutionary tide of the 1940s turned in the mid-1960s amid the bloody showdown between the Army and the Communist Party. A traumatized country now welcomed the New Order goals of Stability and Development. Authoritarian rule was restored, mass politics suppressed, and technocrats brought in to reconnect Indonesia with the world economy. As markets were liberalized, not only for commodities but also for capital, labor, and land, a familiar kind of society reassembled itself in accordance with capitalist market forces like iron filings around a magnet. Probably without being conscious of the parallel, the New Order found itself reinventing the past, not as colonialism, for rule by an ethnic minority was no longer an option, but as an authoritarian state serving as handmaiden to capitalist economic development. Economically the results were spectacular; politically there was growing disenchantment.

As with the Ethical Policy after 1900, the common thread of state action ran through all New Order development policy. As drawn out in chapter 4, the most consistent theme of the whole twentieth century has been the penetration of government into daily life, the increasing role and burden of the state. Development, which has such positive connotations to those in power or serving it, has a more hollow and threatening ring to ordinary people. At the lower levels of society development means not empowerment but disempowerment, having things done to you without consultation or consent and, whatever the rhetoric, usually for the benefit of others. Development is a series of experiments in social engineering that do not stand the test of research ethics. The state applies all its power to insist that things be done in a certain way, however stupid or impractical, and when that does not work it tries something else. As Boeke was honest enough to recognize as long ago as 1927, mistakes are rarely admitted and almost never is there compensation (Boeke 1961). Ordinary people bear the cost and, if they are wise, keep quiet about it. Complaints lead to trouble.

Compared with the colonial state, the New Order was probably worse, because the power of coercion was greater and the scope for evasion less. The colonial state, usually in the form of the Municipality, did increasingly intervene in kampung life but only on the margin. Except for those on land owned by the Municipality, kampungs were not directly subject to local government. Kampung autonomy was, if nothing else, a right to be left alone. On the private estates tenants who duly paid their rent and met any other residual obligations were left even more to their own devices. Not until the Japanese occupation did the writ of the state penetrate to the kampung. Only under the New Order did it become effective. At the kampung level, Stability and Development were not just goals but a top-down process of rule. Stability began in 1966 with the so-called sweeps through the kampungs, a military euphemism for rounding up communists to be arrested and often murdered. "Reliable" people, often with a military background, were brought in to stiffen the local and kampung bureaucracy, so that there would be a smooth chain of command from the Ministry of Internal Affairs in Jakarta to each kampung neighborhood. Development policies could then be implemented with a clear line of authority. Anyone who protested stood to be accused of being a communist remnant, with potentially fatal consequences. The same applied to anyone foolhardy enough to challenge kampung or local officials for their petty embezzlements, which became rampant.

Coercion led easily to expropriation. The main battleground was land. In the case of road widening, the victims were mostly shophouse owners, who were obliged to set back and rebuild at their own expense. Though less common in Surabaya than in Jakarta, inner-city kampung dwellers were removed, either for want of proper title, in the case of squatter communities, or to make way for public or private development projects. Most widespread was conversion of farmland on the urban fringe to industrial or urban use. In the 1910s, after a series of bitter conflicts, the principle had been established that removal of kampung dwellers should be regulated by law. Procedures were established to determine rights of occupancy and the amount of compensation payable to extinguish such rights and fund relocation. This was at least due process. Under the New Order, lip service was paid to process but might usually prevailed. Offers of compensation bore little relationship to the value of the land or to the cost of relocation. Funds earmarked for compensation tended to shake loose into the pockets of bureaucrats all the way down the hierarchy. Kampung dwellers had no redress from an utterly corrupt legal system. Their unofficial leaders were always vulnerable to coercion. Under duress kampung dwellers thereby subsidized development projects, the revenues from which flowed through to the expanding middle class.

The struggle of kampung dwellers came to a head in the real estate booms of the 1910s and 1990s. These were like slow-motion earthquakes, during which urban land use was realigned with changed socioeconomic conditions. Here the very-long-term economic cycle, the changing pattern of urban land use, and social conflict all came into focus. In the late-colonial period social conflict could be portrayed sharply as that between a colonial elite and kampung-dwelling Indonesians. Under the New Order it has been more obviously between the advantaged and the disadvantaged, the former now more diffuse, the latter still kampung dwellers. The line was often drawn between the rich and the ordinary people (*wong cilik,* or *rakyat*), also known as the economically weak (*kaum ekonomi lemah*). The formulation was not primarily racial, because even where the rich were identified with Chinese-Indonesians, the primary fault line was still with Government: Them versus Us. Government here meant the state, the entire apparatus of the state over which ordinary people had no influence and by which they were oppressed.

From a kampung perspective the struggle with the New Order state perpetuates that with the former colonial state. The nationalist movement managed to focus popular energies on a struggle against the Dutch but the accumulation of anger and petty frustrations flowed from the state. Kampung dwellers recognized much sooner than the middle-class bureaucratic cadre that the New Order did not represent their interests. When Sukarno was toppled they lost their stake in the system. This can hardly be overemphasized. In the kampungs of Surabaya, Sukarno was a local hero, "one of us," like his popular minister Ruslan Abdulgani. Soeharto, by contrast, was always a usurper with blood on his hands, the blood of all those relatives, neighbors, and friends who died in the purge of 1966. He was never liked, never trusted, and his very occasional visits to Surabaya caused no ripple in popular consciousness. In the last years of the New Order he came to personify all that was wrong with the state: The Soeharto family and rich Chinese versus the People. In the national elections of June 1999, Surabaya voted overwhelming for Sukarno's daughter, Megawati Sukarnoputri, who inherited her father's aura and popular appeal.

A twentieth-century urban perspective on Indonesia's history thus suggests not a neat sequence of discrete periods—colonialism, Revolution, Old Order, New Order—but a dynamic interaction of very-long-term economic and political forces that still causes an ugly, lurching rhythm. An analogy is the motion of a leaking ship: for a time it may hold a listing course but a small disturbance may tilt it clumsily on the other side. Such a ship cannot be stabilized. Either it has to be pumped out or eventually it sinks. This view of the connection between the New Order and the colonial state, as also between the present and the Old Order, is more complex than continuity or parallelism, or indeed path dependency. Relations with the global economy are sufficient to generate parallelism; the internal dynamics of Indonesian society have given rise to a repeating cycle of reaction and revolution.

This very-long-term analysis also helps explain why the recent Asian crisis together with the domestic political crisis has in Indonesia been so severe and so prolonged. During 1998 the development miracle quickly dissipated. First, the fall of Soeharto was a crisis of authoritarian rule. His New Order had endured almost as long as the late-colonial regime, from the end of pacification in the mid-1900s to the Japanese invasion. Apart from a brief period in the 1950s, Indonesian society has known nothing but authoritarian rule and has been unable to devise a set of institutions to ensure a smooth transfer of power. In the late twentieth century this matters more. Legitimacy now depends not just on lineage and might but also on popular aspirations and international perceptions. This is not, of course, a specifically Indonesian problem.

Second, there is class conflict. The rhetoric of the Indonesian nationalism, the Constitution, and the democratic ideal give rise to an expectation that all citizens will enjoy equal political rights. The actual situation is that some are more equal than others, that the middle class, especially that non-Chinese part of it in living in Jakarta, expects political rights, though not necessarily to be shared with the people. The consumerist middle class has absorbed the old priyayi class of officials and literati. Thus demands for the rule of law, however worthy, are subliminally a demand for rule by the class that would administer the laws, namely the middle class, not a call to enfranchise the people. 'Rule of law' would allow the people to be protected by enlightened civil servants, which harks back to the late-colonial paradigm. The middle class is the class that knows what is best for the rest of society. What makes this distinction such a fault line in Indonesian society is that the middle class and the people live in different places and different types of communities. The middle class live on streets, in suburbs, or in housing estates—nuclear families leading individualized, consumerized, Westernized lifestyles where community is an afterthought; the people live in kampungs and villages as communities, as webs of mutual obligation. And even where suburbs and kampungs may be adjacent, as in Surabaya, middle-class people rarely set foot in those communities, which, except for language, are as foreign as to any Westerner and perhaps more threatening. The threat is not so much physical as psychic: we who live here know that you are a stranger, we deny the construction of your "modern," superior, self-satisfied, Westernized identity. More is at stake here than the distinction between working-class and middle-class communities in Europe, where a common aspiration is to be upwardly mobile. As strongholds of "the people" and the source of Indonesian nationalism, kampung communities hold a moral ascendancy over this dual society.

Third, there is a clash over economic orientation. As in the colonial period, the thrust of New Order development, was integration with the world market. The Jakarta-based technocrats were widely praised for their enlightened economic policies. Statistics showed impressive trends, which were certainly reflected in the tremendous gains in the size and prosperity of the urban middle class, whose members became increasingly cosmopolitan, learned English, gained a university education, traveled abroad, and accumulated consumer durables. Poverty trends suggest that the benefits of development did trickle down, as witnessed by the sharp decline in numbers living in absolute poverty. Nevertheless, village and kampung dwellers did not necessarily see themselves as better off. They were mindful of the greater availability of consumer goods, of motor vehicles, television, better opportunities for education, and improved health care. At the same time they were frustrated by the difficulties of earning a living. Full-time jobs were hard to obtain and, as the crisis layoffs showed so savagely, not at all secure. Those dependent on the informal sector were vulnerable to the relentless encroachment of the formal sector and its supporting apparatus of government policy and regulations. Other sources of frustration were the fragmentation of families and the decline of political and social morality. In short, they were not grateful.

Is the gap between statistics and popular perception simply one of different perceptions or are there different realities not captured in the statistics? One possibility is cognitive dissonance: people did not realize how much better off they were—or how much worse off they would have been without Development. Such views tend to boil down to the old patronizing attitude toward "stupid farmers" (*petani bodoh*). We (of education, status and power) know better what is best for You. This may help to explain why so much official effort went into collecting data and none into finding out what people were actually experiencing. Bureaucrats like the rest of their class confidently took for granted the notion of development as a linear, upward path of mobility and improvement. Their own experience confirmed it. Kampung dwellers, by contrast, tended to see prosperity and poverty as alternating conditions (Jellinek 1991). Hence they were skeptical of the rhetoric of liberalization and globalization, as indeed of Development itself. Fighting a daily battle for livelihood, kampung dwellers were very pragmatic. The crisis of the late 1990s revalidated their view of the world by crippling the modern sector and reinvigorating the informal sector. In Surabaya the cycle may have taken twenty years but it is still a cycle. Kampung dwellers therefore do not see globalization as either inevitable or desirable. Whatever the official statistics, for them the Sukarno years were not so bad, the Soeharto years not so good. They can now lobby through mass political parties for policies to promote small-scale activity, as described by the new phrase People's Economy. Such initiatives are rather derided by the development experts, and for some good reasons, but they represent popular aspiration for a more personalized economy.

Surabaya is not Jakarta. In Jakarta the forces of capital were almost unimpeded and ruthlessly supported—and exploited—by the state. In Surabaya municipal and provincial bureaucracies had more autonomy and were more responsive to social concerns. The Kampung Improvement Program (KIP), which in its New Order guise was pioneered in Surabaya, was followed through more vigorously and consistently, in its later phases with multilateral funding, and involved genuine participation. By the late 1980s most kampungs, including newer ones on the urban fringe, had been involved in the program and several had won prestigious international prizes. The neat and well-ordered appearance of the kampungs and the pride of residents in keeping them that way in turn made it more difficult to argue that they were slums needing to be demolished. The Municipality had a duty of care. This was not a fortuitous result. Johan Silas, the quietly spoken architect who was the driving force behind kampung improvement in Surabaya, promoted the scheme as a low-cost form of development but was also mindful of the long-term objective of gaining the commitment of the Municipality. If the mayor and his senior officials saw themselves as responsible for and proud of the city's kampungs, then developers would not have free rein. Surabaya was also fortunate in the critical 1980s to have as mayor Dr. Poernomo Kasidi, a medical doctor from a military background who had genuine concern for popular welfare. Ir. Moehtadi, a town planner who returned to Surabaya as head of the provincial planning board, was another influential figure. Thus without fuss a small, like-minded group of senior officials and academics managed in Surabaya fairly successfully to deflect the worst excesses of the New Order. They operated within its framework but sought to achieve the ideals of its early reformist years, not to facilitate the ruthless exploitation of its corrupt later years. Only in the 1990s, as the boom gathered strength, were there signs that this compromise was breaking down. The crisis of 1997–98 probably saved many kampungs from redevelopment.

It cannot be proven that Surabaya came through May 1998 without serious rioting because of a more enlightened approach to development. Elements in the military tried to provoke violence as early as 1996, when a Christian church was burned, and there was rioting in the far north of the city during the tense days of May 1998. Very likely the local business community had as rumored paid generously for military protection. In Jakarta and Solo, troops all but disappeared from the streets when the riots broke out, reappearing from barracks only after there had been great destruction. In Surabaya troops remained on station guarding key intersections and buildings. Money and military politics, including the absence of Special Forces (Kopassus) troops, may therefore explain a lot. As does better communication between student leaders, senior officials, and the military. Yet there was also the impression that mass actions on the streets were better controlled, whether during the period of student protests or subsequently during the wave of labor protests. Grievances were clearly stated, the target carefully chosen—usually the provincial or municipal assembly buildings—and there was rarely damage done along the way. These were not dangerous, sullen mobs. People seemed to realize that the problem lay in Jakarta. They would not easily be manipulated into burning their own city, in which they had genuine pride.

Which brings us to the present. There is no end to this story, because life goes on. The end of the century is as arbitrary as the beginning. Nevertheless, in 2001 there is a sense that the future will be different. Still a city on a human scale, Surabaya's experience suggests that there are other possibilities for a more socially integrated and environmentally benign society than the crass and ruthless Jakarta model of the New Order. The authoritarian-developmental phase of the New Order has ended. In June 1999 national elections gave ordinary people a voice in the political system. Demands for a more open and just political system, rule of law, and greater local autonomy are being realized. Perhaps the most interesting aspect is the greater prominence of Islam in public affairs. In Surabaya's kampungs for most of the twentieth century, Islam has been the vehicle for popular aspirations, for hopes of a better society. The affirmation of Islam under the New Order as a code of social morality was a way of rejecting the bland materialism of Development. A society in which ordinary people have a voice and modernist Islam is translated into social and economic policy will not be like the New Order. The kampung society of Surabaya, which generated the first great outburst of the Indonesian Revolution, supported left-wing parties in the Sukarno era, and in June 1999 overwhelmingly voted for Megawati and Islamic parties, may be a better place to look for the shape of a future Indonesia than the high-rise, air-conditioned, moral wastelands of Jakarta. The new era of local autonomy that began on 1 January 2001 gives Surabaya the best opportunity since Independence to assert its identity and chart its own course.

Appendix A

DUTCH FIRMS WITH INDUSTRIAL ESTABLISHMENTS IN SURABAYA, 1958

Taken over by Central Government

Machinefabriek Braat (general engineering)
P. A. Regnault's Verf, Inkt, & Blikfabrieken (paint)
W. A. Hoek's Machine- & Zuurstoffabriek (hydrochloric acid)
Boekhandel & Drukkerij G. Kolff & Co.; Boekhandel & Drukkerij G. C. T. van Dorp & Co. (commercial printing)
Ijs Maatschappij Petodjo (ice)
Begeer van Kempen & Vos (alpaca and luxury goods)
Verenigde Javasche Houthandel Mij (timber)
Van de Pol; HM Europa Azie (furniture)

Taken over by Provincial Government

MACHINERY AND ELECTRICAL

Ned-Indische Industrie; C.V. Machinefabriek de Vulkaan (general engineering)
Smalspoorwerkplaats Ducrobrauns Lindeteves (tramway equipment)
P. Bouman (automobile workshop)
Fa de Oosthonkid (machinery)

Stamefa; Pers & Stampwerk Ngagel (metal cans)
W. Wermuth; Fa Holvast & Co. (electrical and gas fittings)
J. Stokvis

CHEMICAL

HM Electro Galvano (galvanizing)
Surabaya Rubberfabriek Ngagel (rubber goods)
Ruhaak & Co. (paint)
Chemische Industrie & HM (sulfuric acid)
Javaasche Koolzuur (carbonic acid)

PRINTING

Soerabaiasche Handelsblad (newspaper)
De Malanger; Grafika (bibles)
E. Fuhri & Co.; Fa Venco (commercial)

GENERAL

De Ruiter; Maison Stolk (bakery)
Pelangi (biscuits)
HM Concern ter Wolde (chocolate)
HM Morton Java (confectionery)
J. C. van Drongelen (soft drinks)
Textielfabriek Bintang Pari (Bangil) (textiles)
Textielindustrie Java (canvas)
NICKI (firebricks)
Industrie & HM Karangpilang (tiles)
Ligtvoet (asbestos and marble tiles); Asbest (asbestos)
Accu Surabaya (batteries)
"Fiscal C.W." (bicycles)
Oliefabriek Ngagel (coconut oil)

Source: Siahaan 1996 (526–34)

Notes

CHAPTER 2

1. Daendels was a prominent republican who had risen to serve as general in both the French and republican Dutch armies (Schama 1992). In Java he laid the foundations for modern colonial government in place of the ramshackle administration of the collapsed VOC (Furnivall 1944).

2. The literature on the Cultivation System is vast and tortuous. Elson 1994, Fasseur 1975, and the collected writings of Robert Van Niel (1992) provide a good overview.

3. Furnivall 1944 is still a good overview. Creutzberg 1972–75 contains a vast amount of policy detail.

4. This section draws on *KKNS, HVS,* Kraus and de Jongh 1910, ENI 1918 (2:71–72), and Faber 1936.

5. In 1915 there were on Java some 582 private estates with a population of 1.8 million. Most lay in West Java in the residency of Batavia, and neither government nor the literature paid much attention to the rest. *ENI* 1919 (3:345–50) is a good overview and Rapport 1878 contains details of the early history of the estates around Surabaya. Summary statistics are available in *KV* (annual) and *RANI* (annual).

6. The following paragraphs draw on materials from the Oost Java Stoomtram Mij, which in 1912 bought a large estate on the outskirts of Surabaya for suburban development and the laying of tram lines. Two boxes of materials provide a wonderful insight into the troubled affairs of the estates during the 1910s, especially annual reports of the Dermo Land Development Company (Mij tot Exploitatie van Onroerende Goederen "Dermo"), correspondence, an account of difficulties with the inhabitants of the Dermo estate ("Overzicht der moeilijkheden met de opgezetenen op het land Dermo"), a transcript of the joint letter to the governor-general, and summaries of the legal cases involving Salekah and Prawirodihardjo (see ARA, OJS 2.20.16: 14, 20).

7. Sources for this section are Gonggrijp 1957 (153–57), HVS (annual), and ARA, NHM: Verslag (annual).

8. The rest of this section draws upon the source document Vreede 1926 and the excellent account by Ingleson (1986).

9. This paragraph draws on HVS and NHM annual reports and *IV* (annual).

10. The best source is a series of four semiannual reports compiled by A. G. Vreede, head of the Labour Office. Ingleson (1988) relies heavily on these. See also Boomgaard (2000).

11. Vreede (1931b, 248) nevertheless recognized that in the main cities there were "stranded" Indonesian workmen without families or support networks who would need to be treated in the same way as Europeans.

12. Dick (1981) gives some background on the appearance in the early to mid-1930s of small jitneys or autolettes as a cheap form of public transport. Many drivers were probably displaced tradesman.

13. Eng (1993b) estimates for Java and Madura that average per capita calorie supply recovered during the 1930s, almost back to the peak of 1920. The distributional impact is still problematic. See also Boomgaard (2000).

14. Gill 1957 is a good overview of the strategic situation; Vlekke 1945 (chap. 16) details the military preparations in the Indies.

15. This of course coincided with 7 December in Hawaii. The main sources for the rest of this section are Abeyasekere 1976 and ARA, MK (2.10.29, 409: Parindra), which contains a purported last testament of the nationalist party Parindra dated 20 February 1943. This document, reportedly found under a stairway in the governor's office after the hasty evacuation of the republican administration in November 1945, gives a fascinating overview from an Indonesian perspective of events from the outbreak of war with Japan to the end of the first year of the occupation.

16. ROD: IC 072 775 is a typed sheet in which a Tan Ing Hie of Jalan Tegalsarie no. 60 recorded day by day the frequency of Japanese bombings, as later, Allied bombings.

17. Soeparto Brata (1983) gives February 1943 as the first Allied raid.

18. A Japanese version of these events by the commanding officer in Surabaya is Shibata 1986.

19. This account of the fighting draws mainly upon Soeparto Brata 1983, esp. chap. 5. Broeshart et al. 1997 is a good photographic record.

20. Unless otherwise acknowledged, the next few paragraphs are based on BVZ monthly reports (ARA, MK 2.10.29, 447–50).

21. The development of the military situation in East Java after the first Police Action is described in monthly *situatie rapporten* (situation reports) (ARA, MK 2.10.29, 396) and, from March 1949 onward, in *weeko-*

verzichten (weekly overviews) by van der Plas, the civilian head of government (Recomba) (ARA, MK 2.10.29, 397). The economic situation is covered from March 1948 by monthly reports from the East Java representative of the Department of Economic Affairs, Agriculture, and Food (ARA, MK 2.10.29, 408).

22. The enigmatic Charles O. van der Plas (1891–72) was one of the outstanding figures of the last two decades of Dutch colonial rule but apart from Frederick (1994) has been all but ignored in historical writing. Governor of East Java from 1936, he escaped with van Mook to Australia in March 1942 and became a key figure in the government in exile. In 1945–46 he was the intermediary in negotiations with Mountbatten and the British forces in Java. After taking back the reins in East Java as commissioner (recomba) in August 1947, he was one of the main architects of the federal system, which drew on his great knowledge and subtlety. Indonesians respected him but were wary of his talent for manipulation (Kahin 1952, 379n).

23. Kahin 1952 is still a good account of the tortuous process by which the Dutch were dragged to the negotiating table.

24. For background on national politics from 1949 to 1957 see Feith 1962.

25. These estimates were contained in a memo to the high commissioner in Jakarta by J. van der Zwaal, "Aantal Nederlanders in Oost Java," 23 June 1953. This was made available to me by courtesy of Mr. B. van der Zwan of the ARA.

26. Overt anti-Chinese feeling had emerged after March 1956 with the birth of the Assaat Movement of indigenous businessmen (Feith 1962, 481–87). This movement cut across efforts to give the locally born (*peranakan*) Chinese a political voice through the formation in 1954 of the Baperki Party and to resolve the problem of the alien Chinese by the 1955 dual-citizenship treaty with China (Somers 1964, chap. 1; also Siauw 1984).

27. Cribb 1991 is the best survey of events in Java and Bali. Abeyasekere (1987) and Jellinek (1991) both suggest that repression in Jakarta was relatively mild. Although their sources are too patchy for this generalization to be accepted with confidence, Surabaya's communist-controlled municipal government and its strategic importance as a naval base made it an obvious target.

28. From 1965 onward the macroeconomic situation is charted by the four-monthly "Survey of Recent Developments" in the *Bulletin of Indonesian Economic Studies.*

CHAPTER 3

1. The lag may be exaggerated by heavy underenumeration of Surabaya's kampung population in the 1920 census. Between 1920 and 1930 the Indonesian population appears to have grown 6.2 percent per annum, compared with just 1.2 percent between 1905 and 1920 (Steele 1980, 47; Frederick 1989, n18).

2. The population of 20 million cited elsewhere for Greater Jakarta includes another 3 million rural inhabitants (BPS, Supas 1995a).

3. Market analysts sometimes cite the population of Surabaya and immediate environs as 5 million, adding in the rural population of Sidoarjo and Gresik, which no doubt contributes to the estimated daily flow into the city of seven hundred thousand commuters (*SP,* 13/7/95). The number of seasonal workers also continues to be uncertain. The Master Plan Team estimated that such workers might have added another 25 percent to the population at the 1971 census (KMS 1978, 15).

4. The equivalent participation rate (excluding unemployed) was 37 percent for the Chinese population and only 34 percent for Europeans, who had the best access to secondary education and, with their high incomes, could also best afford to support nonworking wives.

5. Squatters may in time form recognized kampung communities. This is partly a matter of internal cohesion and partly of outward manifestations, such as an officially sanctioned kampung government and official slogans emblazoned around the entrances to the pathways leading into the kampung. A squatter kampung, almost a contradiction in terms, poses an awkward dilemma for officials of the city government (see chaps. 4, 6).

CHAPTER 4

1. The bupati of Kabupaten Surabaya (later Gresik) maintained his office in the city on Jalan Genteng Kali until the 1950s.

2. Tiled roofs had been mandatory since 1860 on grounds of fire prevention but the measure had never been enforced (Faber 1931, 107). In consequence of the plague measures, red-tiled roofs are still characteristic of all urban kampungs in the city.

3. The old Simpang hospital remained in subsidiary use until the early 1980s. After lying vacant for some time it was demolished to make way for the Surabaya Plaza shopping mall, which opened in 1988. The last

link to this historic institution is the well-known Apotik (Pharmacy) Simpang on the corner of Jalan Pemuda and Tunjungan.

4. This casual-sex industry would have been much larger if the army and navy had not for health reasons encouraged concubinage as quasi-marriage (Ming 1983).

5. Faber (1931, 243) erroneously attributes the quote to d'Almeida (1864). The correct source is unknown.

6. One of the first tasks of the new section was to translate into Malay some of the more important municipal bylaws (SGS 1928, 109–10). That they had hitherto been unintelligible to kampung society says a great deal about colonial Surabaya.

7. Kampung improvement was later defined to encompass works such as road improvement, the paving of footpaths and kampung lanes along with storm gutters, drains, and local sanitary works but to exclude major sanitary works, housing improvements, malaria control, street lighting, and cemeteries (POJ 1938, 60). Roadways were determined to be inappropriate, the norm being pathways for pedestrians and cyclists (SGS 1930, 315–16; KVC 1939, 28).

8. The flavor of the clash between well-intentioned engineers and social reality can be found in *Locale Techniek*, March 1934, 44–45.

9. As a matter of record, the original eleven markets were Genteng, Turi, Bong, Pabean, Peneleh, Kalianjar, Pegirian, Ampel, Keputran, Babaan, and Kapasan.

10. Sons of high-ranking Indonesian officials (regents) had long enjoyed the privilege of access to Dutch schools as a step to the three Training Schools for Native Officials (Opleidingscholen voor Inlandsche Ambtenaren, OSVIA) in Bandung, Magelang, and Probolinggo (Sutherland 1979, 16–17). Opportunities for the sons of lower priyayi had been limited to the Dokter Jawa (Native Doctor) school in Jakarta and teacher-training schools (*kweekscholen*).

11. The city's first trades school had opened in 1853 (Faber 1931, 265). This private venture soon withered but in an industrial city it had met an obvious need and was succeeded in 1862 by a government institution that from 1877 to 1912 operated as the Burgeravondschool (Faber 1931, 268, 275).

12. This is well illustrated by the faithfulness with which forms, regulations, and the collection of statistics were carried on as before, albeit in Indonesian translation.

13. I am grateful to Johan Silas (pers. comm.) for this insight, as also below clarifying the confusing parallel histories of Opera and the YKP.

14. Most of the information in this and the following paragraph is

taken from information provided by the Kantor (later Dinas) Urusan Perumahan in November 1987.

15. Dengue fever (*demam berdarah*) was again reported in Surabaya in 1968 and has become an annual epidemic at the beginning of the wet season. The fatality rate of about 4.5 percent affects mainly young children; for adults the disease is debilitating and often requires hospitalization. Its vector, the small mosquito *Aedes aegypti,* breeds in clear freshwater, flies no more than about a hundred meters, and settles indoors. Its ability to breed in tiny pockets of water makes eradication virtually impossible (*JP,* 21,27/11/87; *SP,* 11,13/11/86, 1/12/87, 29/3/95, 17/11/95).

16. A controversial project by PT Mandala Citra Umbulan (Tommy Soeharto) to pipe water from the Umbulan springs in the foothills was abandoned in late May 1998 after the downfall of President Soeharto (*SP,* 27/5/98, 27/6/98).

17. Some kampungs, as in the northwest of the city, still have no access to the reticulated water supply and have to buy water containers or drums of water from hawkers.

18. This and the following paragraph draw on interview with engineer and planner Ir. Eddy Indrayana (14/11/87).

19. Pasar Turi was ill-fated. Both new blocks were destroyed by fire in May 1978. In 1980 work began on a bigger replacement project (KMS/Repelita IV, 12.3–12.7).

CHAPTER 5

1. Also referring to Hageman, Faber (1931, 184–5) identifies a workforce in 1859 of only thirty-five thousand, of which about 12 percent may be determined as engaged in industrial activities. However, these data, published by Hageman (1852), refer to the late 1840s.

2. The Wonokromo refinery served the nearby small Djabakota field, the first in Indonesia to be brought into commercial production (*ENI* 1919, 396). The main product was kerosene for use in lighting but byproducts included gasoline, lubricating oil, and heavy residue used by some local factories in place of coal (KV 1890–95).

3. For firms with multiple plants or multiple activities, the local urban component is not identified; coverage of small and household enterprise is uneven, and many firms are listed without the number of employees.

4. ENI (1921, 760) refers to a permanent workforce at the naval base of two hundred Europeans and three thousand Indonesians, plus between

three and eight hundred day laborers. The size of the floating coolie workforce underlines the difficulty, which also shows up in the 1930 census (see chap. 3), of any accurate enumeration of the industrial workforce. The arsenal (sixteen hundred workers) was transferred to Bandung in 1918, so little of its reported workforce may have been left in Surabaya but, against this, no employment figures are recorded for the new drydock company, whose workforce must have approached a thousand (ENI 1921, 761), and several other large firms. On balance a total of around ten thousand for all engineering workshops is likely to be fairly accurate.

5. The naval base and some engineering firms also had woodworking shops, whose workforce is counted under metalworking. Table 5.3 excludes the state prison, which employed about seven hundred prisoners in activities such as cabinetmaking, forging, and pressing tin cans.

6. In 1932 the government brought forward some capital works programs such as rail bridge replacement and placed orders in the Indies instead as previously in the Netherlands (*EWNI,* 25/1/47, 63). These helped to tide over a few engineering firms but the overall impact of reduced government spending and higher real taxation was pro-cyclical.

7. Indonesia was not unusual in remaining a controlled economy well beyond the end of the Second World War. There was no rush to dismantle wartime controls after 1945. Socialist governments believed as a matter of principle that private enterprise ought to be regulated. In Western Europe reconstruction under Marshall aid required bureaucratic intervention as a practical matter.

8. By early 1948 the Martak factory had only 135 hand looms in operation out of a capacity of 600 to 700, the rest of its 2,000 prewar looms having been removed by the Japanese (EWI 1948: 419).

9. Plans for a 120,000-tonne cement plant at Gresik had been announced in 1938 by the trading house Borsumij and the power company ANIEM, with Lindeteves to be involved in distribution (NHM 1944, 81). Indonesia's first cement plant had been opened in 1912 at Padang (West Sumatra)—by 1940 capacity was 340,000 tonnes.

10. The local Heineken subsidiary, Java Brouwerij, had established NV Nederlandsch-Indische Glas Fabrieken (Niglas) in November 1941 to produce glass bottles but war intervened. The project was revived in 1949, deferred in 1950, and finally, in 1956, sold via Bank Industri Negara to PN Iglas (Heineken's 1939–46, 1955; Siahaan 1996, 253).

11. Information in this paragraph is also taken from the local press (*Jawa Pos, Surabaya Post*) and from documentation of the photograph collection of Arsip Nasional.

12. This paragraph is based on interviews in Holland in 1987 with the late Dirk Schaap, former manager of the plant in Surabaya.

13. In East Java the thirty-thousand-spindle Grati spinning mill near Pasuruan opened in October 1965 but construction of the Petrokimia fertilizer plant at Gresik, which began in August 1964 with Italian aid, was suspended—the first stage eventually opened in July 1972 (*SP,* 2/10/65; Siahaan 1996, 452; Petrokimia Gresik ca.1987).

14. This modus operandi was explained by businessmen interviewed in Surabaya in 1987.

15. By 1985 the public sector in Surabaya accounted for only 3 percent of the number of L and M manufacturing firms, though because several were very large, the share of employment was 12 percent and of value added 19 percent (calculated from BPS, *Sensus ekonomi* 1986, tapes).

16. The following analysis is based on the BPS, *Statistik industri* series for L and M establishments, which has the great advantage of being revised back to 1976 on the basis of the 1986 economic census. Little can be gained from earlier published data. Before 1974 medium-scale establishments were classified differently, not as twenty to ninety-nine employees but as five or more employees with power, or ten or more employees without power (McCawley and Tait 1979). The industrial census of 1964 (BPS 1970) offers no data below the provincial level.

17. The decision to proceed was taken in 1972, the land acquired during 1973, and in 1974 vested in the limited liability company PT SIER (Fatima 1981). In the late 1980s a large extension was made across the border into the subdistrict of Berbek, Sidoarjo.

18. The situation as of 1985 is mapped in Dick 1993b.

19. The other high-tech strategic enterprises, all located in Bandung, were the aircraft manufacturer Nurtanio, the arms factory Pindad (which had its origins as the military arsenal in Surabaya—see above), and the railway workshop INKA.

CHAPTER 6

1. Hitherto the small Dutch settlement at Surabaya had been subsidiary to the company's trading establishment at nearby Gresik, which was closer to the vital artery of the Solo River.

2. Bouwmaatschappij means literally building or construction company. Larger firms might be described as developers, or, in contemporary Indonesian parlance, real estate companies.

3. A similar pattern could be observed on the western side, around Sawahan. The most accessible land was taken up by European housing, while further west large plots were taken up for special uses, such as the Native Court (Landraad), schools, the racetrack, and the tram depot and workshops.

4. Jessup (1988) details the main architectural trends, the practitioners, and their buildings in late-colonial Indonesia.

5. Dating from 1813, the Masonic Lodge had been the earliest European building on Tunjungan; since 1850 "de Club," patronized by English and German residents, had stood on the corner of Tunjungan and Embong Malang (fig. 6.4) (Faber 1931, 309, 358).

6. As established in 1906, the municipality had been just 43 square kilometers, which increased to 53 square kilometers in 1911 and 63 square kilometers in 1924 (SGS, annual).

7. In the mid-1990s the official area was increased to 326 square kilometers (KMS, SDA 1995); provincial sources continue to cite 274 square kilometers (*KSP* 1993).

8. On evolution of the town planning framework after Independence, see Niessen 1999.

9. The map is too detailed to reproduce but the updated land use plan to 2005 can be found below as map 6.7.

10. Perhaps by force of habit, the older steam tram continued to run twice daily from the Madura ferry to the Wonokromo bridge and Sepanjang until the 1980s.

CHAPTER 7

An earlier version of this chapter, without the historical introduction but with more detailed analysis of trade data, appeared as Dick 1995.

1. In 1929 Surabaya handled 97 percent (99 percent in 1939) of East Java's imports and around 70 percent of exports (CKS, *Jaaroverzicht*). Without sugar exports diminished, outports lost their base cargo. Pasuruan, which lay closest to Surabaya, ceased to be a deep-sea port of call. Probolinggo and Panarukan remained open in season for the shipment of tobacco. After 1987 tobacco was shipped by container through Surabaya, leaving outports with just low-value residual exports. In 1999, Surabaya (including Gresik, Juanda airport, and the post office) accounted for 98 percent of East Java's exports and 86 percent of imports (BPS, *Exports/Imports*).

2. Paauw (1967, 168) for 1958 estimated average actual rates that adjusted for export taxes and import surcharges. Exporters then received only about 45 percent of the rupiah rate paid out by importers. Applying these adjusted rates to Surabaya's trade figures for 1958 would boost the ratio of exports to imports from 28 percent to 64 percent. Unfortunately, adjusted rates are not available for other years.

3. These reports use an archaic unit of measurement, the last, which may be taken on average to be about two manifest tons (the greater of either weight or volume): one last equaled about twenty sacks of rice or sugar (2 tonnes), 1.8 tonnes of rubber, and 1.2 tonnes of copra. All this makes KPM figures difficult to compare with other sources but does not greatly distort time trends or composition.

4. Opportunities for physical smuggling were much fewer than in the Outer Islands. The main distortion was probably the widespread practice of under-invoicing imports, thereby reducing the recorded deficit on foreign trade.

Glossary

alun-alun	Town square, traditionally in front of the ruler's palace.
AMACAB	Allied Military Administration, Civil Affairs Branch (1946–49).
ANIEM	(Algemeene Nederlandsch-Indische Electriciteit Maatschappij). The General Netherlands Indies Electricity Company.
apotik	A pharmacy.
arak	Rum.
arek Surabaya	(Suroboyo). The people (lit., children) of Surabaya.
atap	Palm thatch.
Bahasa	(Bahasa Indonesia). The national language of Indonesia.
Baperki	(*Ba*dan *Per*musyawaratan *K*ewarganegaraan *I*ndonesia). The Indonesian Citizens Discussion Association, the integrationist Indonesian-Chinese political party (before 1966).
Bappeda	(*Ba*dan *P*erencanaan *Pe*mbangunan *Da*erah). Regional Planning Office.
BAT	British-American Tobacco; a multinational cigarette producer.
becak	A three-wheeled pedicab.
bemo	(*be*cak *mo*tor). A jitney (originally three-wheeled).
benedenstad	A lower town (including port and central business district).
BM	Bouwmaatschappij (q.v.).

bouwmaatschappij	A real estate or development (lit., building) company.
bupati	Regent (of a kabupaten).
BVZ	(Kantoor voor Bevolkingszaken). The Office of People's Affairs (1946–49).
dalem	A palace.
dokar	A pony cart (lit., dog cart), horse-drawn public passenger conveyance.
DPRD	(Dewan Perwakilan Rakyat Daerah). A local people's representative assembly, provincial or municipal.
FDT	The manufacturing sector that produces food, drink, and tobacco.
Fl	(florijn). Guilder.
gemeente	A municipality (colonial era).
godown	A warehouse.
HCS	(Hollandsch-Chineesche School). A Dutch-language primary school for Chinese people.
HIS	(Hollandsch-Inlandsche School). A Dutch-language primary school for Indonesians.
IMF	The International Monetary Fund.
Ir	Ingenieur: A university graduate in engineering, architecture or science.
ITS	(Institut Teknologi Surabaya). The Surabaya Institute of Technology.
Jabotabek	A conurbation of Jakarta and surrounding districts (*Ja*karta-*Bo*gor-*Ta*ngerang-*Bek*asi) that comprise Greater Jakarta.
jalan	A street (e.g., Jalan Niaga).
kabupaten	A district.
kali	A river or canal (e.g., Kali Mas).
kampung	An urban village.
kecamatan	A subdistrict.
KIT	(Koninklijk Instituut voor de Tropen). Royal Tropical Institute.

KITLV	(Koninklijk Instituut voor Taal-, Land- en Volkenkunde). Royal Institute of Linguistics and Anthropology.
KPM	(Koninklijke Paketvaart Maatschappij). The Royal Packet Company, the Dutch owned inter-island shipping firm.
kretek	A clove cigarette.
krupuk	A shrimp cracker.
L and M	Large and medium (referring to the scale of an enterprise).
Landraad	The "Native" or Magistrates' Court.
lighter	An unpowered vessel used mainly to transfer cargo between ship and shore.
Mij	(Maatschappij). A company.
MULO	(Meer Uitgebreid Lager Onderwijs). A junior high school.
NHM	(Nederlandsch Handel Maatschappij). The Netherlands Trading Company.
NV	(Naamlooze Vennootschap). A limited liability company.
OJS	(Oost Java Stoomtram Mij). The East Java Steam Tram Company.
Oosthoek	The east end (corner) of Java, lying east of Probolinggo.
Opera	(*O*esaha *Pe*rumahan *Ra*kyat). The Public Housing Venture.
Pancasila	Sukarno's Five Principles, the state ideology of the New Order.
pasar	A market.
Pasarbedrijf	The (Municipal) Market Authority; see *PD Pasar*.
pasisir	(also *pesisir*). The north coast of Java.
PD	(Perusahaan Dareah). A regional government enterprise.
PD Pasar	The Municipal Market Enterprise (formerly Pasarbedrijf).

Pelni	(*Pel*ayaran *N*asional *I*ndonesia). The state-owned interisland shipping line.
pemuda	A revolutionary (armed) youth of late 1945.
Permesta	(*Per*juangan Se*mesta*). Total Struggle, the late-1950s uprising in Sulawesi.
Perumnas	(Perusahaan Pembangunan *Perum*ahan *Na*sional). The National Housing Corporation.
picul	A measure of weight (just over 60 kg.) used throughout Southeast Asia.
PKI	(Partai Komunis Indonesia). The Indonesian Communist Party.
PLN	(Perusahaan Listrik Negara). The state electricity company.
PN	(Perusahaan Negara). A state (central government) enterprise.
PNI	(Partai Nasionalis Indonesia). The Indonesian Nationalist Party.
prahu	A sail-powered, wooden-hulled interisland or river vessel.
pribumi	Indigenous.
priyayi	An Indonesian aristocrat-official; also, well-educated.
PT	(Perusahaan Terbatas). A limited liability company.
Raad van Justitie	Supreme Court.
recomba	(Regeeringscommissaris voor Bestuursaangelegenheden). A (civilian) commissioner for administrative affairs; equivalent to a prewar provincial governor.
repelita	(*re*ncana *pe*mbangunan *li*ma *ta*hun). A five-year plan.
rust en orde	Law (lit., peace) and order.
Sarekat Islam	The Muslim League (founded in 1912).
sate	Barbecued meat on a skewer.
sawah	Rice fields. May be planted with sugar cane or other crops.

societeit	A club.
soos	Contraction of *societeit* (q.v.).
soto	A clear soup of meat and vegetables.
Supas	(*Su*rvei *P*enduduk *a*ntar *S*ensus). The Intercensal Population Survey.
Susenas	(*Su*rvei *S*osial *E*konomi *Nas*ional). The National Socioeconomic (expenditure and welfare) Survey.
tambak	(Fish or salt) ponds.
TCF	The manufacturing sector that produces textiles, clothing, and footwear.
VOC	(Verenigde Oostindische Compagnie). The United East India Company.
Volkshuisvesting, NV	The Public Housing Corporation.
wali	A revered Muslim religious leader; also prime minister of a negara (1948–50).
warung	A street seller's stall.
YKP	(Yayasan Kas Pembangunan). Lit. Development Fund Foundation, the municipal housing fund.

Bibliography

The bibliography has been divided into four sections: Maps, Periodicals, Government and Corporate Documents, and Books and Articles. Periodicals and documents are arranged alphabetically by the appropriate acronym (followed by the complete name in parentheses), since all sources in those sections are cited that way in text.

MAPS

El Sena, CV. 1997. *Kotamadya Dati II Surabaya menuju metropolitan.* Surabaya. 1: 28,000.

Gemeente Surabaja (Surabaya municipality). 1940. Kon. Instituut voor de Tropen.

KMS. 1977. Team Master Plan, *Surabaya 2000.* May. 1: 30,000.

———. 1986. *Peta penggunaan tanah Kotamadya Dati II Surabaya* (Land use map, municipality of Surabaya). Surabaya: Dinas Tata Kota. 1: 40,000.

Pembina, PT. 1963. *Surabaja* (street plan). 1: 13,200.

PERIODICALS

Business Times. Singapore. Daily.

ERI Economic Review of Indonesia. Department of Economic Affairs, Batavia. Monthly (1947–53).

EWI Economische Weekblad voor Indonesië. Weekly.

EWNI Economische Weekblad voor Nederlandsch-Indië. Weekly.

IDN Indonesian Development Newsletter. Department of Information, Jakarta. Bimonthly.

JC Javasche Courant (Colonial Government Gazette). Batavia.

JP Jawa Pos (JP). Surabaya. Daily.

Kompas. Jakarta. Daily.

New York Times. Daily.

NC Nieuwe Courant. Surabaya. Daily.

PI Properti Indonesia. Jakarta. Monthly.

SA Soeara Asia. Surabaya. Daily.

SH Soerabaiasch Handelsblad. Surabaya. Daily.

Suara Pembaruan. Jakarta. Daily.

SP Surabaya Post. Surabaya. Daily.

GOVERNMENT AND CORPORATE DOCUMENTS

AGS (Allied Geographic Section). 1945. *Southwest Pacific Area: Surabaya Area, East Java*. Special report no. 71.

ARA (Algemeen Rijksarchief Tweede Afdeeling, The Hague). *Algemene Secretarie (AS) van de Nederlands Indische Regeering, geheim en kabinetsarchief, Deel 2* (General Secretariat of the Netherlands Indies government, secret and cabinet archive, Part 2). 1944–50. (2.10.14)

3531. *Stukken betreffende de problemen met de waterstaatkundige toestand in de Sidoarjo-delta als gevolg van Republikeense akties* (Items concerning the problems with water conditions in the Sidoarjo delta in consequence of Republican actions).

1.I.45.1. Commanding Officer AMACAB, Surabaya, Dr F. W. T. Hunger to Lieutenant Governor-General, Batavia, 21 August 1946.

ARA, MK: *Ministerie van Kolonien:*

2.10.29. Rapportage Indonesia. (1945–50).

396. *(Zeer) geheime situatierapporten opgestelde op het centraal kantoor van de Recomba* ([Very] secret situation reports prepared at the central office of the commissioner for East Java). (Monthly, 1947–49).

397. *(Zeer) geheime weekoverzichten samengesteld door de Recomba en de tijdelijke bestuursadviseur* ([Very] secret weekly overviews prepared by the commissioner and the acting government adviser). (Weekly, March–November 1949).

408. *Economische overzichten samengesteld door vertegenwoordiger Oost Java van de Departemen van Economische Zaken* (Economic overviews pre-

pared by the East Java representative of the Department of Economic Affairs). (Monthly, March 1948–July 1949).

409. Diverse stukken betreffende Oost Java (Miscellaneous items concerning East Java).

Memorandum, dd. 30/1/46, Batavia [report on the political situation in East Java, probably by van der Plas].

MR 699/AP03 geheim dd. 3/5/46 (Parindra): *Afscheidswoord van het Dagelijks Bestuur van der Parindra* (Final report of the executive committee of Parindra), dd. 20/2/43.

447–50. Verslagen betreffende de stedelijk bestuursorganisatie in Soerabaja samengesteld door de (Kantoor voor Bevolkingszaken, BVZ). (Reports concerning the urban government in Surabaya prepared by the Office of People's Affairs). (1946–49).

2.10.36. *Mail Rapport (MR), Verbaal (V) and Geheime Verbaal (GV)*:

02: MR 2351/22, *Toelichting op de conclusies genomen door het Volkshuisvesting Congres op 15 tot 17 April 1922 te Semarang gehouden* (Report on the conclusions of the Public Housing Congress held at Semarang). 16 June 1922.

04: V 3–9–35: *Bedrijfsreglemeteering sigarettenfabrieken* (Regulation of cigarette factories).

051: GV 25/4/40 (H26): *Stichting van een chemische industrie in Nederlandsch-Indië* (Establishment of a chemical industry in the Netherlands Indies).

V 20–10–1869–4: *Statistiek van Java en Madoera 1862–1867: Statistiek der residentie Kediri.*

V 20–10–1869–4: *Statistiek van Java en Madoera 1862–1867: Statistiek der residentie Soerabaja.*

ARA, KJCJL 2.29.58.02: Koninklijke Java-China-Japan Lijn: Jaarverslagen van de vertegenwoordingen en agentschappen over 1948: Soerabaja.

ARA, KPM 2.20.58.01: Koninklijke Paketvaart Maatschappij: Jaaverslag van der agentschap Soerabaia. Annual.

ARA, NHM 2.20.01: Nederlandsche Handelmaatschappij: Verslag van den Agent te Soerabaia. Annual.

"De industrialisatie in Nederlandsch-Indië na 1918." Internal report, Amsterdam, 1944.

ARA, OJS 2.20.16: Oost Java Stoomtram Maatschappij, NV: Jaarverslag van de chef de exploitatie (Annual report of the head of operations). Annual. (006–010.)

ARA, OJS, Dermo. 1913–23. Maatschappij tot exploitatie van Onroerende Goederen "Dermo" (Real Estate Company "Dermo"). Jaarverslagen. (020, no. 328.)

———. Verzet. 1913–19. Rechtstoestanden van het land Dermo: Verzet der Opgezetenen van de landen Dermo en Groedo West (Legal conditions of the Dermo estate: Resistance of the inhabitants of the Dermo and Groedo West estates). (014, no. 312.)

ARA, vdPlas 2.21.266.130: van der Plas:

Briefwisseling van der Plas met de CO-AMACAB in Soerabaja inzake de algemeen situatie, de personeelvoorziening en de organisatie van het bestuur [Correspondence between van der Plas and the Allied Commander in Surabaya concerning the general situation, personnel, and government organization], Nov.1945–Aug.1946.

Rijksinstituut voor Oorlogsdocumentatie, Amsterdam (RIOD):

IC 072 775 (Tan Ing Hie): Report on bombing raids.

BIS (Bank Indonesia, Surabaya). 1997. *Statistik ekonomi-keuangan daerah propinsi Jawa Timur* (Economic and financial statistics for the province of East Java). Surabaya, February.

BPS (Biro Pusat Statistik; Central Statistical Bureau).

———. *Statistik industri* (Industry statistics). 1970–. Jakarta. Annual.

———. 1970. *Sensus perindustrian, 1964: Hasil pengolahan sektor industry besar dan sedang, Jawa Timur* (Industry census 1964: Large and medium establishments, East Java). Jakarta.

———. ca. 1977. *Lalu-lintas antar pulau* 1974 (Interisland traffic). Jakarta.

BPS 1984b. *Perpindahan Penduduk antar Propinsi: Hasil Sensus Penduduk 1980* [Interprovincial Migration: Results of the 1980 Population Census], Series S-4, Jakarta.

BPS 1984a. *Lalu-lintas angkutan antar pulau, 1983* (Interisland cargo traffic). Jakarta.

———. 1986. *Sensus ekonomi* (Economic census). Data tapes.

———. 1996. *Sensus ekonomi* (Economic census). Data tapes.

———. 1998a. *Sensus ekonomi 1996: Hasil pencacahan lengkap, Jawa Timur* (Results of the complete count, East Java). Jakarta.

———. 1998b. *Sensus ekonomi 1996: Profil perusahaan tidak berbadan hukum, Jawa Timur* (Profile of legal establishments without legal status: East Java). Jakarta.

———. *Statistical Pocketbook of Indonesia (SPI).* Jakarta. Annual.

———. *Exports: Indonesian Foreign Trade Statistics.* 2 vols. Jakarta. Annual.

———. *Imports: Indonesian Foreign Trade Statistics.* 2 vols. Jakarta. Annual.

BPS. Supas (Survei penduduk antar sensus; Intercensal population census). 1985. Jakarta. Data tapes.

———. 1995a. *Penduduk Jakarta: Hasil survei penduduk antar sensus 1995.* Series S2.09. Jakarta.

———. 1995b. *Penduduk Jawa Barat: Hasil survei penduduk antar sensus 1995.* Series S2.10. Jakarta.

———. 1995c. *Penduduk Jawa Timur: Hasil survei penduduk antar sensus 1995.* Series S2.13. Jakarta.

BPS. Susenas (Survei Sosial Ekonomi Nasional; National socioeconomic survey). 1981. Jakarta. Data tapes.

Braat, Machinefabriek, NV. *Jaarverslag* (Annual report). Surabaya.

CBS (Central Bureau of Statistics). 1947. *Statistical Pocket Book of Indonesia, 1941.* Batavia.

CEI (Changing Economy of Indonesia). 1975. *Indonesia's Export Crops, 1816–1940.* The Hague: Nijhoff.

———. 1978. *Rice Prices.* Ed. P. Creutzberg. The Hague: Nijhoff.

———. 1991a. *General Trade Statistics, 1822–1940.* Amsterdam: Royal Tropical Institute.

———. 1991b. *Population Trends, 1795–1942.* Amsterdam: Royal Tropical Institute.

Census. 1905. "Sterkte de bevolking volgens de opneming van 1905." *Koloniaal Verslag 1907.* Annex A/II.

———. 1920. *Uitkomsten der in de maand November 1920 gehouden volkstelling* (Results of the November 1920 population census). 2 vols. Kantoor voor de Volkstelling, Ruygrok, Batavia, 1922.

———. 1933–36. *Volkstelling 1930.* 8 vols. Departement van Landbouw, Nijverheid en Handel (later Economische Zaken). Batavia. Vol. 3, *Native Population, East Java* (1933); vol. 4, *Europeans* (1935); vol. 7, *Chinese and Other Foreign Orientals* (1935); vol. 8, *Summary* (1936).

———. 1963. *Penduduk Indonesia 1961: Angka-angka tetap* (Population census 1961: Final figures). Jakarta: BPS.

———. 1974. *Sensus penduduk 1971: Series E.* Jakarta: BPS.

———. 1980. *Sensus penduduk 1980.* Jakarta: BPS. Data tapes.

———. 1992. *Penduduk Indonesia: Hasil sensus penduduk 1990.* Series S-2. Jakarta: BPS.

———. 2000a: East Java: Population by kabupaten and sex, print-out, BPS, Jakarta, February 2001.

———. 2000b: *Penduduk Indonesia: Hasil sensus penduduk 2000.* Series RBL1.1. Jakarta: BPS, December.

CKS (Centraal Kantoor voor de Statistiek). 1921–27. *Meerjarige overzicht van de in- en uitvoer van Nederlandsch-Indië* (Annual summary of the imports and exports of N.I.). Batavia.

———. 1928–40. *Jaaroverzicht van de in-en uitvoer van Nederlandsch-Indië, Batavia.*

DBOW (Departement van Burgerlijke Openbare Werken). 1937. *Jaarverslag* (Annual report). Batavia.

DDMS (Droogdok Maatschappij Soerabaja, NV). *Verslag.* Annual.

DEZ (Departement van Economische Zaken, Afdeeling Nijverheid; Department of economic affairs, industry section). 1949. *Bijzonder industrieel welvaartsplan, 1950* (Special industrial welfare plan). Batavia.

DLNH (Departement van Landbouw, Nijverheid en Handel, Afdeeling Nijverheid; Department of agriculture, industry and trade, industry section). 1921. *Adresboek voor de Nederlandsch-Indische nijverheid.* Batavia: Indonesische Drukkerij.

———. 1926. *Landbouwatlas van Java en Madoera* (Agricultural atlas of Java and Madura). Mededeelingen van het CKS, no. 33, Batavia.

DGLC (Directorate-General of Land Communications). 1977. "Surabaya Area Transportation Study." Draft report, Freeman Fox and Associates, London.

DOC (Department of Commerce). 1930. *Handbook of the Netherlands East-Indies.* Buitzenzorg: Kolff.

DOI (Department of Information). 1969. *The First Five-Year Development Plan, 1969/70–1973/74.* 6 vols. Jakarta.

DVT (Dienst van het Veiligheidstoezicht; Inspectorate of safety). *Verslag*, Batavia. Annual.

Encona (Encona Engineering), PT. 1985. "Kali Surabaya Pollution Control Study." Draft final report, in association with Sir M. Macdonald and Partners Asia as consultants to Ministry of Public Works, Jakarta.

———. 1986. "Kali Surabaya Pollution Control Programme: Stage 2, Immediate Improvement Plan." Final report, in association with Sir M. Macdonald and Partners Asia as consultants to Ministry of Public Works, Jakarta.

ENI (*Encyclopaedie van Nederlandsch-Indië*). 1918. 2d ed. The Hague: Nijhoff.

GS (Gemeente Spaarbank; continuation of SMNA). *Verslag.* Surabaya. Annual.

Heineken (Heineken's Nederlandsch-Indische Bierbrouwerij Maatschappij), NV). *Verslag.* Amsterdam. Annual.

HVA (Handelsvereeniging "Amsterdam," NV). *Verslag* Amsterdam. Annual.

HVS (Handelsvereeniging te Soerabaia) (annual), *Verslag* (Annual Report), Surabaya. Annual.

IDI (Industrial Directory of Indonesia). 1957–58. Jakarta: Chamber of Industry of Indonesia.

Internatio (Internationale Crediet-en Handels-Vereeniging "Rotterdam," NV). 1938. *Gedenkboek, 1863–1938* (Commemorative volume). Rotterdam.

IV (*Indisch Verslag;* Colonial report). Annual. (Before 1931, *KV, Koloniaal Verslag.*)

JHS (Javasche Hypotheekbank, Soerabaia, NV). *Jaarverslag* (Annual report). Surabaya.

KG (Kabupaten Gresik). *Kabupaten Gresik dalam angka* (*KGDA*). Annual.

KKNS (Kamer van Koophandel en Nijverheid te Soerabaia). *Jaarverslag* (Annual report). Surabaya.

KMS (Kota Madya Surabaya; Municipality of Surabaya). 1978. *Master Plan Surabaya 2000.* Surabaya.

———. ca. 1984a. *Repelita IV* (Fourth five-year plan). Surabaya.

———. ca. 1984b. *Study keadaan pemukiman dan perumahan di kotamadya dati II Surabaya tahun 1984* (Housing study in the municipality of Surabaya in the year 1984). Surabaya: Bappeda Surabaya/ITS Surabaya.

———. 1994. *Surabaya: Lintas and Langkah.* Surabaya.

———. *SDA. Surabaya dalam angka* (Surabaya in figures). Surabaya. Annual.

KMS. BPP (Badan Perencanaan Pembangunan). 1974. *Monography Kota Surabaya* (Surabaya city monograph). Report prepared in conjunction with Fakultas Ekonomi, Universitas Airlangga, Surabaya.

———. 1975. *Surabaya kota indamardi: Data ilmiah untuk Master Plan Surabaya* (Surabaya, city of industry, trade, shipping, and education: Scientific data for the Surabaya Master Plan). Surabaya.

KMS. Team Master Plan. 1970. *Surabaya: Rencana Pendahuluan* (Outline Plan), Surabaya.

KMS. YKP (Yayasan Kas Pembangunan). 1983. *Brief Explanation on YKPKMS and Its Activities.* Surabaya (1983).

KP (Kementerian Penerangan). 1953. *Republik Indonesia: Propinsi Djawa Timur.* Jakarta.

KPM (Koninklijke Paketvaart Maatschappij, Royal Packet Company). 1903. *Guide through Netherlands India.* London/Amsterdam.

KRN (De Koloniale roeping van Nederland; Holland's colonial call). 1930. The Hague: Nederlandsch-Engelsche Uitgeversmaatschappij.

KS (Kabupaten Sidoarjo). *Kabupaten Sidoarjo dalam Angka* (*KSDA*). Annual.

KSP (Kantor Statistik Provinsi Jawa Timur). *Jawa Timur dalam angka* (East Java in figures). Surabaya: KSP. Annual.

KV (*Koloniaal Verslag;* Colonial report). (KV) (annual) (After 1930, *IV, Indisch Verslag.*)

KVC (Kampongverbeteringscommissie). 1939. "Eerste Verslag van de Kampongverbeteringscommissie" (First report of the Kampong Improvement Commission). Landsdrukkerij, Batavia.

Kodamil (Komando Daerah Militer) VII/Brawijaya. 1976. *Buku Petunjuk: Metropolitan Surabaya and Jawa Timur.* Surabaya.

MES (Marine Etablissement te Soerabaia). *Verslag.* Annual.

MPW (Ministry of Public Works). 1982. "Urban Development Planning Study on Gerbangkertosusila Region (Surabaya Metropolitan Area)." Draft final report, Japan International Cooperation Agency as consultants to Directorate-General of Cipta Karya, Ministry of Public Works, Jakarta, December.

NIF (Nederlandsch-Indisch Fabrikaat). 1934–40. *Officieël orgaan der vereeniging "Nederlandsch-Indisch Fabrikaat."* Batavia. Monthly.

NUDS (National Urban Development Strategy). 1985. *Final Report.* Jakarta: Directorate of Urban and Regional Planning.

OAG (Official Airline Guides). 1997. *OAG World Airways Guide.* London: Reed Elsevier International.

Pakuwon Jati, PT. ca. 1993. Tunjungan City-Tunjungan Plaza III: Pusat Perbelanjaan Era 2000 (Era 2000 Shopping Centre), brochure, Surabaya/Jakarta.

Petrokimia Gresik, PT. ca. 1987. Illus. brochure, Surabaya.

POJ (Provincie Oost Java). *Tien jaar provincie Oost Java, 1928–1938.* Surabaya.

RANI (*Regeeringsalmanaak van Nederlandsch-Indië.* Batavia. Annual.

Repelita VI. 1994. *Rencana Pembangunan Lima Tahun Keenam 1994/95–1998/99* (Sixth five-year development plan). Jakarta: Republik Indonesia.

RPL ("Rapport omtrent de Partikuliere Landerijen beoosten de Rivier Tjimanoek"). *Tijdschrift voor Nijverheid en Landbouw*, no. 22 (1878), 237–701.

Sampoerna (Sampoerna Trading Company), PT HM. 1995. *Annual Report, 1994.* Surabaya.

Semen Gresik, PT. 1980. *Semen Gresik dan perkembangannya* (Gresik Cement and its development). Gresik: PT Semen Gresik.

SGB (Stadsgemeente, Batavia). 1940. "Notulen der vergadering van de Gemeenteraad van Batavia (Minutes of the council meeting). 11 March.

SGS (Soerabaja, Stadsgemeente). *Gemeenteblad* (*GB*) (Municipal gazette), Surabaya.

———. *Verslag (van den toestand) der (Stads)Gemeente Soerabaja* (Report of the conditions in the municipality of Surabaya). Surabaya. Annual.

———. 1936a. *Soerabaia and the Oosthoek: There Lies a Future for Your Business.* Surabaya. Pamphlet.

Singapore, Colony of (later State, Republic). *Annual Report.* Singapore: Government Printer.

SMNA (Spaarbank van den Maatschappij tot Nut van het Algemeen te Soerabaia). *Verslag.* Surabaya. Annual.

Straits Settlements. *Blue Book*, Singapore. Annual.

TSSJ (Toelichting op de "Stadsvormingsordonnantie Stadsgemeenten Java"; Explanation of the Java Municipal Town Planning Law). 1938. Batavia: Landsdrukkerij.

Umbgrove (Umbgrove Commissie). 1862/3. "Stukken betrekkend de suikercultuur op Java." In *Handelingen de tweede kamer van de Staten Generaal*, Zittingen 1862/63, Bijlage I, No. 11.

Waroe (Maatschappij tot Exploitatie der Suikerfabriek). 1920–21. *Jaarverslag* (Annual report). Amsterdam.

World Bank. 1981. *Indonesia: Selected Issues of Industrial Development and Trade Strategy.* 6 vols. Washington, D.C.: East Asia and Pacific Regional Office.

BOOKS AND ARTICLES

Abdulgani, R. 1974. "My Childhood World." Trans. W. Frederick. *Indonesia*, no. 17, 113–35.

Abeyasekere, S. 1976. *One Hand Clapping: Indonesian Nationalists and the Dutch, 1939–1941*. Monash Papers on Southeast Asia, no. 5. Centre of Southeast Asian Studies, Monash University, Clayton.

———. 1987. *Jakarta: A History*. Singapore: Oxford University Press.

Adam, A. B. 1995. *The Vernacular Press and the Emergence of Modern Indonesian Consciousness, 1855–1913*. Ithaca, N.Y.: Southeast Asia Program, Cornell University.

Anderson, B. R. O. 1983. "Old State, New Society: Indonesia's New Order in Comparative Historical Perspective." *Journal of Asian Studies* 42 (3): 477–96.

Anderson, I. H. 1975. *The Standard-Vacuum Oil Company and United States East Asian Policy, 1933–1941*. Princeton: Princeton University Press.

Arndt, H. W. 1970. "Survey of Recent Developments." *Bulletin of Indonesian Economic Studies* 6 (2): 1–30.

———. 1987. *Economic Development: The History of an Idea*. Chicago: University of Chicago Press.

Baardewijk, F. van. 1986. "Rural Response to Intensifying Colonial Exploitation: The forced cultivation of coffee in Central and East Java, 1830–1880." Fifth Dutch-Indonesian Historical Congress, Lage Vuursche, 23–27 June 1986.

Balen, A. van. 1987. "A Survey of the Drinking Water and Sanitation Policy of the Dutch East Indies, 1872–1942." Unpublished report, Klankbordgroep Drinkwatervoorziening Indonesië.

Basu, D., ed. 1985. Reprint. *The Rise and Growth of the Colonial Port Cities in Asia*. Lanham, Md.: University Press of America. Original edition, monograph no. 25, Center for South and Southeast Asian Studies, University of California at Berkeley.

Bauduin, D. C. M. 1941. *Het Indische leven* (Life in the Indies). Rev. ed. The Hague: Leopolds.

Bijlmer, J. 1987. "Ambulante straatberoepen in Surabaya: Een studie naar kleinschalige economische activiteiten." (Mobile street occupations in Surabaya: A study of small-scale economic activity). Ph.D. thesis, Free University of Amsterdam.

Bisschop, P. A. G. 1939. "Het Marine Etablissement." *Locale Techniek* 8 (2).

Boeke, J. H. 1942. *The Structure of the Netherlands Indian Economy.* New York: Institute of Pacific Relations.

———. 1961. "Objective and Personal Elements in Colonial Welfare Policy." In *Indonesian Economics,* ed. W. F. Wertheim et al. The Hague: Van Hoeve.

Bogaers, E., and P. de Ruijter. 1986. "Ir. Karsten and Indonesian Town Planning, 1915–1940." In *The Indonesian City*, ed. P. J. M. Nas, 71–88. Dordrecht: Foris.

Boomgaard, P. 1987. "Morbidity and Mortality in Java: 1820–1880." In *Death and Disease in Southeast Asia*, ed. N. G. Owen. ASAA Monograph no. 14, 48–69. Singapore: Oxford University Press.

———. 2000. "Surviving the Slump: Developments in Real Income during the Depression of the 1930s in Indonesia, particularly Java." In *Weathering the Storm: The Economies of Southeast Asia in the 1930s Depression*, ed. P. Boomgaard and I. Brown. Leiden: KITLV Press.

Booth, A. 1980. "The Burden of Taxation in Colonial Indonesia in the Twentieth Century." *Journal of Southeast Asian Studies* 11 (1) (March 1980): 91–109.

———. 1988. *Agricultural Development in Indonesia.* Sydney: Allen and Unwin.

———. 1993. "Regional Finance in Indonesia: An East Java Case Study." In *Balanced Development: East Java in the New Order*, ed. H. Dick, J. Fox, and J. Mackie, 308–25. Singapore: Oxford University Press.

———. 1998. *The Indonesian Economy in the Nineteenth and Twentieth Centuries: A History of Missed Opportunities.* London: Macmillan.

———, ed. 1992. *The Oil Boom and After: Indonesian Economic Policy and Performance in the Soeharto Era.* Kuala Lumpur: Oxford University Press.

Booth, A., and P. McCawley. 1981. *The Indonesian Economy during the Soeharto Era.* Kuala Lumpur: Oxford University Press.

Broeshart, A. C., J. R. van Diessen, R. G. Gill, and J. P. Zeydner, eds. 1997. *Soerabaja: Beeld van een stad* (Surabaya: Portrait of a city). 3d ed. Purmerend: Asia Minor.

Broeze, F., ed. 1989. *Brides of the Sea: Port Cities of Asia from the Sixteenth–Twentieth Centuries.* Sydney: New South Wales University Press.

———. 1996. *Gateways of Asia: Port Cities of Asia in the Thirteenth–Twentieth Centuries.* New York: Kegan Paul.

Brown, C. 1987. "The Influenza Pandemic of 1918 in Indonesia." In *Death and Disease in Southeast Asia*, ed. N. G. Owen. ASAA Monograph no. 14. Singapore: Oxford University Press.

Brugmans, I. J. 1961. "Onderwijspolitiek" (Education policy). In *Balans van beleid* (The balance of rule), ed. H. Baudet and I. J. Brugmans. Assen: Van Gorcum.

Buitenweg, H. 1980. *Krokodillenstad* (Crocodile city). Katwijk aan Zee: Servire.

Burger, D. H. 1939. "De ontsluiting van Java's binnenland voor het wereldverkeer" (The opening of Java's interior to world commerce). Ph.D. thesis, Wageningen.

Campo, J. N. F. M. à 1992. *Koninklijke Paketvaart Maatschappij: Stoomvaart en staatsvorming in de Indonesische archipel, 1888–1914* (KPM: Shipping and state formation in the Indonesian archipelago). Hilversum: Uitgeverij Verloren.

Carriere, J. D. 1948. "De gas- en electriciteitsbedrijven en de industrie" (The gas and electricity utilities and industry). *Economische Weekblad voor Indonisië* 14:728–33.

Cator, W. J. 1936. *The Economic Position of the Chinese in the Netherlands Indies.* Oxford: Blackwell.

Citroen, C. 1934. "Het Raadhuis te Soerabaja." *Locale Techniek* 3 (1): 12–14.

Cobban, J. L. 1971. "The City of Java: An Essay in Historical Geography." Ph.D. dissertation, University of California, Berkeley.

———. 1974. "Uncontrolled Urban Settlement: The Kampong Question in Semarang, 1905–1940." *Bijdragen tot de taal-, land- en volkenkunde* 130 (4): 403–27.

———. 1988. "Kampungs and Conflict in Colonial Semarang." *Journal of Southeast Asian Studies* 19 (2): 266–91.

———. 1993. "Public Housing in Colonial Indonesia, 1900–1940." *Modern Asian Studies* 27 (4): 871–96.

Colombijn, F. 1994. *Patches of Padang: The History of an Indonesian Town in the Twentieth Century and the Use of Urban Space.* Leiden: Research School CNWS.

Coppel, C. 1983. *The Indonesian Chinese in Crisis.* Kuala Lumpur: ASAA/Oxford University Press.

Creutzberg, P. 1972–75. *Het ekonomisch beleid in Nederlandsch-Indië*

(Economic policy in the Netherlands Indies). 4 vols. Groningen: Tjeenk Willink.

Cribb, R., ed. 1991. *The Indonesian Killings: Studies from Java and Bali.* Centre of Southeast Asian Studies, Monash University, Clayton.

Crouch, H. 1978. *The Army and Politics in Indonesia.* Ithaca, N.Y.: Cornell University Press.

d'Almeida, W. B. 1864. *Life in Java.* 2 vols. London: Hurst and Blackett.

Davis, F. J. H. 1949. "Overzicht van de situatie van de Indonesische nijverheid in 1949" (Survey of the Indonesian industrial situation in 1949). *Economische Weekblad voor Indonesië* 15:1232–42.

Dick, H. W. 1975. "Prahu Shipping in Eastern Indonesia: Parts 1, 2." *Bulletin of Indonesian Economic Studies* 11 (2) (July–November 1975): 69–107, 81–103.

———. 1981. "Urban Public Transport, Parts I and II." *Bulletin of Indonesian Economic Studies* 17 (1): 66–82; 17 (2): 72–88.

———. 1985. "The Rise of a Middle Class and the Changing Concept of Equity in Indonesia." *Indonesia*, no. 39 (April): 71–92.

———. 1987a. *The Indonesian Interisland Shipping Industry.* Singapore: ISEAS.

———. 1987b. "Prahu Shipping in Eastern Indonesia in the Interwar Period." *Bulletin of Indonesian Economic Studies* 23 (1): 104–21.

———. 1989. "Japan's Economic Expansion in the Netherlands Indies between the First and Second World Wars." *Journal of Southeast Asian Studies* 20 (2): 244–72.

———. 1990. "Further Reflections on the Indonesian Middle Class." In *The Politics of Middle Class Indonesia*, ed. K. Young and R. Tanter. Monash Papers on Indonesia, no.19, 63–70. Centre of Southeast Asian Studies, Monash University.

———. 1993a. "East Java in Regional Perspective." In *Balanced Development: East Java in the New Order*, ed. H. Dick, J. Fox, and J. Mackie, 1–22. Singapore: Oxford University Press.

———. 1993b. "The Manufacturing Sector." In *Balanced Development: East Java in the New Order*, ed. H. Dick, J. Fox, and J. Mackie, 230–55. Singapore: Oxford University Press.

———. 1993c. "Nineteenth Century Industrialization: A Missed Opportunity?" In *New Challenges in the Modern Economic History of Indonesia*, ed. J. T. Lindblad, 123–49. Leiden: Program of Indonesian Studies, Leiden University.

———. 1995. "The Transformation of Comparative Advantage: East Java, 1920–1990s." *Bulletin of Indonesian Economic Studies* 31 (1) (April): 41–72.

Dick, H. W., J. J. Fox, and J. A. C. Mackie, eds. 1993. *Balanced Development: East Java in the New Order.* Singapore: Oxford University Press.

Dick, H. W., and P. J. Rimmer. 1998. "Beyond the Third World City: The New Urban Geography of Asia." *Urban Studies* 35 (12) (December): 2302–21.

———. 1999. "Privatising Climate: First World Cities in Third World Settings." In *East West Perspectives in Twenty-First Century Urban Development*, ed. J. Brotchie, P. Newman, P. Hall, and J. Dickey, 305–24. Aldershot: Ashgate.

Diehl, F. W. 1993. "Revenue Farming and Colonial Finances in the Netherlands East Indies, 1816–1925." In *The Rise and Fall of Revenue Farming in Southeast Asia,* ed. J. Butcher and H. Dick, 196–232. London: Macmillan.

Djojohadikusumo, S. 1954. "The Government's Programme on Industries." *Ekonomi and keuangan Indonesia* 7 (November).

Doeppers, D. 1984. *Manila, 1900–1941: Social Change in a Late Colonial Metropolis.* Monograph Series no. 27. New Haven: Yale University Southeast Asia Studies.

Drooglever, P. J., and M. J. B. Schouten, eds. 1981–1991. *Officiele bescheiden betreffende de Nederlands-Indonesische betrekkingen, 1945–1950* (Official documents on Netherlands-Indonesian relations, 1945–1950). Vols. 9–16. The Hague: Nijhoff.

Duparc, H. J. A. 1972. *Trams en tramlijnen: De elektrische stadstrams op Java* (Trams and tram lines: The electric city trams of Java). Rotterdam: Wyt.

"An Economic Survey of East Java." 1971. *Bulletin of Indonesian Economic Studies* 7 (2): 19–37.

Elson, R. E. 1984. *Javanese Peasants and the Colonial Sugar Industry: Impact and Change in an East Java Residency, 1830–1940.* Singapore: Oxford University Press.

———. 1994. *Village Java under the Cultivation System, 1830–1870.* ASAA Southeast Asia Monographs, no. 25. Sydney: Allen and Unwin.

Eng, P. van der. 1993a. "Agricultural Growth in Indonesia since 1880: Productivity Change and the Impact of Government Policy." Ph.D. thesis, Rijksuniversiteit Groningen.

———. 1993b. *Food Consumption and the Standard of Living in Indonesia, 1880–1990.* Economics Division Working Papers 93/1. Research School of Pacific Studies, Australian National University, Canberra.

Faber, G. H. von. 1931. *Oud Soerabaia: De geschiedenis van Indië's eerste koopstad van de oudste tijden tot de instelling van den Gemeenteraad* (Old Surabaya: The history of Indonesia's premier commercial city from the oldest times to the inauguration of the Municipal Council). Surabaya: Gemeente Soerabaia.

———. 1936. *Nieuw Soerabaia: De geschiedenis van Indië's voornaamste koopstad in de eertse kwaarteeuw sedert hare instelling, 1906–1931* (New Surabaya: The history of India's leading commercial city in the first quarter century since her inauguration). Surabaya: Van Ingen.

Fasseur, C. 1975. "Kultuurstelsel en koloniale baten: De Nederlandse exploitatie van Java, 1840–1860" (The politics of colonial exploitation: Java, the Dutch and the Cultivation System). Ph.D. thesis, University of Leiden. Translation, R. Elson and A. Kraal, SEA Program, Cornell University, 1992.

Fatima, S. 1981. "Suatu studi mengenai masalah biaya dalam rangka perhitungan harga pokok tanah pada PT Surabaya Industrial Estate Rungkut" (A study of the cost factor in the context of the calculation of land prices at PT Surabaya Industrial Estate, Rungkut). Thesis, Faculty of Economics, Universitas Airlangga, Surabaya.

Feith, H. 1962. *The Decline of Constitutional Democracy in Indonesia.* Ithaca, N.Y.: Cornell University Press.

———. 1967. "Dynamics of Guided Democracy." In *Indonesia*, ed. R. T. McVey. New Haven: HRAF Press.

Fernando, M. R. 1995. "The Trumpet Shall Sound for Rich Peasants: Kasan Mukmin's Uprising in Gedangan, East Java, 1904." *Journal of Southeast Asian Studies* 26 (2): 242–62.

Firman, T. 1992. "The Spatial Pattern of Population Growth in Java." *Bulletin of Indonesian Economic Studies* 28 (2): 95–109.

Flieringa, G. 1930. "De zorg voor de volkshuisvesting in de stadsgemeenten in Nederlandsch Oost Indië, in het bijzonder in Semarang" (Public housing policy in the municipalities of the Netherlands East Indies and in particular Semarang). Thesis, Technische Hoogeschool, Delft. Printed by Rotterdamsche Boek and Kunstdrukkerij, Rotterdam.

Forster, C. 1988. "Unemployment and the Australian Economic Recovery of the 1930s." In *Recovery from the Depression: Australia and the*

World Economy in the 1930s, ed. R. G. Gregory and N. G. Butlin. Cambridge: Cambridge University Press.

Fouracre, P. R., and D. A. C. Maunder. 1978. *Public Transport in Surabaya, Indonesia.* Crowthorne, England: Transport and Road Research Laboratory.

Fox, J. J. 1993. "The Rice Baskets of East Java." In *East Java in the New Order,* ed. H. Dick, J. Fox, and J. Mackie, 120–57. Kuala Lumpur: Oxford University Press.

Frederick, W. H. 1989. *Visions and Heat: The Making of the Indonesian Revolution.* Athens: Ohio University Press.

———. 1994. "'The Man Who Knew Too Much: Ch. O. Van der Plas and the Future of Indonesia, 1927–1950." In *Imperial Policy and Southeast Asian Nationalism, 1930–1957,* ed. H. Antlov and S. Tonnesson. Richmond, England: Curzon.

Furnivall, J. S. 1944. *Netherlands India: A Study of Plural Economy.* Cambridge: Cambridge University Press.

Geertz, C. 1963. *Agricultural Involution.* Berkeley: University of California Press.

———. 1967. *The Social History of an Indonesian Town.* Westport, Conn.: Greenwood.

George, M. L. 1980. *Australia and the Indonesian Revolution.* Melbourne: Melbourne University Press.

Geursen, G. A. J. 1948. "Rehabilitatie en bevoorrading der industrie sedert de Japanse capitulatie." (Industrial rehabilitation and supply since the Japanese capitulation). *Economische Weekblad voor Indonesië* 14: 715–20.

Gill, G. H. 1957. *Royal Australian Navy, 1939–1942.* Canberra: Australian War Memorial.

Ginsburg, N. S., B. Koppel, and T. G. McGee, eds. 1991. *The Extended Metropolis: Settlement Transition in Asia.* Honolulu: University of Hawaii Press.

Glassburner, B., and K. Thomas. 1965. "Abrogation, Take-over and Nationalization: The Elimination of Dutch Economic Dominance from the Republic of Indonesia." *Australian Outlook* 19 (2): 158–79.

Gonggrijp, G. 1957. *Schets eener economische geschiedenis van Indonesië* (Sketch of an economic history of Indonesia). Haarlem: De Erven F. Bohn.

Gorkom, K. W. van. 1879. "Historische schets van de suikerindustrie op

Java" (A historical sketch of the sugar industry of Java). *Tijdschrift voor nijverheid en landbouw in Nederlandsch-Indië* 23:229–348.

Graaf, H. J. de, and Pigeaud, G. T. 1974. *De eerste Moslimse vorstendommen op Java* (The first Muslim kingdoms on Java). The Hague: KITLV.

Grenville, S. 1981. "Monetary Policy and the Formal Financial Sector." In *The Indonesian Economy during the Soeharto Era,* ed. A. Booth and P. McCawley, 102–25. Kuala Lumpur: Oxford University Press.

Guinness, P. 1986. *Harmony and Hierarchy in a Javanese Kampung.* Singapore: Oxford University Press.

Hageman, J. J. 1852. *Handelingen tot de kennis der geschiedenis, aardrijkskunde, fabeleer en tijdrekenkunde van Java* (Contributions to the knowledge of the history, geography, myths, and chronology of Java). 2 vols. Batavia: Lange.

———. 1859. "Aanteekeningen nopens de industrie, handel en nijverheid van Soerabaja" (Notes on the industy, trade, and crafts of Surabaya). *Tijdschrift voor nijverheid en landbouw in Nederlandsch Indië* 5:137–52.

Hardon, H. J. 1948. "De stand van het industrieel-herstel" (The state of industrial rehabilitation). *Economische Weekblad voor Indonesië* 14:701–9.

Hart, G. H. C. 1942. *Towards Economic Democracy in the Netherlands Indies.* San Francisco: Netherlands and Netherlands Indies Council, Institute of Pacific Relations.

Harvey, B. 1977. *Permesta: Half a Rebellion.* Ithaca, N.Y.: Cornell Modern Indonesian Project, Southeast Asia Program, Cornell University.

Hatta, M. 1960. *Past and Future.* Ithaca, N.Y.: Cornell Modern Indonesian Project, Southeast Asia Program, Cornell University.

Hawkins, E. D. 1963. "Labor in Transition." In *Indonesia*, ed. R. T. McVey. New Haven: HRAF Press.

Heida. 1939. "Soerabaja als woon- en handels-centrum (Surabaya as domicile and trade center)." *Locale techniek* 8 (2) (April): 45–47.

Heneveld, W. 1978. "The Distribution of Development Funds: New School Building in East Java." *Bulletin of Indonesian Economic Studies* 14 (1) (March): 63–79.

Hesselink, L. 1987. "Prostitution: A Necessary Evil, Particularly in the Colonies." In *Indonesian Women in Focus,* ed. E. Locher-Scholten and A. Niehof. Dordrecht: Foris.

Higgins, B. H. 1957. *Indonesia's Economic Stabilization and Development.* New York: Institute of Pacific Relations.

Hill, H. 1988. *Foreign Investment and Industrialization in Indonesia.* Singapore: Oxford University Press.

———. 1992. "Manufacturing Industry." In *The Oil Boom and After*, ed. A. Booth, 204–82. Kuala Lumpur: Oxford University Press.

———. 2000. *The Indonesian Economy since 1966.* 2d ed. Cambridge: Cambridge University Press.

Hindley, D. 1964. *The Communist Party of Indonesia, 1951–1963.* Berkeley: University of California Press.

Hughes, J. 1967. *Indonesian Upheaval.* New York: David Mackay.

Hugo, G. 1996. "Urbanization in Indonesia: City and Countryside Linked." In *The Urban Transformation of the Developing World*, ed. J. Gugler. Oxford: Oxford University Press.

Hugo, G., T. Hull, V. Hull, and G. Jones. 1987. *The Demographic Dimension in Indonesian Development.* Singapore: Oxford University Press.

Hull, T. H. 1987. "Plague in Java." In *Death and Disease in Southeast* Asia, ed. N. G. Owen. ASAA Monograph no. 14. Singapore: Oxford University Press.

———. 1993. "East Java's Family Planning Revolution." In *Balanced Development: East Java in the New Order,* ed. H. Dick, J. Fox, and J. Mackie, 54–74. Singapore: Oxford University Press.

Hull, T. H., E. Sulistyaningsih, and G. W. Jones. 1998. *Prostitution in Indonesia: Its History and Evolution.* Jakarta: Pustaka Sinar Harapan.

Hunter, A. 1967. "Indonesian Oil: A New Generation of Explorers?" *Bulletin of Indonesian Economic Studies*, no. 8: 85–91.

Husin, I. 1993. "Electricity Supply." In *Balanced Development: East Java in the New Order,* ed. H. Dick, J. Fox, and J. Mackie, 256–71. Singapore: Oxford University Press.

Idrus. 1968. "Surabaja" (translation). *Indonesia*, no. 5 (April): 1–28.

Ingleson, J. 1983. "Life and Work in Colonial Cities: Harbour Workers in Java in the 1910s and 1920s." *Modern Asian Studies* 17 (3): 455–76.

———. 1986. *In Search of Justice: Workers and Unions in Colonial Java, 1908–1926.* Singapore: Oxford University Press.

———. 1988. "Urban Java during the Depression." *Journal of Southeast Asian Studies* 19 (2): 292–309.

Jellinek, L. 1991. *The Wheel of Fortune: The History of a Poor Community in Jakarta.* Sydney: ASAA/Allen and Unwin.

Jessup, H. 1988. "Netherlands Architecture in Indonesia, 1900–1949." Ph.D. thesis, University of London.

Johnson, C. 1982. *MITI and the Japanese Miracle: The Growth of Industrial Policy, 1925–1975.* Stanford, Calif.: Stanford University Press.

Jones, G. 1994. "Labour Force and Education." In *Indonesia's New Order,* ed. H. Hill, 145–78. Sydney: Allen and Unwin.

Jones, G., and T. Hull, eds. 1997. *Indonesia Assessment: Population and Human Resources.* Canberra: Research School of Asian and Pacific Studies, Australian National University; Singapore: Institute of Southeast Asian Studies.

Jonkers, A. 1948. *Welvaartzorg in Indonesië* (Welfare policy in Indonesia). The Hague: Van Hoeve.

Kahin, G. M. 1952. *Nationalism and Revolution in Indonesia.* Ithaca, N.Y.: Cornell University Press.

Kamerling, R. N. J. 1982. *De N.V. Oliefabrieken Insulinde in Nederlands-Indië* (The N.V. Insulinde Oil Factory in the Netherlands Indies). Franeker: Wever.

Kawata, T., ed. 1936. *Glimpses of the East: Nippon Yusen Kaisha's Official Guide.* Tokyo: Nippon Yusen Kaisha.

Kerchman, F. W. M., ed. 1930. *25-jaren decentralisatie in Nederlandsch-Indië* (Twenty-five years of decentralization in the Netherlands Indies). Semarang: Vereeniging voor Locale Belangen.

Klinken, G. van. 1997. "Tinder-box or Conspiracy: The Recent Outbreak of Rioting." *Inside Indonesia*, no. 50 (April-June): 6–8.

Koffel, P. 1994. "Riparian Politics: The Case of the Brantas River Clean-up in East Java." Paper presented to Asian Studies Association of Australia biennial conference, Murdoch, Western Australia, 13–16 July.

Korthals Altes, W. L. 1979. "De depreciatie van de Nederlandsch-Indische gulden in 1936" (The depreciation of the Netherlands Indies guilder in 1936). In *Between People and Statistics: Essays on Modern Indonesian History,* ed. F. van Anrooij, D. Kolff, J. van Laanen, and G. Telkamp, 157–73. The Hague: Nijhoff.

Kraus, J., and G. J. de Jongh. 1910. *Verslag over de verbetering van haventoestanden van Soerabaia* (Report on improvement of the harbor conditions at Surabaya). Batavia: Landsdrukkerij.

Kuncoro, M., and H. W. Dick. 1998. "The Dynamics of Industrial Agglomeration in Indonesia and Java." Seminar Paper, Research School of Pacific and Asian Studies, Australian National University, 4 August.

Leeuwen, H. J. M. van. 1948. "De Financiering van het Industrieel Herstel" (The financing of industrial rehabilitation). *Economische Weekblad voor Indonesië* 14, 720–23.

Legge, J. D. 1973. *Sukarno: A Political Biography.* Harmondsworth: Pelican.

Levert, P. 1934. "Inheemsche arbeid in de Java-suikerindustrie" (Native labor in the Javanese sugar industry). Thesis. Wageningen: Veenman.

Lewis, B. D. 1993. "Formal Housing Finance and Low-Income Urban Households in Indonesia: Never the Twain Shall Meet." *Asian Journal of Economics and Social Studies* 12 (4): 257–67.

Lumkeman, E. H. 1939. "Het verkeer in de stad Soerabaja" (Traffic in the city of Surabaya). *Locale Techniek* 8 (2): 66–68.

MacAndrews, C., A. Sibero, and H. B. Fisher. 1982. "Regional Planning and Implementation in Indonesia: The Evolution of a National Policy." In *Regional Development: Essays in Honour of Masahiko Honjo,* ed. R. P. Misra. Tokyo: Maruzen Asia.

Mackie, J. A. C. 1967a. "The Government Estates." In *Sukarno's Guided Indonesia*, ed. T. K. Tan. Brisbane: Jacaranda.

———. 1967b. *Problems of the Indonesian Inflation.* Ithaca, N.Y.: Cornell University.

———. 1993. "Plantations and Cash Crops in East Java: Changing Patterns." In *Balanced Development: East Java in the New Order*, ed. H. Dick, J. Fox, and J. Mackie, 187–213. Singapore: Oxford University Press.

Mackie, J. A. C., ed. 1976. *The Chinese in Indonesia.* Melbourne: Nelson.

Macmillan, A. 1926. *Seaports of the Far East*, 3d ed. London: Collingridge.

McCawley, P. T. 1981. "The Growth of the Industrial Sector." In *The Indonesian Economy during the Soeharto Era,* ed. A. Booth and P. McCawley, 62–102. Kuala Lumpur: Oxford University Press.

McCawley, P. T., and M. Tait. 1979. "New Data on Employment in Manufacturing, 1970–77." *Bulletin of Indonesian Economic Studies* 15 (1): 125–36.

McCoy, A. W. 1982. "A Queen Slowly Dies: The Rise and Decline of Iloilo City." In *Philippine Social History,* ed. A. W. McCoy and E. C. de Jesus. ASAA monograph no. 7. Sydney: Allen and Unwin.

McGee, T. G. 1967. *The Southeast Asian City.* London: Bell.

———. 1991. "The Emergence of Desa Kota Regions in Asia: Expanding a Hypothesis." In *The Extended Metropolis: Settlement Transition in Asia,* ed. N. Ginsburg, B. Koppel, and T. McGee. Honolulu: University of Hawaii Press.

McLeod, R. H. 1998. "Indonesia." In *East Asia in Crisis: From Being a Miracle to Needing One,* ed. R. McLeod and R. Garnaut, 31–48. London: Routledge.

McMillan, M. 1914. *A Journey to Java.* London: Holden and Hardingham.

Meelhuijsen, W. 2000. *Revolutie in Soerabaja, 17 augustus-1 december 1945.* Zutphen: Walburg Pers.

Meijer, H. 1994. *Den Haag-Djakarta: De Nederlands-Indonesische betrekkingen, 1950–1962* (The Hague-Jakarta: Netherlands-Indonesian relations, 1950–1962). Utrecht: AULA/Spectrum.

Middelaer, F. H. V. 1947. "De rehabilitatie van de metaalnijverheid" (Rehabilitation of the metal industry). *Economische Weekblad voor Indonesië* 13:63–65.

Ming, H. 1983. "Barracks Concubinage in the Indies." *Indonesia* 35 (April): 65–93.

Miyamoto, S. 1986. "Jawa shusen shoriki" (An account of the cessation of hostilities in Java). In *The Japanese Experience in Indonesia: Selected Memoirs of 1942–1945,* ed. A. Reid and A. Oki. Monograph no. 72. Athens: Center for Southeast Asian Studies, Ohio University.

Mook, H. J. van 1944. *The Netherlands Indies and Japan: Their Relations, 1940–1941.* London: Allen and Unwin.

Murphey, R. 1969. "Traditionalism and Colonialism: Changing Urban Roles in Asia." *Journal of Asian Studies* 29 (1): 67–84.

Nas, P. J. M. 1986. *The Indonesian City: Studies in Urban Development and Planning.* Dordrecht: Foris.

Neyndorff, E. C. 1939. "Het Gemeentelijk Pasarbedrijf, Soerabaja, 1915–1938" (The municipal market authority). *Lokale Techniek* 8 (2): 55–57.

Nibbering, J. W. 1988. "Forest Degradation and Reforestation in a Highland Area in Java." In *Changing Tropical Forests,* ed. J. Dargavel, K. Nixon, and N. Semple. Canberra: Centre for Resource and Environmental Studies, Australian National University.

Niessen, N. 1999. *Municipal Government in Indonesia: Policy, Law and Practice of Decentralization and Urban Spatial Planning.* Leiden: Research School CNWS, University of Leiden.

Ohmae, K. 1995. *The End of the Nation State: The Rise of Regional Economies.* New York: Free Press.

Oki, A. 1988. "The Transformation of the Southeast Asian City: The Evolution of Surabaya as a Colonial City." *East Asian Cultural Studies* 27 (1–4) (March): 13–47.

Oorschot, H. J. van. 1949. "Moeilijkheden der na-oorlogse industriële ontwikkeling" (Difficulties of postwar industrial development). *Economische Weekblad voor Indonesië* 15:1267–69.

———. 1956. *De ontwikkeling van de nijverheid in Indonesië* (The development of industry in Indonesia). The Hague: Van Hoeve.

Osten, W. J. 1930. "De Suikerafvoer naar Soerabaia" (The sugar transport to Surabaya). *Spoor-en Tramwegen*, I, p. 378 and II, pp. 8–10, 41–2.

Paauw, D. S. 1967. "From Colonial to Guided Economy." In *Indonesia*, ed. R. McVey, 155–247. New Haven: Southeast Asian Studies Program, Yale University.

Palmer, I., and L. Castles. 1965. "The Textile Industry." *Bulletin of Indonesian Economic Studies*, no. 2: 34–48.

Penders, C. L. M. 1968a. *Bojonegoro, 1900–1942: A Story of Endemic Poverty in North-East Java.* Singapore: Gunung Agung.

———. 1968b. "Colonial Education Policy and Practices in Indonesia: 1900–1942." Ph.D. thesis, Australian National University, Canberra.

Poeze, H. 1994. "Political Intelligence in the Netherlands Indies." In *The Late Colonial State in Indonesia,* ed. R. Cribb. Leiden: KITLV.

Post, L. van der. 1996. *The Admiral's Baby.* London: Murray.

Post, P. 1991. "Japanse bedrijvigheid in Indonesië, 1868–1942" (Japanese activity in Indonesia, 1868–1942). Ph.D. thesis, Free University, Amsterdam.

Put, A. H. P. van der. 1939. "De straatverkoop" (Street selling). *Lokale Techniek* 8 (4): 110–12.

Rachbini, D. J. 1995. "Conditions and Consequences of Industrialization in Madura." In *Across Madura Strait,* ed. K. van Dijk, H. de Jonge, and E. Touwen-Bouwsma. Leiden: KITLV.

Reid, A. J. S. 1992. "The Rise and Fall of Sino-Javanese Shipping." In *Looking in Odd Mirrors: The Java Sea,* ed. V. Houben, H. Maier, and W. van der Molen. Leiden: Vakgroep Talen en Culturen van Zuidoost-Azië en Oceanië, Rijksuniversiteit.

———. 1993. *Southeast Asia in the Age of Commerce, 1450–1680: Expansion and Crisis.* New Haven: Yale University Press.

———. 1999. "Economic and Social Change, ca.1400–1800." In *The Cambridge History of Southeast Asia,* ed. N. Tarling, 1 (2): 116–63. Cambridge: Cambridge University Press.

Reijden, B. van der. 1936. "Rapport betreffende eene gehouden enquete naar de arbeidstoestanden in de industrie van strootjes en inheemsche sigaretten op Java: Oost Java" (Deel III) (Report of an inquiry into labor conditions in the native cigarette industry on Java)." Kantoor van Arbeid Publicatie no. 12, Bandung.

Ricklefs, M. C. 1974. *Jogjakarta under Sultan Mangkubumi, 1749–1792: A History of the Division of Java.* London: Oxford University Press.

———. 1993. *War, Culture and Economy in Java, 1677–1726.* ASAA Southeast Asia Monograph no. 24. Sydney: Allen and Unwin.

Robinson, T. 1953. *Piekerans van een straatslijper* (The cutler's apprentice). Bandung: Masa Baru.

Rosendale, P. 1981. "The Balance of Payments." In *The Indonesian Economy during the Soeharto Era*, ed. A. Booth and P. McCawley, 162–80. Kuala Lumpur: Oxford University Press.

Ross, R., and G. J. Telkamp. 1985. *Colonial Cities: Essays on Urbanism in a Colonial Context.* Dordrecht: Nijhoff.

Rothe, C. 1938a. *Industrieën in Nederlandsch-Indië: Keramische, glas- en cement-industrie* (Industries in the Netherlands Indies: The ceramics, glass, and cement industries), Report no. 127, Afdeeling Handelsmuseum van de Koninklijk Vereeniging Koloniaal Instituut, Amsterdam.

———. 1938b. *Industrieën in Nederlandsch-Indië: Textielindustrie* (Industries in the Netherlands Indies: The textile industry), Report no. 125, Afd. Handelsmuseum van de Koninklijk Vereeniging Koloniaal Instituut, Amsterdam.

Ruckert, J. J. G. E. 1930. "De ontwikkeling van de financiën der autonome gemeenschappen" (The development of the autonomous local governments). In *25-jaren decentralisatie in Nederlandsch-Indië* (Twenty-five years of decentralization in the Netherlands Indies). Semarang: Vereeniging voor Locale Belangen.

Rush, J. R. 1990. *Opium to Java: Revenue Farming and Chinese Enterprise in Colonial Indonesia, 1860–1910.* Ithaca, N.Y.: Cornell University Press.

Salmon, C. 1991. "The Han Family of East Java: Entrepreneurship and Politics (Eighteenth–Nineteenth Centuries)." *Archipel* 41:53–85.

Sande Lacoste, A. C. van der. 1939. "Soerabaia: Marine-Basis." *Locale Techniek* 8 (2).

Sardjono. 1986. "Menuju tinggal landas pembangunan nasional di bidang perumahan rakyat" (Toward national development take-off in the field of public housing). *Prisma* 15 (5): 3–16.

Sato, S. 1994. *War, Nationalism and Peasants: Java under the Japanese Occupation, 1942–1945*. ASAA Southeast Asia Publications, no. 26. Sydney: Allen and Unwin.

Schaik, A. van. 1986. *Colonial Control and Peasant Resources in Java: Agricultural Revolution Reconsidered.* Amsterdam: Koninklijk Nederlands Aardrijkskundig Genootschap.

Schama, S. 1989. *Citizens: A Chronicle of the French Revolution.* London: Penguin.

———. 1992. *Patriots and Liberators: Revolution in the Netherlands, 1780–1813*. New York: Vintage Books.

Scheltema, A. M. P. A. 1936. "Zijn minimumloonen voor Java en madoera nu urgenter dan in 1921?" (Are minimum wages for Java and Madura now more urgent than in 1921?). *Koloniale Studien* 20 (3): 81–108.

Schoute, D. 1934–35. "De geneeskunde in Nederlandsch-Indië gedurende de negentiende eeuw" (Medicine in the Netherlands Indies during the nineteenth century). *Geneeskundig Tijdschrift voor Nederlandsch-Indië* 74:880, 75:1562.

Schrieke, J. J. 1918. *Onstaan en groei der stads- en landgemeenten in Nederlandsch-Indië* (Origins and growth of the urban and rural municipalities in the Netherlands Indies). Amsterdam: de Bussy.

Schwarz, A. 1990. "Logjam in Jakarta." *Far Eastern Economic Review*, 22 February, 56–57.

Segers, W. A. I. M. 1987. *Manufacturing Industry, 1870–1942.* Changing Economy in Indonesia, vol. 8. Amsterdam: Royal Tropical Institute.

Shibata, Y. 1986. "Surabaya after the Surrender." In *The Japanese Experience in Indonesia: Selected Memoirs of 1942–1945*, ed. A. Reid and A. Oki. Monograph no. 72. Athens: Center for Southeast Asian Studies, Ohio University.

Shiraishi, T. 1990. *An Age in Motion: Popular Radicalism in Java, 1912–1926.* Ithaca, N.Y.: Cornell University Press.

Siahaan, B. 1996. *Industrialisasi di Indonesia: Sejak hutang kehormatan sampai banting stir* (Industrialization in Indonesia: From the Debt of Honour to the end of the Old Order). Jakarta: Pustaka Data.

Siauw Giok Tjhan. 1982. *Siauw Giok Tjhan Remembers: A Peranakan-Chinese and the Quest for Indonesian Nation-hood.* Ed. and trans. R. Hering. Southeast Asian Studies Centre, monograph no. 11a. Townsville, Australia: James Cook University.

———. 1984. *Siauw Giok Tjhan Remembers: A Chinese Perakanan in Independent Indonesia.* Ed. P. Burns. Book 2, part 3. Southeast Asian Studies Centre, monograph no. 11b. Townsville, Australia: James Cook University.

Silas, J. 1989. *Surabaya: The Fast Growing City of Indonesia.* Surabaya: Municipality of Surabaya.

———. 1996. *Kampung Surabaya menuju metropolitan* (Kampung Surabaya becomes metropolitan). Ed. H. M. Siahaan and T. Purnomo. Surabaya: Yayasan Keluarga Bhakti/Surabaya Post.

———. 1999. "Pasca Krisis: Realitas dan optimisme dalam pembangunan perumahan dan pemukiman" (After the crisis: Reality and optimism in public housing and settlement). Paper presented to Eastern Regional Organization for Planning and Housing, Jakarta, 22 July.

Simons, R. D. G. P. 1939. "Indrukken over de prostitutie en de homosexueele prostitutie, en over het voorkomen van geslachtsziekten in Ned. Oost-Indie en West-Indie" (Impressions of prostitution and homosexual prostitution and of the prevention of venereal diseases in the East and West Indies). *Nederlandsch Tijdschrift voor Geneeskunde* 83 (4): 5574–79, 5689–93.

———. 1941. "Het onrustbarende aantal geslachtziekten en de noodzakelijkheid eener sociaal-hygienische bestrijding hiervan in Nederlandsch-Indië" (The alarming number of venereal diseases and the necessity of a social-hygiene campaign in the Netherlands Indies). *Geneeskundig Tijdschrift voor Nederlandsch-Indië* 1635–46.

Soehoed, A. R. 1967. "Manufacturing in Indonesia." *Bulletin of Indonesian Economic Studies* 8:65–84.

Soeparto Brata. 1983. "Surabaya; 40 tahun yang lalu" (Surabaya, forty years ago). *Jawa Pos*, May–June (twenty issues).

Somers, M. F. 1964. *Peranakan Chinese Politics in Indonesia.* Ithaca, N.Y.: Indonesia Project, Southeast Asia Program, Cornell University.

Stam, A. H. 1930. "De verzorging der stadshygiene door land en gemeente" (The provision of urban hygiene by the state and municipality). In *25-jaren decentralisatie in Nederlandsch-Indië* (Twenty-five years of decentralization in the Netherlands Indies), ed. F. W. M. Kerchman, 124–36. Semarang: Vereeniging voor Locale Belangen.

Steele, R. M. 1980. "Origins and Occupational Mobility of Lifetime Migrants to Surabaya, East Java." Ph.D. thesis, Australian National University, Canberra.

Stevens, T. 1984. "Een zeehaven voor Semarang" (A seaport for Semarang). *Orion* 1 (3): 25–27.

Suhadi, M. 1967. "Industrialization Efforts in Indonesia: The Role of Agriculture and Foreign Trade in the Development of the Industrial Sector." Ph.D. thesis, University of California, Berkeley.

Sulistyaninsih, R. M., and Y. Swasono. 1993. "The Sex Industry: Prostitution and Development in Indonesia." Report to Mahidol University, Bangkok.

Sullivan, N. 1994. *Masters and Managers: A Study of Gender Relations in Urban Java.* Sydney: Allen and Unwin.

Sutherland, H. 1979. *The Making of a Bureaucratic Elite.* Singapore: ASAA/Heinemann.

Sutter, J. O. 1959. *Indonesianisasi: Politics in a Changing Economy, 1940–1955.* Ithaca, N.Y.: Modern Indonesia Project, Cornell University.

Tan, T. K. 1967. *Sukarno's Guided Indonesia.* Brisbane: Jacaranda Press.

Taylor, J. G. 1983. *The Social World of Batavia: European and Eurasian in Dutch Asia.* Madison: University of Wisconsin Press.

Tiedeman, M. B. 1939. "De in aanbouw zijnde nieuwe CBZ te Soerabaia" (The construction of the new central hospital in Surabaya). *Locale Techniek* 8 (2): (March–April): 58–63.

Toer, Pramoedya Ananta. 1980a. *Bumi manusia* (This earth of mankind). Trans. M. Lane. Jakarta: Hasta Mitra.

———. 1980b. *Anak semua bangsa* (Child of all nations). Trans. M. Lane. Jakarta: Hasta Mitra.

Valentijn, F. 1858 [1726]. *Oud en nieuw Oost-Indieen.* Ed. S. Keijzer. 3 vols. The Hague: H. C. Susan.

Van Niel, R. 1984. *The Emergence of the Modern Indonesian Elite.* Reprint. Dordrecht: Foris.

———. 1992. *Java under the Cultivation System: Collected Writings.* Leiden: KITLV Press.

Vlekke, B. H. M. 1945. *Nusantara: A History of the East Indian Archipelago.* Cambridge, Mass.: Harvard University Press.

Vreede, A. G. 1926. "Rapport van het hoofd van het kantoor van arbeid over de arbeidstoestanden in de metaalindustrie te Soerabaja" (Report of the head of the labor office on labor conditions in the metal industry in Surabaya). Weltevreden: Landsdrukkerij.

———. 1931a. "De omvang der werkloosheid in Nederlandsch-Indië over de periode December 1930/Juni 1931" (The extent of unemployment in the Netherlands Indies over the period December 1930/June 1931). *Koloniale Studien* 15 (2): 503–41.

———. 1931b. "Onderzoek naar der omvang der werkloosheid op Java, November/December 1930" (Inquiry into the extent of unemployment in Java, November/December 1930). *Koloniale Studien* 15 (1): 242–73.

———. 1932a. "De werkloosheid in het eerste halfjaar 1932" (Unemployment in the first half-year of 1932). *Koloniale Studien* 16 (2): 668–703.

———. 1932b. "De werkloosheid in Nederlandsch-Indië in het tweede halfjaar 1931" (Unemployment in the Netherlands Indies in the second half-year of 1931). *Koloniale Studien* 16 (1): 183–201.

Vries, H. M. de. 1928. *The Importance of Java Seen from the Air.* Batavia: author; printed by G. Kolff.

Vuldy, C. 1987. *Pekalongan: Batik et Islam dans une Ville du Nord de Java.* Paris: Ecole des Hautes Etudes en Sciences Sociales.

Wal, S. L. van der, ed. 1971–79. *Officiele bescheiden betreffende de Nederlands-Indonesische betrekkingen 1945–1950* (Official documents concerning Netherlands Indonesian relations 1946–1950), Vols. 1–8. The Hague: Nijhoff.

Warr, P. G. 1992. "Exchange Rate Policy." In *The Oil Boom and After,* ed. A. Booth, 132–58. Kuala Lumpur: Oxford University Press.

Warren, J. F. 1993. *Ah Ku and Karayuki-san: Prostitution in Singapore, 1870–1940.* Singapore: Oxford University Press.

Weijerman, A. W. E. 1904. *Geschiedkundig overzicht van het onststaan der spoor- en tramwegen in Nederlandsch-Indië* (Historical review of the origins of the railways and tramways in the Netherlands Indies). Batavia: Javasche Boekhandel and Drukkerij.

Weldon, P. D. 1974. "Indonesian and Chinese Status and Language Differences in Urban Java." *Journal of Southeast Asian Studies* 5 (1) (March): 37–54.

Wirodihardjo, R. S. 1951. *De contingenteeringspolitiek en hare invloed op de Indonesische bevolking* (The quota policy and its impact on the Indonesian population). Jakarta: Nijhoff.

Wit, Y. B. de. 1973. "The Kabupaten Program." *Bulletin of Indonesian Economic Studies* 9 (1): 65–85.

Yong, Mun Cheong 1982. *H. J. van Mook and Indonesian Independence: A Study of His Role in Dutch-Indonesian Relations, 1945–48.* The Hague: Nijhoff.

Yoshihara, K. 1988. *The Rise of Ersatz Capitalism in Southeast Asia.* Singapore: Oxford University Press.

Young, K. 1993. "Kediri and Gudang Garam: An Industrial Enclave in a Rural Setting." In *Balanced Development: East Java in the New Order*, ed. H. Dick, J. Fox, and J. Mackie, 296–307. Singapore: Oxford University Press.

Ziesel, J. H. 1939. "Soerabaia als industriestad." (Surabaya as an industrial city). *Locale Techniek* 8 (2): 52–54.

Index